ASTRAEA

The Imperial Theme in the Sixteenth Century

FRANCES A. YATES

That was the righteous Virgin, which of old
Liv'd here on earth, and plenty made abound;
But after Wrong was lov'd and Justice solde,
She left th'vnrighteous world and was to heauen extold.

ROUTLEDGE & KEGAN PAUL

LONDON AND BOSTON

First published in 1975
by Routledge & Kegan Paul Ltd
Broadway House, 68–74 Carter Lane,
London EC4V 5EL and
9 Park Street,
Boston, Mass. 02108, USA
Set in Monotype Bembo 11pt 1pt leaded
and printed in Great Britain by
The Camelot Press Ltd, Southampton

ISBN 0 7100 7971 0
Library of Congress Catalog Card No. 74–82787

CONTENTS

PREFACE AND ACKNOWLEDGMENTS   xi

PART I   CHARLES V AND THE IDEA OF THE EMPIRE   I

PART II   THE TUDOR IMPERIAL REFORM

QUEEN ELIZABETH I AS ASTRAEA   29

ELIZABETHAN CHIVALRY: THE ROMANCE OF THE
ACCESSION DAY TILTS   88

THE TRIUMPH OF CHASTITY   112

PART III   THE FRENCH MONARCHY

THE IDEA OF THE FRENCH MONARCHY   121

THE ENTRY OF CHARLES IX AND HIS QUEEN INTO
PARIS, 1571   127

THE MAGNIFICENCES FOR THE MARRIAGE OF THE
DUC DE JOYEUSE, PARIS, 1581   149

RELIGIOUS PROCESSIONS IN PARIS, 1583–4   173

CONCLUSION: ASTRAEA AND THE GALLIC HERCULES   208

39309

APPENDICES

Allegorical Portraits of Queen Elizabeth I at Hatfield House   215
Boissard's Costume-Book and Two Portraits   220
Antoine Caron's Paintings for Triumphal Arches   222

INDEX   225

PLATES

Between pages 224 and 225

1 Marcus Aurelius, Capitol, Rome
2 Charles V by Titian, Prado, Madrid. Photo Anderson
3a Device of Charles V. From *Magnifica pompa funerale*, Antwerp (Plantin), 1559
3b Charles V and his Enemies. Engraving by Martin van Heemskerck. From *Divi Caroli V Victoriae*, 1556
4a Initial C. From John Foxe, *Acts and Monuments*, 1563
4b Emperor Constantine embracing Christian Bishops. From Foxe, *Acts and Monuments*, 1570
4c Pope Alexander III and the Emperor Frederick Barbarossa. From Foxe, *Acts and Monuments*, 1570
4d Emperor Henry IV at Canossa. From Foxe, *Acts and Monuments*, 1570
5a Henry VIII and the Pope. From Foxe, *Acts and Monuments*, 1570
5b Henry VIII Enthroned. From Foxe, *Acts and Monuments*, 1570
5c The Monk of Swineshead and King John. From Foxe, *Acts and Monuments*, 1570
5d Henry III and the Papal Legate. From Foxe, *Acts and Monuments*, 1570
6a Mark of the Printer, John Daye. From Foxe, *Acts and Monuments*, 1570
6b Queen Elizabeth I. Engraving by Crispin de Passe, senior
7a Initial C. From John Dee, *General and rare memorials*, 1577
7b Title page. From John Dee, *General and rare memorials*, 1577
8a Queen Elizabeth I. Engraving by Crispin de Passe, senior, after Isaac Olivier
8b Queen Elizabeth I. Engraving by Vertue, after Isaac Olivier
8c Queen Elizabeth I. Engraving by W. Rogers
8d Queen Elizabeth I. Engraving attributed to Remigius Hogenberg

9a   Queen Elizabeth I and the Judgment of Paris, Hampton Court. Reproduced by gracious permission of Her Majesty the Queen

9b   Queen Elizabeth I. Engraving by F. Delaram after N. Hilliard

9c   Queen Elizabeth I. From J. Case, *Sphaera civitatis*, 1588

10a   Queen Elizabeth I. Dover Town Hall

10b   Queen Elizabeth I. Title-page of the Bishops' Bible, 1569

11a   Queen Elizabeth and the Pope as Diana and Callisto. Engraving by Pieter van der Heyden

11b   Queen Elizabeth in Procession. Collection S. Wingfield Digby, Sherborne Castle

12a   Sir Henry Lee. By Antonio Moro, National Portrait Gallery

12b   Sir Philip Sidney. Unknown Artist, National Portrait Gallery

12c   Armour designed for Sir Henry Lee, *Almain Armourer's Album*, Victoria and Albert Museum

12d   George Clifford, Third Earl of Cumberland. By Nicholas Hilliard, National Maritime Museum, Greenwich

13   Queen Elizabeth I, National Portrait Gallery

14a   Queen Elizabeth I, Windsor Castle. Reproduced by gracious permission of Her Majesty the Queen

14b   Procession of Knights of the Garter. By Marcus Gheeraerts, senior, British Museum. Detail

15   Jacopo del Sellaio, The Triumph of Chastity, Museo Bandini, Fiesole. Photo Alinari

16a   Queen Elizabeth I. The Ermine Portrait. Marquis of Salisbury, Hatfield House

16b   Queen Elizabeth I. The Sieve Portrait, Pinacoteca, Siena. Photo Alinari

17a,b   Details from the Sieve Portrait

18a   Design for a Triumphal Arch. Nationalmuseum, Stockholm, Cronstedt Collection

18b   Triumphal Arch at Entry of Charles IX. From Simon Bouquet, *Recueil*, 1572

19a   The Francus and Pharamond Arch. From Simon Bouquet, *Recueil*, 1572

19b   The Castor and Pollux Arch at the entry of Charles IX. From Simon Bouquet, *Recueil*, 1572

20a   The Device of Charles IX. From Ruscelli, *Imprese illustri*, 1560

20b   The Present given to Charles IX. From Bouquet, *Recueil*, 1572

20c   The Gallia. From Bouquet, *Recueil*, 1572

20d   The Juno. From Bouquet, *Recueil*, 1572

21   Antoine Caron, Augustus and the Sibyl, Louvre. Photo Lauros-Giraudon

22a   The Quintain. Drawing by Antoine Caron, Witt Collection, Courtauld Institute

22b   The Quintain with Henri III in the foreground. Valois Tapestry, Uffizi, Florence

23a The Device of Henri III

23b The Device of Catherine de' Medici

23c Castor and Pollux Emblem. From Alciati, *Emblemata*

23d Ship with Lights on Rigging (Castor and Pollux Emblem). From Giordano Bruno, *La cena de le ceneri*, 1584

24–34 Drawings of Religious Processions in Paris, 1583–4, illustrating Henri III's Religious Movements. Bibliothèque Nationale, Cabinet des Estampes, Pd. 29 Réserve. Photo Bibl. nat. Paris

35–9 Drawings of Religious Processions in Paris, 1584, illustrating Queen Louise de Lorraine's visit to the royal charity, Nicolas Houel's House of Love. Bibliothèque Nationale, Cabinet des Estampes, Pd. 30 Réserve. Photo Bibl. nat. Paris

40 The Procession of the League. From B. de Montfaucon, *Monuments de la Monarchie Française*, 1734

41 Entry of Henri IV into Paris, 1594. Engraving by Jean le Clerc after N. Bollery

42a Henri IV as the Gallic Hercules. Print distributed after the Consecration at Chartres

42b Honoré d'Urfé, *L'Astrée*, 1632, title-page

42c Astraea, title-page to Pierre Matthieu, *L'Histoire de la France*, 1605

43a 'Sponsa Thessalonicensis'. From J. J. Boissard, *Habitus variarum orbis gentium*, 1581

43b Queen Elizabeth I. The Rainbow Portrait. Marquis of Salisbury, Hatfield House

43c Lady in Fancy Dress, Hampton Court. Reproduced by gracious permission of Her Majesty the Queen

43d 'Virgo Persica'. From J. J. Boissard, *Habitus variarum orbis gentium*, 1581

44 Charles IX. Bronze bust by Germain Pilon, Wallace Collection, London

FIGURES

1 Woodcut from Hyginus, *De Mundi et Sphere*, Venice, 1502   *page* 30

2 Music from Claude Le Jeune, *Airs*, 1608   158

I had no idea when I began this book as a volume of 'collected essays' that it would take on a life of its own and become a new book. As I sorted the old essays and tried to put them into a meaningful order, they came alive again, and some of them cried out to be rewritten in the light of later experience and knowledge. Others, equally firmly, demanded to be left unaltered as monuments of past experience which still seemed valid for the present. Thus there are different styles in this book. Some essays belong to an early Warburgian period; this applies particularly to the piece after which the volume is named, 'Queen Elizabeth I as Astraea'. Others reflect a French period. The rewriting, and the two short pieces newly written for this book, belong to the present.

The actual work and research represented in the book was done, much of it, more than twenty years ago. None of it is later than the 1950s; even the newly written essays use unpublished lectures of that time. And in going through my notes I have been reminded of even earlier times. The discovery of the Castor and Pollux emblem as an illustration to Giordano Bruno's exposition of heliocentricity must go back to the thirties when I was translating the *Cena de le ceneri*. The preoccupation with Henri III also began in that decade. I have been moving for a very long time among these thoughts and these people. Almost a lifetime has been spent in trying to understand a period which has always seemed, not a dead past, but vitally important for present imaginative and spiritual life. The present book draws close, though indirectly, to Shakespeare; this world of the 'imperial theme' is surely the world in which Shakespeare's imagination operates, and, though I have carefully avoided stressing this, the route followed here may indicate a historical opening towards a new understanding of Shakespeare's religion.

The studies on which these essays are based were written years before my *Giordano Bruno and the Hermetic Tradition* (1964) yet Bruno is already prominent here, wending his way between France and England in search of the ideal imperial ruler who will save the world from tyranny. The close association in the mind of a Renaissance philosopher between the ideal unified governance of human society and the organization of the physical universe is very clear in Bruno's works, in which the politico-religious message is inseparably combined with the Hermetic religious philosophy.

The 'imperial theme' in its relation to French monarchy in the late sixteenth century forms the subject of several of the essays, contrasting and comparing with the Elizabethan imperial theme. As in England, the monarchy served as a unifying symbol in a world in which the rift between Catholics and Protestants threatened chaos. The efforts towards religious conciliation under a liberal French monarchy formed the basis of the movements led by the French Pléiade and by Baïf's Academy of Poetry and Music, and found expression in the great French court festivals, one of which is the subject of one of the essays. In such spectacles, Renaissance magic is invoked to strengthen monarchy and to avert religious war. As the crisis deepened at the end of the century, the French king (Henri III) attempted to lead a religious movement, studied in the essay on religious processions. Henri IV proved the saviour who made possible, at least temporarily, an imperial *pax* from wars of religion.

This book ends at the point at which my last book began, in the early years of the seventeenth century immediately before the outbreak of the Thirty Years' War. Elizabethan Protestant chivalry, studied in one of the essays in this book, and the French Pléiadist movement were among the many ingredients of the Rosicrucian movement in the early seventeenth century in Germany, studied in *The Rosicrucian Enlightenment* (1972).

'Queen Elizabeth I as Astraea', though a central essay, is not more important than the others and connects with them all. In fact, that essay, as published in 1947, seems to contain, towards the end, as it were premonitions of all the other essays and even of many of my other books.

The illustrations are not presented as art history; nor are they picture-book history. They are inseparable from the argument in the text, but do not so much illustrate the text as state the same argument in another medium. They use visual images as historical documents in their own right. Charles V's device of the two columns makes a historical statement which could be made in no other way. So does the 'Sieve' portrait of Queen Elizabeth I. The 'Processions' drawings convey important information through their iconographical argument.

The following is an account of the dates and places of publication of my earlier writings, here reprinted or rewritten, references to which are not given with the essays themselves.

The genesis of the essay on 'Queen Elizabeth I as Astraea' goes back earlier than 1947, the date of its publication in the Warburg *Journal*,[1] to a

---

[1] 'Queen Elizabeth as Astraea', *Journal of the Warburg and Courtauld Institutes*, X (1947), pp. 27–82.

lecture given in 1945 on Queen Elizabeth and her poets which was originally endowed as a *sermon* on the Queen! The 'Astraea' essay is reprinted almost exactly from the article in the *Journal*, except for some omissions, to avoid repetition from other essays, some simplifications in the notes and illustrations, and the addition of a few new references. It belongs to the time when inspiring scholars and an inspiring library were newly arrived from Germany. The manuscript of the article was read by Fritz Saxl not long before his death.

Out of 'Astraea' grew the four 'Empire Lectures', on the imperial theme in the Middle Ages and Renaissance, originally given at London University Senate House in January 1952. They later formed the basis of seminars at the Warburg Institute in 1967–70 and at the Society for the Humanities, Cornell University, in 1968. They have not been published before in their original English form though a French translation was published in 1960.[1] The essays in this book on 'Charles V and the Idea of the Empire' and on 'The Idea of the French Monarchy' are the Empire Lectures as prepared for the French translation.

'Elizabethan Chivalry: The Romance of the Accession Day Tilts' was contributed to a symposium on Philip Sidney arranged by D. J. Gordon at Reading University in March 1954, and was published as an article in the Warburg *Journal*[2] in 1957. The article is exactly reprinted here, except for some slight revisions and two additions to the illustrations.

'The Triumph of Chastity' was newly written for this book, though based on unpublished lectures: 'Petrarch's *Trionfi* and the Elizabethan Poets', given at Reading University in March 1950, and 'Allegorical Portraits of Queen Elizabeth I', given at the Slade School of London University, May 1953. In these lectures I discussed the 'Ermine' and the 'Sieve' portraits in relation to Petrarch's *Trionfi*, with slides of details and comparisons. The identification of the scenes on the column in the 'Sieve' with episodes in Virgil's *Aeneid* was made by Helen Roeder when she was working in the photographic collection at the Warburg Institute in 1949–50; she also helped with 'Tuccia' and the *Trionfi*.

'The Entry of Charles IX and his Queen into Paris, 1571' was the subject of a paper contributed to a colloquium at Royaumont in July 1955, organized by Jean Jacquot and published, in French, in 1956 by the Centre National de la Recherche Scientifique in the volume *Les Fêtes de la Renaissance*.[3] The essay as published here, though it uses the findings of the French article, is really quite a different study, both from the French article and from my

[1] 'Charles Quint et l'Idée d'Empire', *Fêtes et Cérémonies au Temps de Charles Quint*, ed. Jean Jacquot, Centre National de la Recherche Scientifique, Paris, 1960, pp. 57–97.

[2] 'Elizabethan chivalry: The romance of the Accession Day Tilts', *Journal of the Warburg and Courtauld Institutes*, XX (1957), pp. 4–25

[3] 'Poètes et artistes dans les Entrées de Charles IX et de sa reine à Paris en 1571', *Les Fêtes de la Renaissance*, ed. Jean Jacquot, Centre National de la Recherche Scientifique, Paris, 1956, pp. 61–84.

introduction, in English, to the facsimile reprint of Simon Bouquet's account of the Entry.[1] The essay as rewritten for this book is orientated towards the imperial theme in French monarchy symbolism, and towards suggesting comparisons with the Elizabethan imperial theme.

'The Magnificences for the Marriage of the Duc de Joyeuse, Paris, 1581' was a paper in French contributed to an international colloquium in Paris in June–July 1953, organized by Jean Jacquot and others and sponsored by the Centre National de la Recherche Scientifique; it was published in 1954 in *Musique et Poésie au Seizième Siècle*.[2] Some of the music written for these festivals was identified in this article. The original French paper has been very much expanded in the essay to cover the importance of these festivals as a whole, and particularly their aspect as musical incantations aimed at drawing down favourable astral influences on French monarchy.

The drawings of religious processions in the Cabinet des Estampes have fascinated me for years. I published a few of them in *The French Academies of the Sixteenth Century* (1947) and the whole set (Plates 24–39 in this book) was published in my article, in English, written for a French musicological journal and published in 1954.[3] That article has been completely rewritten for the essay in this book on 'Religious Processions in Paris, 1583–4'. In going through the quantities of notes made years ago when working on the processions drawings I found that I was now better able to understand them. The rewriting of 'Processions' for this book has been an exciting experience which has given me new insights into Henri III's royal religious movements as having possible connections with the secret sect known as the Family of Love.

The last essay on 'Astraea and the Gallic Hercules' was newly written for this book; it owes much to the work of Corrado Vivanti on the symbolism used of Henri IV. It attempts to bring together the English and French monarchy symbolism with which the book has been concerned.

The three appendices reprint brief notes related to the themes of the book. 'Allegorical Portraits of Queen Elizabeth I at Hatfield House' was published as a Hatfield House Booklet in 1952.[4] 'Boissard's costume-book and two portraits' appeared as a note in the Warburg *Journal* in 1959.[5] 'Antoine Caron's

---

[1] Simon Bouquet, *Bref recueil*, etc., Paris, 1572, to be reprinted in facsimile in *Renaissance Triumphs and Magnificences*, ed. Margaret McGowan, Theatrum Orbis Terrarum Ltd, Amsterdam, Vol. III. My introduction to this reprint contains material which is not in the quite different essay published here.

[2] 'Poésie et musique dans les Magnificences au Mariage du Duc de Joyeuse, Paris, 1581', *Musique et Poésie au XVIe Siècle*, ed. Jean Jacquot, Centre National de la Recherche Scientifique, Paris, 1954, pp. 241–64.

[3] 'Dramatic religious processions in Paris, in the late sixteenth century', *Annales musicologiques*, II, Publication de la Société de la Musique d'Autrefois, Direction G. Thibault, F. Lesure, Paris, 1954, pp. 215–70, plates I–XX.

[4] Hatfield House Booklet, no. 1, out of print.

[5] 'Boissard's costume book and two portraits', *Journal of the Warburg and Courtauld Institutes*, XXII (1959), pp. 365–6.

paintings for triumphal arches',[1] was also a note in the Warburg *Journal* for 1951.

The body of work represented by this volume belongs in date, roughly, between my two books, briefly known as the *Academies* (1947), and the *Tapestries* (1959). In *The French Academies of the Sixteenth Century*[2] I was concerned with aspects of sixteenth-century French culture, the interest in which was continued in these essays; the *Academies* contains my first study of the French festivals of 1581. My book, *The Valois Tapestries*,[3] carried further the study of sixteenth-century French court festivals, elucidated their representation in the tapestries, and attempted to explore their meaning as expressive of a politico-religious attitude, that of the party of the 'politiques'. Though the present volume is a whole in itself which can be read without any knowledge of my other works, readers of it will find both the *Academies* and the *Tapestries* helpful for further exploration of its themes. In fact, I have incorporated into the essays on French themes in this book material from the *Academies* and from the *Tapestries* which was not present in the essays as originally published.

My thanks are due to all those who have given me permission to use in this volume, either as reprints or in revised form, essays originally published elsewhere. The *Journal of the Warburg and Courtauld Institutes* first gave me the opportunity of publishing two of the essays, and two of the appendices, and I am grateful to the Director of the Institute, Sir Ernst Gombrich, and to the editors, for allowing me to use these essays and notes in the present volume.

Jean Jacquot, of the Centre National de la Recherche Scientifique, kindly gave permission for inclusion here of essays which originally appeared in French in volumes published by the Centre. The colloquies organized in the 1950s for the Centre by Jean Jacquot gave the stimulus for undertaking such studies and much more is owed to him than the actual permission to reproduce them. To his initiative in bringing together gatherings of European scholars to study the European phenomenon of court festival, and other pageantry, much of the revival of interest in these subjects is due. I hope that he will view the present volume as in some sense an outcome of the Anglo-French co-operation in scholarship which he encouraged. Those memorable meetings in Paris were enriched by the participation of the group of French musicologists under whose auspices one of the essays in this book first

---

[1] 'Antoine Caron's paintings for triumphal arches', *Journal of the Warburg and Courtauld Institutes*, XIV (1951), pp. 133–4.

[2] *The French Academies of the Sixteenth Century*, Warburg Institute, no. 15, London, 1947 (Kraus Reprint, 1967).

[3] *The Valois Tapestries*, Warburg Institute, London, 1959; to be reprinted in a revised edition by Routledge & Kegan Paul.

appeared; I am grateful to Madame de Chambure and to François Lesure for permission to republish it here, in revised form. For permission to reprint the Hatfield House Booklet, I am indebted to the Marquis of Salisbury.

Her Majesty the Queen has given her gracious permission to reproduce works in her collections among the illustrations in this book.

I am also grateful to the following for allowing me to reproduce works in their collections: the Marquis of Salisbury; S. Wingfield Digby Esq.; the Town Clerk of Dover; the Trustees of the British Museum; the Directors of the National Portrait Gallery, the Victoria and Albert Museum, the National Maritime Museum, the Courtauld Institute, the Wallace Collection, the Uffizi Gallery, the Louvre, the Prado, the Bibliothèque Nationale (Cabinet des Estampes), the Museo Bandini (Fiesole), the Siena Pinacoteca, the Stockholm Nationalmuseum.

The staff of the Warburg Institute has always given invaluable assistance. To J. B. Trapp and to Jennifer Montague, always ready to help in the library and in the photographic collections, I am most grateful. Elizabeth McGrath has rendered invaluable assistance in tracing photographs, reading the manuscript, and in many other ways, particularly by her enthusiasm. The photographers of the Institute, both past and present, have given of their skills.

To the founder of the Warburg Institute, Aby Warburg, who arranged his library to inspire and facilitate historical studies which should include such subjects as the idea of the Empire, or festivals and their symbolism, this book owes its existence. Though the library of the Warburg Institute has been my base, many days of my life have been spent in the library of the British Museum. And the London Library has been a constant help, with its rich collections of out-of-the-way historical materials. To its staff, both past and present, I am indebted for much assistance.

In Paris, I worked mainly at the Bibliothèque Nationale, particularly at the Cabinet des Estampes, whose director, Jean Adhémar, gave me much kind help.

Many friends have supported me down the years. The late Gertrud Bing took a deep interest in these studies. Ernst Gombrich has encouraged them with sympathetic understanding and with generous sharing of the vast resources of his mind. To Perkin Walker, upon whose profound knowledge of Renaissance music and philosophy I have always been able to draw, I am deeply grateful. My sister's understanding and support have always been with me.

Warburg Institute
August 1973

PART I

CHARLES V AND THE IDEA OF THE EMPIRE

In the middle of the sixteenth century, the Holy Roman Empire, which had seemed to be dwindling more and more rapidly into a local German concern, suddenly takes on once more something of its old significance. The century in which a new Europe, with its great states built up on principles of realistic statecraft and infused with national patriotism, was in process of formation saw also a late manifestation of the Monarch, the potential Lord of the World, in the person of the Emperor Charles V. The patterns of the new Europe take their shape under the shadow, or the mirage, of a recrudescence of the idea of the Empire. The revival of imperialism in Charles V was a phantom revival. That he looked so much like a Lord of the World was due to the Hapsburg dynastic marriage policy which had brought such vast territories under his rule, and when, after his death, Phillip II succeeded to the Spanish monarchy whilst the imperial title passed to another branch of the Hapsburg family, the whole imposing edifice of the empire of the second Charlemagne broke down. The transitory and unreal character of the empire of Charles V is the aspect of it usually stressed by modern historians. Whilst not denying its unreality in the political sense, it is the purpose of the present essay to suggest that it is precisely as a phantom that Charles's empire was of importance, because it raised again the imperial idea and spread it through Europe in the symbolism of its propaganda, and that at a time when the more advanced political thinking was discrediting it.

The following attempt to place the empire of Charles V in a historical context is obviously no more than a slight sketch, or a partial evocation of a vast subject. It is not concerned with political realities, nor with straight political history, but with the idea of empire, or the imperialist hope. As Folz has said, 'A la différence de la notion politique de l'Empire . . . l'espérance impériale demeure extrêmement fluide; elle se meut toujours sur le plan universel.'[1] Every revival of the Empire, in the person of some great emperor, carried with it, as a phantom, the revival of a universal imperialist hope.

[1] R. Folz, *L'Idée d'empire en Occident du Ve au XIVe siècle*, Paris, 1953, p. 178.

These revivals, not excluding that of Charlemagne, were never politically real nor politically lasting; it was their phantoms which endured and exercised an almost undying influence. The empire of Charles V, being a late revival of the 'espérance impériale' in connection with the holder of the imperial title, carried the influence of the phantom on into the modern world.

This is our theme. In order to state it clearly, it is necessary to begin with some discussion, inadequate though this must be, of the medieval imperial idea, and the stages leading to what appeared to be the breakup of the concept under the influences of the new historical and political thinking. In this context, the recrudescence of the imperial idea in Charles V is seen to be a revival of an obsolescent notion.

It is chiefly through its reflection in symbolism and poetic imagery that we shall study the revived phantom of the 'espérance impériale' in the second Charlemagne, and this whole essay is really the preparation for the study of the influence of the imperial idea on the ethos and symbolism of the rising monarchies of Europe. For though the empire of Charles V died away at his death, it succeeded in translating the phantom of the 'espérance impériale' to the national monarchies, particularly those of England and France with which the later essays in this book will be concerned.

The Imperial Idea in the Middle Ages

Romulus Augustulus, the last Emperor of the West in the old succession, was deposed in 475. Thereafter, the Eastern Empire went on alone whilst Western Europe plunged into the Dark Ages and was without a titular emperor until that solemn Christmas Day of the year 800, when, in St Peter's, Pope Leo III placed the imperial crown on the head of Charlemagne. This was the first *renovatio* of the Empire in modern times, and it marked the beginning of modern Europe. The Empire thus renewed in Charlemagne was regarded as indeed the Roman Empire itself through the theory of the translation of the Empire. As Constantine had translated the Empire to the East, so now in Charlemagne it was translated back to the West. Thus Charlemagne's title carried with it in theory the full Roman headship of the world, the universal world rule.[1]

Augustine in his *De civitate Dei* defines human society as consisting of two cities, the *civitas Dei*, the City of God, the church; and the *civitas terrena*, the earthly city, the city of the devil.[2] The earthly city was for him the pagan society, the Roman Empire, the supposed moral virtues of which were incapable of establishing a moral order in this world, given over to

---

[1] See L. Halphen, *Charlemagne et l'Empire carolingien*, Paris, 1947; R. Folz, *Le Souvenir et la légende de Charlemagne*, Paris, 1950.

[2] On Augustinianism and imperialist theory, see H. X. Arquillière, *L'Augustinisme politique*, Paris, 1934; E. Gilson, *Les Métamorphoses de la Cité de Dieu*, Louvain, 1932.

the devil, through which the City of God must make its pilgrimage towards eternity. Why, then, did the Pope, the Vicar of Christ, the head of the *civitas Dei* in its earthly pilgrimage, restore the Empire, the earthly city? The answer is that the Empire thus restored was to be the Christianized Empire; the Emperor was to be the defender of the *civitas Dei*, and to assist it in carrying the message of the church through the world. It was in this light that Charlemagne, whose favourite book was the *De civitate Dei*, regarded his *imperium*, not as a *civitas terrena* in opposition to the *civitas Dei*, but as a city representing the earthly portion of the church, the kingdom of eternal peace in this world, as Alcuin said.

Thus the figures of the Pope and the Emperor were to go through the Middle Ages: the Pope, the head of the church; the Emperor, the head of the world. The Emperor never had a real authority in the world comparable to the real authority of the Pope in the church. He ruled only certain territories, mainly in Germany, with a vaguely defined and often disputed sovereignty over other monarchs. Yet, ineffective though he may seem, his very existence witnessed to the truth that all Europe was descended from one root, the Roman Empire, and kept alive the idea of the headship of Rome over the whole world, the idea of world unity. There was a symmetry in the Pope-Emperor relationship. One cannot say that they were a pair, for the Pope was higher than the Emperor, and from the Pope the Emperor received his crown. Yet the Emperor repeats the spiritual pattern in the temporal order. The Pope is the Vicar of Christ, and the Emperor, too, is in some kind of special relationship to Christ, perhaps best realized by mentally visualizing an emperor, in his capacity of a deacon of the church, standing at the lectern with his imperial crown on his head and his drawn sword in his hand to read one of the lessons on Christmas Day: 'And it came to pass in those days that there went out a decree from Caesar Augustus that all the world should be taxed.' Holding the lowest rank in the spiritual hierarchy, that of deacon, and the highest rank in the temporal hierarchy, the Emperor has a responsibility for supporting the entry of Christ into the world with the sword of his temporal justice. The Emperor Sigismund read that lesson on Christmas Day of the year 1414 before those assembled for the Council of Constance.[1] The rights of emperors in the councils of the Church, and their rights to put forward proposals for the reform of the church, the subject of endless controversy in the Reformation period, have their roots in the religious associations of the imperial office.

The sanctification of the idea of the Empire was enhanced by the tradition of the providential rôle of Rome as a historical preparation for the birth of Christ, a tradition which is not really compatible with the Augustinian view of the *civitas terrena* but which had been elaborated, after the Empire became Christian under Constantine, in the adaptations by Christian

[1] J. Bryce, *The Holy Roman Empire*, London, 1904 ed., p. 398 note.

apologists, particularly Eusebius and Lactantius, of pagan imperial themes. The age of Augustus was the supreme example of a world united and at peace under the Roman Empire, and to that age had also belonged the supreme honour of witnessing the birth of Christ. By consenting to be born into a world ruled by Roman law under the greatest of the Caesars, Christ had consecrated the Roman world order and the Roman justice. Virgil's *Aeneid*, with its glorification of Augustus, thus became a semi-sacred poem glorifying the historical framework of the Saviour's birth. Moreover, Virgil was believed to have spoken with the inspired voice of a prophet when he proclaimed in the Fourth Eclogue that the golden age was about to return, and with it the reign of the Virgin Astraea, or Justice, and that a child would be born destined to rule a reconciled world. These words were understood to refer to the birth of Christ in the golden age of Augustus.[1] Through such associations, it was possible to use pagan imperial rhetoric concerning periodic renovations of the Empire, or returns of the golden age, of medieval Christian emperors, thus retaining something of the cyclic view of history which such expressions imply, though in a Christianized form. A *renovatio* of the Empire will imply spiritual renovation, for in a restored world, in a new golden age of peace and justice, Christ can reign.

This mysticism must not obscure the fact that, as interpreted at the time and as other ages interpreted it, it was the power, the *imperium* in the wordly sense, the right to the world rule, which was renewed or restored in Charlemagne and lived in the medieval emperors. The translation of the Empire was to become the keystone in the traditions of German imperialism, in the form that the Empire was taken away from the Greeks and given to the Germans in the person of Charlemagne. And it was to be the *pièce de résistance* in the arguments by which the French monarchy claimed rights of leadership in Europe, for was not Charlemagne the King of the Franks?

The bestowal of the imperial crown on Charlemagne, though afterwards to be described as the transference of the Empire to the Germans or the Franks, was not so regarded at the time. There was no conscious purpose of settling the office on one nation or dynasty. But we know that in after times the imperial title was in fact to remain with the northern rulers. It might, therefore, be yet another of the interpretations after the event of the translation of the Empire to define it as a translation of the Empire to the North. It was inevitable at the beginning that this should be so, for – to put the situation which afterwards became so highly theorized on its most obvious

---

[1] The Emperor Constantine first publicly interpreted the Fourth Eclogue as a Messianic prophecy. See Constantine, *Oratio ad Sanctorum Coetum*, in Migne, *Patr. graec.*, VIII, 456; Lactantius, *Div. Inst.*, V, v (*Opera omnia*, ed. S. Brandt and G. Laubmann, Vienna, 1890, p. 413). For discussion, see J. B. Mayor, W. Warde Fowler, R. S. Conway, *Virgil's Messianic Eclogue*, London, 1907; A. Bartlett Giamatti, *The Earthly Paradise and the Renaissance Epic*, Princeton, 1966, pp. 23 ff.

For the use of the Christianized *renovatio* theme on imperial coins, see H. Mattingly, 'Virgil's Fourth Eclogue', *Journal of the Warburg and Courtauld Institutes*, X (1947), pp. 14–19.

level – the reason why the Pope needed an emperor was in order to have a temporal ally for his defence, and the temporal power was in the hands of the northern barbarians.

The ideal of the Emperor takes on a northern tinge in those cycles of epic poetry which afterwards grew up about the name and memory of Charlemagne. In them, the emperor-idea is transposed into a feudal world where the imperial *pax* and *justitia* have to be made effective through the fighting qualities of the knights. Thus the Charlemagne of the *Chanson de Roland*, or the Christian Knight-Emperor of the Arthurian romances, is the ideal world-ruler in his northern and feudal transformation. This shifting of the imperial idea to the northern lands casts a haze of romanticism over the classical figure of the Emperor, and that even in Italian eyes. For medieval Italian imperialism looked towards the North for the return of the Emperor, expecting to see him coming thence at the head of an army of shining knights to bring back the golden age of peace and justice, a pathetic but deep-seated illusion which may still account, even in the late fifteenth century, for the delight and admiration with which Italy received the invading armies of Charles VIII, decked out in all the splendid panoply of French chivalry.

Upon the northern and romantic pattern of the ideal Emperor there was superimposed in later medieval times a very precisely defined theory of the imperial office. Amongst the various influences which produced this development, two may be singled out. On the one hand, the remarkable personal ability of certain emperors of the house of Hohenstaufen gave some factual reality to the phantom imperial title. On the other hand, the revival of Roman law at Bologna provided these powerful emperors with a reasoned legal basis for the imperial title.

In Roman law, the Emperor is styled *Dominus mundi*, the Lord of the World. Imperialist students of Roman law, pondering over this title, found that it implied overlordship of all the kings of the world. 'There be many provinces in the Roman Empire, with many kings, but only one Emperor, their suzerain', says Huguccio of Pisa.[1] Here the feudal principle of overlordship is re-interpreted in terms of Roman law. The feudal overlords, or kings, are provincial governors responsible to the Emperor as the one supreme feudal overlord, the one Roman *Dominus mundi* or world ruler.

It was the Emperor Frederick II, who, both by his sensational career and by his intellectual grasp of Roman law, became one of the most significant exponents of imperialism in medieval times. His manifestoes riveted the attention of Europe on the idea of the *Dominus mundi* and its claims, and the counter-manifestoes issued by the papal *curia* made equally clear the claim of the Pope to be the spiritual Lord of the World. For the thirteenth century was the age of law, and if the revival of Roman law had given new clarity to the position of the Emperor, the perfecting of canon law under the great

[1] Quoted by E. Kantorowicz, *Frederick II*, trans. E. O. Lorimer, London, 1931, p. 8.

canonist popes – who were themselves, particularly Innocent III, influenced by the revived Roman law – had equally clarified the position of the Pope.[1] Only if the temporal World Ruler was included within the higher sphere of the spiritual World Ruler in a nicely balanced relation between Pope and Emperor could the medieval ideal of world unity be achieved. If the Pope puts forward a temporal claim encroaching on the Emperor's sphere, or if, conversely, the Emperor puts forward a spiritual claim, encroaching on the Pope's sphere, the balance is destroyed. And the more the two spheres are legalized and defined, the greater becomes the danger of a clash.

Through his mother, Frederick II was the inheritor of the Norman kingdom of Sicily, which included Naples and part of southern Italy. This northern Emperor thus had a very definite foothold in the South, and in his southern realm he developed the blueprint of his ideal of imperial government. From his Book of Laws, the Sicilian constitutions or Constitutions of Melfi, from the pronouncements of the imperial chancery, from the letters and writings of his circle, an idea can be gained as to how Frederick envisaged the office of the emperor. The emperor is more than the representative of God's justice on earth; he is the semi-divine intermediary through whom justice flows from God into the world. To quote Kantorowicz in his book on Frederick:[2]

> All the metaphors of the Book of Laws point in the same direction. The Emperor was the sole source of justice. . . . His justice flows as in a flood . . . he interprets the law . . . From him justice flows through the kingdom in rivulets and those who distribute his rule throughout the state are the imperial officials.

In the model kingdom of Sicily, the law was administered by an official class who had received legal training on the pattern approved by Frederick, and it seems that this new lay class of administrators demanded an almost priestly respect as the channels of the divine imperial justice. New forms and ceremonies were evolved to express this hieratic conception, involving what amounted to a revival of emperor worship. Witnesses have described the Emperor presiding over the courts of justice. 'The *Sacra Majestas* of the Emperor was enthroned on inaccessible heights; over his head was suspended a gigantic crown; all who approached him must prostrate themselves before the *Divus Augustus*.'[3]

The philosophical justification for this imperial law state was based on three forces, defined as *Necessitas, Justitia, Providentia*.[4] The existence of a ruler to guide the affairs of the state is a necessity, a law of nature; it is a divine law that such rule must be just; and through divine *providentia*, or foresight, the Roman Emperor is the just and necessary ruler. Frederick's

---

[1] See W. Ullmann, *Medieval Papalism*, London, 1949.
[2] *Frederick II*, trans. Lorimer, pp. 234–5.   [3] *Ibid.*, p. 236.   [4] *Ibid.*, pp. 254 ff.

conception is derived partly from Roman law; partly from ancient philosophy coming in from those Arabic sources with which he was very familiar; and partly it is an imitation of the ecclesiastical theory of world government, with the Emperor substituted for the Pope as God's representative on earth, and the hierarchy of legal officials substituted for the hierarchy of the priesthood.

It may have been Frederick's dream to enforce the pattern of government which he established in the kingdom of Sicily, and the imperial ideals which it embodied, throughout the whole world, but in fact he was not able to extend it even throughout his own domains. In his northern dominions he was still simply the feudal overlord. One might perhaps say that as a great Hohenstaufen emperor he belongs to the northern, the feudal, the knightly, imperial pattern. But as Monarch of Sicily he leads a new type of *renovatio*, more southern and classical in its clear outlines, in which a closely reasoned legal, philosophical, and theological argument on the necessity for One Ruler finds its expression in a closely knit absolutist state. The two types are united in the character of the Emperor himself, for the court with which he was surrounded in Sicily was a chivalrous court, and the administration was partly recruited from it.

Perhaps it is the combination of these two types or patterns of imperial *renovatio* which forms the essence of Ghibellinism. The Ghibelline looks for the renovation of the Empire, the coming of the ideal World Ruler, and the reign of peace and justice in a new golden age. He looks for it towards the North, for there the Empire was first reborn and there the imperial title remained. A breath of chivalrous romance is in his expectation, but within the Ghibelline romanticism is a hard core of clear-cut legalistic thinking. The government of the world under One Ruler must reflect the government of the universe under One God in no vague and generalized way. It must be an ordered dispensation of justice within an organized state.

The balance between popes and emperors, always an uneasy one, becomes in Frederick's times a balance between two world monarchies, the one organized on a basis of canon law, the other beginning to be organized on a basis of Roman law, and each claiming that its head was the direct channel of divine influence. The theoretical subjection, of Emperor to Pope, which Frederick always publicly acknowledged, could not conceal the dangers of this situation, and Europe echoed with the awe-inspiring quarrel between the two heads of Christendom. The most sensational episodes were the banning by the Pope of the Emperor's crusade, and the confiscation by the Emperor of whole shiploads of ecclesiastics coming to attend a council summoned by the Pope. Things came to open conflict when, during the Emperor's absence on the banned crusade, papal armies invaded the kingdom of Sicily. In that campaign the two monarchies are actually at war with one another, and there falls upon men's ears the dreadful sound – fraught with apocalyptic fears – of the clash of the spiritual sword against the temporal sword.

The phases of the quarrel were publicized in manifestoes issued by Pope and Emperor. Frederick, as representative of the imperial *pax*, makes the Pope the sole disturber of the peace of Europe – an argument later taken up by the Reformers. Indeed, as the quarrel takes its fearful course, the Emperor tends to assume more and more a moral and reforming line.[1] It was the acknowledged rôle of emperors to be crusading leaders, and the apostolic duty of converting the heathen was part of the imperial office. Now, as the gap yawns between Pope and Emperor, the missionary side of that office begins further to take the shape of a reforming rôle, as the Emperor deplores in his public declarations the belligerent spirit, the pride, the avarice, of the Vicar of Christ and his cardinals. Thus there begins to emerge that notion of an imperial reform of the church which was later to be so strongly developed in connection with the religious sanctions claimed by Protestant national monarchs.

A way of expressing the religious side of the imperial mission, as understood in Frederick's circle, was through a form of Adam mysticism. According to these notions, the first Just World Ruler was Adam before the Fall; it is therefore the function of the Just Emperor to establish such a rule upon earth as will lead men back to the state of Adam before the Fall, that is to say, to the Earthly Paradise.[2] This implies a Christ-like redemptive rôle for the Emperor, though limited to the temporal sphere, and it is related to that interpretation of the golden age as being identical with the Earthly Paradise which Lactantius,[3] among others, had worked out in the time of Constantine. It would seem that what is developing here is a species of secular mysticism, or mystical secularism, with the Emperor as a kind of temporal Christ, redeeming man back to the Earthly Paradise with his justice, bringing in a full golden age with his imperial order. Such notions are a very extreme development out of that process of sanctifying the *civitas terrena*, the wordly society, which was implicit in the medieval emperor-idea.

With the death of Frederick II, the fullest and most consistent attempt to restore the Roman Empire collapsed in failure. Yet this extraordinary being lived in the imaginations of men for many years to come. The Guelph and Ghibelline factions perpetuated the memory of his gigantic contest with the Papacy. The tyrants of Italy were his spiritual descendants – some of them, his physical descendants through his illegitimate children – supporting, like him, their despotic claims with the panoply of imperialist rhetoric. How far the ideal of universal monarchy lived, if only as a rhetorical appendage, in the claims of the Sforza or the Medici to be the restorers of the golden age within their domains is a question which might be worth investigating.

Dante places the Emperor Frederick and his chancellor, Pietro della

---

[1] *Ibid.*, pp. 614 ff.   [2] *Ibid.*, pp. 258 ff.   [3] *Div. Inst.*, V. viii (*ed. cit.*), p. 421.

Vigna, in Hell.[1] Yet whilst in the *Divina Commedia* he thus carefully disassociates himself, theologically speaking, from the great protagonist of Ghibelline imperialism, in his *Monarchia* he expounds a theory of the Monarch which seems to be influenced by Frederickian theory and may owe something of its inspiration to the memory of the pattern of the Sicilian state. Kantorowicz puts the case even more strongly when he says that the dream of enforcing the Sicilian pattern on the whole earth was not fully advanced until Dante painted his picture of the one Roman World Monarchy.

Dante defines the monarchy, or empire, thus: 'The temporal monarchy, which is called Empire, is one Principate above all the others which are in time or in those things which are measured in time.'[2] That is to say, the temporal monarchy belongs to the history of this world, not to the spiritual world which is outside time. He proceeds to demonstrate from analogy with the order of the physical universe that it is necessary in the order of things that there should be a political order corresponding to the natural order, and that this order must be a universal world monarchy under one ruler. He then uses analogies from smaller social units. As all the powers within an individual man must be under one ruler, his intellectual power; as there must be one to rule a family, the paterfamilias; one to rule a city; one to rule a kingdom; so there must be one to rule the universal world.[3]

A major argument for the necessity for a World Ruler is that only so can war be avoided. To quote from the fourth book of the *Convito*, where Dante gives in abbreviated form the gist of the *Monarchia*:[4]

> In order to prevent wars and to remove the cause of them through all
> the earth . . . there must of necessity be Monarchy, that is to say one
> sole principality; and there must be one Prince, who, possessing all,
> and not being able to desire more, holds the kings content within the
> limits of the kingdoms, so that peace may be between them . . . and
> in this love . . . men can live happily, which is the end for which
> man was born.

Within this universal peace man may develop his intellectual powers. As the individual man, when quiet and in repose, may prudently operate, so the whole human race, when peace and tranquillity reign, may freely and easily pursue its proper functions. The world, then, is best disposed for the felicity of the human race and the development of its powers, in which development true liberty consists, when it is ordered under one ruler. This is what Virgil meant when, wishing to praise his own age, the age of Augustus, he says in the Fourth Eclogue, 'Now returns the Virgin, now return the ages of Saturn'.

[1] *Inferno*, X, xiii. [2] *Monarchia*, I, ii. [3] *Ibid.*, I, v. [4] *Convito*, IV, iv.

Iam redit et Virgo redeunt Saturnia regna

By the Virgin, explains Dante, Virgil means the Virgin Astraea, or Justice, who left the world when men grew evil in the ages of iron; by the ages of Saturn, he means the best ages, which are also called the golden ages.[1]

The World Monarchy, continues Dante in the second book of the *Monarchia*, belongs of right to the Roman people, and the office of World Ruler to the Roman Emperor. This is because the Roman people were the most just of peoples, and because their rule was a rule of reason, which is equated with justice. The Roman imperial claim is also supported by the argument from Providence. That the Romans were providentially called by God to the World Rulership is shown by the success which followed them, and by the fact that the Son of God chose to be born into the world at a time when it was united under the rule of one prince, and that prince a Roman prince.[2] The argument from Providence is thus stated in the *Convito*:[3]

> And since at Christ's advent into the world . . . earth must be in the best disposition . . . and the best disposition of the earth is when it is a Monarchy, that is to say all subject to one Prince . . . by Divine Providence it was ordained what people and what city should fulfil this, and that people was the Roman nation, and that city was glorious Rome.

Thus Dante's argument has developed the three cardinal points of the Frederickian theory of monarchy, *Necessitas, Justitia,* and *Providentia*.

In the third and last book of the *Monarchia*, Dante maintains that the authority of the monarch depends immediately upon God, thus plunging into those dangerous issues between the spiritual monarchy and the temporal monarchy which had convulsed the age of Frederick II. He undertakes detailed arguments against the canon lawyers and denies the validity of the Donation of Constantine. He rejects the symbolism of the sun and moon – that the Emperor derives his authority from the Pope as the moon borrows her light from the sun – and makes Pope and Emperor both directly derivative from the divine sun. Yet he emphasizes the strict division between the spiritual and the temporal spheres. Man has two ends: the one the attainment of blessedness in this temporal life by the operation of his own powers, and this is figured by the Earthly Paradise; the other the attainment of blessedness in eternal life, to which he cannot rise by his own powers unaided by grace, and this is figured by the Celestial Paradise. To these two ends and these two Paradises correspond the ends and offices of the temporal monarchy and the spiritual monarchy.[4]

It would be unwise to over-emphasize the resemblances between Dantesque and Frederickian theory, some of which may well be due to independent

---

[1] *Monarchia*, I, xi. [2] *Ibid.*, II, viii–xii. [3] *Convito*, IV, v. [4] *Monarchia*, III.

drawing on similar sources. Nevertheless, Dante's *Monarchia* is most certainly an imperialist document, and the most striking statement of imperialist theory in medieval times.

The channel through which Dante expected the return of the Just Empire was the emperor of his day, the Emperor Henry VII. He awaited his coming to Italy from the North to fulfil the mission to which his office called him.[1]

> We have wept long by the waters of confusion [he cries in a letter to Henry urging him to come to Italy] and unceasingly prayed for the protection of the just king, who should destroy the satellites of the cruel tyrant and should stablish us again under our own justice . . . But when thou, the successor of Caesar and Augustus . . . didst bring back the venerable Tarpeian standards, forthwith our deep sighing was stayed . . . Then many sang with Maro of the Reign of Saturn and the Return of the Virgin.

The words show that Dante fully accepted as a reality the translation of the Empire to Charlemagne and to his descendants, the northern emperors. For Dante, Henry VII truly represents Eternal Rome; he is the true successor of Caesar and Augustus; and therefore only he can restore justice and so bring back the Virgin Astraea and the golden age.

The ideal of the World Ruler as it emerges in Dante is the ideal of the full headship of the world in the Roman Emperor, which had been preserved – and as it were carried on through the Middle Ages in potentiality – in the medieval emperor-figure, but which is now released, expanded, and clarified, under the influences of revived ancient law and ancient philosophy, into a complete theory of the world fully ordered under the justice of the one *Dominus Mundi*. No tincture of nationality or of nationalism in the modern sense enters into this. The contemporary emperor is for Dante neither a German nor an Italian; he is a Roman, the true successor of Caesar and of Augustus, the living witness to the survival of the unity of the ancient world, the living channel through which unity will be restored in some new *renovatio*, rebirth, return of the justice of the golden age.

Dante's notions are far from being characteristic of medieval thought as a whole on these matters. In the *De regimine principum*, part of which, at least, is by Thomas Aquinas, the doctrine of the two powers necessary for the two ends – which *is* a characteristically medieval doctrine – is set forth. Though this duality converges into unity in Christ, who is both *rex* and *sacerdos*, in this world the two powers are committed separately, the one to earthly rulers, the other to priests and to their head, the Pope.[2] In his political theory in the *Summa*, Aquinas seems to be envisaging a number of

[1] Dante, *Epistolae*, ed. P. Toynbee, Oxford, 1920, pp. 89–90, 101.
[2] *De reg. princ.*, I, xiv; cf. A. P. D'Entrèves, *The Mediaeval Contribution to Political Thought*, Oxford, 1939, p. 40.

individual states to which the temporal power is committed. He believes that monarchy is the best form of government, and uses the 'one' argument in support of this but in relation to the rule of a king, not of a universal monarch or emperor.[1] Though all his thought implies a fundamental unity of human life under the supreme principle of justice and a supreme divine government of the world, he nowhere puts forward the idea of one universal monarch.[2] On the whole, the influence of classical political thought upon him is not in the direction of imperialism.

An instructive confutation of Dante's *Monarchia* from the Guelph point of view was written in 1327 by a Dominican of the name of Guido Vernani.[3] Vernani announces that he will demolish all Dante's arguments from Augustine's *De civitate Dei*. The argument that the rule providentially belongs to the Roman people is destroyed by quotations from Augustine on the idolatry, pride, and vainglory of the worldy city. The Age of Augustus is qualified as an age of growing vices, a falling-off from the virtues of the Republic, which explodes the golden age of imperial rule as the divinely appointed setting for the birth of Christ. The notion that the imperial justice can lead man back to the Earthly Paradise is annihilated by the statement that the original sin of Adam is not touched by any human legislation. And finally, it is emphatically denied that man has two ends after the manner formulated by Dante: the one the attainment of temporal bliss in this world by the full exercise of his powers, the Earthly Paradise to which the temporal monarchy tends: the other the attainment of blessedness in eternal life, the Celestial Paradise to which the spiritual monarchy tends. This is to make, says Vernani, a double beatitude for the corruptible and the incorruptible parts of man, and this is an impossibility, for in the corruptible part there cannot be, properly speaking, either virtue or beatitude, wherefore man is not ordained by God to the end of temporal bliss which cannot satisfy his true nature. For the heart of man is satisfied in no creature, but only in the vision of the *summum bonum*, his one true end.

This uncompromising statement may help to clarify the situation. The elements in Dante's imperialist theory to which Vernani objects are perhaps more characteristic of that *renovatio* which we call 'the Renaissance' than of the Middle Ages, although they are developed out of something which had existed in the Middle Ages ever since Pope Leo III translated a sanctified *civitas terrena* to Charlemagne.

Renaissance Humanism and the Imperial Idea

It has been said that universalism, or rather the never-realized ideal of universalism, breaks down at the Renaissance. Men begin to limit their

---

[1] *De reg. princ.*, II; cf. D'Entrèves, *op cit.*, p. 37.   [2] *Ibid.*, p. 36.

[3] Guido Vernani, *De Potestate Pontificiis et de reprobatione Monarchiae compositae a Dante Alighieri*, 1327; cf. D'Entrèves, *op cit.*, p. 28.

hopes of achieving unity to within the boundaries of national states. National patriotism arises to take the place of the old vaguely defined universal loyalties which experience had shown to be only at rare intervals even partially workable, and which usually led – as in the futile intervention of emperors in Italy in the fourteenth century – to no golden age but to increased confusion and disaster. Petrarch is contrasted with Dante as representing the newer point of view. In place of the tremendous vision of the *Monarchia* of the one *Dominus mundi* establishing a reign of peace and justice throughout the world, Petrarch would seem to transfer his enthusiasm to a vision of a united Italy, no longer torn by rivalries between petty states but at peace within herself. The poem 'Italia mia', on this view, becomes a patriotic poem, an appeal to the Italian people to rise as a nation.

Yet Petrarch's Italian patriotism really arises within the old universal framework, though his view of history is essentially different from that on which medieval imperialism was based.[1] The belief in the unbroken continuity of the Roman Empire through the theory of the translation of the Empire to Charlemagne is an illustration, in this particular field, of what we know to be, roughly speaking, true of the Middle Ages as a whole, namely that the medieval centuries were hardly aware of a break between their own times and the classical past.[2] Petrarch's attitude to history reflects what has been called the humanist's new sense of historical distance. With his increased knowledge of classical civilization, the humanist is unable to regard this as having continued unbroken up to the present (his present). He thinks of it as having come to an end with the destruction of ancient civilization by the barbarians, whereupon there set in a period of darkness which has lasted up to his own time, but which it is the mission of the humanist to dissipate by discovering and studying anew the literary and other monuments of the ancient world. This should bring about a renewal, a rebirth, a new period of classical light dispersing the barbarous darkness extending from the fall of the ancient world, through the Middle Ages, to the present. There is still in this the notion of the cyclic returns, of the periodic renovations, of imperialist rhetoric, but the humanist demands a much fuller renovation of classical civilization, the true nature of which he has begun to perceive.

What becomes, on this view, of the medieval theory of the continuity of the Empire? That Petrarch did not actually contest the theory of the translation of the Empire, and therefore its continuity, is suggested by the

---

[1] On Petrarch and the Empire, see T. E. Mommsen, 'Petrarch's conception of the Dark Ages', *Speculum*, XVII (1942), pp. 226–42; C. C. Bayley, 'Petrarch, Charles IV, and the *Renovatio Imperii*', *Speculum*, XVII (1942), pp. 323–41; W. K. Ferguson, *The Renaissance in Historical Thought*, Cambridge, Mass., 1948, pp. 8 ff.

[2] As Ferguson says (*op cit.*, p. 7), though many medieval historians were aware of the decline of the Roman Empire, they thought of this as a symptom of the general ageing of the world nearing its end.

prophecy which he puts into the mouth of Lucius Scipio in his Latin poem *Africa*.[1] Yet elsewhere he seems to view with scorn some of the most cherished notions of medieval imperialism. For him, the barbarous influences which had destroyed Rome live on in the barbarized Empire of the Middle Ages. In an early letter, he calls Charlemagne '*King* Charles, whom by the cognomen of "the Great" barbarous peoples dare to raise to the level of Pompey or Alexander'.[2] By denying to Charlemagne his imperial title, and by suggesting that only barbarous peoples call him 'the Great', Petrarch seems, as T. E. Mommsen pointed out, to be implying disregard of the whole institution of the medieval empire and its claim to be the true successor of the *imperium Romanum*. Perhaps also his words in *Africa* about 'the strangers who steal the sceptre and the glory of the Empire',[3] though used of the non-Italian emperors of ancient Rome, might have an implied application to the translation of the Empire to the Franco-German strangers of the North.

The weakness of the medieval empire from the humanist point of view was that its centre was not Rome. Ideally, Rome was acknowledged as the centre through the coronation of the emperors at Rome by the Pope; nevertheless, politically, its centre was in the North. With the lessening of respect for the notion of the translation of the Empire, the inconsistency in the idea of a so-called Roman Emperor who does not govern from Rome becomes apparent. 'If the Roman *imperium* is not in Rome', asks Petrarch in the *Liber sine nomine*, 'where is it?'[4]

The historical visions and emotions aroused in Petrarch by his visits to Rome and by the actual sight of its majestic ruins intensified his new concept of history. This found a political outlet in his enthusiastic response to the movement which Cola di Rienzo attempted to initiate in 1347.[5] Calling himself a 'Tribune of the People', Rienzo issued a series of excited manifestoes inviting all Italy to unite under a new-born Rome. The type of revival which Rienzo seemed primarily to envisage was a revival of the Republic. The ancient civic *virtus* of the Roman people was, he proclaimed, re-emerging under his leadership, and this rebirth of Rome, although its appeal was primarily to Italy, had wide connotations, for he sent his manifestoes to nearly all the monarchs of Europe. Rienzo's republicanism was, however, only a prelude to an intended revival of the Empire based on Rome. The Roman people, rising in their revived strength and *virtus*, were to elect a Roman emperor who should dwell in Rome. In this way a renovated Empire would arise in Rome. Hence the imperial golden age rhetoric which Rienzo used of his movement.

[1] *Africa*, II, ll. 288–93.   [2] *Le Familiari*, ed. V. Rossi, 1926, I, 25.   [3] *Africa*, II, ll. 274–8.
[4] *Liber sine nomine*, IV, in P. Piur, *Petrarcas 'Buch ohne Namen' und die papstliche Kurie*, Halle, 1925, p. 126; cf. Ferguson, *op cit.*, p. 9.
[5] See C. Burdach, *Rienzo und die geistige Wandlung seiner Zeit* (in *Vom Mittelalter zur Reformation*, II, i), Berlin, 1913; P. Piur, *Cola di Rienzo*, Vienna, 1913; I. Origo, *Tribune of Rome*, London, 1938.

The rights of the Roman people to confer authority on the emperor had not infrequently been urged on medieval emperors. Under the influence of Arnold of Brescia, the Roman senate wrote a letter to the first Hohenstaufen emperor, Conrad III, claiming the right to nominate him and demanding that he should dwell in Rome. Rienzo issued a similar letter to the emperor of his day, Charles IV.[1]

Rienzo's republicanism has within it no real understanding of the constitutional differences between the Roman Republic and the Roman Empire. The point, for Rienzo, of his republicanism was that through it he would revive the *virtus* of Roman citizens and inspire them to claim the return of the Empire to Rome. In this way, the titular emperor would become a truly Roman Emperor. His movement implies, of course, that the preceding medieval emperors had not been truly Roman Emperors. Nevertheless, by calling himself, not only 'Tribune of the People', but also 'Knight of the Holy Spirit', Rienzo retained those chivalrous associations belonging to the northern pattern of imperial renewal, which were hardly consonant either with republicanism or with a more purely Roman type of imperialism.

Petrarch pinned his faith to Rienzo's movement. He believed that both the weakness and the disunion of Italy and the fact that Rome had ceased to be the seat of the Empire were caused by the 'fickleness of the Goddess Fortuna' who was no longer controlled by the antique virtue of the *Populus Romanus*. Rienzo's career had inspired the hope that the antique virtue was reviving, but the citizens of Rome proved broken reeds, and his movement petered out in failure. In his disappointment, Petrarch, remembering his Ghibelline origins (his father, a contemporary of Dante, had like Dante suffered exile from Florence for his imperialist views) turned to the titular emperor of his day, Charles IV. Petrarch implores the Emperor himself to do what Rienzo's movement had failed to do, to unify Italy and restore the *imperium* to Rome.[2] It is thus clear that the so-called Italian nationalism of Petrarch arises within the old framework and implies the universal ideals. For both Rienzo and Petrarch the unification of Italy – whether achieved through pseudo-republicanism or the traditional Ghibelline appeal to the emperor – was but the prelude to the return of the *imperium* to Rome; and the *imperium* meant in theory the World Ruler, the *Dominus mundi*, the universal peace and justice.

What then is the difference between this and the Dantesque Ghibellinism? Had not Dante also called upon the Emperor to come to Italy to restore her? Yes, but for Dante the Holy Roman Emperor was the true successor of Caesar and Augustus; he did not need re-Romanizing for, though he might be a German by birth, by virtue of his office he was a Roman, in true line of descent from the emperors of ancient Rome. The necessity for the re-Romanizing of the Empire which Petrarch feels so strongly is related to the poor

[1] See Bayley, *op cit.*, pp. 324–5.   [2] *Ibid.*, pp. 328 ff.

view which he took of the medieval empire as a semi-barbarian institution, and to his doubtful attitude to the theory of the translation of the Empire.

The Emperor failed Petrarch, no less than did the Roman citizens. Italy was not united, nor was the *imperium* translated back to Rome in a *renovatio* which should be the political counterpart of the humanist Renaissance, or rebirth, of classical culture. Nevertheless, the phantom of imperial *renovatio* is a driving force behind the work of the Italian humanists. They strive to make the dream, unrealized in the political sphere, come true in the sphere of letters. One need only think, for example, of the language in which Poggio Bracciolini describes his discovery of a manuscript of Quintilian in the monastery of St Gall, lying in a heap of rubbish, 'hardly a fit residence for a condemned criminal and most unworthy of its noble inhabitants'.[1] Leonardo Bruni, writing to congratulate Poggio on his find, says that he is eagerly awaiting the arival of the Quintilian manuscript in Italy, adding that when 'after having delivered him [that is Quintilian] from his long imprisonment in the dungeons of the barbarians, you transmit him to this country, all the nations of Italy ought to assemble to bid him welcome'.[2] The vision is that of the noble Roman author, Quintilian, rescued by humanist hands from neglect and barbarization, re-entering his native land where he is welcomed with a triumph. There was some historical injustice in this vision, since it was the Carolingian Renaissance, now relegated to the ages of barbarism, which had copied and transmitted the classical manuscripts which the Italian humanists rediscovered.[3]

The proudest achievement of the Italian humanists, the rediscovery and re-creation of the Latin tongue, which – cleansed from its barbarization in the ages of darkness – now shone forth again upon the world in classical purity, is motivated by similar enthusiasms. The universal ideals of humanism come out clearly in Lorenzo Valla's eloquent preface to his treatise 'on the Elegance of the Latin Tongue',[4] where he proclaims that the revived and purified Latin is to be the world language, the vehicle for the transmission of the light of the classical revival to all peoples.

The dismissal of the Middle Ages, and the medieval empire, as a dark

[1] Poggio to Guarino, December 1416; cited W. Shepherd, *Poggio Bracciolini*, Liverpool, 1837, pp. 97–8.

[2] Bruni to Poggio, cited Shepherd, *op. cit.*, pp. 95–6.

[3] See G. Billanovich, 'Petrarch and the textual tradition of Livy', *Journal of the Warburg and Courtauld Institutes*, XIV (1951), pp. 137–208.

[4] L. Valla, *De elegantia latinae linguae lib. VI*, Rome, 1471, preface. In this preface, the phantom of Roman imperial *renovatio* can be clearly distinguished behind the enthusiasm for the Renaissance of classical letters, and many other such passages can be found in the works of Italian humanists.

The ideology behind the artistic transformation of the Capitol in the Renaissance is studied by F. Saxl, 'The Capitol during the Renaissance, a symbol of the imperial idea', *Lectures*, London, Warburg Institute (1957), pp. 200–14.

period between classical antiquity and the humanist Renaissance was a notion less congenial to the northern nations, and particularly to the Germans, who were naturally unwilling to take the view that the translation of the Empire to the Germans meant its barbarization. Amongst German historians, therefore, however fully under the influence of the classical revival emanating from Italy, the attitude to the history of the Empire is different from that of Petrarch and his followers.[1] In the *Chronicle of Nauclerus*, published in 1516, the coronation of Charlemagne is hailed as proof of the divinely ordained superiority of the German people; it marks the passing of the Roman Empire to the Germans. God has chosen the Germans to dominate the nations and to have sovereignty over the whole world. And he has chosen wisely, for are not the Germans the most sincerely noble, the most just, the most prolific, the strongest and most tenacious in war of all peoples?[2] The argument from Providence, of God's providential choice of the Roman people, is here transferred to the virtuous German people as those to whom the Empire is rightly translated.

Thus in both the North and the South, the ideal of the World Ruler takes on a particularist tinge. The transmission of the Empire to the North means that the German people are the true successors of the Romans, whilst the South insists that the Empire must be translated back to Italy, away from the barbarous North. The abstract Ghibellinism of Dante had contained no such distinctions. Though Dante damns Frederick II to Hell, it is for his heresy that he damns him, not as a stranger, a barbarian, or a German. For Dante, Frederick is none of these things; he is Caesar Augustus. And speaking of the culture of the Sicilian court in his *De vulgare eloquentia*, he says:[3]

> Those illustrious heroes Frederick Caesar and his well-born son, Manfred, displaying the nobility and rectitude of their natures, so long as fortune permitted them, followed humane things and disdained the ways of the brute. And so the gifted and the noble-hearted strove to be guided by the majesty of these great princes, so that every work of excellence produced at that time by a Latin author first issued from the hall of these great kings.

In the fifteenth century, there grew up new schools of historical thought and political theory, particularly in Florence, which make a very definite break with the phantom of the Empire and its periodic renewals. These currents are nourished partly from the fuller knowledge opened up by humanist studies of ancient political history and theory, and partly by the

---

[1] Ferguson, *op cit.*, pp. 33 ff.

[2] J. Nauclerus, *Memorabilium omnis aetatis et omnium gentium chronici commentarii*, Cologne, 1544 (1st ed., Tübingen, 1516), pp. 619–20, 630; cf. Ferguson, *op cit.*, p. 35.

[3] *De vulgare eloquentia*, I, xii.

object-lessons in different types of government provided by that very dis-unity of Italy which Rienzo and Petrarch deplored.

Leonardo Bruni[1] in his *History of Florence* shows that clear grasp of the difference between republic and empire the absence of which is noticeable in Rienzo. An ardent believer in republican liberty as opposed to imperialist despotism, Bruni dates the decline of Rome from the suppression of the Republic. Like Vernani, though for different reasons, he disbelieves in the Augustan golden age. According to Bruni, Rome 'began to go to ruin when first the name of Caesar fell like a disaster upon the city, for freedom ended with the imperial title and, following liberty, virtue departed'.[2] This smashes the whole theory of the divinely appointed imperial golden age in which Christ was born, and all the sequences of subsequent imperialist history. It hardly matters to learn, after this, that Bruni did not believe in the translation of the Empire to Charlemagne; for if the Roman Empire itself was a deg-radation from the Republic, the translated and barbarized form of it must obviously be of still less significance.

Through these views, Bruni develops a slant on medieval history which is different, not only from that of a northern imperialist chronicler admiringly tracing the careers of Holy Roman Emperors, but also from that of Petrarch for whom the Middle Ages were a dark period of barbarism. For Bruni, the Middle Ages are not dark, for they witness the gradual rise of the spirit of liberty in the free cities of Italy, the communes. This fortunate and hopeful movement flourished when the Empire was weak and when emperors withdrew their influence from Italy. It was at the times when the despotic imperial influence was not strong that the communes developed their free-dom and their powers.

Apart from its anti-imperial tone, Bruni's *History of Florence* is an example of a more exact and scholarly type of historiography, which was leading to a more realistic and secular view of both history and politics, a climate of opinion in which it began to seem less and less desirable to base either history or action on mystical interpretations of the Roman Empire.

It was Machiavelli, of course, who put *Realpolitik* on a scientific basis. Animated by an intense patriotism, he wished for the creation of a strong, well-organized state in Italy which should become the nucleus of Italian unity. He used his reading of Roman history and his close observation of contemporary events as material from which to deduce practical guidance for a ruler as to how to obtain, and retain, power. This realistic approach of necessity ruled out the old idealist and universalist conceptions. The two foci of medieval history – the Papacy and the Empire – are neither of them conducive, in Machiavelli's view, to the welfare of Italy. He regarded the

---

[1] See Ferguson, *op cit.*, pp. 10–11; J. W. Thompson, *History of Historical Writing*, New York, 1942, I, pp. 473 ff.; H. Baron, *The Crisis of the Early Italian Renaissance*, Princeton, 1966, pp. 94 ff.
[2] Quoted Ferguson, *op. cit.*, p. 10.

Papacy with active dislike as the chief cause of Italy's weakness and disunity; and the Empire as an outworn, obsolete institution, an irritating excuse for foreign intervention in Italian affairs.[1] Nevertheless, by taking Roman history, whether republican or imperial, as the store-house whence he draws empirical observations for the guidance of the modern politicians' work for Italy, he implies that Italian history is Roman history, with its universal implications. And there is embedded in Machiavelli's thought a survival of the old cyclic views, for he believes in an organic process of rise and decline in the life of states, and that their renovation consists in a return to a pristine *virtù*.

So we have arrived at a time when the new orientations of historical thinking set going by Italian humanism seem to have finally dismissed the Empire, even as a myth or a phantom testifying to the universal idea. Henceforward the national states will learn from Machiavelli how to build up their separate powers on a basis of realistic thought and observation.

Northern humanism, which, of course, developed later than in the South, reached its fullest and finest flowering in Erasmus. As a political thinker, Erasmus is a Christian idealist, far removed from the Machiavellian realism. His ideal for Europe is that all its princes should have received a Christian education, with special emphasis on instruction in the virtues necessary for a ruler, to be acquired from moral pagan writers such as Plato, Cicero, Seneca, or Plutarch. Thus trained, the monarchs of the individual states would act in concert to defend and maintain an international *pax* in Europe. He develops these ideas in his *Education of a Christian Prince*,[2] written in 1516 for the instruction of the youth who was afterwards to become the Emperor Charles V.

Though Erasmus, too, would seem to have discarded the Empire, substituting for it the concert of Christian princes as the instrument for preserving universal peace, a vestigial survival of the imperial idea can be detected in some of his writings. In a letter written to Dukes Frederick and George of Saxony in 1517 (and used as a preface to his edition of Suetonius printed in 1518),[3] Erasmus says that the name of empire, once sacrosanct throughout the world, carries with it even now religious and venerable associations, though but a shadow of its former self. Even in ancient times, he points out, the Roman Empire was never really universal; many parts of the world,

---

[1] The first book of Machiavelli's *Istorie fiorentini* discusses Italian history in relation to the disasters arising from the ambition of popes and the interventions of emperors: in the following books he insists on the deplorable results for Florence of the incessant strife between the Guelph and Ghibelline factions.

[2] Erasmus, *The Education of a Christian Prince*, trans. L. K. Born, Columbia University Press, 1936. See also Erasmus's *Querela Pacis* (1517), English trans. W. J. Hirten, New York, 1946.

[3] Erasmus, *Opus epistolarum*, ed. P. S. Allen *et al.*, 1906–47, II, 586. This important letter was pointed out to me by the late Barbara Flower.

recently discovered, were unknown to it. Its majesty paled before the light of the gospel, as the moon before the sun. In the invasions of the barbarians it was extinguished, though after many centuries the Roman Pontiffs restored it 'but in name rather than in fact'. He doubts whether it is now either possible or desirable to restore the Empire, though he admits that, in theory, a universal monarchy would be the best state for the world. This seems now quite unrealizable, and, in any case, the office of universal monarch is too heavy a responsibility for one man to bear. Moreover, the universal monarchy will not be necessary 'if concord joins the Christian princes among themselves'. The true monarch of the world is Christ, and, if our princes consent to His teachings, all will flourish under one prince.

Written three years before Charles V was elected emperor, this letter of Erasmus is a valuable document for the state of feeling about the Empire in enlightened northern circles just before that event. Erasmus is realist in the sense that he realizes that the modern states of Europe, with their modern princes, render the Empire but a shadow and a phantom; he is idealist in the sense that he translates to the concert of Christian princes the imperial functions of maintaining universal *pax* and *justitia*. Yet the name of empire, which has never been more than a name, even when translated to emperors by popes (there is nothing in Erasmus of the *Romanitas* which the early Italian humanists developed out of the imperialist tradition), still has august and religious associations, and the universal monarchy subsists as a shadow behind the Christian dream of the universal rule of Christ.

The phenomenon of the Empire of Charles V was about to infuse new potency into the idea of empire.

Charles V and the Idea of Empire

Let us very briefly remind ourselves of the family connections through which Charles V inherited the most extensive territory in Europe held by any monarch since Charlemagne. On the paternal side, he was heir to the domains of the dukes of Burgundy, including the Netherlands and Austria; through his mother, the daughter of Ferdinand and Isabella, he was ruler of Spain and Sicily. Thus, almost fortuitously as it seemed, Charles stepped into an inheritance which ran from the centre of Europe up into German lands in a manner recalling the Carolingian empire; which, through the Sicilian title, gave him the foothold in southern Italy of which Frederick II had made such use; and which also included the wealthy and recently united monarchy of Spain with its vast spheres of influence in the newly discovered continent beyond the Atlantic. When, in 1519, on the death of his grandfather Maximilian, the princes of Germany elected Charles to the imperial title, it was realized – in some quarters with fear, in others with hope – that this emperor, inheriting territories in Europe which linked together (though not exactly covering) the area of what had once been the Roman Empire, and territories beyond the seas in lands unknown to the Romans, was one through whom the Holy Roman Empire might revive its universal claim, one who might indeed become Lord of the World in a larger sense than was conceived, even by the Romans.

Later events served but to increase the number of benefits showered on this monarch by the goddess Fortuna. His great rival was the French king, who not only commanded large material wealth and territory but who also claimed to be the true descendant of the Frankish Charlemagne, therefore having a right to leadership in Europe – a claim which was acknowledged in many quarters outside France, particularly in Italy, where the French monarchy as saviour was always an alternative to the imperial influence. When at the battle of Pavia, in 1525, the imperialist forces defeated the French and captured their king – so that François Ier actually became Charles's prisoner – the portentous destiny of Charles seemed further underlined, for by that victory not only was France vanquished but also all Italy lay at his feet.

Meanwhile in Rome, the head of the spiritual monarchy viewed these events with dread. The threat to the papal territories which the alliance between the Sicilian kingdom and the North – as in the days of Frederick II – had revived, was now made immediate by the great imperialist victory. And when in those terrible days of 1527 the imperialist armies took and sacked Rome, and Pope Clement VII himself became Charles's prisoner, it seemed that Europe of the sixteenth century – in spite of the complex influences of Renaissance and Reformation, of the rise of nationalism, or of modern schools of thought in the interpretation of history and politics – had re-simplified itself to the medieval pattern of Empire and Papacy, and in that uneasy balance the Empire had at last turned the scale. The sack of Rome by the armies of the new Charlemagne was the devastating answer of history to the dream of the Italian humanists. Whether regarded realistically as the latest, and not the least destructive, of the barbarian invasions, or apocalyptically as the portent of a new dispensation, that event put the idea of universal empire back into the centre of the stage.

It was not the Romanized and re-Italianized empire longed for by the humanists that Charles's career seemed to be renovating, but the medieval idea of empire, based on the northern holder of the title. At last the armies of the Holy Roman Emperor, whose advent Dante, the Ghibelline dreamer, had sighed for, came down from the North to Rome – and sacked it! Dantesque ideas were consciously entertained in Charles's entourage. His first tutor, and his confidential adviser through life, was the Italian, Mercurio Gattinara, who was a student of Dante's *Monarchia* and who expected from Charles V the realization of Dante's hope of universal monarchy.[1] The

[1] On Gattinara's sources, see Carlo Bornate in *Miscellanea di storia italiana*, 3rd series, XVII, Turin, 1915, pp. 233–568.

Spanish bishop, Antonio Guevara, court preacher and historiographer to the Emperor, wrote a work on imperial and royal virtue, the *Relox de principes*, which was widely read all over Europe. Guevara repeats the old imperialist arguments for the rule of One Monarch from analogy with the rule of one in smaller social units.[1] These were the Ghibelline and Dantesque arguments for the rule of the universal monarch.

Yet many-sided Renaissance influences also fashioned the new imperialist propaganda, and are to be found in Guevara's work. He cast his treatise in the form of an imitation of the meditations of the Emperor Marcus Aurelius, the great Stoic emperor. Stoicism, a strong tradition in Spain, was widely revived in the Renaissance, when Seneca and Plutarch were amongst the most admired authors.[2] Stoic thought encourages a universal outlook on affairs, and Marcus Aurelius was the great exemplar of stoic moral idealism and universalism.

In Titian's famous portrait of Charles V (Plate 2), which recalls the antique statue of Marcus Aurelius (Plate 1) we have one of the most striking presentations of Charles in his imperial rôle. He is Romanized as the stoic emperor, the World Ruler on whose domains the sun never set. Yet he is also the northern ruler, the Christian and chivalrous emperor, wearing the collar of the Order of the Golden Fleece.

Charles's intensive cult, after the manner of his Burgundian ancestors, of the Order of the Golden Fleece tended to restore something of their international character to the Orders of Chivalry and to place Charles himself in an international setting as the Knight-Emperor of Christendom, pledged to maintain the Christianized imperial virtues and to spread them throughout the world.

For the career of the new Charlemagne was evoking afresh the memories of the first pattern of imperial *renovatio*, the feudal and chivalrous pattern. At the court of Ferrara, always noted for its devotion to the traditions of chivalry, Ariosto composed his modern chivalrous epic, the *Orlando furioso*, first published in 1516. The whole subject of Ariosto's poem, being a revival of the twelfth-century romances of the Charlemagne cycle, is a revival of the medieval idea of the Empire translated to the North in Charlemagne, which certain aspects of Italian humanism had tended to depreciate as a barbarized form of the Roman Empire. In the first stanza of the *Orlando furioso* the translation of the Empire is confirmed by the description of Charlemagne as 're Carlo imperator romano'. This reaction from the scepticism concerning the medieval empire, and its basis in the theory of translation, which humanist study had encouraged, is connected with the reaction which

[1] Guevara's book was translated into English by Thomas North with the title *The Diall of Princes*. The passage here indicated on the rule of One is quoted, in North's English translation, below, p. 52.

[2] They were important sources for Erasmus in *The Education of a Christian Prince*; see L. K. Born's introduction to his translation.

was taking place in contemporary history, for Ariosto's poem includes a glorification of the new Charlemagne, Charles V. In the fifteenth canto of the poem, Astolfo hears the prophecy of the future empire of Charles V. The prophetess foretells that the world will be put under a universal monarchy by one who will succeed to the diadem of Augustus, Trajan, Marcus Aurelius, and Severus. This ruler will spring from the union of the houses of Austria and of Aragon; and by him Astraea, or Justice, will be brought back to earth, together with all banished virtues.[1]

Thus, in Italy itself, Ghibellinism revives anew, and Ariosto's words may be compared with those with which Dante had hailed the Emperor Henry VII as destined to bring back the rule of Astraea, or Justice, and the golden age. If it is objected that Ariosto's choice of the Carolingian epic as the vehicle for what he has to say is a poetic fiction, and not to be taken seriously as a political statement, the reply can be made that the re-feudalization of the imagination which his poem represents is in itself symptomatic of a new state of affairs, as compared with earlier efforts to dispel the Dark Ages by re-classicizing the imagination.

Ariosto speaks, too, of those new worlds, unknown to the Romans, which have lately been discovered, repeating the widely held belief that these discoveries were themselves a portent of a new world monarchy. According to the prophetess in the poem, it has pleased God to keep the ways to these as yet undiscovered lands unknown until the time when he will raise up a new emperor. She foresees the time when these discoveries will be made, and when the World Ruler will appear in the person of Charles V.[2] These passages fill out for us the meaning of Charles's famous device of the two columns, with its motto *Plus Oultre* (Plate 3a). As well as its obvious meaning that his was an empire which extended further than that of the Romans, which had been bounded by the columns of Hercules, the device carried with it also this prophetic implication that the discovery of the new worlds was providentially timed to coincide with the coming of one who should be the *Dominus mundi* in a wider sense than was known to the Romans. Ruscelli hints at this in his commentary on the device.[3] Thus the old argument from Providence was brought up to date to cover the new geographical situation.

Spread by magnificent pageantry, Charles's device was known throughout Europe. It raised again the phantom of empire which had haunted the Middle Ages, but in a modernized form.

---

[1] *Orlando furioso*, XV, xxv, xxvi. The passage is quoted below, p. 53, in Sir John Harington's English translation.

[2] *Orlando furioso*, XV, xxi, xxiv, quoted below, pp. 54–5, in Harington's English translation.

[3] G. Ruscelli, *Le imprese illustri*, Venice, 1572, p. 20. On the device of Charles V, see Marcel Bataillon, 'Plus Oultre: La cour découvre le nouveau monde', in *Fêtes et cérémonies au temps de Charles Quint*, ed. Jean Jacquot, Centre National de la Recherche Scientifique, Paris, 1960, pp. 13–27; Earl Rosenthal, '*Plus ultra, Non plus ultra*, and the columnar device of the Emperor Charles V', *Journal of the Warburg and Courtauld Institutes*, XXXIV (1971), pp. 204–28.

Charles's own character did something to help the dream, or the delusion, that the Holy Roman Empire in its holy aspect was reviving. Perhaps the second Charlemagne was a little like his namesake, rather a slow and simple man but dignified by his sincere respect for his office. Deeply imbued with the Hapsburg religious temperament, he bore himself with modesty in his great position and with a profound sense of responsibility to the divine powers whence he believed that he held it. The world recognized the vein of integrity in him and was impressed by that abdication scene when he laid aside all his greatness in order to pass his remaining days in a monastery. His weaknesses do not diminish the genuineness of that gesture which was of a piece with his lifelong attitude to his work. Charles's own attitude towards his office revived respect for the religious side of the imperial dignity.

That side carried with it traditionally the duty of spreading the gospel among the heathen and defending it from heathen attack. This is represented, in Charles's case, by the carrying of the cross into the New World with the imperial banner and by his victories over the Turk. In earlier imperialist controversies with the Papacy, as we saw, the imperial office came also to imply a mission of reforming the church – a notion with which Dante is deeply imbued[1] and which is also present in Petrarch's re-Romanized Ghibellinism. The reforming mission of the empire comes very much to the forefront again with Charles V. Though stiff in his attitude to Luther's violent rebellion, there was reason to believe that the Emperor was not unsympathetic to some of the views of Erasmus, and Spanish Erasmians saw a connection between Erasmian reform and the mission providentially fallen to this emperor.[2]

Antonio de Valdes was chiefly responsible for the imperialist apologies after the Sack of Rome, and these show traces of the old Ghibelline arguments for imperial reform now put forward by an Erasmian imperialist. In his remarkable dialogue between Lactantius and an archdeacon,[3] the two speakers discuss the sack. The archdeacon was present at it, and is profoundly shocked. Lactantius (significantly named after the imperialist Christian of Constantine's day) argues that it was the Pope who stirred up the war and made trouble between Christian princes: he points to the scandalous life of the clergy and to their notorious avarice. God, he says, sent the excellent Erasmus to argue the need for reform; he was not listened to, so God raised the violent Luther. The church listened to neither, so God was obliged to

---

[1] In a letter addressed to the Italian cardinals, urging them to undertake the reform of the Church, Dante accuses them of being wedded neither to charity, justice, or Astraea, but only to avarice (*Epistolae*, ed. Toynbee, pp. 134, 145).

[2] See the chapter on 'L'Erasmisme au service de la politique espagnole' in Marcel Bataillon, *Erasme et l'Espagne*, Paris, 1937, pp. 395 ff.

[3] There is an English translation of this work; see A. de Valdes, *Dialogue of Lactancio and an Archdeacon*, trans. J. E. Longhurst, University of New Mexico Press, 1952.

allow the sack of Rome as a final providential warning. He suggests that now that the Pope is in the Emperor's hands he will be prevented from doing evil. Finally, the archdeacon, whom these arguments have converted, urges that the Emperor should now take his opportunity and reform the church. This was an extreme position which Charles himself (who was worried and regretful about the sack) might not have approved, but such talk flying over Europe raised in men's minds the powerful phantom of the Reforming Emperor.[1]

Charles never did take the step, urged on him by some of his advisers, of summoning a council of the church to carry through a reform movement and end the schism. Yet he was known to be interested in projects, such as those put forward by Melanchthon, for exploring ways and means of reconciling Catholics and Protestants. His very serious and painstaking approach to such problems certainly associated the imperial title with vague hopes for a general reunion of Christendom, a restoration of the *universitas Christiana*, an imperial *pax* in the theological sphere. In relation to the religious problems discussed at the Diet of Augsburg in 1530, Charles spoke of the 'peculiar Imperial grace and gentleness and desire for peace'.[2]

The position of Charles as the most powerful and significant emperor since Frederick II raised again the Pope-Emperor situation of Frederick's times, though in a modified and modernized form. Modified, because Charles's Catholic orthodoxy was never impugned, as Frederick's was; modernized, because Renaissance and Reformation have intervened to change the face of Europe. Yet this modern emperor, politically successful against the Papacy, where former emperors had failed, and in his spiritual capacity leading a reform movement, began to appear like the age-long Ghibelline dream of the Just Emperor. In his temporal aspect he would restore the imperial rule of justice and peace throughout the world; in his spiritual aspect he would reform the avarice (those indulgences against which Luther had protested) and the pride (the temporal power of the Papacy which the events of 1527 had humbled) of the popes. An extraordinary concatenation of circumstances seemed to have marked Charles out for this rôle. He was the holder of the consecrated title of Holy Roman Emperor. He had providentially inherited territories in Europe which recalled the Roman Empire; he had providentially appeared at the time when the new worlds were discovered. He was even providentially endowed with the imperial virtues; Aleander said of him that he had 'the best disposition of any ruler for a thousand years'.[3] In such a phenomenon might not men expect to see some latent manifestation of universal monarchy, reducing to

---

[1] Gattinara was one of those who nourished the hope that the Emperor would reform the Church; see K. Brandi, *The Emperor Charles V*, trans. C. V. Wedgwood, London, 1939, p. 256.

[2] Quoted by E. Armstrong, *The Emperor Charles V*, London, 1910, I, p. 252.

[3] Quoted, *ibid.*, I, p. 79.

the ideal One, not only the temporal world, but even the spiritual and temporal monarchies in some new Pope-Emperor solution, and providing some imperial approach to the problem of religious schism? It is significant that Ariosto, in the passage about Charles V already indicated, uses the words of St John's Gospel, usually applied to Christ, or to the Pope: 'And there shall be one flock and one shepherd.'

> E vuol che sotto a questo imperatore
> Solo un ovile sia, solo un pastore.

The 'imperatore', in his Christ-like rôle, seems here to dominate the 'pastore', and the words of the poet may be compared with those which the Chancellor, Gattinara, addressed to Charles after his election to the imperial title:[1]

> Sire, God has been very merciful to you: he has raised you above all the Kings and princes of Christendom to a power such as no sovereign has enjoyed since your ancestor Charles the Great. He has set you on the way towards a world monarchy, towards the uniting of all Christendom under a single shepherd.

It has been pointed out, with truth, that Charles V did not entertain the ambition of achieving a world empire by conquering other states; and it has therefore been argued that the Dantesque monarchical ideas of Gattinara were not really consonant with the mind of Charles.[2] We need, however, a fuller study of what the Spanish Erasmians really meant by their use of Dantesque universalism in connection with Charles. It is curious to recall that in 1527 Gattinara requested Erasmus to prepare an edition of Dante's *Monarchia* as a service to the imperial cause.[3] Erasmus seems not to have complied, but would Gattinara have made this request to the scholar whose detestation of war was so well known had he been thinking of the Dantesque imperialism in terms of conquest? More probably it was the religious side of the imperial idea that he had in mind, particularly its reforming side, and perhaps in some form not incompatible with the Erasmian *pax Christiana*, to be maintained by the concerted Christian princes with the Emperor at their head.

The set of 'providential' circumstances which had seemed to raise the Holy Roman Empire out of the backwaters into which it had been receding soon passed away, and the mirage dissolved. But the point is that in Charles V and in the symbolism of his propaganda, the *phantom* of the Empire *did*

---

[1] Quoted Brandi, *op cit.*, p. 112. Brandi emphasizes (p. 269) that Gattinara's ideas originate in Dante.

[2] This is argued by Menendez Pidal, *Idea imperial de Carlos V*, Madrid, 1940. P. Rassow (*Die Kaiser-Idee Karls V dargestellt an der Politik der Jahre 1528–40*, Berlin, 1932) agrees with Brandi that it was Gattinara who formed Charles V's 'imperial idea'.

[3] See the letter to Erasmus, attributed to Gattinara, in *Opus epistolarum*, VI, 1790a; and cf. Bataillon, *Erasme et l'Espagne*, p. 249.

revive, and that in itself is a historical fact deserving careful study. It is a striking one for several reasons. In the first place, the phantom had been dying under the critical examination of the new types of political and historical thinking. To those intelligent and patriotic Florentines, Machiavelli and Guicciardini, talking together after the victory of Pavia, the unexpected recrudescence of the Holy Roman Empire may well have seemed a devastating reaction, foreboding the end of Italian independence and blocking all forward and liberal movements of the human spirit.[1] It did, of course, mark the beginning of the Austro-Spanish domination of the peninsula. Second, the imperial phantom which revives with Charles V is not the Romanized phantom which had haunted the earlier humanists. It is the northern phantom which returns with the second Charlemagne, and which finds congenial expression in the revived chivalrous epic, though it also drapes itself in the classical formulae which humanist studies had enriched.

Further, it is important to ask why the revived phantom found a wide acceptance in men's imaginations. This may itself be symptomatic of a psychological need of the times, the need for order. For all the breakages in the old order of things brought with them fears as well as hopes, fears of a general collapse into chaos. Such fears made men ready to turn again – if only in thought, in their mental imagery – to the rope to which their medieval ancestors had clung, to the idea of the undying Roman Empire, the continued existence of which, as renovated in Charlemagne and his successors, held the world together. The symbolism of the empire of Charles V, which seemed able to include the whole world as then known and to hold out the promise of a return to spiritual unity through a revival of the cementing power of the Christianized imperial virtues, was a comforting phantom in the chaotic world of the sixteenth century.

After Charles's reign, the imperial title, which was not held by his son Philip, receded once more into a local concern, and Europe was left with only the memory of the psychologically comforting revival of the idea of imperial universality and continuity which Charles as the new Charlemagne had seemed to represent. Yet the need for an ordered refuge was even greater than before, for the latter half of the sixteenth century was a time of political instability, the anxieties of which were greatly increased by being interpreted in terms of theological menace. The onslaughts of the Reformers on the corruptions of the Papacy, using the terrifying language of the Apocalypse, seemed to have weakened the spiritual monarchy almost beyond repair, for, although the Counter Reformation was under way, its effects were not yet fully felt. Thus the spiritual monarchy was diminished by the Reformation, which withdrew large parts of Europe from its spiritual control. And the temporal monarchy was diminished, and had no longer

---

[1] Machiavelli's violent reactions to the invasion of the imperialist armies of Charles V are described in F. Ercole, *Da Carlo VIII a Carlo V*, Florence, 1932, pp. 268 ff.

much temporal control. Without the twin props of Pope and Emperor, how was the world to be held together in the growing confusion, unless the national monarchs – representing the ordered rule of the One within their individual realms – took over something of the imperial rôle in its universal and religious aspect?

It is the theme of this book, or one of its themes, that some study of the history of the imperial idea in the Middle Ages and Renaissance, such as has been briefly attempted in this introductory essay, is a necessary preliminary to the study of the ethos and symbolism of the national monarchies of Europe as they developed in the Renaissance period. Particularly is this true of the Tudor monarchy, and of its most famous representative, Queen Elizabeth I. In the next essay it will be shown that the key to the complex symbolism used of this queen, the key to the many images under which she was presented to the world, is the imperial idea, and particularly the idea of imperial reform.

PART II

THE TUDOR IMPERIAL REFORM

QUEEN ELIZABETH I AS ASTRAEA

In the prologue to Thomas Dekker's *Old Fortunatus*, two old men meet one another and before entering the queen's presence hold the following conversation:[1]

> Are you then travelling to the temple of Eliza?
>
> Even to her temple are my feeble limbs travelling. Some call her Pandora: some Gloriana: some Cynthia: some Belphoebe: some Astraea: all by several names to express several loves: Yet all those names make but one celestial body, as all those loves meet to create but one soul.
>
> I am of her own country, and we adore her by the name of Eliza.

The conversation suggests that Queen Elizabeth as a symbol, as a celestial object of worship, appears under various aspects to different worshippers and yet is not herself incoherent.

It would be reassuring if we could believe that there is indeed some Ariadne's thread to guide us through the labyrinth of Elizabethan symbolism which, whether studied in the pictures of the queen or in the poems about her, presents many apparently insoluble problems. Perhaps some of the difficulty might be cleared up through fuller study of her names; perhaps we are over-familiar with some of these and relatively ignorant of others. We know her well, for example, as the moon-goddess, Cynthia or Diana, exquisitely sung by Ben Jonson as the 'Queen and huntress, chaste and fair,' and obscurely worshipped by the adepts, Raleigh and Chapman. We have often heard of Gloriana and Belphoebe, the pivots of Spenser's *Faerie Queene*. But what of Pandora, what of Astraea? What 'loves' did these names express? Over Pandora as a name for Elizabeth we shall not linger, but the Virgin Queen as Astraea is the subject of this essay.

Astraea: Classical and Christian Interpretations

There is a famous description in the first book of Ovid's *Metamorphoses* of

[1] T. Dekker, *Works*, London, 1873, I, p. 83.

29

the four ages. In that first golden age, under the rule of Saturn, men gathered their food without labour in an everlasting spring, all were virtuous by nature, and peace universal reigned. After the golden age of Saturn came the silver age of Jove when the eternal spring gave place to the seasons, men felt for the first time the extremes of heat and cold and the labour of tillage began. The third was the age of brass, sterner than the first two, but yet not impious. Finally came the iron age, when evil was let loose. Modesty, truth, and faith fled from the earth; men travelled greedily over the seas for gain; delved into the earth for metals. War came, and brandished in its bloody hands the clashing arms. Piety lay vanquished, and the virgin Astraea, last of the immortals, abandoned the blood-soaked earth:[1]

Virgo

Figure 1   Woodcut from Hyginus, *De Mundi et Sphere*, Venice, 1502

Victa iacet pietas, et virgo caede madentis
ultima caelestum terras Astraea reliquit.

Ovid is drawing on Greek sources. The golden age tradition, hinted at by Hesiod,[2] was expanded by the Greek astronomical poet Aratos when treating of the constellation Virgo, the sixth sign of the zodiac.[3] Aratos explains that when the virgin Justice left the world in the iron age she took up her abode in the heavens as the constellation Virgo; the figure of the

[1] Ovid, *Metamorphoses*, I, 149–50.
[2] Hesiod, *Works and Days*, 199. The decay of everything in the evil days to come described here is similar in sentiment to Ovid's description of the departure of the Virgin.
[3] Aratos, *Phaenomena*, 96–136.

just virgin now shines in the sky, bearing an ear of corn in her hand. The attribute of the ear of corn – *virgo spicifera* – is repeated by the Latin translators and imitators of Aratos, and a traditional representation of the constellation is a winged woman holding corn. The ears of corn mark the position of Spica, a particularly bright star in the constellation.

The Latin poets in general continue this identification of Astraea, the just virgin of the golden age, with Virgo, the sign of the month of August; Seneca, for example, speaks of 'the lion giving to Astraea the flying year',[1] meaning that the sun is passing from Leo to Virgo in his course along the zodiac. The Elizabethan poets know this tradition, and they also equate Astraea with Virgo. This can easily be proved from Spenser. In the procession of the months in the seventh canto of the *Faerie Queene*, August is accompanied by Virgo-Astraea:[2]

> The sixt was *August*, being rich arrayd
>   In garment all of gold downe to the ground
>   Yet rode he not, but led a louely Mayd
>   Forth by the lilly hand, the which was cround
>   With eares of corne, and full her hand was found;
>   That was the righteous Virgin, which of old
>   Liv'd here on earth, and plenty made abound;
>   But after Wrong was lov'd and Justice solde,
> She left th' vnrighteous world and was to heauen extold.

And again at the beginning of *Mother Hubbard's Tale* we are told that:

> It was the month in which the righteous Maid
>   That for disdaine of sinful world's upbraide,
>   Fled back to heaven, whence she was first conceived,
>   Into her silver bower the Sun received . . .

That is to say, it was the month of August in which the sun enters the constellation Virgo. And we hear the whole story of Astraea-Virgo at the beginning of the fifth canto of the *Faerie Queene*, the canto on Artegal, or Justice:[3]

> Now when the world with sinne gan to abound,
>   Astraea loathing lenger here to space
>   Mongst wicked men, in whom no truth she found,
>   Return'd to heauen, whence she deriu'd her race;
>   Where she hath now an euerlasting place,

---

[1] Seneca, *Hercules Oetaeus*, 69.

[2] *Faerie Queene*, Bk VII, canto VII, xxxvii (*Works*, eds Greenlaw, Osgood, and Padelford, Baltimore, 1932, VI, p. 175).

[3] *Faerie Queene*, Bk V, canto I, xi (*Works, ed. cit.*, V, p. 7). Spenser took the description of the zodiac as a 'balteus' from Manilius, *Astronomicon*, I, 677; III, 334.

> Mongst those twelue signes, which nightly we doe see.
> The heauens bright-shining baudricke to enchace;
> And is the *Virgin*, sixt in her degree,
> And next her selfe her righteous ballance hanging bee.

The last lines refer to the position of Virgo in the zodiac, of which she is the sixth sign, standing between Leo, or the Lion, on the one hand, and Libra, or the Balance, on the other.

The Greek astronomical poem of Aratos had numerous imitators and translators among the Latins. It was translated by Cicero, by Germanicus Caesar, and by Festus Avienus, and it influenced the work of Hyginus. Germanicus Caesar's *Aratea* renders the flight of the Virgin by the line[1]

> Deseruit properè terras iustissima virgo.

A *scholion* on Germanicus's *Aratea* quotes an exposition by Nigidius Figulus, the Neo-Pythagorean teacher, of the Virgo-Astraea myth. This version seems to have attracted a good deal of attention in the Renaissance;[2] it resumes the story of the flight of the just virgin and speaks of her having been given a place in heaven as the reward of her piety.[3]

The astronomical poems and their commentators discuss the various genealogies and changing aspects of Virgo-Astraea. The parentage of the Virgin is obscure; some call her the daughter of Jove and Themis;[4] others the daughter of Astraeus and Aurora; others call her Erigone, daughter of Icarus, a pious virgin whose little dog led her to her dead father's body. She has affiliations with several deities. The corn in her hand suggests that she must be Ceres. Sometimes she is affiliated to Venus. Others think that she is Fortune, because her head disappears amongst the stars.[5] There is a hint of Isis in her nature,[6] a hint later followed up by Martianus Capella,[7] but the female diety whom she perhaps most resembles is Atargatis,[8] the Syrian goddess, worshipped under the name of Virgo Caelestis at Carthage,[9] and asso-

---

[1] Germanicus Caesar, *Aratea cum scholiis*, ed. A. Breysig, Berlin, 1867, p. 137.

[2] See the linking of the name of Nigidius Figulus with the Virgo story in the passages from Guevara and Sir R. Barckley, quoted below, pp. 51–2.

[3] Germanicus Caesar, *op. cit.*, p. 126.

[4] Hyginus, *Poet. Astron.*, II, 25. Hesiod is the origin of this genealogy, who makes Dike (Justice) the dauther of Jove and Themis, and gives her Eunomia (Order) and Eirene (Peace) as sisters.
For a discussion of the various genealogies and associations of Virgo, see A. Bouché-Leclercq, *L'Astrologie grecque*, Paris, 1899, pp. 139 ff.; and Cumont's article on the zodiac in C. Daremberg and S. Saglio, *Dictionnaire des antiquités grecques et romaines*, Paris, 1875–1917.

[5] Valeriano follows this tradition, and shows Astraea as a headless figure between Leo and Libra (P. Valeriano, *Hieroglyphica*, Cologne, 1614 ed., p. 743).

[6] Cf. F. Boll, *Sphaera*, Leipzig, 1903, pp. 129–30, 212. Dike-Virgo has affinities with Isis or Eleithya.

[7] Martianus Capella, *De Nupt.*, II, 174; cf. Bouché-Leclercq, *op. cit.*, pp. 139–40.

[8] Germanicus, *Aratea, ed cit.*, p. 125. Cf. Bouché-Leclercq, *op. cit.*, p. 139; Cumont, *op. cit.*

[9] See the discussion in F. Dölger, *Antike und Christentum*, Munster, 1929, I, pp. 92 ff., on the worship of the Carthaginian Virgo Caelestis in imperial times. Virgo Caelestis was assimilated to Juno and made patroness of the Roman people.

ciated with Urania,[1] and, like Isis, with the moon.[2] The just virgin is thus a complex character, fertile and barren at the same time; orderly and righteous, yet tinged with oriental moon-ecstasies.

It is to Virgil that she owes her greatest fame. Together with the Cumaean Sybil, the virgin of the golden age stands at the beginning of the famous Fourth Eclogue. Virgil prophesies that the golden age is about to begin anew. It is even now returning as he writes; now comes back the virgin, now returns the reign of Saturn:[3]

> Iam redit et virgo, redeunt Saturnia regna.

Those are words which have never been forgotten in the history of the West. A child is about to be born, continues the poet-*vates*, 'beneath whom the iron brood shall first begin to fail and the golden age to arise in all the world'. This child is destined to rule a reconciled world and during his life-time the four ages will run back to the golden age. May that child come quickly, prays Virgil, and receive his sovereign honours, for all the world awaits him.

The question as to what Virgil himself may have meant by the child of this Eclogue does not come within our province. Later ages have read the Eclogue in the light of subsequent history and seen it in the context of Virgil's position as the prophet of the imperial mission of Rome. In the sixth book of the *Aeneid*, Aeneas, in the course of his journey through Hell in the company of the Cumaean Sybil, hears from the lips of Anchises the prophecy of the return of the golden age under Augustus Caesar.[4]

> This, this is the hero, who oft you hear is promised you, Augustus
> Caesar, of deified Caesar's race who shall establish in Latium a second
> time the golden age throughout the fields where Saturn once was
> king: beyond the Garamantae and beyond the Indians he shall extend
> his empire.

The golden age is the Augustan rule, the Augustan revival of piety, the peace of the world-wide Augustan empire. Astraea-Virgo, the just and pious virgin, whose return in the Fourth Eclogue heralds the golden age of empire, thus takes on a Roman gravity of aspect. She becomes an imperial virgin.

In Manilius's astrological poem, so widely read in the Renaissance, can be studied the influences of Virgo. To those born under her she gives great

---

[1] 'La Vierge Céleste de Carthage est proche parente de la Mère des Dieux, au même titre que l'Ouranie syrienne', H. Graillot, *Le culte de Cybèle*, Paris, 1912, p. 529. Cf. Dölger, *op. cit.*, p. 97.

[2] For some Renaissance mythographers, Astraea was a name for the moon. Amongst the names of Luna, Zucchi gives 'Diana, Hecate, Lucina, Proserpina, Astraea . . .' F. Zucchi, *Discorso sopra li dei de' gentili*, 1602, reprinted in F. Saxl, *Antike Gotter in der Spätrenaissance, Studien der Bibl. Warb.*, VIII, 1927.

[3] *Eclogue* IV, 6.   [4] *Aeneid*, VI, 791-5.

facility in eloquence and all branches of rhetoric, including shorthand.[1] These influences are probably due to her association with the planet Mercury.[2] Although a virgin, she gives fertility, a contradiction which Manilius finds surprising. In the moral sphere she is just and reasonable, and also pious and skilled in sacred mysteries. In noble lines Manilius describes the virgin of the golden age, whom he calls by the name of Erigone.[3] The association of the virgin 'quae rexit saecula prisca' with justice and imperial rule comes out strongly in Manilius's lines, and this, together with her piety, fits her to become the object of a state cult.

Curiously enough, one of the few, if not the only, archaeological evidences of a cult of Virgo is to be found in Roman Britain. The prefect of a cohort stationed at the eleventh fort on Hadrian's Wall in Northumberland in the time of the Severus emperors (third century) raised an inscription to Virgo, in which the familiar figure, bearing her usual attribute, the ear of corn (*spicifera*), is the object of a syncretist worship which amalgamates the Carthaginian Queen of Heaven, Virgo Caelestis, with the Mother of the Gods, with Ceres, with Atargatis, the Syrian goddess, yet she is still the just virgin of the golden age, 'inventress of justice, foundress of the city'.[4] Her worship has taken on a state aspect; she represents Virtus and Pax, those much emphasized features of Roman imperial rule. Had Elizabethan archaeologists known of this inscription, they might have seized upon it as a classical sanction for the state worship of the imperial Virgo, Elizabeth.[5]

There is, of course, another side to the fame of the Fourth Eclogue. This paean to the golden age of empire was adapted by the Christians as a Messianic prophecy. The child whose advent it foretells becomes Christ, born during the reign of Augustus, beneath whose spiritual reign the iron brood of sin should first begin to fail and the golden age of Christian piety and justice should arise. And the virgin who 'returns'

Iam redit et virgo, redeunt Saturnia regna

becomes, not merely the virgin Astraea returning to earth in the new golden age of empire, but the Virgin Mary, Mother of God and Queen of Heaven, whose appearance with her divine Son ushers in the Christian era.

So far as one can discover, the first person to make a detailed and public claim for the Fourth Eclogue as a Messianic prophecy was the Emperor

---

[1] Manilius, *Astronomicon*, IV, 189–202.

[2] The signs Gemini and Virgo are allotted to Mercury (Ptolemy, *Tetrabiblos*, I, xx). The association with Mercury accounts for Virgo being sometimes represented with the caduceus (see Figure 1, p. 30).

[3] *Astronomicon*, IV, 542–6. The name Erigone for Virgo is also used by Servius in his commentary on Virgil.

[4] *Corpus Inscriptionum Latinarum*, VII, 759. See Graillot, *op. cit.*, p. 473; Dölger, *op. cit.*, pp. 99ff.

[5] Considerable learning on the cult of Virgo Caelestis in Britain is, however, displayed by John Selden in his *De diis syris* (p. 247 in the Leipzig, 1662 edition). See also his remarks on Virgo and the Virgin Mary, *ibid.*, p. 105.

Constantine. 'Who is that virgin who returns?' enquires the Emperor, and answers his own question; she is the Virgin Mother of Christ.[1] The Emperor associates his Christian interpretation of the Eclogue with his exposition of the Sybilline prophecies as also relating to the advent of Christ. The first Christian emperor is anxious to amalgamate imperial and Christian traditions as much as possible; the Sybils and Virgil are pressed into service to this end. The Virgo of the Fourth Eclogue is Christianized as the Virgin Mary, but she retains the strong imperial and pagan undertones of Constantinian Christianity.

Lactantius hardly goes quite so far as his imperial master; he does not state that Virgo is the Virgin, but he relates the golden age and the just virgin to Christian piety in general. The poets taught, he says, that justice reigned in the golden age of Saturn and left the earth. This is not to be regarded as poetic fiction but as the truth.[2] God was manifestly worshipped in the golden age, and men loved a simple way of life, 'and this is peculiar to our religion'. In the later ages piety deteriorated, until finally, the just virgin left the earth. Lactantius continues:[3]

> But God, as a most indulgent parent, when the last time approached,
> sent a messenger to bring back that old age, and justice which had
> been put to flight. . . . Therefore the appearance of that golden time
> returned, and justice was restored to the earth, but was assigned to a
> few; and this justice is nothing else than the pious and religious worship
> of the one God.

The Christian religion is the golden age, but it is known only to a few and not apparent to the many. Therefore people should not vainly look for justice as though she were some image who would fall from heaven (Lactantius is here surely thinking of the return of Virgo-Astraea from the skies). Justice is already amongst us and in our midst, and the golden age will come to every individual soul which accepts the Christian religion.[4]

> Be just and good, and the justice which you seek will follow you of
> her own accord. Lay aside every evil thought from your hearts, and
> that golden age will at once return to you, which you cannot attain to
> by any other means than by beginning to worship the true God.

Here the foundation is laid for the assimilation of the description of the golden age to the language of Christian mysticism. The abundance of wine and corn, the peace among the animals, the aroma of spices become metaphors of the experiences of the pious soul. The pastoral language of the

---

[1] Constantine, *Oratio ad Sanctorum Coetum*, cap. XIX (Migne, *Patr. graec.*, VIII, 456).
[2] Lactantius, *Div. inst.*, lib. V. cap. v, 'De iustitia'.
[3] Lib. V, cap. vii.
[4] Lib. V, cap. viii: I am indebted to Peter Eden for this quotation.

Fourth Eclogue, already curiously close, as has always been noted, to the language of the Hebrew prophet Isaiah, can take its place with the Canticle amongst the vocabulary of Christian mysticism. For Lactantius, the return of the just virgin is a type of a spiritual state.

In more sober mood, St Augustine takes up again the problem of the Fourth Eclogue. He believes that it does indeed prophesy the coming of Christ, but that Virgil was repeating the prophecy from the Cumaean Sybil[1] and did not himself understand what he was saying. Thus the seal was set upon the tradition of the Messianic character of the Fourth Eclogue.

That tradition continues through the Middle Ages. The poem by the Carolingian bishop Theodulf on the truths 'hidden' in the fables of pagan poets, where the medieval theory of hidden Christian meanings in pagan poetry is clearly stated, includes the just virgin amongst the examples of pagan myths which beneath a 'false covering' conceal divine truths.[2] The approximation of Virgo to the Virgin sometimes went so far as to influence the symbolism of the latter. Types of the Virgin exist showing her clothed in a garment covered with ears of corn; as has been pointed out,[3] this is a borrowing by the Holy Virgin of Virgo's ear of corn.

Dante's treatment of Virgo-Astraea is of the utmost importance. In the *Purgatorio*, Statius tells Virgil that he was converted to Christianity by the prophecy in the Fourth Eclogue, a prophecy made by one who could not see his own way but held a light behind him to illumine the paths of others:[4]

> Facesti come quei che va di notte,
>   che porta il lume retro e sè non giova,
>   ma dopo sè fa le persone dotte,
>
> quando dicesti: 'Secol si rinnova;
>   torna giustizia e primo tempo umano,
>   e progenie discende dal ciel nuova.'

This is the correct Augustinian reading of the Eclogue as a true Messianic prophecy made by the poet without a full understanding of what he was saying. The 'giustizia' which here 'returns' is the Virgin Astraea in her prophetic character as an intimation in pagan poetry of the birth of Christ from the Virgin.

As we have seen, Dante's treatment of Astraea in his *Monarchia* tends

---

[1] *Civ. Dei*, X, 27. Cf. J. B. Mayor, W. Warde Fowler, R. S. Conway, *Virgil's Messianic Eclogue*, London, 1907, p. 24.

[2]
> Plurima sub falsa tegmine vera latent . . .
> Sic Proteus verum, sic *iustum Virgo* repingit,
> Virtutem Alcides, furtaque Cacus inops.

(*Theodulfi Carmina*, in *Mon. German Hist.*, *Poetarum latinorum medii aevi*, I, p. 543.)

[3] K. Rathe, 'Ein unbeschriebener Einblattdruck und das Thema der "Ährenmadonna"', *Mitteilungen der Gesellschaft fur vervielfältigende Kunst*, Vienna, 1922.

[4] *Purgatorio*, XXII, 67–72.

very strongly to sanctify and Christianize the imperial idea. The just virgin is the sacred empire, justified in its own right because it produced the Augustan golden age when the world was most one, and justified by God because it was the fullness of time in which Christ chose to be born. The moon of empire borrows its light direct from the sun of God's approval. The just virgin becomes an imperial virgin, sacred and divine. She is, moreover, a virgin of distinctly Ghibelline tendencies who boldly makes herself almost the equal of the Pope. In some of Dante's letters she even takes on the aspect of a reforming virgin whose mission it is to protest at the vices of the clergy.[1]

The letter to the Emperor in which Dante seems to associate some imperial reformatory action with Virgil's prophecy of the return of the Virgin Astraea had a fairly wide currency, for it was published in a prominent position by that much-read author, A. F. Doni. Doni produced in 1547 a volume[2] which is a collection of letters and short pieces by various authors, some of them famous, such as Petrarch and Cola di Rienzo, others less well known. Many of the items satirize the vices of the clergy and some of them discuss possibilities of reform. The volume begins with Dante's letter to the Emperor, and the poet's quotation from Virgil on the Return of the Virgin occurs on the very first page.

Imperial themes and symbols used by Cola di Rienzo in his movement, briefly touched on above, were to have a wide currency and are suggestive for later developments. Imbued with notions ranging from Joachimist and Franciscan mysticism to belief in Merlin[3] and other prophecies, all combined with profound scholarly reverence for antique Rome, Rienzo's movement fused pagan and Christian influences in a striking manner. His invitations to all the towns and provinces of Italy to participate in the justice, *pax*, and *concordia*, which reborn Rome and the spiritual rebirth in the Holy Spirit will spread throughout the world, are couched in the most extravagant language. Tyrants will disappear in the new reign of justice, destroyed as Judith destroyed Holofernes.[4] The detestable names of Guelf and Ghibelline will be wiped out in the new age of peace and union.[5] He urges Charles IV of Bohemia to lead, as emperor, a renovated world towards the new era of 'universal reformation'.[6] In another letter he deplores the corruptions of the church and the grave faults of the popes.[7]

Elsewhere he quotes the famous lines:[8]

[1] See above, p. 11.

[2] *Prose Antiche di Dante, Petrarcha, et Boccaccio, et di molti altri nobili et virtuosi ingegni*, Florence, 1547.

[3] Rienzo constantly cites Merlin, whom he often brackets with Joachim; see Cola di Rienzo, *Epistolario*, ed. A. Gabrielli, Rome, 1890, pp. 120, 126, 131, 201.

[4] Rienzo frequently uses this biblical illustration of his movement (see *ibid.*, pp. 84, 88, 155, 213).

[5] *Ibid.*, p. 59.

[6] *Ibid.*, p. 94.

[7] *Ibid.*, pp. 145 ff.

[8] *Ibid.*, p. 212. Cf. K. Burdach, *Vom Mittelalter zur Reformation* II, i, Berlin, 1928, p. 511.

Iam redit et virgo, redeunt Saturnia regna

and associates them with his mission. The first of the ceremonies celebrating his elevation to the dignity of 'Knight of the Holy Spirit' took place on 1 August 1347. He attributed importance to the imperial name of the month in which this culminating event of his life took place, which he associated with prophecies relating to Virgo and Libra.[1] On the preceding evening he had undergone a ritual immersion in the font in which, according to tradition, the Emperor Constantine had been baptized a Christian,[2] thus emphasizing the Christian aspect of his knightly and Roman mission.

Rienzo looks for a *renovatio urbis*, a rebirth of Rome, combined with spiritual rebirth, inspired by the Holy Spirit, and there are thus elements in his movement leading to both Renaissance and Reformation. He believes that the time for the *renovatio* is due, and he associates this belief with the 'Phoenix period' of five hundred years. He seems to have known of the antique use of the phoenix as the symbol of *renovatio*: it appears on a coin of Constantine the Great; on one of Constans I with the motto *Felix Temporum Reparatio*; and on one of Hadrian with the inscription *Saeculum Aureum*.[3] The return of the golden age and the rebirth of the phoenix are symbols with parallel meanings.

Elizabethan Imperialism

But what, it may be asked, has all this to do with Queen Elizabeth I? The answer is that the 'imperial' idea, whether in the Renaissance, the Reformation, or the nationalist sense, plays a vital part in the thought of the Elizabethan age.

It has been said of the Italian Renaissance that 'it starts from the medieval conception of world-empire'.[4] The whole process of the 're-naissance' of art and letters is intimately bound up with the return to a classical golden age, or rather with the more vital idea of the eternal survival and living rebirths of that age. The Elizabethan age is the great age of the English Renaissance, and in this sense the golden age theme lies behind it. It is also an age of national expansion, and the universal medieval aspirations turn in a

---

[1] Rienzo, *Epistolario*, p. 175. The month of August, over which Virgo rules, owes its name to Augustus, who changed the name of the month Sextilis in honour of his victories (Suetonius, *Divus Augustus*, XXVI, XXXI).

[2] This symbolic act was connected with his notions on reform; it was to cleanse the Empire of its stains and initiate a general reform; *Epistolario*, p. 107; cf. I. Origo, *Tribune of Rome*, London, 1938, pp. 128–9.

Rienzo's cult of Constantine, as 'knight' of the Holy Spirit, may be interestingly compared with Elizabethan imperialism and religious chivalry.

[3] See the article by H. Mattingly, 'Virgil's Fourth Eclogue', *Journal of the Warburg and Courtauld Institutes*, X (1947), pp. 14 ff.

[4] K. Burdach, 'Dante und das Problem der Renaissance', *Deutsche Rundschau*, 50, Berlin, 1924, p. 262.

nationalist direction, towards a golden age for England. But it is in its religious use of the imperial theme that Elizabethan imperialism is, perhaps, most strongly characterized, for the royal supremacy over both church and state – the key-stone of the whole Tudor position – owed its sanction to the tradition of sacred empire. Elizabethan Protestantism claims to have restored a golden age of pure imperial religion.

The doctrine of the Divine Right of Kings arose out of the medieval controversies concerning the respective powers of Popes and Emperors. Theoretically, both Pope and the Emperor depended upon Christ; and the two together, working in harmony, were to 'combine all that was of lasting value in the system of the Roman Empire with all that was essential to the realization of the City of God'.[1] But the dual system proved unworkable. The Papacy gradually encroached upon the Empire, weakening the imperial power by encouraging individual sovereigns and putting forward its claim to universal monarchy under which the unity of the world was alone possible. The imperialists developed a counter-claim, maintaining that the Emperor had a divine right to the universal monarchy by which the peace and union of all mankind would be achieved. The imperialist writers, such as Marsilio of Padua and Ockham, stress unity as the goal of humanity; and Dante, by emphasizing the right of the divinely appointed Holy Roman Empire to lead man to this goal, completes the imperial counter-claim to the world-wide authority of the Papacy.

The arguments for kingship – such as that sovereignty must be vested in one head to preserve unity – were related to the arguments for empire, and the 'imperial' title of English kings to complete sovereignty within their dominions had long been associated with the struggles of the English crown against papal interference.[2] With the Reformation, the imperialist arguments became of the greatest importance in England. It is as successors to the divine imperial power that kings claim the right to throw off papal suzerainty. As one seventeenth-century writer puts it, the 'Brittanic Church was withdrawn from the Roman Patriarchate by the Imperial authority of Henry VIII'.[3]

The close connection between politico-theological theory in the time of Elizabeth and the earlier imperialist doctrines can be exemplified from the writings of Bishop Jewel. Jewel is much saddened by the decay of the Empire:[4]

[1] J. N. Figgis, *The Divine Right of Kings*, 2nd ed., Cambridge, 1934, p. 38.

[2] The position of English kings was regarded as 'imperial' (cf. Freeman, *Norman Conquest*, I, 132, 3; Figgis, *op cit.*, pp. 42–3). The 'imperial rights' of English kings were the equivalent of 'sovereign rights'—the right to be the One and only ruler within one's dominions. Figgis remarks that the use of the term 'imperial rights' as equivalent to 'sovereignty' shows that 'there was a belief that true sovereignty, i.e. independence and unquestioned authority, had been derived from an appropriation by each kingdom of rights originally confined to the Empire' (p. 43, note 3).

[3] I. Basire, *Ancient Liberty of the Britannick Church*, 1661, p. 44.

[4] John Jewel, *Defence of the Apology of the Church of England*, in *Works*, Parker Society, Cambridge, 1847, II, p. 916.

The empire of Rome contained sometimes a great part of the world as England, France, Spain, Germany, &c. Where is England now? It is divided from, and is no part of the empire. Where is France, Spain, Italy, Illyricum? Where is Rome itself? They are taken away from it, and are now no part of the empire. Where is Macedonia, Thracia, Graecia, Asia, Armenia, &c.? We cannot think of them but with heaviness: they be now under the Turk: they are taken away, and are no part of the empire. What is become of the great countenance which the emperor had in all the world? He is now in comparison nobody. What part of all the empire is left unto him? Not one. He hath not left him one city or town. What is become of all which did belong to him? They are dissolved; taken from him; and his estate is brought to nothing.

In marked contrast to this decay is the growth of the temporal power of the Pope. Jewel gives a list of his possessions, exclaiming after each item that it was obtained 'by the spoil of the empire'. 'We see then', he concludes, 'that the emperor is abated; that the bishop is increased, and so increased that he hath made the emperor to be his man, to bear his train, to wait upon him, to kneel down and kiss his foot.'[1]

Jewel's contention that the Pope is Antichrist rests on the words of St Paul, in the second epistle to the Thessalonians, that lawlessness is restrained by one who holds the power and that when he is taken out of the way chaos will come. This restraining power of order was interpreted as the Empire whose fall would usher in the reign of Antichrist.[2] The decay of the Empire and the growth of the Papacy is proof to Jewel that the latter is Antichrist.

In his *Apology for the Church of England* (1560)—the official apology for Elizabethan Anglicanism—Jewel had already pitted Pope against Emperor. From motives of ambition, he maintains, the Popes have distracted the Roman Empire and torn the Christian world in pieces.[3] Who was it, he asks, who poisoned the Emperor Henry VII (this was Dante's emperor) even in the act of receiving the Sacrament?[4] With this offence against an emperor he brackets the poisoning 'of our King John of England in a drinking-cup'. He adduces many examples of the contemptuous attitude of Popes to Emperors, and complains of the suppression of the Emperor Ferdinand I at the Council of Trent,[5] and of the usurpation by modern Popes of the Emperors' place of authority in General Councils.[6]

[1] *Ibid.*, II, p. 917.
[2] 'For the mystery of lawlessness doth already work: only there is one that restraineth now, until he be taken away' (2 Thessalonians, 2, vii). Cf. Jewel, *Works*, II, p. 913. That the restraining power here referred to was the Empire rested on the authority of Tertullian, Augustine, Ambrose, and Chrysostom. The interpretation was current among the continental Reformers; see T. N. Veech, *Dr. Nicholas Sanders and the English Reformation*, Louvain, 1935, pp. 159 ff.
[3] 'To feed his ambition and greediness of rule, hath he pulled in pieces the empire of Rome, and vexed and rent whole Christendom asunder' (*Works*, III, p. 75).
[4] *Ibid.* [5] *Ibid.*, p. 99. [6] *Ibid.*, pp. 98–9; cf. Figgis, *op. cit.*, p. 43.

The Christian Emperors in old time, appointed the Councils . . . We now therefore marvel the more at the unreasonable dealing of the bishop of Rome, who, knowing what was the emperor's right, when the church was well ordered, knowing also that it is now a common right to all princes, forsomuch as kings are now fully possessed in the several parts of the empire, doth so without consideration assign that office alone to himself, and taketh it sufficient, in summoning a general council, to make a man that is prince of the whole world no otherwise partake thereof than he would make his own servant.

This is a crucial passage. All kings have come into a share of the emperor's majesty and this gives them the religious rights of emperors in councils of the church. This legitimizes the national council under royal authority by which the Church of England was reformed. One can hardly over-emphasize the importance for the understanding of Tudor and Stuart symbolism of the fact that the Divine Right of Kings to rule over both church and state was a derivation from the claims of Roman Emperors to be represented in the councils of the church.

Jewel seizes on every Catholic writer who had ever criticized the Pope as a supporter for the Anglican reform, probably using as his guide the catalogue of extracts from anti-papal writers compiled by Flacius Illyricus.[1] In the *Defence* (1567) of his *Apology for the Church of England* he urges his readers to see what 'Dantes, Petrarcha, Boccace, Mantuan, Valla', and others have said about the Pope, even though they were his own 'dearlings', that is, Catholics.[2] 'Franciscus Petrarcha calleth Rome the whore of Babylon, the mother of all idolatry and fornication.'[3] He repeats this on another page and attributes the same expression to Dante: 'Dantes, an Italian poet, by express words calleth Rome the Whore of Babylon.'[4] Others whom he regards as supporters are St Bernard of Clairvaux, the Abbot Joachim, Marsilio of Padua, and Savonarola.[5] The Greek Church and the Greek empire were also pressed into service.[6] Anglican theologians drew many of their arguments from the Greek, rather than from the Latin, fathers. In their endless discussions concerning the authority of emperors in early councils, upon which hinged the imperial right of monarchs to call national councils, the eastern emperors play a large part. Most important of all were the precedents set by the Emperor Constantine. In reply to the Catholic Thomas Harding's criticism

[1] Mathias Flacius Illyricus, *Catalogus testium veritatis, que ante nostram aetatem reclamarunt Papae*, Bâle, 1556; Strasbourg, 1562. This book includes Dante and Petrarch (pp. 868 ff. in the 1556 ed., pp. 505 ff. in the 1562 ed.) amongst those who have written against the Pope. For a discussion of it see P. Polman, *L'élément historique dans la controverse religieuse du XVIᵉ siècle*, Gembloux, 1932, pp. 185 ff.

[2] *Works*, IV, p. 628.   [3] *Ibid*.

[4] *Ibid*., p. 744. Jewel is no doubt, like Foxe (see below), thinking of *Purgatorio*, XXXII.

[5] *Works*, III, p. 81.

[6] Jewel regards the Greek church as a whole as anti-papal; see *ibid*,, III, p. 196; IV, pp. 739-40.

that the supreme pastorship and authority in things spiritual has been entrusted into lay hands in England, Jewel says:[1]

> We flatter not our prince with any new-imagined extraordinary power, but only give him that prerogative and chiefty that evermore hath been due unto him by the ordinance and word of God; that is to say, to be the nurse of God's religion: to make laws for the church; to hear and take up cases and questions of the faith, if he be able; or otherwise to commit them over by his authority unto the learned; to command the bishops and priests to do their duties, and to punish such as be offenders. Thus the godly emperor Constantinus sat in judgement in a cause ecclesiastical ... Greater authority than Constantinus the emperor had and used our princes require none. This, I trust, hitherto is no great heresy.

We thus find that the official apologist for the Church of England bases the right of the crown to be head of both church and state on the position of the early Christian emperors in the early church. Moreover, he appears to know of Dante's writings, a surprising fact, for we are usually told that Dante was little read in Elizabethan England. This theologian has provided us with a hint which can be followed up in greater detail, and with the added advantage of visual illustrations, by referring to one of the most important works of the English Reformation, namely John Foxe's *Acts and Monuments*, more popularly known as 'Foxe's Book of Martyrs'.

The first English (1563) edition of Foxe's monumental history of the sufferings of the martyrs in the Marian and other persecutions in England, contains a dedication to Queen Elizabeth in which the ending of the sufferings of the Reformed church in her reign is compared to the ending of the persecution of the early church by the first Christian emperor, Constantine. The peace and happiness of Constantine's reign is altogether to be compared, thinks Foxe, with the blessings now enjoyed by the subjects of Queen Elizabeth. 'Briefly, let Constantinus be never so great, yet wherein is your noble grace to him inferiour?'[2] And if Elizabeth is Constantine, Foxe himself is Eusebius, writing the Ecclesiastical History of the sufferings of the early church. What made this parallel still more neat and convincing was the fact that Constantine was born in England, supposedly of an English mother, a point to which Foxe alludes in the opening words of his dedication:[3]

> Constantine the greate and mightie Emperour, the sonne of Helene an Englyshe woman of this your realme and countrie (moste Christian and renowned Pryncesse Queene Elizabeth). . . .

[1] *Defence of the Apology, Works*, III, p. 167.
[2] John Foxe, *The Acts and Monuments*, ed. Josiah Pratt with introduction by John Stoughton, 4th ed., London, 1877, I, pp. vii*–viii*.
[3] *Ibid.*, p. vi*.

The capital C of 'Constantine' encloses a portrait of the queen (Plate 4a). She sits on the throne holding the sword of justice and the orb of rule. On her right stand three men (possibly representing the Three Estates of the realm). The two roses of York and Lancaster lead to the Tudor roses above the virgin's head, and the top curve of the C ends in cornucopiae. The lower part of the letter, beneath Elizabeth's feet, is formed by the body of the Pope, wearing the papal tiara and holding broken keys. The just virgin, trusting in an 'imperial' authority like that of Constantine, has subdued and overpowered the Pope; the royal crown triumphs over the papal tiara.

In the 1570 edition of the book this dedication was replaced by another which opens with the words:[1]

> Christ, the Prince of all princes, who hath placed you in your throne of majesty, under him to govern the church and realm of England, give your royal highness long to sit, and many years to reign over us . . . .

These words imply the divinely ordained right of the queen to rule over both church and state; and the capital C of 'Christ' contains the same picture.

The arguments and other illustrations of Foxe's book bear out the theme succinctly stated in this initial. Put very briefly, his point of view is that the English reform is no new development but represents a pure Catholic church which had always existed[2]. In the early ages of Christianity, the church as a whole was pure; in later ages wickedness crept into high places in Rome, and the impious 'Whore of Babylon' oppressed the true church. But in the present happy dispensation in England the true church once more triumphs. Roughly speaking, for Foxe the church was pure when persecuted under the pagan emperors and when early Christian emperors guided its councils; impure when the bishops of Rome took the lead. Through this convenient simplification he is able to tell the history of the kings of England from the earliest mythical times of King Lucius, said to have been the first Christian king of England, to the time of Queen Elizabeth, by relating all the problems to the one theme of Pope versus Emperor, or Emperor versus Pope, and the part played by English kings in that eternal see-saw.

The main outline of the argument can be followed in the illustrations. These must have been very familiar to the Elizabethan public because the book was placed in most churches.[3] Popes owe their whole position to the kindness of devout emperors to them, as is shown in the picture of the

---

[1] *Ibid.*, p. vi.   [2] This was, of course, a common Protestant thesis.

[3] It was resolved at a convocation meeting at Canterbury in 1570 that copies of the 1570 edition (this is the edition from which all the illustrations here reproduced, except Plate 4a, are taken) should be placed in cathedral churches, and in the houses of archbishops, bishops, deacons, and archdeacons. Although this resolution was never enforced, the advice contained in it was very widely carried out (*D.N.B.*, article Foxe).

H. J. Cowell (*The Four Chained Books*, London, 1938) states that Jewel's *Defence of the Apology* and Foxe's *Acts and Monuments* were often chained in churches, together with the Bible and Erasmus's Paraphrases.

Emperor Constantine embracing Christian bishops (Plate 4b). This origin of their power is acknowledged by the papalists themselves, who have forged the 'Donation of Constantine' to account for it. Later popes, having grown rich and powerful through the imperial kindness, turned proud and insolent and became the oppressors of the emperors to whom they owed everything. Notable examples of papal oppression of emperors are illustrated; for example, Pope Gregory VII (Hildebrand, the origin and fountain-head of all the evils for Foxe) making the Emperor Henry IV and his wife wait in the snow at Canossa (Plate 4d); or another pope treading on the neck of the great Emperor Frederick Barbarossa (Plate 4c). These things can also be illustrated from the behaviour of popes to Kings of England. We see the monk of Swineshead poisoning King John (Plate 5c) and Henry III being obliged to kiss the knee of the Pope's legate (Plate 5d).

Though not satisfied with Henry VIII's religious settlement, which is not sufficiently reformed for his taste, Foxe hails with joy the ending in his reign of the Pope's 'usurped power'.[1] We see Henry sitting in royal state on his throne of majesty (Plate 5b); and Henry trampling on the Pope (Plate 5a).

The picture of Queen Elizabeth trampling on the Pope in the initial C is thus the climax of the whole book. She represents the return to the Constantinian, imperial Christianity, free from papal shackles, the kind of religion which Foxe regards as alone pure. The intensely evangelical utterances of Foxe's martyrs, and the fascination of his detailed descriptions of their sufferings, have drawn away attention from the fact that the politico-religious position which he propounds derives its sanction from the traditions, Christianized it is true, of the worldly empire of Rome. The Virgo of the Fourth Eclogue, with her vaguely Christian associations, would be an admirable symbol for such a position.

Even more clearly than in Jewel, one can study in Foxe how this reading of history, which culminated in the Elizabeth-cult, claimed sanctions from the most various quarters. Foxe quotes as witnesses to the true and pure church or as in some way allied to his own position (the following is a selection only of the names which he mentions): Joachim of Flora, the Albigenses, Raymond of Toulouse, Marsilio of Padua, Arnold de Villa Nova, Robert Grosseteste, William of Ockham, Jean of Jandun, Buridan, Dante, Petrarch, Nicholas Oresme, Nicholas of Lyra, Cardinal Cusanus, Aeneas Sylvius, Wickliff, Gower, Chaucer, Huss, Savonarola, Laurentius Valla, Pico della Mirandola.[2] These names include the greatest of the theorists of imperialism, Marsilio of Padua, Ockham, Dante; the most celebrated poet of the Italian Renaissance, Petrarch; the philosopher of Renaissance

---

[1] *Op. cit.*, IV, p. 167.

[2] *Ibid.*, I, pp. xxi–xxiii, 303; II, pp. 659, 661, 705; III, p. 607. The story of Savonarola (whom Foxe seems to regard as a martyr almost on a par with those made by 'Bloody Mary') is recounted at length, IV, pp. 8 ff.

Neo-Platonism, Pico della Mirandola.[1] Troubadours and philosophers, poets and humanists, all could witness to the wickedness of the Church of Rome and therefore, by implication, to the righteousness of the virgin of imperial reform. He does not mention Cola di Rienzo whose cult of Constantine might, one would have thought, have appealed to him.

Foxe's main reference to Dante is so curious, though not original, that it seems worth while to quote it in full:[2]

Dante, an Italian writer, a Florentine, lived in the time of Louis the emperor, about the year of Our Lord 1300, and took his part with Marsilio of Padua against three sorts of men, which he said were enemies to the truth. That is, the pope: Secondly, the order of religious men, which count themselves the children of the church, when they are the children of the devil their father: Thirdly, the Doctors of decrees and decretals. Certain of his writings be extant abroad, wherein he proveth the pope not to be above the emperor, nor to have any right or jurisdiction in the empire. He refuteth the Donation of Constantine to be a forged and a feigned thing, as which neither did stand with any law or right. For the which he was taken of many for an heretic. He complaineth, moreover, very much of the preaching of God's word being omitted; and that instead thereof, the vain fables of monks and friars were preached and believed of the people, and that so the flock of Christ was not fed with the food of the gospel, but with wind. 'The pope,' saith he, 'of a pastor is made a wolf, to waste the church of Christ, and to procure with his clergy not the word of God to be preached, but his own decrees.' In his canticle of purgatory, he declareth the pope to be the Whore of Babylon. And to her ministers, to some he applieth two horns, to some four. As to the patriarchs, whom he noteth to be the tower of the said Whore Babylonical [sic]. Ex libris Dantis Italice.

Hereunto may be added the saying out of the book of Jornandus, imprinted with the aforesaid Dante; that forsomuch as Antichrist cometh not before the destruction of the empire, therefore such as go about to have the empire extinct, are forerunners and messengers in so doing of Antichrist. 'Therefore let the Romans,' saith he, 'and their

---

[1] With Pico, Ficino and Politian are mentioned (IV, p. 4) as amongst the 'excellent wits' who flourished in the time of the Emperor Maximilian I.

That these Elizabethan theologians seem to regard the Florentine Neo-Platonists as allied to the 'imperialist' position is interesting. Hints to this effect are let fall by Flacius Illyricus, who quotes a letter from Pico della Mirandola urging the Emperor Maximilian to reform the church (Catalogus, 1556 ed., p. 996). It might be useful to follow up this suggestion and to enquire, for example, why Ficino chose to translate Dante's Monarchia into Italian.

[2] This passage first appeared in the 1570 edition of the Acts and Monuments (I, p. 485) on which the above quotation is based, and is repeated in many later editions. Pratt's text (ed. cit., II, pp. 706–7) differs considerably from that of the 1572 ed.

bishops beware, lest, their sins and wickedness so deserving by the just judgment of God, the priesthood be taken from them.'

This account is derived almost verbally from Flacius Illyricus.[1] Unoriginal though it is, it is revealing as to the position of Dante in the thought of an Elizabethan theologian; he is to Foxe above all the imperialist writer, belonging to the tradition of which Marsilio and Ockham were also representatives.

Dante's *Monarchia* first saw the light as one of several imperialist tracts published in one volume at Bâle in 1559. The first item in this volume is by Alciati,[2] and the collection includes, besides Dante's work, the treatise by Aeneas Sylvius *De Ortu & Authoritate Imperii Romani*,[3] and a work of a similar character by Jordanus.[4] The latter is the 'Jornandus' to whom Foxe attributes the argument, which we have already met with in Jewel, that the restraining power, to which St Paul alludes in 2 Thessalonians as preventing the coming of Antichrist, is the empire. Therefore take note, says Jordanus, 'That since Antichrist will not come until the empire is destroyed; therefore all those who work towards the disappearance of the empire are precursors and announcers of Antichrist.'[5] But Foxe's reference to 'Jornandus' does not in itself prove that he had closely studied the volume in which Dante's work first appeared,[6] for he is simply quoting this quotation from Flacius Illyricus.

Similarly, his allusions to the *Divina Commedia* derive from the quotations from that poem given by Flacius Illyricus,[7] and follow that writer's inter-

[1] Foxe was using the 1562 Strasbourg edition of the *Catalogus* in which the account of Dante (pp. 505 ff.) is fuller than in that of 1556. The association of Dante with Marsilio of Padua is not stated in Flacius's main account of the poet, but Foxe could have found it implied in other parts of the *Catalogus*, where Dante is represented as one of those who, like Marsilio of Padua, wrote books in defence of the cause of the Emperor Louis of Bavaria against the Pope.

[2] A. Alciati, *De formula Romani Imperij Libellus*, etc., Bâle, 1559.

[3] Reprinted in Goldast's collection of imperialist writings; see M. Goldast, *Monarchia S. Romani imperii*, Hanover, 1611, pp. 1558 ff.

[4] *Chronica magistri Iordanis, qualiter Romanum Imperium translatum fuit in Germanos, & primo quare Romanum imperium sit honorandum* by Jordanus, Canonicus Osnaburgensis. Reprinted in Goldast, *op. cit.*, II, pp. 1462 ff.

[5] P. 225 in the Bâle collection of 1559. There is a similar argument in the tract in the same volume by Aeneas Sylvius, the eighth chapter of which is entitled 'Antichristum non uenturum donec Imperium Romanum steterit'.

[6] Paget Toynbee (who pointed out Jewel's and Foxe's allusions to Dante in his British Academy Lecture, *Britain's Tribute to Dante in Literature and Art*, London, 1921, pp. 4, 5) assumed from Foxe's mention of Jordanus in association with Dante that the martyrologist must have seen through the press the volume containing the first edition of the *Monarchia* (see his note 'John Foxe and the editio princeps of Dante's "De Monarchia"' in the *Athenaeum* of 14 April 1906). Toynbee was unaware that Foxe quotes all his remarks on Dante, including the Jordanus reference, from Flacius Illyricus, which makes this supposition less probable. Foxe was, however, in Bâle at the time when Oporinus published the volume and both he and Jewel were certainly familiar with its contents.

[7] Flacius quotes (in the 1562 edition of the *Catalogus*) from *Paradiso* IX, XVIII, and XXIX, giving the Italian text with a Latin translation. He does not quote from *Purgatorio* XXXII, but

pretation of them. Nevertheless, this passage from the Book of Martyrs, though borrowed, is probably one of the earliest, if not the earliest, attempts at Dante exegesis from an English pen. Foxe has no doubts about the hidden meaning of the vision of the Gryphon and the Harlot in the thirty-second canto of the *Purgatorio*. His useful historical simplifications again come to his aid and make the most complex subject as clear as day to him. Like the whole of English history, the Divine Comedy is simply the drama of Pope versus Emperor, with the pope as the villain of the piece – the wicked wolf, the Whore of Babylon, the Antichrist.[1]

Foxe and Jewel guide us to the books that we ought to read if we want to understand the Elizabeth cult. Dante's *Monarchia* and the tracts published with it are of primary importance; so also is Marsilio of Padua's *Defensor Pacis*, with its argument that the imperial power is the sole guarantee of peace. The sacred One Ruler of these Catholic imperialist writers became in the hands of imperialist Protestant Elizabethan theologians the sacred One Virgin whose sword of Justice smote down the Whore of Babylon and ushered in a golden age of pure religion, peace and plenty. The fact that Astraea for Dante is a symbol of imperial reform and is also a name for Elizabeth is more than a merely literary parallel.

The religious side of the imperial legend was easily turned in a nationalist direction as England's power and greatness expanded under Elizabeth's rule. This can be strangely exemplified from another use of the same initial C and its picture.

As we have seen, Anglican theologians drew many of their arguments from the Greek rather than from the Latin fathers. In their discussions con-

---

mentions it with the résumé which Foxe follows; though Foxe makes nonsense of the last phrase, where Flacius describes some ministers with two horns and four others with one horn each, all of them together being the 'fortress' of the *meretrix* (cf. *Purgatorio*, XXXII, 145–50).

These passages, together with *Monarchia* III, iii and x, provide all the material for Flacius's, and Foxe's, presentation of Dante's views.

Flacius Illyricus was a Lutheran theologian, associated at one time with Melanchthon, though more uncompromising than the latter. His *Catalogus*, a convenient collection of anti-papal ammunition, was very popular with Elizabethan theologians.

[1] Like Jewel, Foxe calls on Petrarch, as well as on Dante, for support. He says that Petrarch 'in his works and his Italian metre, speaking of the court of Rome, calleth it Babylon, and the whore of Babylon sitting on the waters, the mother of idolatry and fornication . . . and saith further that she extolleth herself against her founders, that is, the emperors who first set her up, and did so enrich her; and seemeth plainly to have thought that the pope was Antichrist . . .' (*op cit.*, II, pp. 707–8). Flacius Illyricus (*Catalogus*, 1556 ed., pp. 871–2) gives the source of these statements, namely the twentieth epistle (i.e. the letter beginning 'Et quid adhuc haeres' which is the twentieth of the *Seniles* in the edition of the letters published at Venice in 1503) and the ninety-second (or ninety-first) poem in the *Canzoniere*, beginning 'De l'empia Babilonia'.

Flacius Illyricus, in his survey of opponents of the papacy, lists, next but one after Dante and Petrarch, an English king (Edward V) with the remark that England is a firm opponent of the 'papal tyranny' (*Catalogus*, 1556 ed., p. 873).

cerning the authority of emperors in early councils, upon which hinged the imperial right of monarchs to call national councils, the eastern emperors play a large part. In Jewel's complaint on the collapse of the empire he laments above all that the eastern empire has fallen into the hands of the Turk. Jewel believed that the eastern churches disapproved of the pope. Graecia complains, he says, 'how the bishops of Rome with the marts of their purgatories and pardons have both tormented men's consciences and picked their purses'.[1]

These sympathies with the Greek empire were used in a most curious way in connection with the nascent maritime ambitions of Elizabethan England by John Dee, the queen's learned astrologer.

Dee's *General and rare memorials pertayning to the Perfect Arte of Navigation* was the only one published (in 1577, he wrote it is 1576) of a series of volumes which he planned should be an exposition of, and plea for, Elizabethan imperialism. (The idea of the work as a whole was that it should be a 'Hexameron or Plat Politicall of the Brytish Monarchie.') It consisted partly of practical tables for the use of mariners, but the theoretical pages of the work are interlarded with impassioned pleas for the establishment of a strong navy both to defend the country and to aid expansion. The learned man brings the most varied historical arguments to bear upon his theme, of how to maintain and increase the 'Royal Maiesty and Imperiall Dignity of our Souerayn Lady Elizabeth'.[2] The tale of the lands and seas to which she can lay claim is based both on the dominions mythically reported to have been held by the British King Arthur and on those over which the Saxon King Edgar ruled. The Roman Pompey and the Greek Pericles are quoted with approval for their views on the importance of sea sovereignty. But strangest of all is the use which Dee makes of the Byzantine Neoplatonic philosopher, Gemistus Pletho.

As is well known, it was Gemistus Pletho who gave the impulse to those philosophical studies which, as developed by Ficino and the Florentine Academy, had such a far-reaching influence on Renaissance thought. There was a political as well as a philosophical side to Gemistus Pletho. About the year 1415, he addressed two orations to the Emperor Manuel and to his son Theodore on the affairs of the Peloponnesus and on ways and means both of improving the economy of the Greek islands and of defending them.[3] A Latin translation of these orations had recently been published,[4] and Dee is of the opinion that they would be of use 'for our Brytish Iles, and in better and more allowable manner, at this Day, for our People, than that his Plat

[1] *Works*, III, p. 81; IV, pp. 738–40.
[2] John Dee, *General and rare memorials pertayning to the Perfect Arte of Navigation*, London, 1577, p. 24.
[3] The orations are reprinted in Migne, *Patr. Graec.*, CLX, pp. 822 ff.
[4] The orations, with a Latin translation by Gulielmus Canterus, were printed in the volume containing the *Eclogues* of John Stobaeus, published at Antwerp by Plantin in 1575.

(for Reformation of the State at those Dayes) could be found, for Peloponnesus avaylable.'[1] In spite of the difficulties of Dee's style and punctuation his meaning is clear, a meaning which he repeats on subsequent pages, namely that the advice given to the Byzantine Emperor by Pletho is good advice for Elizabeth, the Empress of Britain. He therefore reprints at the end of his work the greater part of the Latin translation of the first oration, and the whole of the second, with curious marginal notes.

The first words of the first oration are 'Cum in navi gubernator',[2] words which remind one that Dee's book consists of 'Tables Gubernaticke', that is, tables for pilots and mariners which he believes will be widely used and will form a 'world-wide monument to the Eternall and Heroical Renown of Q. Elizabeth'.[3] It is therefore not unnatural that the capital C contains a picture of Queen Elizabeth (Plate 7a). It is the same initial as that used in Foxe's dedication comparing Elizabeth to Constantine, the first emperor to make Constantinople his seat. Here it introduces the opening words of Gemistus Pletho's advice to the last Greek emperor, advice which is to be applied to Queen Elizabeth's empire.

It may be objected that the use of initials from Foxe's book in Dee's *Memorials* might be purely fortuitous, the printer of both books (John Daye) happening to have such initials at hand and making use of them regardless of whether they suited the context. But an argument against such a theory is the fact that the frontispiece to Dee's book (Plate 7b) takes the picture from the C initial and expands it to cover the theme of his book. On this frontispiece we see again the figure of Elizabeth accompanied by the three men, but now they are all in a ship of which the queen holds the rudder (recalling the words 'Cum in nave gubernator', for the C of which the figures are used in the text). The ship is labelled 'Europa', and Europa rides beside it on the bull. Ships and armed men are defending the land. On a fortress stands a figure of *Occasio*. From the sun, moon, and stars descends St Michael, a flying figure with sword and shield. An ear of corn is seen reaching the land upside down. The Greek inscription round the whole explains that it is a 'British Hieroglyphick', and a further explanation is to be found on one of the pages of the book.[4] The practical moral is that Britain is to seize

---

[1] *Op. cit.*, p. 63.   [2] *Ibid.*, p. 69.   [3] *Ibid.*, 'Advertisement to the Reader'.

[4] 'Why should we not hope, that, Respublica Britannica, on her knees, very Humbly, and ernestly Soliciting the most Excellent Royall Maiesty, of our Elizabeth, (Sitting at the Helm of this Imperiall Monarchy: or, rather, at the Helm of the Imperiall Ship, of the most parte of Christendome: if so, it be her Graces Pleasure) shall obteyn, (or Perfect Policie, may perswade her Highnes,) that which is the Pyth, or Intent of Res-Publica Brytanica, Her Supplication? Which is, That, ΣΤΟΛΟΣ ΕΞΩΠΛΙΣΜΝΟΣ may helpe us, not onely to ΘΡΟΥΡΙΟΝ ΤΗΣ ΑΣΦΑΛΕΙΑΣ: But make us, also, Partakers of Publik Commodities Innumerable, and (as yet) Incredible. Unto which, the Heavenly King, for these many yeres last past, hath, by Manifest Occasion, most graciously, not only inuited us: but also, hath made, even now, the Way and Means, most euident, easie, and Compendious: Inasmuch as (besides all our own sufficient Furniture, Hability, Industry, Skill and Courage) our Freends are become strong: and our Enemies, sufficiently weake, and nothing Royally furnished, or of Hability, for Open Violence Using:

Occasion by the forelock and grow strong at sea to strengthen Elizabeth's 'Imperiall Monarchy' and perhaps even to make her the pilot of the 'Imperiall Ship 'of Christendom. The kneeling figure of 'Res-publica Britannica' is aspiring earnestly to rule the waves.

The religious imperial theme of Foxe's initial C[1] has here developed into a nationalist imperial theme. Foxe's virgin claims theological sanction for her opposition to the papacy from the traditions of imperial influence in the church. Dee's virgin seeks practical advice from the traditions of the Greek empire for the defence and expansion of her realm. The reformed Virgo representing the pure imperial religion is also the British Virgo aspiring to empire through sea power.

There is yet another strand in the complex tissue of Elizabethan imperialism through which Virgo-Astraea becomes the perfect symbol for the British Virgo, namely the Tudor claim to Trojan descent.

As is well known, according to Geoffrey of Monmouth, in very ancient times a mythical being called Brutus, a Trojan and a relative of the pious Aeneas who founded Rome, founded London as Troynavant, or New Troy, and from him were descended the British kings. Though rejected by Polydore Vergil, this story was accepted by most Elizabethan poets as part of the Tudor myth. The Tudors were of Welsh or ancient British descent. When the Tudors ascended the throne of England, so runs the myth, the ancient Trojan-British race of monarchs once more resumed the imperial power and brought in a golden age of peace and plenty. As Greenlaw says, 'The descent of the Britons from the Trojans, the linking of Arthur, Henry VIII, and Elizabeth as Britain's greatest monarchs, and the return under Elizabeth of the Golden Age are all commonplaces of Elizabethan thought.'[2] This legend gives the framework within which Elizabeth, as one who could trace an ancestry going back, via ancient British romance, to the founders of Rome, claims as by right the title of the imperial virgin who brings in the golden age of pure religion and national peace and prosperity.

Closely related to the imperial theme of the Trojan descent of the Tudors is the theme of the united monarchy which they established through joining the houses of York and Lancaster. It is an all-pervasive commonplace of Elizabeth symbolism that she is the one Tudor Rose in whom the red and

---

Though their accustomed Confidence, in Treason, Trechery, and Disloyall Dealings, be very great. Wherein, we beseche our Heavenly Protector, with his Good Angell to garde us, with Shield and Sword, now, and euer. Amen' (*op. cit.*, p. 53.) The original drawing by Dee himself for this frontispiece has been discovered: see Peter French, *John Dee: the World of an Elizabethan Magus*, London, 1972, Plate 14.

[1] Other initials from Foxe's book are used in the *General and rare memorials*. The C initial is also used in Gabriel Harvey's *Gratulationum Valdinensium*, London, 1578, a collection of poems in praise of Elizabeth (see F. M. O'Donoghue, *Descriptive and Classified Catalogue of Portraits of Q. Elizabeth*, 1894, p. 36).

[2] E. Greenlaw, *Studies in Spenser's Historical Allegory*, Baltimore, 1932, p. 46; cf. also D. Bush, *Mythology and the Renaissance Tradition in English Poetry*, New York, 1932, pp. 39 ff.

white rose of York and Lancaster are united. In the poets the allusion sometimes takes the form of the red and white of the virgin's complexion, as for example in one of Greville's sonnets:[1]

> Under a throne I saw a virgin sit,
> The red and white rose quartered in her face,
> Star of the north, and for true guards to it,
> princes, church, states, all pointing out her grace.

After reading these lines, it is interesting to look again at the C initial (Plates 4a, 7a) where the three men (perhaps representing 'princes, church, states' as already suggested) are turned towards the enthroned queen, above whose head the allusion is made to the union of the two roses in the one Tudor rose.

That union was in itself an 'imperial theme', because it established *pax* under One Monarch, in place of discord and war under two rival houses. And the Tudor Rose symbolism blended admirably with the mystic worship of the one, pure, imperial, British virgin.

Elizabethan imperial symbolism is influenced in many ways by imitation, conscious or unconscious, of the dazzling figure of Charles V, in whom the imperial theme, in all its aspects, had shone forth with renewed splendour.

The earlier part of the sixteenth century had seen the ascendancy of one in whom the age-long traditions of Holy Roman Empire bore a real relation – perhaps for the last time – to the political and religious destinies of Europe. The universal empire, which for Dante was but wishful thinking, came within an ace of realization by the Emperor Charles V with his huge dominions in both the old and the new worlds. Nor was Charles, though not without his faults, an altogether unworthy representative of that office of sacred emperor in which, ideally, the virtues of imperial Rome should be combined with Christian fervour. Though it may be that Charles himself was too wise and too politically practical to pursue the chimera of universal empire, there is no doubt that the spectacle of this peace-loving Caesar who, mainly through peaceful inheritance, was so nearly lord of all the world, raised again in many minds the old dream of the golden age restored. Charles's apologists dwell on the Dantesque and Ghibelline arguments, and their works – particularly those of Guevara and Ariosto – were another channel (besides the studies of Elizabethan theologians) through which those arguments, now combined with the Virgo-Astraea image, could have become familiar to the Elizabethan public.

Antonio de Guevara was court preacher and historiographer to Charles V. The famous *Relox de prencipes* – so popular in England in the sixteenth

---

[1] Fulke Greville, *Caelica*, sonnet 82 (ed. U. Ellis-Fermor, Gregynog Press, 1936, p. 103); cf. also the April eclogue of Spenser's *Shepheards Calendar*.

century as to be three times translated – is a guide to imperial and royal virtue based on the example of Marcus Aurelius. The *Diall of Princes* (to give it its English title in Sir Thomas North's translation) repeats the abstract arguments for universal empire:[1]

> God without great mystery did not ordain, that in one family there should be but one father; among one people there should be but one citizen that should command; in one province there should be but one governor alone; and also that one king should govern a proud realm; and likewise that by one onely captain a puissant army should be led. And furthermore, and above all, he willeth that there should be but one Monarchial king and Lord of the World.

Such a passage as this suggests that Guevara belongs to the tradition of the medieval imperialist writers, including Dante, and from the popular translations of his book the ordinary Elizabethan reader could have become acquainted with this 'One' argument of imperialist theologians.

Guevara introduced his treatment of the royal and imperial virtue of Justice by quoting Nigidius Figulus on Virgo-Astraea:[2]

> Nigidius Figulus, one of the most famous and renowned philosophers of Rome, said that between two of the zodiacal signs (Leo and Libra) is a virgin named Justice: the which in times past dwelled among men on earth, and after she was of them neglected, she ascended up to heaven. . . . During the time that men were chaste, gentle, pitiful, patient, embracers of virtue, honest and true, Justice remained on earth with them: but since they are converted unto adulterers, tyrants, given to be proud, unpatient, liars, and blasphemers, she determined to forsake them. . . . Though this seem to be a poetical fiction, yet it comprehendeth in it high and profound doctrine: the which seemeth to be very clear, for where we see justice, there are few thieves, few murderers, few tyrants and few blasphemers . . . Homer desirous to exalt justice, could not tell what to say more, but to call kings the children of the great god Jupiter: and that not for the naturality that they have, but for the office of justice which they minister. So that Homer concludeth, that a man ought not to call just princes other, but the children of God.

It is significant that the treatment of Virgo-Astraea in this work, which it would be fair to call one of the most widely-read books in Elizabethan England, leads up to the doctrine of the divine origin of kings.

[1] *The Diall of Princes*, trans. Thomas North, Bk I, cap. xxviii.
[2] *Ibid.*, Bk III, cap. i. John Florio's *First Fruites*, London, 1578, affords glimpses of the material from which the Elizabeth cult was built up. By far the largest number of literary extracts in it are from Guevara, and Guevara's views on the One Monarch, or on chivalry, are interspersed with praises of the Virgin Queen.

Guevara does not make the obvious application of his theme to his contemporary situation by saluting Charles V as the one Lord of the World who has induced Astraea-Virgo, or Justice, to return to earth. But that application is made by Ariosto in the famous verses of the *Orlando furioso* where the English duke, Astolfo, hears the prophecy of the future empire of Charles V.[1] The prophetess tells him that the world will be put under a universal monarchy beneath the wisest and most just emperor since Roman times; this ruler will spring from the union of the great houses of Austria and Aragon; and by him Astraea will be brought back again to earth from her exile in heaven, together with all other banished virtues.[2] The words can be quoted in their Elizabethan dress, as translated by Sir John Harington:[3]

> I see the will of heav'n doth so incline,
>> The house of *Austria* and of *Arragon*,
>> Shall linke together in a happie line,
>> And be by match united both in one:
>> I see a braunch grow by the banke of *Ryne*,
>> Out of this house, as like there hath bene none,
>> Whose match (thus much to say I dare be bold)
>> May not be found in writers new or old.

> By him againe *Astrea* shall be brought,
>> And be restored from her long exile,
>> And vertues that have long been set at nought,
>> Shall raigne and banish fraud deceit and guile:
>> For which great works by him so nobly wrought,
>> God meanes to grant him all this earthly Ile,
>> And under this wise Prince his deare anointed,
>> One shepheard and one flocke he hath appointed.

The branch growing 'by the banke of *Ryne*' is Charles V, offspring of the union of the houses of Austria and Spain; it is he who will put the world under its best rule, that of the One Monarch, and so reinstate Astraea-Justice and all virtues.

It was easy for a panegyrist of Elizabeth to transform the union of the houses of Austria and Aragon into the union of the houses of York and Lancaster, and to foretell the advent, not of an emperor who should bring back Astraea, but of a virgin queen who should be Astraea-Virgo personified. Spenser's *Faerie Queene*, constructed round the figure of Elizabeth, was, as is well known, strongly influenced by Ariosto's epic. Merlin's prophecy to Britomart of the advent of Queen Elizabeth is reminiscent of the prophecy in the *Orlando furioso* of the advent of Charles V. It tells of the return of the imperial, Troy-descended, British line to power; of the union of the houses

---

[1] Ariosto, *Orlando furioso*, canto XV, stanzas 21 ff.   [2] *Ibid.*, XV, 25.
[3] *Orlando furioso*, trans. Sir John Harington, London, 1634, ed., XV, 18.

of York and Lancaster in the Tudors; and foretells the eventual advent of a 'royal virgin' who shall establish peace:[1]

> Thenceforth eternal union shall be made
> Between the nations different afore,
> And sacred Peace shall lovingly perswade
> The warlike minds, to learne her goodly lore,
> And ciuile armes to exercise no more;
> Then shall a royal virgin raine . . .

The small world of the Tudor union and the Tudor *pax*, personified in the Tudor Virgo, have here behind them the vaster European perspectives of the Hapsburg union and the Hapsburg *pax*; and behind these again is the august concept of Holy Roman Empire, reaching out in ever-widening influence to include the whole globe, both the old and the new worlds, under the rule of the One Monarch and the returned just virgin Astraea of a new golden age.

Ariosto's prophecy of the coming of Charles V and Astraea is full of reminiscences of the Fourth Eclogue, though with one curious difference. In the Fourth Eclogue, the golden age was a time when men did not travel restlessly hither and thither, voyaging over the sea in ships. But in Ariosto, the advent of an age of voyaging and discovery is prophetic of the rise of a new golden age of universal empire. 'God has kept secret', says the prophetess, 'the way to the new worlds beyond the ocean until the time which he had ordained for the appearance of the new universal monarchy.'[2] Charles's famous device – the two columns and the words *Plus oultre* (Plate 3a) – emphasized the vast extension into the new world of his sacred empire, the intensification of the imperial idea through maritime discovery and adventure. The columns are the Columns of Hercules, boundary of the ancient world, which Charles's empire is to exceed[3] (this appears to be the meaning of *Plus ultra* or *Plus oultre*), including in its sway new worlds of which the ancients knew nothing.

The transference to Elizabeth of the maritime side of the prophecy relating to Charles is implicit in Harington's translation of the *Orlando furioso*. The Prophetess foresees in a visionary trance the coming of new mariners and new masters who shall find new stars, new skies, and sail round the world:[4]

> Yet I foresee, ere many ages passe,
> New marriners and masters new shall rise,

---

[1] *Faerie Queene*, Bk III, canto III, xlix; *Works, ed. cit.*, III, p. 46.

[2] *Orlando furioso*, XV, 21; Harington's translation XV, 14 (*ed. cit.*, p. 114).

[3] Cf. the interpretation of the device given by G. Ruscelli, *Le imprese illustri*, Venice, 1566, pp. 112 ff. Ruscelli quotes Ariosto in connection with this device. See further the studies of the device referred to above, p. 23, note 3.

[4] Harington's translation, *loc. cit.*

That shall find out that erst so hidden was,
And shall discover where the passage lies
And all the men that went before surpasse,
To find new lands, new starres, new seas, new skies,
And passe about the earth as doth the Sunne,
To search what with Antipodes is done.

In a marginal note against this verse, Harington refers to the circumnavigation of the globe by Sir Francis Drake, thus transferring to a subject of Queen Elizabeth those maritime adventures which Ariosto's prophetess regards as a portent of the coming of the new universal empire. He very freely translated the stanza in order to make it fit Drake's exploit.

Thus the theme of nautical adventure and overseas expansion, purely nationalist and aggressive though it may be in practice, has behind it for these sixteenth-century minds some memory of empire in the ancient and religious sense. The discovery of new worlds raises the problem of the expansion of the concept of holy empire under the One to fit a world larger than that known to Virgil or to Dante.

Even on its purely 'reformation' or 'Protestant' side, the portentous figure of Charles V, devout Catholic though he was, may be discerned looming behind the Elizabethan imperial theme.

Under Injunctions promulgated in the reign of Edward VI and confirmed in that of Elizabeth, it was laid down that two books should be placed in every church in England for all to read. These two books were the Bible in English, and Erasmus's Paraphrases on the New Testament, also in English.[1] Erasmus had dedicated his Paraphrases on the four Gospels to four monarchs: St Matthew to the Emperor Charles V; St Mark to Francis I, King of France; St Luke to Henry VIII, King of England; St John to the Archduke Ferdinand of Austria (later the Emperor Ferdinand I), brother of Charles V. English translations of Erasmus's prefaces were included in the English translation of the Paraphrases. Every parishioner might therefore read how Erasmus had told the Emperor Charles V that 'where as no prince is so secular, but that he hath a doe with the profession of the gospell, the Emperours are anoynted sacred for this very purpose, that they may eyther maynteyne or restore, or elles enlarge and spredde abrode the religion of the gospell'.[2] They might read, too, in the dedication to Francis I, how Erasmus had thought it right that the four gospels should be dedicated to the four chief princes and rulers of the world, adding:[3]

God sende grace that the spirite of the ghospell maye lyke wyse ioyne the heartes of you all fower together in mutuall amitie and concorde,

[1] E. Cardwell, *Documentary Annals of the Church of England*, Oxford, 1839, I, pp. 9, 181.

[2] *The first tome or volume of the Paraphrase of Erasmus upon the newe testamente*, London, 1548 (there were later editions). Erasmus's preface before the paraphrase on St Matthew.

[3] *Ibid.*, Erasmus's preface before the paraphrase on St Mark.

as your names are in this ghospell boke aptely conioyned. Some there
be whiche extende the byshoppe of Romes dominion euen unto hell or
purgatory: other some giue him impery and power ouer the aungels.
And so far am I from enuying him this preeminente auctoritie, that I
woulde wishe hym to haue a great deale more, but yet woulde I desyre
withall, that the worlde might once fele this his power, good and
holsome, in settyng christian Princes at one, and in conseruing the
same in peace and amitie, whiche haue a long season with no lesse
dishonour, then slaughter and effusion of Christian blood, warred one
agaynste another to the utter decay of Christes religion.

One may perhaps fancy that the Erasmian irony here plays about the
'Bishop of Rome', suggesting that he tends to set Christian princes at variance
with one another;[1] it is, in a way, a continuation of the imperialist argument
that the imperial or monarchical power is the 'Defensor Pacis', and that the
Papacy is a stirrer up of war. And by dedicating his Paraphrases to monarchs,
Erasmus implies that he is calling upon the imperial and royal powers to
restore the purity of the Gospel.

The presence of this book in all parish churches must have associated
Charles's name in Elizabethan minds with the Erasmian reform which had
started the train of events which led to England's break with the Papacy.
Imperial reform, both in its beginnings and in its subsequent developments,
was, in fact, by no means a Protestant monopoly. Charles, though always a
fervent Catholic, had been interested in the earlier part of his career in
liberal movements for reform and for influencing Councils in the direction
of conciliation with Protestants[2] (a policy continued by some of his successors
on the holy imperial throne).[3] In his political capacity as emperor he had
come into conflict with the temporal power of the Pope, a conflict which
once led him to the sad extreme of sacking Rome. This event could be
regarded by ardent imperialists as a revenge for the former insults of popes
to emperors.

There is a well-known set of twelve engravings which celebrates the
victories of Charles V.[4] One shows the defeat of Francis I at Pavia in 1525.
Another illustrates the capitulation of Pope Clement VII to the imperial
army which sacked Rome in 1527. The Pope is seen looking disconsolately
out of the windows of the Castel S. Angelo at the guns of his besiegers. This

---

[1] Cf. Erasmus, *The Complaint of Peace* (Thomas Paynell's translation), Scholar's Facsimiles and
Reprints, New York, 1946, pp. 33 ff.

[2] See E. Armstrong, *The Emperor Charles V*, 1910, II, pp. 200 ff.

[3] Cf. my article 'Paolo Sarpi's history of the Council of Trent', *Journal of the Warburg and
Courtauld Institutes*, VII (1944), pp. 132 ff., and the references there given.

[4] The series was designed by Martin van Heemskerck, engraved by Dirck Coornhert, and first
published by Hieronymus Cock in 1556. It is reproduced, with notes and other valuable illustrative
material, in Sir W. Stirling Maxwell's *The Chief Victories of the Emperor Charles V*, London and
Edinburgh, 1870.

is indeed a complete reversal of the Pope versus Emperor situation at Canossa (see Plate 4d). Other designs in the series show the Emperor's triumphs over Solyman, the Turk, and over his German adversaries. And in one we see the Emperor's Catholic navies bring the blessings of Christianity to the savage inhabitants of the New World.

All these themes are summed up in the picture with which the series opens (Plate 3b). Charles is seen seated in a triumphant attitude between the two columns of his device, holding the sword and orb of empire. His opponents are bound at his feet by leashes attached to rings in the eagle's beak. On his right are Clement VII and Francis I, and the retreating figure of the Sultan Solyman; on his left are John Frederick, Elector of Saxony; Philip, Landgrave of Hesse; and William, Duke of Cleve. It is a bringing together in a composite group of all the victories which the individual pictures celebrate; even the scene in the New World is hinted at by the device.

This Catholic Emperor is placed on a distinctly higher level than the Pope whose temporal power he has subdued. Indeed he seems to threaten, not only the Turk, but also the Pope with the sword of imperial justice. Such a presentation of the wearers of the imperial crown and the papal tiara is a step in the direction of the Pope's fall under the feet of a reformed just virgin, wearing a royal crown, such as we see depicted in the initial C (Plates 4a, 7a).

Yet of course Erasmus himself never dreamed – and the most Catholic Emperor Charles V never approved – of the extreme development which the imperial reform was to take in England, the tone of which can be studied in Nicolas Udall's dedication to Edward VI of that same volume of Erasmian paraphrases which was in all the parish churches. Addressing Edward's 'Emperiall Maiestie', Udall reminds him that his father Henry VIII 'playnly saw that no waye there was to a reformation, but by this onely meane, yf the authoritie and usurped supremitie of the See of Rome were extirped, abolished, and clene extincte.[1]' The disgraced Pope has now fallen under the 'imperial' feet of Henry VIII (cf. Plate 5a).

But in spite of this divergence in their paths, the Catholic imperial symbolism of Charles V influences the Protestant Tudors. John Daye, the printer, to whose close association with Foxe 'may in large part be attributed the eventual triumph of the Reformation in England',[2] used as his printer's

---

[1] Erasmus, *Paraphrases*, ed. cit.

Udall's vision later in this dedication of the monstrous beast which has been cast out of England is still more extreme. The dragon of Papistry hisses out his curses and his ex-communications, and the contagious infection of idolatry and superstition. This dragon has ceased not to persecute the 'woman clothed in the sun', that is to say the Church of England, until he was finally put to flight by the 'English St Michael', King Henry VIII, who with his 'angels, the lords and godly prelates', cast the dragon out of England.

For the printer's mark representing the 'woman clothed with the sun' and the dragon, used in some English editions of the *Paraphrases*, see R. B. McKerrow, *Printers' and Publishers' Devices*, London, 1913, no. 107.

[2] C. H. Garrett, *The Marian Exiles*, Cambridge, 1938, p. 157.

mark in the *Acts and Monuments* a device (Plate 6a)[1] which is singularly close to some forms of Charles V's two columns device (cf. Plate 3a). And variations on that device turn up from time to time in representations of Queen Elizabeth, for example in a well-known engraving of 1596.

Elizabeth stands between two columns (Plate 6b) on which are a Pelican and a Phoenix,[2] She holds the orb and sceptre of rule, and behind her is an island with smoking forts, surrounded by shipping. This refers to the defeat of the Armada and of the might of Spain and the Pope by the virgin queen, and, it may be suggested, transfers to her the imperial destiny at which the two columns hint.[3]

'Eliza Triumphans', as she stands between two obelisks with a world-view in the background in an engraving by William Rogers,[4] holds the orb in her left hand, and in her right the olive-branch. Figures on the obelisks hold crowns, one of palm, the other of oak-leaves, which with the gold crown on the queen's head makes three crowns – the triple crown of empire?

Elizabeth's victory over the Spanish Armada was a victory, not only over a national enemy, but also over a spiritual power which made a total claim on men's allegiance. To defeat it required not only a strong navy but also a strong symbolism. By claiming for the national church that it was a reform executed by the sacred imperial power as represented in the sacred English monarchy, the Elizabeth symbol drew to itself a tradition which also made a total, a universal claim – the tradition of sacred empire. The extravagant language used of Elizabeth need not necessarily imply that Elizabethan hopes went so far as to expect a world empire for the queen. The arguments for sacred empire – that the world is at its best and most peaceful under one ruler and that then justice is most powerful – are used

[1] The letters I.D. at the base of the columns stand for John Daye's initials. Daye had already used this device in the reign of Edward VI (McKerrow, *op. cit.*, no. 115).

The printers' marks ought not to be left out of account in any study of Elizabethan symbolism. The mark of Giovanni Giolito of the Phoenix with the motto *semper eadem*, used by him on the title-page of Ludovico Dolce's life of Charles V, was often copied by Elizabethan printers (see McKerrow, *op cit.*, nos 252, 254, 297). *Semper eadem* was the motto used by Elizabeth with her Phoenix badge.

[2] F. M. O'Donoghue, *op. cit.*, p. 45; R. Strong, *Portraits of Queen Elizabeth I*, Oxford, 1963, Engravings, 23. It has been suggested that this engraving may be by Crispin de Passe. The verses below the picture are as follows:

> Immortalis honos Regum, cui non tulit aetas
> Ulla prior, veniens nec feret ulla parem,
> Sospite quo nunquam terras habitare Britannas
> Desinet alma Quies, Iustitia atque Fides,
> Queis ipsae tantam superant reliqua omnia regna,
> Quantum tu maior Regibus es reliquis,
> Viue precor felix tanti in moderamine regni,
> Dum tibi Rex Regnum coelica regna paret.

[3] The Phoenix and Pelican signs, seen on these columns, appear on another well-known representation of the queen, which hails her as 'Th'admired Empresse, through the world applauded' (O'Donoghue, *op. cit.*, p. 72).

[4] O'Donoghue, *op. cit.*, p. 65; Strong, *op. cit.*, Engravings, 17.

to buttress her religious rights as an individual monarch. The monarch who is One and sovereign within his own domains has imperial religious rights, and he can achieve the imperial reform independently of the Pope.[1] The lengths to which the cult of Elizabeth went are a measure of the sense of isolation which had at all costs to find a symbol strong enough to provide a feeling of spiritual security in face of the break with the rest of Christendom.

Through these associations, the imperial theme in relation to Queen Elizabeth has overtones which soar beyond the individual destinies of the Tudors and their realm. The details of the Tudor story, such as the union of York and Lancaster, become intensified into mystic harmonies where the angular features of the *Rosa Electa* (Plate 8c) are revealed. The unmarried state of the Queen is exalted into a symbol of the imperial virgin Astraea which fills the universe.

Queen Elizabeth as Astraea[2]

It would seem that from the very beginning of her reign the Virgo-Astraea symbol was used of Elizabeth.[3] We read in Camden that 'In the beginning of her late Majesties Reign, one upon happy hope conceived, made an half of the Zodiack, with *Virgo*, rising, adding JAM REDIT ET VIRGO. . . .'[4] But the use of the image was at its height in the years following the Armada.

The play *Histrio-Mastix* (1589?) contains pageant-like scenes in glorification of Elizabeth's reign. Peace, Bacchus, Ceres, and Plenty enter at one door, bearing the cornucopiae, and Poverty and her attendants vanish by the other door. After speeches in praise of Peace, Astraea enters 'Ushered by Fame, supported by Fortitude and Religion, followed by Virginity and Artes'. Peace does obeisance to Astraea for her justice and virginity and the latter then 'mounts unto the throne'. A note in the margin explains that Astraea represents Queen Elizabeth, and she is hailed by the following paean:[5]

[1] The representation of Elizabeth, engraved by Crispin de Passe after Isaac Olivier (Plate 8a), which influences many cult pictures of her, contains a representation of the imperial reform in the form of the Sword of Justice resting on the Word of God, the Bible. The purity of the Gospel has been restored by the sacred imperial power, represented by the sword. There is an allusion to Constantine in the verses accompanying this picture, and in view of the icon-like stiffness of the figure of the queen it is interesting to realize that there is indeed some Byzantine influence in the Elizabethan conception of sacred imperialism.

One fancies that some of the jewels in the queen's hair are in the form of stars, a feature which becomes exaggerated in an eighteenth-century descendant of the picture (Plate 8b); and here above the virgin's head is the Phoenix sign in a circle of stars.

[2] Warburg drew attention in a note to the use of Astraea as a name for Elizabeth (see A. Warburg, *Gesammelte Schriften*, Leipzig-Berlin, 1932, I, p. 415).

[3] E. C. Wilson, *England's Eliza*, Cambridge, Mass., 1939, is a useful survey of imagery used of Queen Elizabeth by the poets.

[4] W. Camden, *Remains*, London, 1674, ed. p. 466.

[5] *The School of Shakespeare*, ed. R. Simpson, New York, 1878, II, pp. 84–7; cf. Wilson, *op. cit.*, pp. 109–10.

Mount, Emperesse, whose praise for Peace shall mount,
Whose glory which thy solid vertues wonne,
Shall honour Europe whilst there shines a Sunne.
Crown'd with Heavens inward beauties, worlds applause
Thron'd and repos'd within the loving feare
Of thy adoring Subjects: live as long
As Time hath life, and Fame a worthy tongue!
Still breath our glory, the worlds *Empresse*,
Religions Gardian, *Peaces* patronesse!
Now flourish Arts, the Queene of *Peace* doth raigne;
Vertue triumph, now she doth sway the stemme,
Who gives to Vertue honours Diadem.
All sing Paens to her sacred worth,
Which none but Angels tongues can warble forth:
Yet sing, for though we cannot light the Sunne,
Yet utmost might hath kinde acceptance wonne.

Song.
Religion, Arts and Merchandise
triumph, triumph:
Astraea rules, whose gracious eyes
triumph, triumph.
O're *Vices* conquest whose desires
triumph, triumph:
Whose all to chiefest good aspires,
then all triumph.

Here we have Elizabeth-Astraea as the empress of the world, guardian of religion, patroness of peace, restorer of virtue; she is hailed with a Roman triumph which extols the wealth and prosperity which her golden age have brought.

George Peele's *Descensus Astraeae*, a pageant given to welcome a new lord mayor of London in 1591, brings out strongly the reforming side of Astraea's mission. The presenter of the pageant describes it as an emblem of Elizabeth as Astraea 'descended of the Trojan British line'. At the top of the pageant Astraea appeared as a shepherdess, with her sheep-hook, speaking these words:[1]

Feed on, my flock among the gladsome green
Where heavenly nectar flows above the banks . . .

She is opposed by Superstition, a Friar, and Ignorance, a Priest, who attempts in vain to poison the fountain from which her flock is drinking. One of the Graces thus describes Astraea:[2]

[1] George Peele, *Works*, ed. A. H. Bullen, London, 1888, I, p. 363. [2] *Ibid.*, p. 364.

Whilom, when Saturn's golden reign did cease,
  And iron age had kindled cruel wars,
Envy in wrath perturbing common peace,
  Engendering canker'd hate and bloody jars;
Lo, then Olympus' king, the thundering Jove,
  Raught hence this gracious nymph Astraea fair:
Now once again he sends her from above,
  Descended through the sweet transparent air;
And here she sits in beauty fresh and sheen,
Shadowing the person of a peerless queen.

Peele clearly associates the return of the virgin of the golden age with reformation in religion. She is the shepherdess of her people's souls, guarding them with her sheep-hook. She is exercising that supreme pastorship and authority in things spiritual at which the Catholic Harding protested and which Jewel defended on the ground of the authority of emperors to judge ecclesiastical causes. Her golden age is the age of purified religion. She is the simple shepherdess, contrasting with the superstitious friar and the ignorant priest. It is in a somewhat similarly controversial vein than an anonymous poet lamented after Elizabeth's death that:[1]

Righteous *Astraea* from the earth is banish't.
And from our sight the morning star is vanish't
Which did to us a radiant light remaine,
But was a comet to the eye of *Spaine:*
From whose chaste beames so bright a beautie shin'de,
That all their whorish eyes were stricken blinde.

Peele was a purveyor of both town and court pageantry and in both spheres the Astraea image holds good. In a poem which reflects one of the Accession Day tilts, held in 1595, Peele urges Clio to bring the Muses to Elizabeth-Astraea's court:[2]

Conduct thy learnèd company to court,
Eliza's court, Astraea's earthly heaven;
There take survey of England's emperess,
And in her praise tune your heroic songs . . .

And after his description of the tilt, and of the devices and accoutrements of the knights, he concludes on the same note:[3]

Long may they run in honour of the day!
Long may she live to do them honour's right,

---

[1] John Lane, *An Elegie upon the death of the high and renowned Princesse, our late Soueraigne Elizabeth,* Fugitive Tracts, second series, no. 2, London, 1875.
[2] *Anglorum Feriae*; Peele, *Works, ed. cit.,* II, p. 343.   [3] *Ibid.,* pp. 354–5.

> To grace their sports and them as she hath done,
> England's Astraea, Albion's shining sun!

In a very similar poem, describing the Accession Day tilt of 1591,[1] we know that Peele's allusions to Elizabeth as a Vestal Virgin related to an elaborate presentation of the Temple of Vesta erected for the occasion.[2] Very possibly his references to the queen as Astraea in the 1595 Accession Day poem may also refer to some visual presentation of the Astraea theme on that occasion.[3]

The Misfortunes of Arthur is a pageant play produced in honour of Queen Elizabeth by the young law students of Gray's Inn in 1588, the Armada year. The prologue states that students of the law are the servants of Dame Astraea, or Justice. The play, the scene of which is laid in ancient Britain, concludes with an impassioned prophecy:[4]

> Let Virgo come from Heaven, the glorious Star:
> The Zodiac's Joy: the Planet's chief delight:
> The hope of all the year: the ease of skies:
> The airs relief, the comfort of the earth.
> That virtuous Virgo born for Britain's bliss:
> That peerless branch of Brute: that sweet remain
> Of Priam's state: that hope of springing Troy:
> Which time to come, and many ages hence
> Shall of all wars compound eternal peace.
> Let her reduce the golden age again,
> Religion, ease and wealth of former world.
> Yea let that Virgo come and Saturns reign
> And years oft ten times told expired in peace.

---

[1] *Polyhymnia*; *ibid.*, pp. 287 ff.

[2] The pavilion 'made of white Taffeta . . . being in proportion like unto the sacred Temple of the Virgins Vestall' erected for this occasion is described by Sir W. Segar, *Honor, military and civill*, London, 1602, Bk III, ch. 54. See E. K. Chambers, *Sir Henry Lee*, Oxford, 1936, pp. 135 ff. and below pp. 102–3, 117.

[3] The prevalence of the Virgo idea in the *imprese* reported by Camden rather supports the notion that this may have been a leading theme at one or some of the Accession Day tilts. For example: 'A very good invention was that to shew his stay and support by a Virgin Prince, who presented in his shield, the Zodiack with the characters only of *Leo and Virgo*, and this word, HIS EGO PRAESIDIIS' (Camden, *Remains, ed cit.*, pp. 460–1).

'The Star called *Spica Virginis*, one of the fifteen which are accounted to be of the first magnitude among the Astronomers, with a scrole inwritten, MIHI VITA SPICA VIRGINIS, declared thereby haply, that had that Star in the Ascendant at his Nativity, or rather that he lived by the gracious favour of a Virgin Prince' (*ibid.*, p. 461).

'It may be doubtful whether he affected his Sovereign or Justice more zealously, which made a man hovering in the Air, with FEROR AD ASTRAEAM' (*ibid.*, p. 462).

Possibly the jewel of a woman 'called virtute or virgo' with compasses in one hand, a garland in the other, and standing on a rainbow may have been a representation of some 'Virgo' *impresa* (the jewel is described in John Nichols, *The Progresses of Queen Elizabeth*, London, 1823, II, p. 79).

[4] Thomas Hughes, *The Misfortunes of Arthur*, ed. H. C. Grumbine, Berlin, 1900, p. 190; Tudor Facsimile Texts, 1911, pp. 45–6.

A Rule most rare, unheard, unseen, unread,
The sole example that the world affords.

It is the prophecy of the advent of a British Virgo of Trojan descent, such as is found in the *Faerie Queene*. The crude lines are full of echoes of the solemn words of the Fourth Eclogue; this Virgin will bring back the reign of Saturn; she will establish an eternal peace, restore religion, and her people shall live in the ease and wealth of the golden age.

One may perhaps see in pictorial form in an engraving illustrating Christopher Saxton's *Survey of England* (1579) something of the atmosphere of mysterious prophecy surrounding the advent of the Virgo. Queen Elizabeth enthroned (Plate 8d)[1] is flanked by figures of astrologers, holding spheres; in the bottom left-hand corner a man with compasses draws a map; in the right-hand corner a man gazes through a telescope at a sign in the starry heavens. Here we see a representation of Virgo-Elizabeth as a celestial portent whose advent has been mysteriously foretold.

The writer of *The Misfortunes of Arthur* uses Virgo as a sign of the zodiac in rather a loose sense. Astronomically speaking, Virgo is simply one of the twelve signs of the zodiac, which the sun enters in August; astrologically speaking she rules a certain part of the body and dispenses certain, mainly mercurial, influences. Those born under her may have imperial destinies, but it is quite unwarranted, from any scientific point of view, to speak of Virgo as the 'Zodiac's Joy', as though she were some queen of the zodiac; or as the 'Planets' chief delight'. The Virgo of the Elizabethans is, however, so closely bound up with the Astraea of the Fourth Eclogue and her imperial connections, that they extend to the Virgo of the skies, the sign of the zodiac, the commanding position in the heavens of her royal incarnation on earth. The full implications of this will become apparent in other examples.

Richard Barnfield's *Cynthia* (1595) is based on a theme quite common in Elizabethan literature, which found visual expression in the picture at Hampton Court (Plate 9a), which is dated 1569. It consists of a revised Judgment of Paris in which the golden apple is awarded to neither Juno, Venus, nor Minerva, but to the Virgin Queen, a goddess who excels them all. Barnfield's poem, which shows throughout the influence of Spenser, describes Elizabeth as a 'Fairy Queen' reigning in peace and union amidst the ocean. To this sacred virgin Jove (not Paris) awards the golden ball, and it is as Virgo that she receives this distinction:[2]

[1] This engraving is attributed to Remigius Hogenberg (Strong, *op. cit.*, Engravings, II).

[2] R. Barnfield, *Poems*, ed. E. Arber, 1896, pp. 54–5. Other examples of Judgments of Paris in which the prize is awarded to Elizabeth are, Francis Sabie, *Pan's Pipe*, 1595; George Peele, *Arraignment of Paris*, 1584. Cf. Wilson, *op. cit.*, pp. 147, 431.

The award to the mysterious 'Avisa' of a place above Juno, Minerva, or Venus (*Willobie His Avisa*, 1594, ed. G. B. Harrison, London, 1926, pp. 23 ff.) ought to be placed in the context of all these Judgments of Paris.

Thus, sacred Virgin, Muse of chastitie,
This difference is betwixt the Moone and thee:
Shee shines by Night; but thou by Day do'st shine:
Shee monthly changeth; thou dost nere decline:
Yet neither Sun, nor Moone, thou canst be named,
Because thy light hath both their beauties shamed:
Then, since an heauenly Name doth thee befall,
Thou Virgo art: (if any Signe at all).

Here Virgo, whilst still remembering her connection with the sign, has become even more than the 'Zodiac's joy' or the 'Planets' chief delight'. She is a being greater than the sun and moon.

This tendency of Virgo-Astraea-Elizabeth to expand until she fills the universe is very curiously represented in visual form in an illustration to J. Case's *Sphaera civitatis* published in 1588 (Plate 9c).[1] It is a diagram showing the central earth surrounded by the spheres of the moon, sun, and planets, and the sphere of fixed stars – in short a diagram representing the universe according to the Ptolemaic system. This universe is held by the crowned figure of Queen Elizabeth. An accompanying Latin poem alludes to the 'wonderful year' of the defeat of the Armada and to Elizabeth as the Virgin Astraea:[2]

Quis verum neget augurium mirabilis anni?
Aurea iam redijt post ferrea secula proles.
Caelicolae liquere polum, terraque locantur.
Infima supremis concertant sidera signis
Una Deos eademque heroas sphaerula pandit.
Virgo tenet solium, virgo tenet inclyta centrum.
Utraque complexu virtutem continet omnem.
Altera ut Astraea est, sic altera ad astra feretur.

It is therefore as Virgo-Astraea that Elizabeth here holds the world; the virtues of her golden age which radiate through the spheres; her *Iustitia immobilis* which reigns on the central earth.

The clue to this picture is to remember the analogy with the physical world by which the imperialist argument for the One ruler was established. 'As the heaven is regulated in all its parts . . . by the one first mover who is God, so the world of men is at its best when it is ruled by one prince.' In the dedication of his book to Sir Christopher Hatton, Case explains that the diagram represents the *sphaera civitatis* of which the Prime Mover must be the Prince, the representative of the Deity. Elizabeth-Virgo-Astraea is here the One Monarch of Dantesque tradition under whom individual countries,

[1] J. Case, *Sphaera civitatis*, London, 1588. The work is an Aristotelian treatise on political moral philosophy.
[2] *Ibid.*, sig. gg 5 *verso*.

or better still the whole world, are at their best, and Justice, together with all other virtue, reigns.[1]

If the virtues named on the diagram are examined, it will be found that some of them may be regarded as Virgo influences, for example *Ubertas rerum*, Facundia, Religio, and Justitia. To the two imperial virtues Pietas (Religio) and Justitia, the diagram adds the other two, namely Virtus (Fortitudo) and Clementia,[2] together with Prudentia, whilst the sphere of Saturn represents the all-embracing imperial or royal 'Maiestas'. The sphere of fixed stars is labelled *Camera stellata Proceres Heroes Consiliarii*.[3]

The attribution to Elizabeth of all the virtues was a commonplace which fits very easily into the Astraea theme, for Justice is an imperial virtue, and also the virtue which is theoretically supposed to include all the others. When Astraea comes again she brings with her, not only Justice, but all other banished virtues, as Ariosto says. The portrait of Elizabeth in Dover Town Hall (Plate 10a) shows, behind the queen, a column on which can be seen the three theological and the four cardinal virtues; Faith, Hope, Charity, Justice, Fortitude, Temperance, Prudence. The central position is held by Justice with the sword, and this virtue seems to be wearing a dress similar to that of Elizabeth herself. Perhaps one may imagine that this might be a picture of the Virgin Queen as Astraea-Justice, including all the virtues.

In Case's diagram we saw the One Virgo, holding the world. Verses on the queen written on the occasion of her visit to Audley End in 1578, and alluding to her Phoenix motto of *semper eadem*, make still clearer the relation of her name of Una, or One, to the concept of Princeps, or Monarch:[4]

Semper Una

Una quod es semper, quod semper es Optima Princeps,
    Quam bene conveniunt hae duo verba tibi:
Quod pia, quod prudens, quod casta, quod innuba Virgo
    Semper es, hoc etiam *Semper* es *Una* modo.
Et Populum quod ames, Populo quod amata vicissim
    Semper es, hic constans *Semper* et *Una* manes.
O utinam quoniam sic *semper* es, *una* liceret,
    Una te nobis *semper*, Eliza, frui.

If these verses on One, with their allusion to the Phoenix symbol's motto of *semper eadem*, are compared with the verses on the One Virgo holding the

---

[1] The 'sphere' theme turns up in several portraits of Elizabeth. There is a sphere on the queen's sleeve in the 'Rainbow' portrait at Hatfield House (Plate 43b), a sphere as an ear-drop in the Ditchley portrait (Plate 13), and in another portrait, spheres are embroidered on the sleeves of the dress.

[2] The four imperial virtues are *Pietas, Justitia, Clementia, Virtus*. (See M. P. Charlesworth, *The Virtues of a Roman Emperor*, Raleigh Lecture, 1937.)

[3] From one of the commendatory poems, it would seem that this is a reference to the members of the Court of Star Chamber.

[4] Nichols, *op. cit.*, II, p. 112; cf. Wilson, *op. cit.*, p. 78.

sphere, where the allusion was to Virgo-Astraea, it will be realized how close is the connection between Elizabeth as the Phoenix and Elizabeth as Astraea. Both are symbols of imperial *renovatio*, implying the return of that best rule under the One, when the world is most at peace, and justice, together with all other virtue, reigns.

The 'one' theme is always strong in Eliza worship. The royal virgin is 'unique'; the 'one and only'. Her one-ness staggers the universe:[1]

> I weepe for ioy to see the Sunne looke old,
> To see the Moone mad at her often change,
> To see the Starres onely by night to shine,
> Whilst you are still bright, *still one*, still diuine . . .

cries one of her adorers in ecstasy.

It is by now already apparent that the elucidation of Astraea as a name for Elizabeth throws beams of illumination upon many of her other epithets and aspects. This can be still further emphasized by turning to Sir John Davies of Hereford's *Hymnes to Astraea*.

The hymns to Astraea are a series of twenty-six fifteen-lined poems; in each poem the first letters of each line, when read downwards, spell the words ELISABETHA REGINA. This is a very neat formulation of Astraea-worship in its relation to Eliza-worship, and the various peoms bring out various aspects of the cult.

The first is merely the general statement, that Elizabeth Regina is the Virgin of the golden age returned to earth:[2]

> E arly before the day doth spring
> L et us awake my Muse, and sing;
> I t is no time to slumber,
> S o many ioyes this time doth bring,
> A s Time will faile to number.
>
> B ut whereto shall we bend our layes?
> E uen vp to Heauen, againe to raise
> T he Mayd, which thence descended;
> H ath brought againe the golden dayes,
> A nd all the world amended.
>
> R udenesse it selfe she doth refine,
> E uen like an Alychymist diuine;
> G rosse times of yron turning
> I nto the purest forme of gold;
> N ot to corrupt, till heauen waxe old,
> A nd be refined with burning.

[1] Thomas Dekker, *Old Fortunatus*, *Works*, ed. cit., I, p. 84.
[2] Sir John Davies, *Complete Poems*, ed. A. B. Grosart, London, 1876, I, p. 129.

It is, on the whole, a courtly interpretation of the theme. Astraea has refined the rude manners of the age of iron and ushered in a more civilized epoch.

One side of the Astraea theme upon which we have not hitherto touched comes out very clearly in these hymns, namely her relation to Spring. In the golden age, Spring eternal reigned, and the virgin of the golden age brings Spring with her:[1]

E arth now is greene, and heauen is blew,
L iuely Spring which makes all new,
I olly Spring doth enter;
S weete yong sun-beames doe subdue
A ngry, agèd Winter.

B lasts are milde, and seas are calme,
E uery meadow flowes with balme,
T he Earth wears all her riches;
H armonious birdes sing such a psalme,
A s eare and heart bewitches.

R eserue (sweet Spring) this Nymph of ours,
E ternall garlands of thy flowers,
G reene garlands neuer wasting;
I n her shall last our *State's* faire Spring,
N ow and for euer flourishing,
A s long as Heauen is lasting.

Two of the other poems also relate to Elizabeth-Astraea as Spring; one is addressed to her as May, where she is called 'May of Maiestie'; and another to her as Flora, 'Empresse of Flowers'.

That Virgo can represent the Spring might seem at first sight something of an anomaly, for, as we know, she is an autumnal sign, bearing corn in her hand. The cornucopiae overflowing with fruitful abundance and *ubertas rerum* would seem to be more properly her own than the flowers of Spring. It is, however, the conflation of Virgo the sign of autumn with Astraea the virgin of the golden age which brings about this seeming anomaly, for in the eternal spring of the golden age flowers and fruits grew together at the same time: 'Then spring was everlasting, and gentle zephyrs with warm breath played with the flowers that sprang unplanted. Anon the earth, untilled, brought forth her stores of grain. . . .'[2] Astraea's spring is not the ordinary season but the eternal spring of the golden age. This is very clearly brought out by Sir Philip Sidney's sister, Mary, Countess of Pembroke, in her poem entitled *Dialogue between two shepherds Thenot and Piers, in praise of Astraea*, written in honour of the queen's visit to Wilton. Thenot's

---

[1] *Ibid.*, I, p. 131.
[2] Ovid, *Metamorphoses*, I, 107–10.

compliments to Astraea are contradicted by Piers, yet the contradiction always turns out to be an even greater compliment. Thus Thenot says:[1]

> Astraea may be justly said,
> A field in flowery robe arrayed,
> In Season freshly springing.

to which Piers replies:

> That Spring endures but shortest time,
> This never leaves Astraea's clime,
> Thou liest instead of singing.

The Astraea-Elizabeth garlanded with spring flowers of Davies's poem represents 'our State', the state of England renewed in a golden age, a *renovatio temporum* which the poet hopes will last for ever. She is here the state virgin, the 'Renaissance' princess, centre of a newly refined court.

Her aspect as the representative of the virtues is not forgotten in these hymns, which tell of her moral virtue in the control of her passions ('Of the passions of her heart', XX);[2] of her innumerable intellectual virtues which no mathematician can count ('Of the innumerable virtues of her minde', XXI);[3] of her wisdom, ('Right princely vertue fit to reaigne', XXII);[4] and above all, of her justice:[5]

> Of her Justice
> E xil'd *Astraea* is come againe,
> L o here she doth all things maintaine
> I n *number*, *weight*, and *measure*;
> S he rules vs with delightfull paine,
> A nd we obey with pleasure.
>
> B y *Loue* she rules more then by *Law*,
> E uen her great mercy breedeth awe;
> T his is her sword and scepter:
> H erewith she hearts did euer draw,
> A nd this guard euer kept her.
>
> R eward doth sit at her right-hand,
> E ach vertue thence taks her garland
> G ather'd in Honor's garden;
> I n her left hand (wherein should be
> N ought but the sword) sits Clemency
> A nd conquers Vice with pardon.

---

[1] *A Dialogue betweene two Shepheards, Thenot, and Piers, in praise of Astraea, made by the excellent Lady, the Lady Mary Countesse of Pembroke, at the Queenes Maiesties being at her house*, reprinted in *A Poetical Rhapsody*, ed. H. C. Rollins, Cambridge, Mass., 1931, I, pp. 15 ff.

[2] Davies, *ed. cit.*, I, p. 148.   [3] *Ibid.*, p. 149.   [4] *Ibid.*, p. 150.   [5] *Ibid.*, p. 151.

The justice of Astraea is here tempered with mercy, and she appears in this poem as a combination of the imperial virtues of Justitia and Clementia.

The hymns to Astraea as a whole cover nearly all the points included in the cult of the imperial virgin. There is an engraving of Queen Elizabeth which shows her in a glory and with a crown of stars encircling her head. In its original version it was accompanied by verses by Sir John Davies (Plate 9b),[1] and so is perhaps a representation of her under that poet's favourite image, as the starry virgin of the golden age returned to earth. The contrast between the crudity of this representation and the accomplished poetic imagery which flows from Sir John's pen, is typical of the strange gap in quality between the visual arts and the literature of the period.

Spenser and Astraea

Spenser is the Virgil of the Elizabethan golden age, and the *Faerie Queene* its great epic poem. Here, if anywhere, we should expect to find Astraea enshrined, and here in fact we do find her, not only under that name but under many names. The concept of Elizabeth as the imperial virgin is the lynch-pin of the poem; it is the Prime Mover, round which its whole elaborate universe of moral allegory revolves.

The ground-plan of the *Faerie Queene*, as Spenser explained in his letter to Raleigh, was that it should present in an allegorical framework every virtue, both public and private. Of the projected twelve cantos on the private virtues we have only six and part of a seventh; whilst the section on the public virtues, which would probably also have had twelve parts, is non-existent. All these virtues were summed up in the queen, or rather in the 'most high Mightie and Magnificent *Empresse*' to use the words of the dedication. Gloriana, the fairy queen, represented, so Spenser informs Raleigh, Queen Elizabeth in her public character as the just and righteous ruler; whereas Belphoebe was Elizabeth in her private character as a most beautiful and virtuous lady. The combination Gloriana-Belphoebe is Elizabeth as all the virtues, public and private. Belphoebe, the queen as private virtue, symbolized above all her chastity; Gloriana – the queen as

---

[1] See O'Donoghue, *op. cit.*, p. 62; Strong, *op. cit.*, Posthumous portraits, 9. The picture was engraved by F. Delaram, and the verses accompanying it by Sir John Davies are as follows:

> Lo here her type, who was of late,
>   the Propp of Belgia, Stay of France:
> Spaine's Foyle, Faith's Shield, and Queen of State;
>   of Armes and Learning, Fate and Chance:
> In briefe; of women, neere was seene,
>   so great a Prince, so good a Queene.

Reduced in size and with the inscription cut off, this engraving became the frontispiece to Camden's *Annales, or the Historie of the Most Renowned and Victorious Princess Elizabeth*, London, 1630. I talso appears in Nichols, *op. cit.* (See O'Donoghue, *op. cit.*, pp. 62–3; Strong, *op. cit.*, Posthumous portraits, 16.)

public virtue—symbolized the glory of her just government. Elizabeth is implored by Spenser not to refuse[1]

> In mirrors more than one her self to see,
> But either Gloriana let her choose
> Or in Belphoebe fashioned to be:
> In th'one her rule, in th'other her rare chastity.

Belphoebe-Gloriana is the Virgin-Ruler, religiously adored for her virginity and her justice.

The historical framework of the poem also brings out the theme of the advent of a just, imperial virgin. The British virgin whose advent is prophesied to Britomart by Merlin (in that prophecy which is a transference to Elizabeth of the prophecy of the *Orlando furioso*) is to be a descendant of Britomart and Artegal, the representatives of the virtues of Chastity and Justice. And she comes of an 'imperial' Trojan line. The descent of Gloriana from the Trojan Brut is the theme of the tenth canto of Book I, and the story is told by Merlin to Britomart in Book III when he foresees that out of her 'ancient Trojan blood' will spring a line of kings and 'sacred Emperors' culminating in the royal virgin Elizabeth.

Thus the dominant themes in Spenser's glorification of Elizabeth correspond to the leading characteristics of Astraea.

As might be expected, Spenser's most open treatment of Virgo-Astraea in relation to Elizabeth comes in the fifth book which treats of Justice. The book opens with a lament for the golden age:[2]

> For during *Saturnes* ancient reigne it's sayd,
>   That all the world with goodness did abound:
> And loued vertue, no man was affrayd
>   Of force, ne fraud in wight was to be found:
> No warre was known, no dreadful trumpets sound,
> Peace universall rayn'd mongst men and beasts,
> And all things freely grew out of the ground:
> Iustice sate high ador'd with solemne feasts,
> And to all people did diuide her dred beheasts.

> Most sacred vertue she of all the rest,
>   Resembling God in his imperiall might;
> Whose soueraine powre is herein most exprest,
>   That both to good and bad he dealeth right,
>   And all his workes with Iustice hath bedight.

[1] *Faerie Queene*, Bk III, v; *Works, ed. cit.*, III, p. 2.

[2] Bk V, introduction, ix, x; *Works, ed. cit.*, V, p. 3. Cf. also the stanza quoted above, p. 31. Another allusion to Saturn and Virgo is probably to be found in Bk III, XI, xliii, where we are told that Saturn loved Erigone (another name for Virgo, see above, p. 34). This has been regarded as a mythological mistake on Spenser's part (*Works, ed. cit.*, III, p. 296).

> That powre he also doth to Princes lend,
> And makes them like himselfe in glorious sight,
> And rule his people right, as he doth recommend.

This paean in honour of Astraea-Justice is the corner-stone of the poem, for it lays down the 'imperialist' theory of the divine right of kings. Justice is the key virtue, the most sacred of all, for it reflects the 'imperiall might' of God which he 'lends' to princes, giving them a divine right, like his own. Spenser now naturally turns to the just goddess who reigns in England:[1]

> Dread Souerayne Goddesse, that doest highest sit
> In seate of iudgement, in the'Almighties stead,
> And with magnificke might and wondrous wit
> Doest to thy people righteous doome aread . . .

It is a vision of the enthroned imperial virgin.

Other visions of, and names for, the queen in the poem embody different aspects of the theme. In this same fifth book on Justice there is a picture of the queen as Mercilla. She is seated on a high throne. Little angels hold back the cloth of state; in her hand she holds the sceptre; at her feet is the sword of justice.[2] Here the queen represents justice tempered with mercy, hence the name Mercilla. Spenser's Mercilla is, in fact, Elizabeth as Justitia-Clementia, both imperial virtues.

The title-page of the Bishops' Bible of 1569 (Plate 10b),[3] shows Justice and Mercy holding the crown over the enthroned queen's head. If we turn back to one of Sir John Davies's hymns, we learn that 'exil'd Astraea' when she returns as Elizabeth rules by mercy, and that[4]

> In her left hand (wherein should be
> Nought but the sword) sits Clemency . . .

And the portrait of Elizabeth, attributed to Marcus Geeraerts, in a flowery

---

[1] *Ibid.*, Bk V, introduction, xi; *Works, ed. cit.*, V, p. 4.

The last lines of this stanza state that Artegal is the instrument of Elizabeth's justice; and a little later (Bk V, I, v; *Works, ed. cit.*, V, p. 6) we are told that Artegal was instructed in justice in his infancy,

> By faire *Astraea*, with great industrie . . .

It clearly follows from these two statements that Elizabeth is Astraea.

Spenser does not make the crude statement that Astraea and the golden age have automatically returned with Elizabeth. His is the loftier conception that Elizabeth is the celestial justice for which Artegal, and her other knights, have to fight in the wicked world.

[2] *Ibid.*, Bk V, viii, xvii ff.; ix, xxvii ff.: *Works, ed. cit.*, V, pp. 93 ff., 108 ff. Attendant on Mercilla are

> Just *Dice*, wise *Eunome*, myld *Eirene*

Justice, Order, and Peace, the three daughters of Jove, according to Hesiod (see above, p. 32, note 4).

[3] O'Donoghue, *op. cit.*, p. 39; Strong, *op. cit.*, Woodcuts, 70.

[4] See above, pp. 68–9.

robe with the sword of justice at her feet and what appears to be an olive-branch in her right hand[1] might be a representation of the queen as Justitia-Clementia, or Astraea-Mercilla.

One of the most striking of all the names used by Spenser in this poem is that of Una, the One, the heroine of the first book which is dedicated to Holiness, or pure religion. Philosophical emphasis on the One may here be combined with idealist politics and connected with the imperial theme of the One sovereign ruler under whom Justice is the most powerful in the world and the peace and unity of the golden age return to mankind. Una is descended of a royal lineage. Her ancestors were[2]

> Ancient Kings and Queenes, that had of yore
> > Their scepters stretcht from East to Westerne shore,
> And all the world in their subjection held;
> Till that infernal feende with foule vprore
> Forwasted all their land, and them expeld:
> Whom to auenge, she had this Knight from far compeld.

Una can lay claim to a world empire (she is always called a 'royal virgin') and it is the mission of the Red Cross Knight to restore her to her heritage.

He is, however, temporarily seduced from her allegiance by another lady, also daughter of an emperor, who, in contrast to the simplicity and humility of Una's bearing, is proudly and richly attired:[3]

> A goodly lady clad in scarlot red,
> Purfled with gold and pearl of rich assay,
> And like a *Persian* mitre on her hed
> She wore, with crownes and owches garnished . . .

This lady was of light reputation, and entertained her lover all the way with 'mirth and wanton play', in marked contrast to the gravity and seriousness of Una.

It is generally admitted that the false Duessa stands in Spenser's eyes for the scarlet woman of Rome and false religion; whilst Una is the purity of reformed religion. But the full significance of the contrast now comes out more clearly. Both are emperors' daughters; both make a universal claim. Duessa wears a 'Persian mitre';[4] Una a royal crown. Duessa and Una

---

[1] O'Donoghue, *op. cit.*, p. 12; Strong, *op. cit.*, Paintings, 85.

It is perhaps too fanciful to suggest that the little dog by the sword might indicate that this is Astraea under her name of Erigone, daughter of Icarus, whose little dog symbolized her piety to her father's memory (see above, p. 32).

[2] *Ibid.*, Bk I, I, v; *Works, ed. cit.*, I, p. 6.   [3] *Ibid.*, Bk I, II, xiii; *Works*, I, p. 22.

[4] Jewel refers to the 'Persian' pride of the Bishop of Rome; cf. *Works*, IV, pp. 81, 104.

M. Y. Hughes ('England's Eliza and Spenser's Medina', *Journ. of Eng. and Germ. Philol.*, 1944, pp. 1-15) suggests that in the name Medina, Spenser alludes to Elizabeth's *via media* in religious policy. This interesting interpretation need not conflict with the above; the imperialist religious policy was always conciliatory in theory.

symbolize the story of impure papal religion and pure imperial religion. Una is the royal virgin of the golden age of pure religion and imperial reform; she is the One Virgin whose crown reverses the tiara.

There is yet another side to Spenser's Astraea, by which she becomes approximated to the Renaissance vision of beauty, of the celestial Venus.

In the sixth book of the *Faerie Queene*, that devoted to the legend of Sir Calidore, or the virtue of Courtesy, the knight comes upon a little wooded hill, said to be the haunt of Venus, and there he sees the Three Graces, and a hundred other naked maidens, dancing around a 'faire one' in the centre. She is crowned with a rosy garland, and the damsels as they dance throw flowers and sweet odours upon her. These nymphs and graces, as they move in solemn yet sweet attendance on the 'faire one', are rather strangely compared to stars moving round the constellation of Ariadne's Crown (*Corona borealis*):[1]

> Looke how the Crowne, which *Ariadne* wore
>   Vpon her yuory forehead that same day,
>   That *Theseus* her vnto his bridale bore,
>   When the bold *Centaures* made that bloudy fray
>   With the fierce *Lapithes* which did them dismay;
>   Being now placed in the firmament,
>   Through the bright heauen doth her beams display,
>   And is vnto the starres an ornament,
> Which round about her move in order excellent.
>
> Such was the beauty of this goodly band,
>   Whose sundry parts were here too long to tell;
>   But she that in the midst of them did stand,
>   Seem'd all the rest in beauty to excell,
>   Crown'd with a rosie girlond, that right well
>   Did her beseeme. And euer, as the crew
>   About her daunst, sweet flowers, that far did smell,
>   And fragrant odours they vppon her threw;
> But most of all, those three[2] did her with gifts endew.

Through the comparison with Ariadne's Crown, the Venus of this vision can be connected with Virgo-Astraea. Ariadne, like Astraea, was a maiden who became a constellation. When deserted by Theseus, she was loved and crowned by Bacchus and found a place in heaven, not very far from Virgo, as the group of stars known as the Northern Crown. Several classical writers, including Lucian,[3] and above all, Manilius, seem to identify Virgo with Ariadne.

---

[1] *Faerie Queene*, Bk VI, X, xiii–xiv; *Works, ed. cit.*, VI, p. 117.   [2] The Three Graces.

[3] Lucian, *Deor. conc.*, LXXIV, 51; Propertius, III, 17, 6 ff. For other references and a discussion of the whole point see Boll, *Sphaera*, p. 276.

Manilius introduces Ariadne's Crown in association with Erigone (his name for Virgo) and then describes Erigone surrounded and crowned with flowers of many hues and painting the grassy meadows on a wooded hill with all the colours of Spring. This love of flowers and of sweetly mingled odours in those born under her symbolizes their love of elegance and of all the gentler arts and graces of life.[1] Spenser has fused this flowery Virgo, associated with Ariadne's Crown, with Venus and the Graces,[2] and thereby creates a vision eminently suited to the knight who represents the virtue of Courtesy. And there can be no doubt that this Virgo-Ariadne was also Elizabeth-Virgo when we learn from William Camden that:[3]

> *Sir Henry Lea* upon some Astrological consideration, used to her late Majesties honour, the whole constellation of *Ariadnes* Crown, culminant in her Nativity, with this word: CAELUMQUE SOLUMQUE BEAVIT.

The picture of Elizabeth seen by Sir Calidore represents her as a vision of celestial beauty, decked with all the flowers and scents of the civilizing arts and graces of a Renaissance court. There was no Elizabethan Botticelli to give this vision an enduring place in art, but Spenser's is an intensely visual imagination, and he invests the fierce anti-papal Virgo of the Protestant theologians with the gentle elegance of Neoplatonic allegory.[4]

Shakespeare and Astraea

Shakespeare twice mentions Astraea, once in *Henry VI*,[5] where she is associated with Joan of Arc, and again in *Titus Andronicus*.

Titus, the good, the noble Roman, maddened by his wrongs, rushes on to the stage, accompanied by his friends. They all carry bows and arrows, with letters attached to the arrows. Titus is looking everywhere for Astraea who has left the earth. Almost his first words are the Latin words:[6]

> Terras Astraea reliquit . . .

Amongst Shakespeare's 'small Latin', the Ovidian description of the four ages evidently had a place. Wrung with anguish, Titus implores his companions to seek everywhere for Astraea, on land, on sea, and even in the lower world:[7]

---

[1] Manilius, *Astronomicon*, V, 251–69. Cf. Sir John Davies on Astraea as Flora, *op. cit.*, p. 137.

[2] In the preceding stanzas the vision is that of a medieval Realm of Venus, which, in the stanzas quoted, melts into reminiscences of the Manilius passage on Ariadne-Virgo. There were precedents for the affiliation of Virgo to Venus (see Cumont's article, cited above).

[3] *Remains, ed. cit.*, p. 470; cf. Chambers, *Sir Henry Lee*, p. 141

[4] We have seen how the Elizabethan theologians can regard Dante, Petrarch, Savonarola, Ficino, Pico della Mirandola, as supporters of their imperial reform. A poet like Spenser would therefore feel justified in drawing for his glorification of the imperial Virgo upon those Florentine philosophical, poetic, and religious currents which were also the inspiration of Botticelli.

[5] *I Henry VI*, I, vi, 4.   [6] *Titus Andronicus*, IV, iii, 4.   [7] *Ibid.*, ll. 13–18.

> . . . when you come to Pluto's region,
> I pray you, deliver him this petition;
> Tell him, it is for justice and for aid,
> And that it comes from old Andronicus,
> Shaken with sorrows in ungrateful Rome.
> Ah, Rome!

But Justice is nowhere to be found, and at last he determines to drag her down again by force from heaven. Then follows a most extraordinary scene. Titus and his friends proceed to shoot their arrows, with the prayers or letters attached to them, up into the sky, trying to reach the gods. They hit some of the signs of the zodiac which begin to fall out of their places. One of the arrows, that shot by Lucius, hits Virgo.[1]

There must be a connection between the search for Astraea on earth and the hitting of Virgo in heaven, for Virgo, as we know well, was Astraea after she had fled to heaven from the wicked world.

The play is throughout concerned with the Empire. The good Titus ought to have been emperor, instead of the wicked Saturnine (whose name is the evil opposite of the golden age of Saturn).[2] The noble and chaste Roman virgin, Lavinia, daughter to Titus, has been most shamefully abused and mutilated. It was the treatment of Lavinia which drove Titus mad and made him shoot at the stars for Justice. But the good empire returns with Lucius. He is the just man who in the end assumes the purple, and his reign will 'heal Rome's harms, and wipe away her woe'.[3] It is therefore perhaps a very significant detail that it was Lucius who hit Virgo in the shooting scene, and therefore, presumably, brought her down to earth. The apotheosis of Lucius at the end of the play thus perhaps represents the Return of the Virgin – the return of the just empire and the golden age.

Shakespeare can hardly have failed to know the popular identification of Elizabeth with Astraea. He can hardly have failed to know the arguments in the books which it was more or less obligatory to read in one's parish church and in which Lucius was presented as the first Christian King of England.[4] Foxe's 'Book of Martyrs', it will be remembered, begins with Lucius and ends with Elizabeth. The suggestion may therefore be proffered that the appearance of Astraea-Virgo in *Titus Andronicus* might definitely connect Shakespeare with the topics which we have been discussing.

Shakespeare was deeply concerned with monarchy, particularly in relation to English history. The discussions as to whether an 'imperial theme' can

---

[1] *Ibid.*, ll. 48 ff.

[2] When they are shooting at the stars for Justice, one of the archers is adjured to shoot to Saturn, not to Saturnine (IV, ii, line 56).

[3] V, iii, line 147.

[4] See Foxe, *Acts and Monuments, ed. cit.*, I, pp. 87, 151, 305, 307–10, 328, 397, 404–6; Jewel, *Works, ed. cit.*, I, p. 305; III, p. 163. The Lucius story turns up throughout Elizabethan literature.

be traced running through the imagery of his plays[1] have left out of account the real imperial theme which no one living in Tudor England could escape. Was the imperial theme, for Shakespeare, not only national but also religious, in a Dantesque sense?

Shakespeare's treatment of the Astraea image – so utterly surprising and unconventional, so remote in its passion and wildness, not only from the stock-in-trade Astraea of a Lord Mayor's pageant, but also from the more subtle Neoplatonic Virgo of a court poet – leaves him with the eternal question-mark still against his name.

Astraea; the Imperial Moon; and the Virgin Mary

Astraea is a symbol which links easily with other symbols used of the queen. The suggestion made at the beginning of this study that Astraea as a name for the queen might prove an Ariadne's thread to guide us through Elizabethan symbolism as a whole has already been found to have some substance in it and might be carried still further.

Take, for example, the moon symbolism. The goddess of the moon under various names – Diana, Cynthia, Belphoebe – is the most popular of all the figures employed by Elizabeth's adorers, and in the minds of certain poets the Cynthian cult appears to take on some kind of esoteric philosophical significance.

Our studies have reminded us that the moon is the symbol of empire, and the sun of papacy. The virgin of imperial reform who withstood the claims of the Papacy might therefore well become a chaste moon-goddess shedding the beams of pure religion from her royal throne. Moreover, the imperial cult has constantly drawn to itself a philosophical justification: the ideal ruler is always the Philosopher King. The so-called Elizabethan 'School of Night', with its worship of Cynthia and its devotion to intellectual contemplation,[2] might have been drawing on the 'imperialist' tradition, not only in the political, but also in the religious, philosophical, and poetic sense.

To work this suggestion out fully would require a separate study; here there is not space to support it by quotation from more than one poem. In George Chapman's *Hymnus in Cynthiam*, which may be fairly said to be the quintessence of the Cynthian cult, Elizabeth-Cynthia is thus adjured:[3]

> Then set thy Christall, and Imperiall throne,
> (Girt in thy chast, and neuer-loosing zone)

---

[1] *Cf.* G. Wilson Knight, *The Imperial Theme*, Oxford, 1931.

[2] The existence of a 'School of Night', of which Raleigh, Chapman, and others were members and which was opposed by Shakespeare, the Earl of Southampton and others, is based, perhaps rather insecurely, on a phrase in *Love's Labour's Lost*. See my *A study of Love's Labour's Lost*, Cambridge, 1936, pp. 89 ff.; M. C. Bradbrook, *The School of Night*, Cambridge, 1936.

[3] George Chapman, *Poems*, ed. P. B. Bartlett, New York and London, 1941, p. 33.

> Gainst Europs Sunne directly opposit,
> And giue him darknesse, that doth threat thy light.

Here, under the image of an eclipse, the imperial moon is set up against the sun of Europe, in the kind of antithesis which we are accustomed to see visualized in the crown versus the tiara. And later in the same poem we find what appears to be a description of a moon device, beginning with these lines:[1]

> Forme then, twixt two superior pillers framd
> This tender building, Pax Imperij named . . .

One is reminded of the two columns of Charles V's imperial device, and they here frame a 'Pax Imperii' symbolized by the moon. To these quotations it would be possible to add others in support of a theory that the contemplative world of night and moonshine, in which some intellectual Elizabethan poets seem to find their spiritual home, might be a Ghibelline world, ruled by a moon of imperial reform.

Another virgin image frequently used of Elizabeth is that the 'Vestal Virgin'. The interesting 'Sieve' portraits of the queen,[2] which portray her as the Vestal Virgin Tuccia bearing her attribute, the sieve, are a reference to this image. The Roman and religious connotations of vestal virginity need little elaboration.[3] It is as a vestal virgin that Elizabeth swims into our ken in one of the very few certain allusions to her by Shakespeare, as 'a fair Vestal, throned by the West'.[4] The 'imperial' character of this vestal is emphasized, and it is perhaps no accident that she appears in *A Midsummer Night's Dream* – a play bathed from beginning to end in moonlight.

The symbols used of Elizabeth are not always virgin symbols. In her capacity as the just and peaceful ruler she brings wealth and plenty to her people, and can be hailed as Ceres, a mother-goddess:[5]

[1] *Ibid.*, p. 35. [2] See below, pp. 114–19. Plate 16b.

[3] John Florio in his *First Fruites* (London, 1578, dialogue 28), shortly after celebrating the virtues of Elizabeth, laments the pure golden age of imperial Rome in terms of Vestal virginity: 'O golden worlde . . . then was chastitie knowen in the Temple of Vesta. Then the Emperours dyd frequent the Chappel of Iupiter, then Lust durst not come to the Court of Cesar, then abstinence walked through the markette in euerye Cittye, then the worlde was chaste, then the world dyd triumph, but nowe euery thyng goeth contrary. Certis it is a lamentable thyng, to consider the state of this world.' Florio probably has in mind here Petrarch's *Trionfo della Castità* (in which Tuccia is mentioned).

In view of the Elizabethan interpretation of Petrarch as a Protestant ally in the fight with the Whore of Babylon the *Trionfo della Castità* might be a useful guide to Elizabeth symbolism (see below pp. 112–14 and Plates 15, 16). Another figure, besides the chaste Tuccia, who occurs in that poem is the chaste 'Judit ebrea', slayer of the tyrant Holofernes. Judith is a name often used of Elizabeth.

For the use of the Judith story in Protestant and Catholic controversy, see E. Purdie, *The Story of Judith in German and English Literature*, Paris, 1927.

[4] *A Midsummer Night's Dream*, II, 158; see below, pp. 117–18.

[5] *Oxonienses academiae Funebre Officium in memoriam honoratissimam serenissimae et beatissimae Elizabethae*, Oxford, 1603, sig. S 4 v.; cf. Wilson, p. 381.

Mater Eliza, meae, dum viverat alma, parentis,
Dives eram, placidae Pacis alumna, Ceres . . .

lamented a university poet at her death. But it will be remembered that
the just virgin of the golden age carries corn and is compared to Ceres.[1]
She is a virgin yet her influences are fruitful, and so also are Eliza's. This
applies not only in the material but also in the spiritual sphere, where we
find Jewel describing Elizabeth as the nursing mother of the church in
England.[2]

The notion of a fruitful virgin in relation to the virgin queen brings in
the most daring comparison of all. Many of the symbols of this virgin – for
example the Rose (the Tudor Rose, badge of union, of peace, of mystic
empire), the Star, the Moon, the Phoenix, the Ermine,[3] the Pearl[4] – were
also symbols of the Virgin Mary. There is a good deal of evidence that some
Elizabethans did not flinch from such a comparison. A song in John Dowland's *Second Book of Airs* gives this advice:[5]

> When others sing *Venite exultemus!*
> Stand by and turn to *Noli emulari!*
> For *Quare fremuerant* use *Oremus!*
> *Vivat Eliza!* for an *Ave Mari!*

'Long live Eliza!' instead of 'Hail Mary'! The startling suggestion makes
one begin to ask oneself whether the cult of the virgin queen, was, perhaps
half-unconsciously, intended to take the place of the cult of the Virgin,
one of the most abiding characteristics of the ancient faith. There is an
engraving of the queen, with her device of the Phoenix, below which is
written 'This Maiden-Queen Elizabeth came into this world, the Eve of the
Nativity of the blessed virgin Mary; and died on the Eve of the Annunciation
of the virgin Mary, 1602.' This statement is accompanied by the following
couplet:[6]

---

[1] See above, pp. 32, 34.

[2] Addressing Elizabeth, Jewel can call her 'now the only nurse and mother of the church of
God within these your majesty's most noble dominions,' expressing the hope that she may live
to be 'an old mother in Israel'(*Works*, III, p. 118).

This aspect of the queen, as the source of spiritual nourishment to her church, may account for
her appropriation of the sacred 'Pelican' symbol (for an example see Plate 6b).

[3] The ermine is a symbol of chastity and of the Virgin Mary. Its appearance in the portrait of
Elizabeth at Hatfield House (see below, p. 114, and Plate 16a), in close proximity to the sword of
state, makes of that picture a variation on the just virgin theme.

[4] The pearl as a symbol of Elizabeth, for which there is plenty of literary material, ought to be
fully worked out. It may have something to do with the marked predominance of pearl jewellery
in the portraits.

[5] *An English Garner*, IV, 1882, pp. 524–5; cf. Wilson, *op. cit.*, p. 206. (On this and the preceding
pages, Wilson discusses the analogies between the Elizabeth cult and the worship of the Virgin.)
This poem has been attributed to Sir Henry Lee, see E. K. Chambers, *Sir Henry Lee*, Oxford, pp.
142–3; and below, p. 103.

[6] O'Donoghue, *op. cit.*, p. 79.

> She was, She is (what can there more be said?)
> In earth the first, in heaven the second Maid.

This staggering remark seems to imply that the defunct Queen Elizabeth is now a second Blessed Virgin in heaven. What more can there be said indeed? Except to add that implications of this kind are not uncommon in Elizabethan literature. For other examples one need only turn to the chants of the university poets at her death:[1]

> Lux ea quae divae festum natale Mariae
> Iuncta praeit, fuit illa dies natalis Elizae . . .

Or:[2]

> Virgo Maria fuit, fuit illa: beata Maria,
> Inter foeminum Beta [i.e. Elisabeta] beata genus.

Here one of the names used of Elizabeth by her poets, namely 'Beta', is assimilated to 'Beata Maria'. In the memorial poems the death of Elizabeth becomes a kind of Assumption of the Virgin, followed by a Coronation of the Virgin in heaven.[3] She who was virgin queen and goddess on earth is invested with the glory of a Virgin Queen of Heaven:[4]

> Quae fuit in terris Dea, Virgo, Regia virgo
> Nunc est in coelis Regia, Virgo, Dea.

To emphasize the worship of 'diva Elizabetta', the imperial virgin, in place of that of the Queen of Heaven, to carry her gorgeously arrayed through street and countryside (Plate 11b) that she might show her divine Justice and Clemency to the people, was a way by which the virgin of the imperial reform might draw ancient allegiances to herself. The bejewelled and painted images of the Virgin Mary had been cast out of churches and monasteries, but another bejewelled and painted image was set up at court, and went in progress through the land for her worshippers to adore. The cult of the Virgin was regarded as one of the chief abuses of the unreformed church,[5] but it would be, perhaps, extravagant to suggest that, in a Christian country, the worship of the state Virgo was deliberately intended to take its place.

These strange tones and colourings in the Elizabeth symbolism can,

---

[1] *Oxoniensis academiae*, sig. T. i; cf. Wilson, *op. cit.*, p. 381.

[2] *Oxoniensis academiae*, sig. P. 2; cf. Wilson, *op. cit.*, p. 382.

[3] Such an allusion is perhaps present, as well as the Astraea reference, in Plate 9b. Representations of the Virgin Mary with a crown of stars are, of course, common.

[4] *Threno-thriambeuticon. Academiae Cantabrigiensis ob damnum lucrosum, & infaelicitatem faelicissimam, luctuosus triumphus*, Cambridge, 1603, sig. D. I; cf. Wilson, *op. cit.*, p. 383.

[5] Cf. Jewel's controversy with the Catholic Harding. Jewel reproaches the Catholics with worshipping the Virgin Mary as 'lady of angels', 'queen of heaven' and 'God's most faithful fellow'; this, says Jewel, is to make 'a creature equal in fellowship with God' (*Works*, III, p. 121).

perhaps, once again be best understood by reference to Astraea-Virgo. That many-sided figure also had affinities with moon-cults – with Astarte or Isis; she also, though not the Virgin Mary, was an echo of her.[1] Queen Elizabeth as a symbol draws to herself a mysterious tradition.

The Ambiguous Virgo

Like the Elizabethan settlement itself, the virgin of the imperial reform was an ambiguous symbol, capable of being read in different ways. Between the two poles of the extreme Protestant view, which sees her as the pure opponent of Antichrist, the Pope, and the extreme Catholic view which exactly reverses this position and will have no dealings with the Antichrist of Protestantism or with the blasphemous claims of the illegitimate daughter of Henry VIII, there is a middle way, the way of those who wait and hope for vague developments, perhaps the marriage of Elizabeth to a Catholic prince and a mass return of England to the fold, perhaps even a general reunion of all Christendom. The various types of approach can be very briefly illustrated from the following examples drawn mainly from England's relations with foreign powers.

The Protestant Dutch, seeking Elizabeth's support in their quarrel with Philip of Spain, saw her in the same light as Foxe and Jewel, as the royal virgin triumphing over the Pope. There is a well-known Dutch engraving (Plate 11a) which presents this basic theme in a singularly repulsive manner, and in a mythological setting which is of considerable interest, after our study of the imagery of the poets. It tells the story of Diana discovering the unchastity of the nymph Callisto, with Elizabeth in the rôle of Diana, wearing the crown and the Pope in the rôle of Callisto, wearing the tiara. It is, of course, suitable that the Whore of Babylon should appear as the lewd nymph, who is discovered to have laid a number of baneful eggs, such as Inquisition, etc. Elizabeth is not only Diana; she is also the naked Truth which Time has brought to light.[2] On her left, the provinces of Holland are rejoicing in her discomfiture of the Pope.

It is as the chaste moon of reformed religious truth that we see Elizabeth here, and it is somewhat startling to be confronted with this crude rendering of the blend of politico-theological satire with mythological imagery such as we have tried to suggest in the poets.

The diametrically opposed point of view to this one could find no open expression in Elizabethan England, though many books against the Anglican theologians, written by the English Catholic exiles, circulated, in spite of the

---

[1] See above, pp. 3–4.

[2] On the image of Truth the daughter of Time used as a symbol of the triumph of both Protestant and Catholic Truth in England see F. Saxl, 'Veritas Filia Temporis', in *Philosophy and History*, essays edited by R. Klibansky and H. J. Paton, Oxford, 1936, pp. 197–222.

danger. Such a book is Nicholas Sanders's *The Rocke of the Churche* which refutes the imperialist theory of the rights of emperors in councils, and finds the setting of the temporal prince above the lawful successor of St Peter to be the very mark and badge of Antichrist, who 'setteth the world aboue the Churche, and the earthly power aboue the heauenly.'[1] The Catholics certainly had excellent material to hand for their Antichrist argument, for one of the interpretations of the Beast of the Apocalypse is that it represents the world, or the Roman Empire, in opposition to the church. They might have said that the burning of poetic incense to the 'diva Elizabetta' was a restoration of the emperor cult in protest against which the early Christian martyrs had laid down their lives. For Sanders, another sure indication of the presence of Antichrist in England was the storm of destruction caused by the Reformation, for it is the mark of the beast to make an abomination of desolation in holy places. In the reign of Edward VI he had seen statues of Christ on the Cross, flanked by the Virgin Mary and St John, torn down and in their place set up the royal arms with its supporters the Greyhound and the Dragon.[2] Thus, he says, in place of Christ they set up a Lion (alluding to the lions and lilies on the royal coat-of arms); in place of the Virgin, a Dog; and in place of St John, a Dragon.[3] Thus, beasts took the place of the sacred figures of the Christian faith. He enquires sarcastically of Jewel why, if the images of Christ are to be destroyed, the images of rulers are to be respected, and urges him to 'breake . . . if you dare the image of the Queenes Maiestie, or the Armes of the realme'.[4] All this is but an indication of the distinctive form which heresy takes in England.[5]

> The worlde, toward the coming of Antichrist is grown so wise, that these men haue found now, that euery Emperor, King, Prince, or Duke (who hath any temporall state of his owne) is greater, euen in Ecclesiasticall causes, then the lawfull successour of S. Peter. This, I say, is the divinity of England. For therein, our countrie maketh a peculiar Secte of his owne, wherein they disagree, euen from their fellow Caluinists.

For Sanders the only cure for these blasphemies was the invasion of England by Philip of Spain, and the restoration of Catholic truth by force.

So the situation is exactly reversed, and the pure imperial virgin becomes the lewd worldly power, the *civitas diaboli*, the Antichrist, which wars against the *civitas Dei*. It gave a strange edge to the Elizabeth cult to know that this reverse side of the picture was circulating underground.

[1] Nicholas Sanders, *The Rocke of the Churche*, Louvain, 1567, p. 517.
[2] For the Dog and the Dragon supporting the royal arms, see Plate 5b.
[3] Nicholas Sanders, *De visibili Monarchia Ecclesiae*, Louvain, 1571, p. 824.
[4] Nicholas Sanders, *A Treatise of the Images of Christ and his saints . . .* , Louvain, 1567, p. 109. Quoted by Veech, *op. cit.*, p. 185.
[5] *Rocke of the Churche*, p. 500.

Elizabethan relations with France are more complex than with the two clear opposite poles of the Protestant Low Countries and Catholic Spain.

The French monarchy, by virtue of its leading position in Christendom and its connections with the Carolingian empire, had maintained a comparatively independent attitude towards the Papacy throughout the Middle Ages.[1] Medieval French kings were more successful in this respect than English kings, and the French monarchy was regarded with great respect by medieval imperialist writers as a bulwark of the imperial idea. In the sixteenth century, Gallican Catholicism maintains this tradition to some extent.

It would take us too far afield to attempt here to trace the uses of Astraea in France as a symbol of the imperial justice of the French crown, but there is no doubt that it was so used. Favyn, writing in 1620, when speaking of the origin of the *main de justice* carried before the kings of France – the wand with a hand at the end of it, a derivation from the Roman standard – says that the hand is made of white ivory to denote the 'innocence of the Virgin Astraea', and he also states that Astraea is the sign of the horoscope of France.[2] In this connection it is interesting to remember that Shakespeare uses Astraea in relation to Joan of Arc.

The centre royalist Catholic party in France had supported at the Council of Trent the policy of the Emperor Ferdinand[3] (the contemptuous treatment of whom is deplored by Jewel) – a policy in some ways a derivative of the Erasmian tradition. This policy failed at the Council, but Gallican Catholicism did not officially endorse the decrees of the Council of Trent and so it survived in some French royalist Catholic circles. Royalist Gallican Catholicism sometimes took a very liberal turn, veering very close to Anglicanism. This led to the development of three religious parties in France – the Protestant Huguenots, the Catholic League which supported Spain and the full

---

[1] Figgis brings out the resemblances and differences between Anglican and Gallican royalism. As against the temporal claims of the Pope, the Gallican doctrine is as uncompromising as the Anglican, and has a stronger historical tradition, for French kings had, on the whole, been much more successful than English kings in maintaining through the Middle Ages an independent attitude. Yet the French 'politique' Catholic admitted the spiritual claims to the Papacy 'and it is far from easy to do this, while denying *in toto* its pretensions to political supremacy. It was impossible for the supporters of the king to take the line of the Imperialists and boldly to claim that the Pope was amenable to the jurisdiction of their master.' (Figgis, *op. cit.*, pp. 110 ff.)

Figgis goes on to suggest that the Gallican opponents of papal claims were, owing to the ambiguity of their position, less clear than Englishmen or than medieval imperialists in their statement of the necessary unity of the sovereign power. I believe this to be true. In the 'imperial' mysticism surrounding the French king (see below, pp. 121–5). I have not found that emphasis on the One which exists in England.

[2] A. Favyn, *Théatre d'honour et de chevalerie*, Paris, 1620, pp. 275 ff.

It would be fascinating to collate and compare the treatment of the Astraea theme in France and England. Ronsard (see below pp. 210–11, author of *La Franciade*, the epic glorifying the Trojan descent of the Kings of France (below, pp. 130–3), was also author of sonnets to 'Astrée'.

[3] This has been touched upon in my article on Sarpi, cited above, and is treated at much greater length in my book *The French Academies of the Sixteenth Century*, Studies of the Warburg Institute, no. 15, London, 1947 ; Kraus Reprint, 1967.

claims of the Papacy, and the central or loyal royalist 'politique' party. The last was mainly Catholic, admitting the spiritual authority of the Pope, but developing a theory of sacred kingship which comes very close to the English theory of divine right.[1]

In the time of Henri III, this royalist Gallicanism, or 'politique' Catholicism, takes on considerable power as the spirit of Counter Reform enters France.[2] Influenced by Carlo Borromeo, Henri becomes the leader of a penitential movement of baroque intensity. With this is associated an 'imperialist' mysticism related to the sacred imperial destiny of the French crown. Medieval authors, including Joachim of Flora and Dante, are studied in his circle, and efforts are made to increase the spiritual ties between France and England by appeals to the 'ancient piety' of English, as well as of French, kings. A new religious order of chivalry, the Order of the Holy Spirit, is created; Favyn somewhat mysteriously suggests that it was originally intended to call this order the 'Order of the Phoenix' alluding to the position of the king of France, who is 'unique' amongst the princes of Christendom.[3]

Henri's idea seems to have been to put forward a purely mystical and contemplative conception of sacred empire, as opposed to the aggressively martial ambitions of Spain under Philip II, with which, or so it seemed to many, the Papacy had associated itself. It was as the missionary of this movement that Giordano Bruno came into England a few years before the Armada, offering French sympathy against Spain and a common ground between France and England in a religious conception of non-aggressive empire.

Bruno's attitude when in England shows how an imperialism such as this could be utterly different in temper from the Protestant imperialism such as we have studied in Jewel and Foxe. Bruno detests the reformed English church and its doctors and speaks with longing of the vanished English medieval past, of the learned philosophers and mystics who flourished of old in Oxford and Cambridge and whose place is now taken by ignorant and quarrelsome pedants; of the ancient 'Egyptian' rites, now replaced by others of less efficacy.[4] Nothing could be more remote from Bruno's nostalgia for

---

[1] Figgis, *op. cit.*, pp. 120 ff.

[2] I have attempted to study, in *The French Academies of the Sixteenth Century* (pp. 152 ff.), Henri III's royalist Gallican Counter Reformation and its relations with England. This movement, which was violently attacked by the papalist and pro-Spanish Catholic League, provided a version of the royalist–imperialist tradition which, on the religious side, was permeated by the new influences of Catholic Counter Reform (see below, pp. 173 ff.) and was totally different in temper from Protestant imperialism. I believe that it had a great influence in the later sixteenth century in England, and would have attracted English Royalists of a Catholic temperament.

[3] Favyn, *op. cit.*, p. 678; cf. *French Academies*, p. 157.

These 'Knights of the Holy Spirit' who might have taken the unique Arabian bird as their emblem, rather than the Dove of the Holy Spirit, recall Cola di Rienzo's atmosphere (see above, pp. 37–8).

[4] For quotations of Bruno's strictures on the English Reformation see my articles 'Giordano Bruno's conflict with Oxford', *Journal of the Warburg Institute*, II (1939), pp. 227 ff.; and 'The

the old forms of Catholic culture in England than the delight with which Bishop Jewel hails the casting of great lumps of rubbish out of the church by the reformed virgin queen.[1] Yet – and this is the curious point – Bruno can join enthusiastically in the worship of the queen.

Bruno, who was in England from 1584 to 1586, writes with as much fervour of Elizabeth as do her subjects. He praises her for having kept the peace in her realms when the rest of Europe was at war. He speaks of her as the 'unique Diana' and as 'diva Elizabetta'.[2] It is significant that this afterwards got him into trouble with the Inquisitors. When asked by them whether he had ever praised heretic princes he replied:[3]

I have praised many heretic princes, but not as heretics but solely for their moral virtues. And in particular I praised the Queen of England and called her 'diva' not as a religious attribute but as the epithet which the ancients used to give to princes. And in England where I then was it was customary to give the title of 'diva' to the Queen.

In one of his dialogues, the *Cena de le ceneri*, Bruno joins in the lament for the lost golden age, using the words of Seneca:[4]

The golden world our fathers have possessed,
Where banished fraud durst never come in place,
All were content to live at home in rest . . .

One would think that this might lead up to Astraea, and although Bruno does not mention that name he later in the book assigns to Elizabeth a dominant place in the heavens and an imperial destiny. The English queen is a 'peerless and most rare Lady who shines in this cold sky, so close to the arctic parallel, and thence gives light to the whole terrestrial globe'.[5] Bruno

religious policy of Giordano Bruno', *Journal of the Warburg Institute*, 1939–40, III, pp. 181 ff. In the latter article, I have suggested that Bruno's exposition of the Copernican theory hides a conciliatory religious offer from Henri III's movement. See also *French Academies*, pp. 225 ff.

[1] Jewel, *Works*, III, p. 117.

[2] *Opere italiane*, ed. G. Gentile, Bari, Laterza, 1925–7, pp. 172–3; II, pp. 316–17.

[3] *Documenti della vita di Giordano Bruno*, ed. V. Spampanato, 1933, p. 121. The passage is translated and quoted in full in 'The religious policy of Giordano Bruno', pp. 204–5. All these discussions of Bruno's mission in England were later taken up, expanded, and revised in my *Giordano Bruno and the Hermetic Tradition*, London, 1964. See further, below, pp. 167–9, 213.

Bruno had said in *De la causa, principio, e uno*, 1584, that all the virtues were feminine, for example, 'la prudenza, la giustizia, la fortezza, la temperanza, la bellezza, la maestà, la dignità, la divinità,' and this led up to the enquiry as to where could be found 'un maschio megliore o simile a questa Diva Elizabetta, che regna in Inghilterra' (*opere italiane*, I, pp. 172–3).

[4] *Opere italiane*, I, p. 25. The quotation is from Seneca, *Medea*, lines 375–77, and the translation is taken from *Seneca his Tenne Tragedies*, translated into English, ed. Thomas Newton, 1581 (Tudor Translations, I, 1927, p. 204).

On this page, Bruno is contrasting himself, as a discoverer of new worlds in the heavens, with the mariners of the age, who have discovered new worlds beyond the ocean.

[5] 'Non hai qui materia di parlar di quel nume de la terra, di quella singolare e rarissima Dama, che da questo freddo cielo, vicino a l'artico parallelo, a tutto il terrestre globo rende si chiaro lume . . .' (*Opere italiane*, I, p. 52).

prophesies for the celestial virgin a monarchy extending far into new worlds:[1]

> Of Elizabeth I speak, who by her title and royal diginity is inferior to no other monarch in the world; who for her wisdom and skill in sound government is second to none of those who hold the sceptre. I leave it to the world to judge what place she takes among all other princes for her knowledge of arts and sciences and for her fluency in all the tongues. . . . If her earthly territory were a true reflection of the width and grandeur of her spirit this great Amphitrite would bring far horizons within her girdle and enlarge the circumference of her dominion to include not only Britain and Ireland but some new world, as vast as

With this worship of the queen by an emissary of the French 'politique' party, may be compared Sir John Davies's eighth Hymn to Astraea (in *op cit.*, I, p. 136):

> To All the Princes of Europe
> E urope, the earth's sweet Paradise,
> L et all thy kings that would be wise,
> I n *politique deuotion*;
> S ayle hither to obserue her eyes,
> A nd marke her heauenly motion.
>
> B raue Princes of this ciuill age,
> E nter into this pilgrimage;
> T his saint's tongue is an oracle,
> H er eye hath made a Prince a page,
> A nd works each day a miracle.
>
> R aise but your lookes to her, and see
> E uen the true beames of maiestie,
> G reat Princes, marke her duly;
> I f all the world you doe suruey,
> N o forehead spreades so bright a ray,
> A nd notes a Prince so truly.

[1] *Opere italiane*, I, p. 523. With this passage may be compared a phrase of Dante's on the expansion of sacred empire: 'For although it has been constrained by violence to narrow the bounds of its government, yet by indefeasible right it everywhere stretches as far as the waves of Amphitrite, and scarce deigns to be circumscribed by the ineffectual waters of Ocean' (*Epistolae*, ed. Toynbee, pp. 92, 102).

It is now possible to identify an allusion to Elizabeth in Bruno's *Spaccio della bestia trionfante* (*Opere italiane*, II, pp. 181–2).

Bruno warns Virgo to stay near the Beasts, Leo and Scorpio, where she is at present, and not to associate with gods and heroes who might be less willing to support her than are the beasts.

This is clearly an allusion to political alliances. Some slight help towards deciphering it is provided by the dedication to Elizabeth of Sir R. Barckley's *A Discourse of the Felicite of Man*, London, 1598. Barckley recalls the account given by 'Figulus' (see above, p. 52) of Virgo, and continues, 'May not this allegoricall speech (most excellent Prince) of this learned man, be aptly and liuely applied to your Maiestie that are . . . a virgin truly representing Iustice . . . that haue on the one side one that arrogateth superioritie ouer all, representing Leo: on the other side another that by weighing his Indian gold representeth *Libra*'. Here Leo seems to mean the King of France, and Libra the King of Spain.

One may therefore probably infer that the Leo whose support Bruno offers to Virgo is the King of France. He appears to be trying to melt the Virgo out of her isolation and coldness. Cf. also the allusion to the French King as a lion whose 'liberal and courteous love' warms the colder regions of the heavens (*Opere italiane*, I, p. 14).

the universal frame, where her all-powerful hand should have full scope to raise a united monarchy.

It is a vision of 'united monarchy' for the 'diva Elizabetta'. Bruno constantly quotes from the *Orlando furioso* in this dialogue, and one cannot but think that he is giving Elizabeth part in an imperial destiny in the new world such as was prophesied by Ariosto for Charles V.

Bruno was full of hopes of some vast, vague, unifying, reforming movement. After the death of Henri III he put his faith in Henri IV. D'Aubigné reports the strange hopes that were entertained of Henri IV whose conversion, to the imperially minded, seemed to foreshadow that some universal solution of the religious problem might come from the sacred French monarchy. D'Aubigné says that it was rumoured that Henri IV would die Emperor of all the Christians, that he would convert the hierarchies to the empire, the keys into swords, and that there would be a reunion of religions, or a toleration of them all.[1]

The Astraea symbol was associated with Henri IV in one of the most influential books of the early seventeenth century. Honoré d'Urfé's long pastoral romance of *Astrée* is dedicated to that monarch, and in the dedication 'Astrée' is identified with the justice which his rule has brought back to Europe.[2] The illustrated edition has a picture of Astraea, the innocent shepherdess of the golden age, with the ears of corn in her hair (Plate 42b).

It may be suggested, therefore, that Elizabeth-Virgo was a flexible symbol. From the blatantly Protestant anti-Papal Virgin, she could become a more elusive goddess, not altogether remote from that Reformation-hating mystic, that curious combination of Gothic revival and incipient baroque – Giordano Bruno. By these double meanings she could attract both Protestants and 'politique' Catholics among her subjects into her orbit, the latter perhaps hoping for her marriage to a Catholic prince or for some development, analogous to the conversion of Henri IV, which never materialized. Religious royalism already has in her reign the two flavours of ultra-Protestantism or of sub-Catholicism which recur again and again in English history.[3]

The virginity of the queen was used as a powerful political weapon all

---

[1] Agrippa D'Aubigné, *Œuvres complètes*, ed. Réaume and Caussade, Paris, 1887, II, p. 326 (see below, pp. 222–3).

The notion of the imperial idea as promising a solution to the problem of religious disunity seems also to have been present in Charles V's device of the two columns, of which Ruscelli says that one of its meanings referred to the 'Christian monarchy, or to the union of all religions in one' (*Imprese illustri*, p. 116).

[2] Honoré d'Urfé, *L'Astrée*, ed. H. Vaganay, Lyons, 1925–8, I, p. 4.

D'Urfé offers *Astrée* 'a ce grand Roy, la valeur et la prudence duquel l'a rappelée du Ciel en terre pour le bonheur des hommes'.

[3] With Charles I, of course, the sub-Catholic trend strengthens, and it is interesting to remember that his wife, Henri IV's daughter, brought with her to the English court a French Neoplatonic cult which owed much to Honoré d'Urfé's *Astrée*. See G. F. Sensabaugh, 'Love ethics in platonic court drama 1625–42', *Huntington Library Quarterly*, 1937–8, pp. 277–304.

through her reign. Many foreign potentates hoped to win her hand. She coquetted with them, played them off against one another, and never married. Whatever the love shafts aimed at her, the imperial votaress passed on, in maiden meditation, fancy free. This ambiguity of the Virgo served the double purpose of keeping foreign powers at bay, and confusing the religious issue in the minds of her own subjects.

The complex and opposite mythological ingredients of Elizabeth Virgo as a symbol are thus a suitable reflection of the conflicts and antitheses which the Elizabethan settlement tried to evade. Her 'imperial peace' covered, not without deep internal strains, divided religious opinions.

Tudor imperialism is a blend of nascent nationalism and surviving medieval universalism. The symbol of the Virgin Queen – in whatever way understood, and all the more intensely because of the conflicts inherent in it – touched tremendous spiritual and historical issues. The destiny of all mankind is at stake in the idea for which the virgin of the golden age stands, and above both papacy and empire is Christ, praying in the words of St John's gospel, 'that they may all be one; even as thou, Father, art in me, and I in thee'. This is the sacred imperialism of the Prince of Peace, the Christian blend of Hebrew and Virgilian prophecy, uttered by the Messiah in the universal peace of the Roman Empire, that time of which Dante says that there will never be another like it for then 'the Ship of the Human Family by a sweet pathway was hastening to its rightful haven'.[1] In the Elizabethan imperial theme, universal concepts are never far below the surface in the interpretation of history. A great comic and tragic genius, surrounded by such a symbolism and such a view of history, would be inclined to dwell, in place of the facile optimism of official propaganda, upon the contrast between these highest hopes of mankind and their constant disappointment, upon the spectacle of the lust and bloodshed of the iron age perpetually dispelling the vision of justice and of peace. Shakespeare's narration of the crimes of monarchs or of the agony and death of lovers gains its poignancy from the imagery, which so often suggests universal possibilities forever betrayed.

[1] *Convito*, Fourth Treatise, chap. v.

ELIZABETHAN CHIVALRY: THE ROMANCE OF THE ACCESSION DAY TILTS

On the anniversary of the Accession Day of Queen Elizabeth I on 17 November 1558, it became the custom to hold an annual tilt at which the Queen's loyal knights jousted before her. Though material for the reconstruction of the Accession Day Tilts is scarce and scattered, there is reason to believe that this annually enacted romance of chivalry of which the Queen was the heroine exercised a very potent influence on the Elizabethan imagination. Unfortunately, we have no visual records of these brilliant scenes, such as the Valois tapestries in the Uffizi show us of ceremonial tilting in fancy dress at the French court, but the richly woven word-picture of the Iberian annual jousts in Sir Philip Sidney's *Arcadia* is a reflection of Accession Day Tilt pageantry.

Accession Day Tilts and Sidney's 'Arcadia'

The Iberian annual jousts, as described in the *Arcadia*,[1] were held every year on the anniversary of the marriage day of the Iberian queen. To them had come, on a certain year, knights from the court of Queen Helen of Corinth in order to tilt with the Iberian knights. This queen of Corinth was a young and fair woman; she carried herself among a people 'mutinously proud' so that they respected her authority. She kept her country at peace at a time when 'many countries were full of wars'. Yet she encouraged 'continual martial exercises without blood', for by this means she made her courtiers 'perfect in that bloody art'. These military exercises were at the same time brilliant spectacles full of learned allusions, for 'her sports were such as carried riches of knowledge upon the stream of delight'. Thus this queen, through her court pageantry, 'used so strange and yet well succeeding a temper, that she made her people by peace war-like; her courtiers by sports learned; her ladies by love chaste'.[2]

Coming from such a court, it is no wonder that the Corinthian knights won a prize for their tilting at the Iberian annual tournament. The accoutrements of the knights at this event were most strange and ingenious. The entry of one Iberian knight into the lists is described in some detail. He was

---

[1] Sir Philip Sidney, *The Countesse of Pembroke's Arcadia*, 1590 ed., Bk II, chap. 21 (ed. A. Feuillerat, Cambridge University Press, 1922, pp. 282 ff.). All quotations are from the 1590 edition, in modernized spelling. There was a revised edition of the work in 1593. The earliest version of the romance, known as the *Old Arcadia* and written about 1580, does not contain the accounts of the ceremonial jousts.

[2] *Arcadia*, ed. cit., p. 283.

announced by bagpipes instead of the usual trumpets, preceded by one attired as a shepherd's boy, and accompanied by a dozen others also dressed as shepherds and carrying lances which very prettily represented sheep-hooks. The appearance of the knight himself was in harmony with his rustic pageant, for his furniture was 'dressed over with wool' and 'enriched with jewels artificially placed'. His *impresa*, too, carried on the shepherd theme, for it was a sheep marked with pitch, with the motto *Spotted to be known*. Amongst the ladies watching the tilt was one who, they say, was the star by which the course of this knight was directed. The shepherds attending on Philisides— for this was the name of the Shepherd Knight—went in amongst the ladies and two of them sang an eclogue to the accompaniment of recorders played by the other shepherds.[1]

Philisides' opponent in the tilt was Lelius, a knight who 'was known to be second to none in the perfection of that art'.[2] The tilting costume of Lelius is not described, unless that of some of the other tilters applies to him. One entered like a wild man 'full of withered leaves which though they fell not still threatened falling'.[3] Another came in hidden, both man and horse, in a figure representing the Phoenix, which, apparently, was set on fire so that the knight appeared to rise 'as it were out of the ashes thereof'. Against this fiery Phoenix Knight there ran a 'Frozen Knight' whose armour naturally represented ice, and all his furniture corresponded to this idea.[4]

The episode of the Iberian annual jousts comes into the *Arcadia* with an accent of reality. Queen Helen of Corinth sounds so very like Queen Elizabeth. Philisides is certainly Philip Sidney himself; we know that by external evidence from Spenser and others,[5] as well as by the internal evidence afforded by the name Star or Stella of this knight's lady. And Lelius is undoubtedly Sir Henry Lee, that most accomplished man-at-arms, who appears to have been mainly responsible for starting and organizing the Accession Day Tilts.

The identification of the Lelius of the *Arcadia* as Sir Henry Lee was made by J. H. Hanford and S. R. Watson in an article published in 1934.[6] The main piece of evidence for this identification is that fact that Joshua Sylvester uses the name 'Laelius' for Lee.[7] Into his *Divine Weekes and Workes* (which is a free translation of *Les Semaines* of Du Bartas) Sylvester inserted many allusions to Queen Elizabeth and her mythology, and these allusions – in a poem whose theme is the divine creation of the world – have the effect of

[1] *Ibid., ed. cit.*, pp. 284–5.   [2] *Ibid.*   [3] *Ibid.*, p. 286.   [4] *Ibid.*

[5] The name 'Philisides' is used for Sidney by Spenser in the *Ruins of Time*; and also by Lodowick Bryskett in his poem in the volume of elegies on Spenser's death.

D. Coulman proves that the 'Spotted to be known' device belonged to Sidney and throws light on its meaning in her note 'Spotted to be Known', *Journal of the Warburg and Courtauld Institutes*, xx (1957), pp. 179–80.

[6] J. H. Hanford and Sara R. Watson, 'Personal allegory in the Arcadia: Philisides and Lelius', *Modern Philology*, XXXII (1934), pp. 1–10.

[7] *Ibid.*, p. 6; they also point out that Lee had an estate called Lelius.

investing the days of Elizabeth with a kind of cosmological significance. Du Bartas has just described the creation of the heavens; he is discussing Sol, the greatest of the planets, and has quoted the nineteenth Psalm on the Sun as a bridegroom coming out of his chamber and rejoicing as a strong man to run his race. At this solemn moment in creation's story, Sylvester inserts into his translation a description of Sir Henry Lee, under the name of Laelius, tilting before Queen Elizabeth at one of the Accession Day Tilts:[1]

> (As Hardy Laelius, that great Garter-Knight,
> Tilting in Triumph of Eliza's Right
> Yearly that Day that her dear reign began
> Most bravely mounted on proud Rabican,
> All in gilt armour, on his glistring Mazor
> A stately plume of Orange mixt with Azur,
> In gallant Course, before ten thousand eyes,
> From all Defendants bore the Princely Prize)
> Thou glorious Champion, in thy Heavenly Race,
> Runnest so swift we scarce conceive thy pace.

Thus the Sun running his course through the heavens becomes a champion who recalls the splendour of the Accession Day Tilts of Eliza's reign and the impressive appearance of Hardy Laelius, alias Henry Lee, on these occasions.

The other piece of evidence for the identification of Lee as the Laelius of the *Arcadia* is that we know from a document that Sidney tilted against Lee at the Accession Day Tilt of 1581. A manuscript in the Bodleian gives the names of the tilters on that occasion, and in the list Sidney's name is opposite to that of Lee.[2]

The Philisides and Laelius of the Iberian annual joust are thus Philip Sidney and Henry Lee at an Accession Day Tilt. The portrait of Lee by Antonio Moro (Plate 12a) shows a man undoubtedly handsome in a somewhat bold and flashy style; we can well imagine this confident personage as a striking and dramatic figure at the Tilts. We can further help our imagination by looking at one of the designs for armour (Plate 12c) in the *Almain Armourers Album*.[3] This splendid suit in white and gold, and decorated with suns and phoenixes, was made for Sir Henry Lee. Perhaps this is the actual

---

[1] J. Sylvester, *Divine Weekes and Workes*, London, 1605, p. 135. E. K. Chambers also notes that the passage refers to Lee, but does not make the connection with the 'Lelius' of the *Arcadia*; see E. K. Chambers, *Sir Henry Lee*, Oxford, 1936, p. 141.

Rabican is the name of a horse in Ariosto's *Orlando furioso*, XXII, 227 (noted by Chambers, *loc. cit.*). Sir John Harington in his notes to canto XLI of his translation of the *Orlando furioso* mentions the Accession Day Tilts.

[2] Ashmole, 845, fols 164–5; quoted by Hanford and Watson, pp. 9–10.

[3] The original of this volume of designs for armour by German armourers settled in England is in the Victoria and Albert Museum; it was published in facsimile by H. A. Dillon, *An Almain Armourer's Album*, London, 1905. Parts of this suit made for Lee are in existence; see Chambers, *op. cit.*, pp. 131–2.

suit of 'gilt armour' in which Lee so much impressed Sylvester by his sun-like appearance.

The portrait of Philisides here reproduced (Plate 12b) shows him as a partially armed knight. Though probably a late copy, it is a good example of the 'knight' type of portrait of Sidney, and is of particular interest here because it came, like the portrait of Lee, from Ditchley, the home of Sir Henry Lee.[1]

There is an eye-witness account of the Accession Day Tilt of 1584 which suggests that the shepherd get-up of Philisides, as described in the *Arcadia*, and the pageant of shepherds which accompanies him, may reflect the kind of thing which was actually done at these tilts. Describing the tilt of 17 November 1584, Von Wedel says that the tilters entered the tilt-yard, which adjoined the palace at Whitehall, in pairs; trumpets or other musical instruments were blown as they entered. (The entrance of Philisides in the *Arcadia* is heralded by bagpipes.) The combatants had their servants clad in different colours; these servants did not enter the barriers but arranged themselves on both sides. Some of the servants were disguised like savages, or like Irishmen, with hair hanging down to the girdle like women; others had horse-manes on their heads. Some came driving in a carriage, the horses being equipped like elephants. When a gentleman with his servants approached the barrier, he stopped at the foot of the staircase leading to the Queen's room, while one of his servants, in pompous attire, mounted the steps and addressed the Queen in well-composed verses, or with a ludicrous speech, making her and her ladies laugh.[2]

This account confuses what was probably the fact, namely that the 'pageant' of servants with which the tilters were accompanied was in harmony with the character which the knight assumed in the tilt, and with the *impresa* which he had adopted. (The *imprese* were painted on paste-board shields which were given up before the tilt began.)[3] Thus the servants as savages or wild men whom Von Wedel saw probably accompanied a knight who was tilting as a wild man, like the one in the Iberian tournament who came in 'like a wild man . . . full of withered leaves'. The appearance of Philisides, as described in the *Arcadia*, as a Shepherd Knight with a sheep *impresa* and with his pageant of shepherd attendants – some of whom went in among the ladies and sang them an eclogue – is probably not more strange than the spectacles to be seen at actual Accession Day Tilts, when Elizabeth's courtiers dramatized themselves as knights of romance, and appeared in

[1] See R. Strong, *Tudor and Jacobean Portraits*, London, 1969, I, p. 291; II, Plate 369. It was presented to the National Portrait Gallery from the Ditchley collection in 1925, when the portrait of Lee was also presented.

[2] For full quotation of Von Wedel's account of the 1584 Tilt, see E. K. Chambers, *Elizabethan Stage*, Oxford, 1932, p. 143, note 3.

[3] A gallery at Whitehall was hung with *impresa* shields which had been used at Accession Day Tilts; see Chambers, *loc. cit.*

costume pageants expressive of the character they had assumed and of their romantic relation to the Queen and to the ladies of the court.

The character of the Shepherd Knight suited Sidney very well. If the *Arcadia* description refers to his appearance at the 1581 tilt, this would be two years after the publication of Spenser's *Shepherd's Calendar*, with its dedication to Sidney and its use of the shepherd formula for conveying a Protestant theological moral. As will appear later, it would seem to have been a part of Sir Henry Lee's plan for the Accession Day Tilts that their imagery should build up, in terms of chivalrous romance, the political and theological position of Protestant England. There may well, therefore, have been quite a serious purpose behind Sidney's appearance as the Shepherd Knight. For at the court of Elizabeth, as at that of Queen Helen of Corinth, the 'sports were such as carried the riches of knowledge upon the stream of delight'.

The 1581 Accession Day Tilt is the first of which there is a definite documentary record, though they almost certainly started earlier. If Sidney made a rather sensational appearance at it as a Shepherd Knight, this may have been a factor in the making of the Sidney legend – a legend which is woven into the legend of the Accession Day Tilts. Perhaps Spenser commemorated it in Sir Calidore, who doffed his bright arms, addressed himself in shepherd's weed,[1]

> and in his hand he took
> In stead of steel-head spear, a shepherd's hook.

As others have pointed out, the Iberian annual joust in the *Arcadia* may not represent any one Accession Day Tilt but may introduce elements from other occasions.[2] It has been suggested that there may also be an allusion to the entertainment called *The Four Foster Children of Desire* given in May 1581, on the occasion of the visit of the French commissioners about the French match for Elizabeth.[3] This entertainment was in the form of a tournament in which Sidney took part as one of the challengers, and one of the defendants appeared as a Frozen Knight (it will be remembered that there is a Frozen Knight in the Iberian joust). Sir Henry Lee was involved in *The Four Foster Children of Desire* as an 'unknown knight who came in in the midst of the running'.[4] This, therefore, was also an occasion on which both Sidney and Lee were present and may be reflected, mingled with the Accession Day Tilt allusion, in the Arcadian affair.

The Iberian tournament takes place in Book II of the *Arcadia*; the wars of Amphialus in Book III, though in part real and bloody wars, are also in

[1] *Faerie Queene*, VI, 9. xxxvi.   [2] Hanford and Watson, *op. cit.*, pp. 7–9.

[3] *Ibid.*, p. 7; and see also E. Welsford, *The Court Masque*, Cambridge, 1927. *The Four Foster Children of Desire* is printed in John Nichols, *The Progresses of Queen Elizabeth*, London, 1823, II, pp. 310–29.

[4] Nichols, *op. cit.*, II, p. 319.

part ceremonial jousts at which knights appear in highly elaborate and un-practical attire. The fight between Amphialus and Phalantus of Corinth, in particular, is very like a tilt, for it is watched by ladies. The furniture of Amphialus was[1]

> made into the fashion of the branches of a tree, from which the leaves were falling: and so artificially were the leaves made, that as the horse moved, it seemed indeed that the leaves wagged, as when the wind plays with them; and being made of pale cloth of gold, they did bear the straw-coloured livery of ruin.

His armour was tawny and gold, and the *impresa* painted on his shield was the torpedo fish.

He must have been a remarkable sight, but nothing in comparison to his opponent Phalantus of Corinth, who was on a white horse whose mane and tail were dyed carnation.[2]

> His reins were of vine branches, which engendering one with the other, at the end, when it came to the bit, there, for the boss, brought forth a cluster of grapes, by the workman made so lively, that it seemed, as the horse champed on his bit, he chopped for them, and that it did make his mouth water, to see the grapes so near him. His furniture behind was of vines, so artificially made, as it seemed the horse stood in the shadow of the vine. . . . His armour was blue like the heaven, which a Sun did with his rays . . . gild in most places.

One wonders whether Phalantus of Corith in his sun armour might again be a reflection of Sir Henry Lee, for Peele's description of Lee at the Accession Day Tilt of 1590 – the last in which he took an active part – is as follows:[3]

> Mighty in arms, mounted on puissant horse,
> Knight of the crown in rich embroidery,
> And costly fair caparison charged with crowns,
> O'ershadowed with a wither'd running vine,
> As who should say, 'My spring of youth is past,'
> In corselet gilt of curious workmanship,
> Sir Henry Lee, redoubted man-at-arms,
> Leads in the troops . . .

Did Lee recognize himself as the vine-encircled Phalantus of Corinth of the *Arcadia* and present himself at his last tilt as the vine now withered with age? That tilt was full of memories of Sidney, for Essex (as described by Peele) wore black armour at it, and was accompanied by an all-black pageant,[4]

---

[1] *Arcadia, ed. cit.,* p. 415.   [2] *Ibid.*

[3] George Peele, *Works,* ed. A. H. Bullen, London, 1888, II, p. 288. The quotation is from Peele's *Polyhymnia.*

[4] Peele, *Works, ed. cit.,* II, p. 292.

As if he mourn'd to think of him he miss'd,
Sweet Sidney, fairest shepherd of our green.

Thus Philisides, the Shepherd Knight, was remembered at the Accession Day Tilt at which Lelius retired from active service.

Sir Henry Lee and the Woodstock Entertainment, 1575

The elaborate descriptions of ceremonial chivalry are not in the original version of the *Arcadia* and do not appear until the 1590 and subsequent versions. It was during the decade of the fifteen-eighties that the Accession Day Tilts, of which the moving spirit was Sir Henry Lee, seem to have reached a high point of development. Chambers has given us a useful book on the life of Lee, but we need to study also Lee's imagination, Lee as the expert on humanist chivalry, Lee as one of the builders of the Elizabethan mythology.

The source for the statement that the Accession Day Tilts were Lee's idea is Segar in his *Honor Military and Ciuill*, published in 1602;[1] Segar also states that these Tilts began with the reign. As we have seen, the first recorded one was in 1581. They almost certainly began earlier than that, perhaps, as Chambers suggests, not at Whitehall but at Woodstock, of which Lee was Ranger, or elsewhere near Oxford.[2] Until 1590, when Lee officially resigned the championship of the Crown to the Earl of Cumberland, he was chief challenger at the tilts; and even after his resignation he continued to preside over them as a kind of Master of the Ceremonies. It is Segar who gives this information; but, unfortunately, the only one of these annual events which he describes in any detail is the resignation tilt of 1590, and the elaborate mythology in which Lee clothed his retirement.

The mythology of the 1590 tilt connects with that of the two great entertainments which Lee gave to the Queen, the one at Woodstock in 1575; the other at Ditchley in 1592, after he had retired from active service in the tilt. The Ditchley Entertainment refers to and recalls the imagery of the Woodstock Entertainment, given so many years before, and it also recalls the imagery of the resignation tilt of 1590. In it Lee, as it were, looks back down the arches of the years which he had decorated with his pageantry, and reminds the Queen of his part in the building of her legend, of the chivalrous romance which he had woven around her at Woodstock and at the Accession Day Tilts. The imagery which he used at Woodstock is, therefore, a most important clue to the imagery of the Accession Day Tilts as a whole.

[1] '... these annual exercises in Arms, solemnized the 17. day of November, were first begun and occasioned by the right vertuous and honourable Sir Henry Lee ... who ... in the beginning of her happy reigne, voluntarily vowed ... during her life, to present himselfe at the Tilt armed, the day aforesayd yeerly ...': W. Segar, *Honor Military and Ciuill*, London, 1602, p. 197.

[2] Chambers, *Lee*, pp. 38, 84, 133–4. In the absence of any evidence to the contrary there seems no reason to disbelieve Segar's statement that they began with the reign.

In 1575, the Queen went on that summer Progress which included the famous visit to Kenilworth where she was entertained by the Earl of Leicester. Sidney was present at it in Leicester's suite. No expense was spared for the Kenilworth Entertainment with its Ladies of the Lake, sibyls, and other mixed romantic and classical paraphernalia. Yet one has the impression that it fell rather flat. Its classicism was slightly university-wittish and provincial; its romanticism slightly ridiculous, as indicated by the song of Deepe Desire concealed with a consort of music in a hollybush as the royal party left:[1]

> If death or dole could daunt a deepe desire,
> If privie pangs could counterpoise my plaint . . .
> Then farewell sweet, for whom I taste such sower:
> Farewell delight for whom I dwell in dole . . .

This was rather old-fashioned stuff.

A few weeks later the Queen and the court arrived at Woodstock, there to be entertained by Sir Henry Lee.[2]

The first sight which greeted the Queen at Woodstock was a combat between two knights called Contarenus and Loricus. This fact has been obscured by the defect in the only surviving copy of the printed account of the Woodstock Entertainment in which the opening of the Tale of Hemetes the Hermit, in which these two knights were characters, is missing. The text begins with the Hermit Hemetes intervening to stop their fight. The Hermit 'speaketh to two knights that fought there' and says 'No more most valyant knights.'[3] Now Loricus – like Lelius – was one of Sir Henry Lee's pseudonyms. He calls himself Loricus at the Ditchley Entertainment of 1592.

Here, then, at Woodstock in 1575, the entertainment opens with the spectacle which was to be so famous – the spectacle of Sir Henry Lee fighting under the eyes of his Queen in a mock combat of chivalrous display. The combat forms part of a romance, the Tale of Hemetes the Hermit. When the knights had stopped fighting, the Hermit, addressing himself to the Queen, began his Tale:[4]

Not long since in the country of Cambaya, which is situate near the mouth of the rich river Indus, a mighty duke bare dominion, called Occanon, who had heir to his estate but one only daughter named

[1] Nichols, *op. cit.*, I, pp. 522–3.

[2] For the programme of the 1575 tour, see Chambers, *Elizabethan Stage*, IV, pp. 91–2. The court arrived at Woodstock on 11 September.

The Woodstock Entertainment was published in 1585; only one copy of the print survives; it has been edited by A. W. Pollard, *The Queen's Majesty's Entertainment at Woodstock, 1575*, Oxford, 1910. The first part of the Entertainment, the 'Tale of Hemetes', is printed from Gascoigne's copy in Nichols, *op. cit.*, I, pp. 553–82.

[3] Nichols, *op. cit.*, p. 557; *Entertainment, ed. cit.*, p. xv (in this version it is said that the knights had to dismount, which shows that they had been tilting).

[4] Nichols, *op. cit.*, I, p. 558; *Entertainment, ed. cit.*, p. xvi (spelling modernized in quotation).

Gaudina.[1] This lady then, more fair than fortunate, lived most dear to her father, and most beloved of his people. But to prove that beauty is not ever a benefit, nor high estates be always the happiest, it happened within a little while, Gaudina sought by many that were great, and served by many that were worthy, had more competitors of her beauty than did either well content her or prove commodious unto her; for Love, which is not led by order, nor chooseth by appointment, limed her affection unmoveably with the liking of a Knight (of estate but mean but of value very great) called Contarenus, who exceedingly loved her. . . . In small process of time (the secret fires of their fancies discovered) the smoke of their desires betrayed this matter to her father long before they would.

This quotation must suffice to give an impression of the style of the Hermit's Tale, which goes on to relate the measures which Duke Occanon took to prevent his daughter's marriage to Contarenus; how Gaudina went in search of her lover and came to the grotto of the Sibyl where she met Loricus; how Loricus loved a lady of very high degree but coloured his passion by pretending to love one of her attendant ladies; how the Sibyl advised Gaudina and Loricus to keep together and foretold that when they came to the best country in the world and the one which had the most just ruler all would be well. The Hermit then rambles on to tell his own tale and adventures. The gist of it all was that he too had once been a famous knight, loved of ladies, but was now old and wrinkled and 'cast into a corner' and had settled down in a hermitage on a hill hard by.[2] The *dénouement* is that the Sibyl's prophecy is now verified; all the personages in the Tale are now in the best country in the world and in the presence of the best ruler; the hardy knights Contarenus and Loricus have here fought (this proves that the missing opening was the fight between these two knights); the constant lovers Contarenus and Gaudina have here met; and Hemetes the Hermit, who had been blind, has here received his sight.[3]

The Tale of Hemetes may seem to us somewhat prosy, but it was received as a striking novelty and made a great impression. It was rumoured to contain important secret meanings. The Queen desired to have a copy of it, and of the whole entertainment. George Gascoigne – eagerly following up a possible line into royal favour – presented the Queen the next Christmas with a copy of the Tale as given in English at the Entertainment, to which he pedantically added Latin, Italian, and French translations of it.[4] This shows that it was admired as an example of style. Gascoigne, however, says definitely that he was not the author of the Tale. Who then was its author?

There exists a manuscript volume, formerly at Ditchley and now in the

[1] Variant 'Gandina'.   [2] Nicholls, *op. cit.*, I, pp. 560, 562; *Entertainment, ed. cit.*, p. xix.
[3] Nichols, *op. cit.*, I, p. 562; *Entertainment, ed. cit.*, p. xxi.
[4] See C. T. Prouty, *George Gascoigne*, Columbia University Press, 1942, pp. 221 ff.

British Museum, which is a collection of Lee's devices for tilts and other entertainments.[1] This volume contains a manuscript copy of the Tale of Hemetes[2] (the manuscript also lacks the opening pages of the Tale). The presence of the Tale in the Ditchley Manuscript, apparently as one of Lee's devices, would seem to suggest very strongly that Lee was its author. If so, he takes a not unimportant place in Elizabethan literary history, for in its mixture of Greek and chivalrous romance,[3] its ramblingly attractive prose style, the Tale of Hemetes foreshadows the *Arcadia* (even the first version of which was not yet written in 1575).

Woodstock was a wonderful experience and it was not yet ended. When the Tale was over, the Hermit conducted the Queen and her suite to a banqueting house specially erected on a hillock in the wood for the occasion and formed of turves and boughs of greenery bedecked with ivy, flowers, and 'spanges of gold plate' which glimmered astonishingly.[4] It was under a great oak, the branches of which were hung with emblems and posies. These excited much interest and were carefully examined by the French ambassador.[5] Here they dined at tables, one of which was round and the other in the shape of a half-moon, both covered with green turves. Sitting there, raised well up above the level of the ground and amongst the glittering hangings, the Queen and her ladies must have seemed like celestial creatures (through intentional stage-management). Presently, in the midst of the merry cheer of the banquet, was heard a divine sound of unacquainted instruments coming from below the banqueting house, and at this auspicious moment the Fairy Queen made what Chambers believes to be her first appearance in Elizabethan literature.[6] It was perhaps not her first appearance at Woodstock for she says in the verse speech which she now makes that she has very recently seen the Queen appeasing a cruel fight near this place.[7] This may mean that the Fairy Queen had been present at the fight between Contarenus and Loricus with which the entertainment began. The Fairy Queen's verses are not very good, but she will learn to do better in later years. For we are here probably close to the living springs in living pageantry whence both Sidney's *Arcadia* and Spenser's *Faerie Queene* drew their emotional nourishment.

On the homeward way through the forest more music was heard 'closely in an oak' whence issued a sound both of voice and instrument 'the excellentest now living'. The Song in the Oak echoed the song of Deepe Desire

[1] Additional MS., 41499 A (modern transcript, Additional 41499B). Chambers gives an abstract of its contents in his *Lee*, pp. 268–75.

[2] Fols 4–5 *verso*; cf. Chambers, *Lee*, pp. 84, 270.

[3] The element of Greek romance in the 'Tale of Hemetes' has been noted by Prouty, *op. cit.*, p. 228, note 127; he points to Underdowne's translation of Heliodorus (1569) as the possible influence. The introduction of the strong chivalrous element into the Greek romance foundation is the notable characteristic of the second version (1590) of the *Arcadia*.

[4] *Entertainment, ed. cit.*, p. xxii. [5] *Ibid.*, p. xxiii. [6] *Lee*, p. 88.

[7] *Entertainment, ed. cit.*, p. xxiv.

in the hollybush at Kenilwoth, but the difference in quality between this song and that is such that it seems that between Kenilworth and Woodstock a new age has been born:[1]

> I am most sure that I shall not attain,
> the only good wherein the joy doth lie.
> I have no power my passions to refrain,
> but wail the want which nought else may supply.
> > Whereby my life the shape of death must bear
> > that death, which feels the worst that life doth fear.
>
> But what avails with tragical complaint,
> not hoping help, the furies to awake?
> Or why should I the happy minds acquaint
> With doleful tunes, their settled peace to shake?
> > O ye that here behold infortune's fare,
> > there is no grief that may with mine compare.

The Song in the Oak is attributed in a manuscript anthology of verse to Edward Dyer, and this may be correct, for a document proves that Dyer was at Woodstock at about this time.[2]

On the second day of the entertainment there was a play which carried the story of Contarenus and Gaudina to a rather unexpected conclusion.[3] With the sympathy, but also the strong approval, of the Fairy Queen, Gaudina gave up Contarenus for reasons of state. It is a stiff little play in poor verse (perhaps by Gascoigne) but it seems to have profoundly moved the audience, 'in such sort,' says the narrator, 'that her Grace's passions, and other the ladies could not but show itself in open place more than ever hath been seen'.[4]

Sidney was probably at Woodstock, and Mary Sidney his sister for whom the *Arcadia* was written was certainly there, a little girl of twelve who had just become a lady of the court; she was handed a posy from the oak above the banqueting hall in the wood.[5]

The Woodstock Imagery in Speeches for Accession Day Tilts

There exist a number of speeches, obviously composed for delivery at Accession Day Tilts, the themes of which relate to the romance of Woodstock. Some of these speeches are to be found in the third volume of Nichols's *Progresses of Queen Elizabeth*, his source being the texts printed by William Hamper from a manuscript in his possession which is now lost.[6] Others are

---

[1] *Ibid.*, pp. xxvii–xxviii.   [2] Cf. Chambers, *Lee*, pp. 90–1.
[3] *Entertainment, ed cit.*, pp. xxix ff.   [4] *Ibid.*, p. xxviii.   [5] *Ibid.*, p. xxvi.
[6] Nichols, *op. cit.*, III, pp. 193–213; cf. Chambers, *Lee*, p. 268.

in the Ditchley Manuscript (already referred to as containing a copy of the Tale of Hemetes) which was formerly at Lee's home, Ditchley, and was presented to the British Museum by his descendant, Lord Dillon, together with a modern transcript of it. The Ditchley Manuscript begins with items which are also to be found in Nichols, but goes on to give more material; it has never been published in full, though Chambers gives an abstract of its contents in his book on Lee.[1] One can be sure that the speeches which we are about to examine were composed for Accession Day Tilts, for they expressly refer to assemblies of knights of the Queen's Accession Day. Unfortunately it is not at present possible to decide to which years they belong, as they are undated. Their style is very like that of the Hermit's Tale of Woodstock.

One of these compositions (found both in Nichols and in the Ditchley Manuscript) is a 'Message of the Damsel of the Queen of the Fairies' delivered on behalf of an 'Enchanted Knight' to Queen Elizabeth.[2] It states that in celebration of the day of Her Majesty's entrance into the government many knights are gathered 'not far from hence' to show their prowess in her honour. The Enchanted Knight, being temporarily incapacitated in some way not specified, sends the Damsel with apologies and a present. We learn from this speech that the Fairy Queen myth was an accepted part of Accession Day Tilt romance.

In another of these speeches (found only in the Ditchley Manuscript)[3] we meet again the Hermit of Woodstock. A hermit has come from his cell to make a petition to Her Majesty on behalf of a homely, rude company, no better than shepherds, and their leader, a knight who is 'clownishly clad'. We have to picture a scene in which a hermit introduces to the Queen a knight, apparently in some kind of rustic fancy-dress, and accompanied by a band of rustics or shepherds. The hermit himself was, so he says, formerly also a knight but is now old and 'cast into a corner'. To comfort him, the hermit reads him a little lecture on Mutability:[4]

> I discoursed with him of the stability of the world and the mutability
> of things. I told him how Seneca said that Eternity stood by change and
> contrariety. I showed him how the earth has her summer and winter;
> the water her ebbs and flows; the air his heat and cold.

He advises the knight to leave the court and live in the country; this in fact the knight has already done, and a crowd of country people have attached themselves to him. He and they spend much time in prayer for the Queen

[1] *Ibid.*, pp. 268-75.

[2] Nichols, *op. cit.*, III, pp. 198-9; Ditchley Manuscript (B.M. Additional 41499 A), fols 1 verso-2. It would be very important to date the Tilt to which this speech refers.

[3] Ditchley Manuscript, fols 2-3 *verso*; cf. Chambers, *Lee*, p. 270. In the modern transcript of the Ditchley Manuscript (B.M. Additional 41499 B) this speech is on fols 9-19. I have modernized the spelling in the following quotations.

[4] Ditchley Manuscript, original, fol. 3 *verso*; transcript, fol. 17.

by whose holy government they enjoy the gospel of grace. I continue from here in the hermit's own words:[1]

> Now most gracious Queen, as they were of late making melody with this homely melody they have brought with them, one that came from the Church told them, how the Curate had showed his parishioners of a holiday which passed all the Pope's holidays, and that should be on the seventeenth day of November. The Knight remembering then the vow he had made, which was whilst he could set on a horse, and carry a staff in his hand, to sacrifice yearly the strength of his arm in honour of her that was mistress of his heart, told these his neighbours he must go from them for a while. Nay by St Mary quoth they then we will go with you, and take such part as you do, so we shall see for the expense of a few pence, the godliest lady (God bless her) that ever man set eye on; so we shall see jousting (they say) and we will joust too, as well as we can, if you will have us. Nay my good neighbours quoth the Knight, this noble exercise appertains not to men of your birth and bringing up, neither can any joust at the feast but he that is a gentleman, except he have license. Why master, quoth one of them, though we know not of pedigrees perhaps we come of as gentle blood as some of them, and rather than fail, you shall speak for us.

The hermit next explains that the knight has commissioned him to petition the Queen on behalf of the country people, the petition being first that they may see her, and second that 'they might have leave tomorrow, amongst your noble gentlemen, to run if they cannot the Tilt, yet at least the Quintain.'[2]

What are we to make of this peculiar speech? In the first place, it is certain that it relates to an Accession Day Tilt on the seventeenth of November to which the knight is going (he goes annually) and to which the country people want to go 'tomorrow'.

Second, this speech seems to be very much in the atmosphere of the Woodstock Entertainment. It is a long tale by a hermit who is 'cast into a corner', the very words used by the hermit of Woodstock. The knight clownishly clad[3] is a knight with leanings towards the retired life, in the nostalgic vein of Woodstock rusticity. In the Ditchley Manuscript, this speech is immediately followed by the 'Tale of Hemetes', and immediately preceded by the 'Message of the Damsel of the Queen of the Fairies'. Both the 'Fairy' speech and the 'Hermit and Clownish Knight' speech are almost certainly by Lee and and are composed for Accession Day Tilts. It is clear

[1] *Ibid.*, original, fol. 3 *verso*; transcript, fol. 17.

[2] *Ibid.*, original, *loc. cit.*, transcript, fol. 19.

[3] The knight sounds like Lee himself, but at one time is addressed by intitials (original, fol. 3 *recto*, transcript, fol. 16) which the transcript, with a question mark, reads as 'CH'; Chambers (*Lee*, p. 270) accepts this doubtful reading. I think myself that the 'H' is an 'L'.

that the imagery of Woodstock was very closely bound up with that of the Tilts.

Most curious of all, we seem to have learned from the hermit's remarks that an Accession Day Tilt may have been given out as a forthcoming event in the parish church by the curate, who had possibly even preached a sermon on it, showing his parishioners that this was a holiday which surpassed all the Pope's holidays. This is an extremely interesting indication that this annual institution of Protestant chivalry was deliberately offered as a substitute for the old Popish saints' days and holidays.[1] For the expense of a few pence (we know from Von Wedel that the charge of admission to Accession Day Tilts was twelve pence)[2] the rude country people may now instead behold the worship of Elizabeth by her knights. Further, we note from this speech how Protestant chivalry in its religious aspect lends itself to pastoral allegory. The prayer for the queen and her gospel of grace passes immediately to rustic merry-making with a homely melody. With the knight 'clownishly clad' and his rustic retinue we are in the world of the pastoral theology, the homely Protestantism of the *Shepherd's Calendar*, of the pastoral eclogues in the *Arcadia*, of Philisides with his shepherd pageant at the Tilt.

This speech is undoubtedly of importance to students of Spenser's *Faerie Queene*. It will be remembered that Spenser himself derives the genesis of his poem from the Fairy Queen's 'annual feast' at which a 'clownish young man' presented a petition to the Queen.[3] With its philosophy of mutability, its clownishly clad knight going to the Queen's annual feast, its Protestant moral, this speech seems to be using the same kind of vocabulary as Spenser. This man Lee, as year by year he produced the Elizabeth show, must have helped to fashion through pageantry the imagination of the age.

There is other material about the Tilts in the Ditchley Manuscript which must be passed over more briefly. A poem dated 17 November 1584 must belong to the Tilt of that year, as may also a long address to the Queen which immediately follows it.[4] It is spoken on behalf of some 'wandering knights' who at last year's Tilt were represented by a Black Knight and now come again in their own persons. One of them has a conference with an old hermit by whose oracles he is directed (again the hermit motif). Another speech which immediately follows in the manuscript may also belong to an Accession

---

[1] For evidence that Protestant festivals were deliberately organized, see the note by S. Anglo on 'An early Tudor programme for plays and other demonstrations against the Pope', *Journal of the Warburg and Courtauld Institutes*, XX (1957), pp. 176–9.

[2] Quoted Chambers, *Elizabethan Stage*, I, p. 143, note 3.

[3] *Faerie Queene*, dedication to Raleigh.

I. L. Schulze ('Elizabethan chivalry and the Faerie Queene's annual feast', *Modern Language Notes*, 50 (1935), pp. 158–61) argues a connection between the *Faerie Queene* and the Accession Day Tilts. The speech quoted above seems to me to prove such a connection beyond dispute. It would however be premature to attempt to formulate what the connection was or how it worked; this must await further research on the Tilts.

[4] Fols 6–7; cf. Chambers, *Lee*, pp. 271–2.

Day.[1] It speaks throughout of a Temple of Peace in which some knights who have been quarrelling will be reconciled. This may refer to some real erection put up in the tiltyard and expressive of the leading allegory of the occasion; we know that something of the kind was done at the Tilt of 1590, to which we shall come shortly.

But we must first pause respectfully for a moment over an entry in the Ditchley Manuscript which Chambers prints in full, but without comment.[2] It is headed 'A remembrance of Sir Philip Sidney Knight the 17th November 1586'. The date shows that it must relate to a commemoration of Sidney at the Accession Day Tilt of 1586, the year of his death. It consists of three short sets of Latin verses which are headed respectively, in English, 'the first', 'the second,' and 'upon the mourning horse'. Since the first verse alludes to three friends, one of whom is dead, it is possible that the first and second sets were spoken by Dyer and Greville, the surviving two of the three-cornered friendship. The third set was evidently placed in some way on the 'mourning horse'. We can only wonder how Lee stage-managed this no doubt deeply moving celebration. Was a horse led in to pause in the usual way before the Queen – but a riderless mourning horse, because the Shepherd Knight was dead?

The Retirement Tilt of 1590

Tilting is a pretty tough exercise, and not suitable for middle-aged knights. At the age of forty-seven, Lee thought that it was time for him to retire, and at the Tilt of 1590 he dramatized himself as an aged knight in an elaborately produced spectacle, which is thus described by Segar.[3]

Lee had chosen the Earl of Cumberland as his successor as chief challenger on behalf of the Crown, and on 17 November 1590 these two presented themselves to the Queen at the foot of the stairs under her gallery window; this was the window from which the Queen and her ladies were accustomed to watch the tilting in the tiltyard.

> Her Majesty beholding these armed knights coming toward her did
> suddenly hear a music so sweet and secret as every one thereat greatly
> marvelled. And hearkening to that excellent melody, the earth as it
> were opening, there appeared a pavilion, made of white taffeta . . .
> being in proportion like unto the sacred Temple of the Virgins Vestal.
> This Temple seemed to consist upon pillars of Pourferry, arched like
> unto a Church, within it were many lamps burning.

Before the Temple stood a crowned pillar on which were Latin verses extol-

[1] Fols 7–7 verso; cf. Chambers, ibid., p. 272.   [2] Fol. 7 verso; Chambers, ibid.
[3] Honor Military and Ciuill, pp. 197 ff. Peele's Polyhymnia also describes this Tilt (Works, ed. Bullen, II, pp. 288–301).

ling the crowned Vestal Virgin and her Empire, which was spreading out beyond the Columns of Hercules into the New World. For, of course, by 1590, the Armada year had come and gone. This added a new note of ecstasy to Lee's queen-worship, and the Vestal Virgin set-up of this year's Tilt is a paean of victory.[1]

In this splendid setting, the aged knight sentimentally retired from the Tilt, with the song 'My golden locks time hath to silver turned' sung by Mr Hales, a gentleman in that art excellent:[2]

> My helmet now shall make a hive for bees,
> And lover's songs shall turn to holy psalms:
> A man at arms must now sit on his knees,
> And feed on prayers that are old age's alms.
> And so from court to cottage I depart,
> My Saint is sure of mine unspotted heart.

Those who had been at Woodstock would catch the allusion. The splendid Loricus of those days has now himself become the ancient hermit.

When Lord Dillon presented the Ditchley Manuscript to the British Museum, he gave at the same time another manuscript also evidently from among Lee's papers.[3] This is a copy of the verses from Sidney's *Old Arcadia* in the form and in the order in which they are given in the original version of the romance. This volume of extracts is rather loosely bound into a parchment cover on which is the inscription 'Sir Henry Lee delivered being champion to the Queen delivered to my Lord Cumberland by William Simons.' Chambers supposes that this means that the cover once contained matter relating to the 1590 Tilt at which Lee resigned to Cumberland, and that the *Arcadia* extracts were afterwards slipped into this cover.[4]

Yet it is not impossible that the *Arcadia* contents of the volume do belong to its cover, and that Lee intended to hand to Cumberland at his resignation Tilt these copies of Sidney's verses as representing, as it were, the true Bible or inspiration of the Tilt, the scriptures of the perfect knight of Protestant chivalry. We know that books were sometimes given at the Tilts. Philip Gawdy says in his diary that at the Accession Day Tilt of 1587, books were given to the spectators.[5] Chambers supposes that Peele's *Polyhymnia* was

---

[1] The 'Sieve' portrait of Elizabeth at Siena shows her as a Vestal Virgin standing beside a column on which is an imperial crown (the note goes on to suggest a connection between this picture and the Retirement Tilt of 1590, on which see now pp. 124 ff., below).

In my Hatfield House Booklet (reprinted below in Appendix 1, pp. 215-19) I have suggested that the 'Rainbow' portrait of Elizabeth at Hatfield House may refer to some allegorical show in her honour at an Accession Day Tilt.

[2] Segar, *op. cit.*, pp. 198-9. There are various copies of this poem extant; one set to music in Dowland's *First Book of Airs*. A variant version (set in Dowland's *Second Book of Airs*) contains the lines which compare the cult of Elizabeth with that of the Virgin Mary, see above, p. 78.

[3] Now British Museum, Additional MS., 41498.

[4] *Lee*, p. 268.   [5] Philip Gawdy, *Letters*, ed. I. M. Jeayes, London, 1906, p. 25.

distributed at the 1590 Tilt.[1] There is therefore nothing inherently impossible in the idea that Lee might have intended to present extracts from the *Arcadia* to Cumberland at a Tilt. On the other hand, this actual copy was evidently not given to Cumberland, for if it had been it would not have stayed at Ditchley. More research is needed to solve the problem of this mysterious manuscript, if it can be solved. It is a tantalizing document, presenting as it does a copy of a vitally important body of Elizabethan poetry in a cover relating to the Tilts.

We have a splendid portrait of the man to whom Lee resigned his position at the Tilts in Nicholas Hilliard's presentation of George Clifford, Third Earl of Cumberland, in a magnificent suit of star-decorated armour, and holding a tilting-lance in his right hand (Plate 12d). He wears the Queen's glove in his hat, and, almost certainly, stands here as Lee's successor as challenger for the Crown at the Accession Day Tilts. On the tree hangs a shield on which is painted a celestial device. We have here one of those paste-board *impresa* shields used at the Tilts. The pattern of celestial spheres on the lining of the Earl's sleeves is almost exactly the same as that on Lee's sleeves in Moro's portrait (Plate 12a). Cumberland is carrying on the Lee tradition. We know from Segar that, at the request of the Queen, Lee continued after his resignation to preside over the Tilts as Master of the Ceremonies,[2] and this probably preserved the continuity of his imagery in them.

The Ditchley Entertainment, 1592

We do not propose to pursue the track of the Accession Day Tilts after 1592, but to round off the story of Loricus, the Hermit, and the Fairy Queen, we must look at the entertainment which Lee gave to the Queen when she visited him at his home, Ditchley, in 1592.[3] Lee deliberately designed the Ditchley Entertainment to remind the Queen of Woodstock, and of all that had happened since.

There were first of all some despairing enchanted knights and ladies singing sad songs in a grove of trees. Then the Queen is led to a hall hung with allegorical pictures where an old knight lies sleeping. As she looks at the pictures and divines their meaning, the knight awakes and utters an 'old Knight's Tale' which is full of reminiscences of Woodstock.[4]

> Not far from hence nor very long ago
> The Fairy Queen the fairest Queen saluted.

---

[1] *Elizabethan Stage*, I, p. 145.

[2] *Honor Military and Ciuill*, pp. 199–200.

[3] The Ditchley Entertainment is printed in full by Chambers in his *Lee*, pp. 276–97. Parts of it are in Nichols, *op. cit.*, III, pp. 199–210. Its author was possibly Richard Edes, writing under Lee's direction (Chambers, *op. cit.*, pp. 145, 268).

[4] *Ibid.*, p. 282.

Woodstock is not far from Ditchley. It was perhaps tactful to say that it was 'not very long ago' that the Fairy Queen had saluted the Queen there. It was seventeen years ago, and the Queen who had then been a young thing of forty-one was now fifty-nine. The sports and plays then enacted, continues the Old Knight, are famous; amongst them were jousts and feats of arms; and a banquet in a bower full of enchanted pictures which many curiously examined and tried to construe. These enchanted tables of the Fairy Queen have been transported hither, and the Old Knight has been enjoined to keep them.[1]

Does this mean that the emblems and posies which had hung on the tree at Woodstock had been preserved by Lee at Ditchley and were now shown to the Queen again as the Old Knight revives these nostalgic memories of that wonderful day? Or is the Old Knight merely claiming that, in general, he has been the true keeper of the Fairy Queen tradition begun at Woodstock? The curiously vague and riddling style in which the Ditchley Entertainment is written makes precise interpretations of this and other points difficult. But of the allusion to Woodstock there can be no doubt.

Even clearer were such allusions on the second day at Ditchley, when a chaplain addressed a long speech to the Queen describing how an old knight called Loricus has now become a hermit.[2] He once had his adventures told 'by a good father of his own coat not far from this coppice',[3] alluding to how the hermit Hemetes had told the story of Loricus at Woodstock. Loricus, continues the chaplain, has since then led an active life, consorting with courageous gentlemen in open Jousts 'the yearly tribute of his dearest love'.[4] Now he has retired his tired limbs into a 'corner of quiet repose in this country'. In short, Loricus has now become, like the Hemetes of the Woodstock Tale, a hermit 'cast into a corner'. Here he lives in heavenly meditation adoring the Crown in the Crown Oratory.

The chaplain's speech shows clearly enough that the Woodstock story of Loricus, the Hermit, and the Queen, is at Ditchley repeated with the retired Loricus now in the rôle of the Hermit; whilst the jousts of the intervening years were 'yearly tributes' of Loricus's love. In other words, the Accession Day Tilts were annual instalments in the story of chivalrous romance begun at Woodstock in 1575, or possibly earlier, and now retrospectively summed up at the Queen's visit to Ditchley.[5] A meandering story, told in episodes, this enormously publicized romance lived out in scenes of pageantry built round Elizabeth by her admiring knight-hermit, must have been familiar

---

[1] *Ibid.*, p. 283. [2] *Ibid.*, pp. 290 ff. [3] *Ibid.*, p. 290. [4] *Ibid.*, p. 291.

[5] It may not have ended there. An 'Old Knight', obviously Lee, is the speaker in an Accession Day Tilt speech which must be later than 1590, and perhaps belongs to the Tilt of 1593. This speech is in both Nichols and the Ditchley Manuscript; cf. Chambers, *Lee*, p. 269. The 'romance' may have begun at Tilts held in years before 1575 (the date of the Woodstock Entertainment); and may have continued after 1592 (the date of the Ditchley Entertainment). This uncertainty makes the undated Accession Day Tilt speeches very difficult to place.

to every courtier, knight, and poet in the little world of Elizabethan England.

The well-known portrait of Elizabeth standing on the map of England (Plate 13), with her feet on the county of Oxfordshire near Woodstock, is usually connected with the Queen's visit to Ditchley in 1592. Like so much of the material with which we have here been concerned, this picture was originally at Ditchley. The Queen stands fairy-like and majestic; light streams from her, defeating the dark clouds in the sky; riddling and only partially decipherable verses on the picture seem to refer to her as a 'prince of light'.[1] One cannot but feel that the retired Loricus-Lee might have designed this picture to commemorate, not only the Queen's visit to his home, but also the great day at Woodstock, the story of which, annually continued in the intervening years, he so touchingly wound up at Ditchley.[2]

The Hermit in an Elizabethan Textbook of Chivalry

The hermit as the adviser of knights is a familiar figure in romances of chivalry, but one can point more directly to what was probably the main source for the hermit idea which had such a strong hold on the imagination of Sir Henry Lee. A hermit as an authority on the rules of chivalry holds a prominent place in a work the importance of which as a source-book for Elizabethan chivalry has not been sufficiently recognized. This is the *Book of the Ordre of Chyvalry* by the medieval Catalan philosopher, Ramon Lull, which was translated into English by William Caxton and was one of the first books which he printed (between 1483 and 1485). Caxton's interest in chivalry is shown by his choice of books for printing, one of which was Malory's *Morte d'Arthur*.

The *Book of the Ordre of Chyvalry* opens with a description of how a wise knight, who had long maintained the order of chivalry in jousts and tournaments, had retired into a hermitage in a wood:[3]

> For nature failed in him by age . . . and he . . . made his habitation or dwelling place in a great wood abundant of waters and great trees . . .
> And fled the world by cause that the feebleness of body in the which he was by old age fallen.

One day, a young squire arrived at the old knight's hermitage. The two talked with one another, and it transpired that the squire knew little about

---

[1] Spenser's lines on Elizabeth at the beginning of the *Faerie Queene* (I, introduction, iv) express the same idea as this picture:

> Great lady of the greatest isle, whose light,
> Like Phoebus lamp throughout the world doth shine

[2] The imagination of Lee may be behind several of the more complex of the portraits of the Queen; see below, p. 117.

[3] *Book of the Ordre of Chyvalry*, translated and printed by W. Caxton, ed. A. T. B. Byles, Early English Text Society, London, 1926, p. 4.

the rules of chivalry. 'Friend,' said the old hermit-knight, 'the rule and order of chivalry is written in this little book which I hold here in my hands.'[1] Whereupon the squire asked to be instructed from the book, and so is introduced the textbook of knightly theory and practice.

At the end of his English translation of this work, Caxton added an urgent appeal for the revival of chivalry in England, rather on the lines of the similar appeal in his preface to Malory. The knights of England, he says, have been famed throughout the universal world, both in the old Roman times and in the times of King Arthur, but they are now fallen from their former glory.[2]

> Oh ye knights of England where is the custom and usage of noble chivalry that was used in those days. . . . Some not well advised use not honest and good rule against all order of knighthood . . . leave this, leave it, and read the noble volumes of St. Graal, of Lancelot, of Galahad, of Tristram, of Perseforest, of Percival, of Gawain, and many more . . .

Caxton advises, as the best means of reviving chivalry, that public jousts or tourneys should be held regularly, at least annually, and if possible more often. This will cause gentlemen to resort to the ancient customs of chivalry, and also to be ready to serve their prince when he should call them or have need.[3]

Sir Henry Lee had made it his business to revive English chivalry by an annual Tilt, as Caxton advised in his translation of Lull's textbook in which a hermit is the repository of knightly wisdom. Thus the story of a Hermit in relation to Knights suited Lee perfectly; in his active life he was the knight advised by a wise hermit; in his retired life, he himself became the wise hermit.

In its opening words, Lull's *Book of the Ordre of Chyvalry* puts chivalry into a cosmological context. God rules over the seven planets, says Lull, and the seven planets dominate all terrestrial things. Hence, by analogy, the Prince, like God, rules over the knights, the planets, upon whom in turn depend the terrestrial bodies or lower orders.[4] Lull's decided formulation of this analogy (not of course original to him) at the beginning of the textbook on chivalry most easily accessible to the Elizabethans, may have been influential on the imagery of the Tilts. The majority of the *imprese* listed by Camden[5] (which are probably mostly Accession Day Tilt *imprese*) are based on the celestial bodies. Around the Fairy Queen revolved the knights as planets, themselves again infinitely remote from the terrestrial lower orders. This which one might describe as, quite literally, the quintessence of snobbery, makes it

---

[1] *Ibid.*, p. 11.   [2] *Ibid.*, pp. 122–3.   [3] *Ibid.*, p. 124.   [4] *Ibid.*, pp. 1–2.

[5] Among them are Lee's device of Ariadne's Crown with the motto *caelumque solumque beavit* (W. Camden, *Remains*, London, 1674 ed., p. 470). This device may be connected with the Crowned Pillar of the Retirement Tilt (cf. Chambers, *Lee*, p. 141). For a suggested comparison with Spenser's use of Ariadne's Crown, see above, p. 74.

possible to transpose the magnificent spectacle of Sir Henry Lee thundering down the tilt in his sun-armour into the spectacle of Sol issuing as a bridegroom to run his race around the zodiac. Elizabethan chivalry transposed its imagination with great facility into the heavens and the world of the stars.

The ethic in which Lull's hermit instructs his knights is the Aristotelian ethic of the mean. 'Virtue and measure abide in the middle between two extremes,' and knights must be virtuous by 'right measure'.[1] Lull carefully works out his definitions of the virtues which a knight must have as means between opposite extremes. The point is of some importance because it shows that the Aristotelian ethic and the ethic of chivalry, which are sometimes treated as separate strands of influence in Spenser's *Faerie Queene*, are one and the same thing in Lull's textbook, which Caxton had naturalized in English and made the programme for the revival of English chivalry.

Lullism as a philosophy had an immense vogue in the Renaissance. Giordano Bruno, who claims to have known Sidney, was influenced by it; and so was John Dee, Sidney's instructor in philosophy. There would therefore be nothing archaistic in Lee's adoption of Lull's hermit as one of the bases of the legend he constructed around the Accession Day Tilts. On the contrary, this would link contemporary chivalry with contemporary philosophy; and we have seen that Lee's hermit was a bit of a philosopher, with his talk of mutability, the seasons, and the elements.

Some General Reflections on Elizabethan Chivalry

The passion for the trappings of chivalry in court spectacle and pageantry was by no means peculiar to England in the sixteenth century. Something like an imaginative re-feudalization of culture was going on all over Europe, witness the *Orlando furioso*. One can call it an 'imaginative' re-feudalization, since, though feudalism as a working social or military structure was extinct, its forms were still the vehicle of living emotions. In France and England, this phenomenon had something to do with the rise of the national monarchies which used the apparatus of chivalry and its religious traditions to focus fervent religious loyalty on the national monarch.

In Elizabethan England, the ceremonial of chivalry was one of the few important traditional forms of pageantry surviving from pre-Reformation times. A saint who outlived the Reformation was St George, as patron of the Order of the Garter, and he did not do so without a struggle. Under Edward VI, the Garter Statutes were re-written and the name of St George obliterated throughout; his appearance on the badge was described as that of an 'armed knight'.[2] Mary Tudor, as one would expect, immediately put

[1] *Book of the Ordre of Chyvalry*, pp. 56–7.
[2] N. H. Nicolas, *History of the orders of Knighthood of the British Empire*, London, 1831, pp. 178ff.

St George back into the Statutes; but it is a less obviously to be expected fact, and one on which one may ponder, that Elizabeth left him there.[1] She can be seen in the portrait at Windsor (Plate 14a) significantly pointing to the Garter badge of St George and the Dragon which hangs on its blue ribbon round her neck; this was, after all, to wear the image of a saint in a Protestant country. Her position as head of the Order, which, with its Arthurian associations, had been made a vehicle for the glorification of the national monarchy established by the Tudors, was a very important aspect of her legend. Garter festivals and processions were a prominent feature of the public life of her times (Plate 14b). 'Hardy Laelius', as Sylvester reminds us, was a 'great Garter-Knight.' His Accession Day Tilts were not a specifically Garter occasion, but open to any member of the order of knighthood; yet in their glorification of the Queen as a romantic heroine they are a kind of fanciful extension of the Garter cult of her.[2]

The cessation of the observance of saints' days and other festivals of the church, with their religious pageantry and their occasions for merry-making, must have been felt as a great lack. We have had evidence from one of the Accession Day Tilts speeches that these annual occasions were presented as a substitute for, or an improvement on, 'the Pope's holidays'. The annual pageant of Protestant chivalry, in honour of the holy day of the Queen's accession, skilfully used the traditions of chivalrous display to build up the Queen's legend as the Virgin of the Reformed Religion (witness Lee's 'imperial Vestal Virgin' set-up at the Resignation Tilt) and to present the spectacle of the worship of her by her knights in the ritual of chivalry as a new kind of regularly-recurring semi-religious festival.

Yet, at the same time, the pageantry of chivalry could also cover the blurred religious outlines of the 'Elizabethan Settlement'. Since the romance tradition was independent of the religious changes, this would allow those not whole-heartedly in favour of the latter to join in chivalrous occasions. How far the ceremonial of chivalry could bridge religious gaps is shown by the fact that in 1585 English Knights of the Garter combined in the streets of Paris with Knights of the Order of the Holy Spirit; and the Catholic and Protestant Orders were able to attend Vespers (but not Mass) together in the Church of the Grands Augustins. The occasion was the investiture of Henri III with the Order of the Garter.[3]

The peculiar flavour, the peculiar passion and intensity of Elizabethan chivalry, may be due not only to its being a vehicle for patriotic devotion to the popular national monarchy and zeal for the Protestant cause, but also to

---

[1] Nicolas, *op. cit.*, p. 186. An interesting defence of the retention of St George in a Protestant country is to be found in Gerard de Malynes, *Saint George for England allegorically described*, London, 1601; see also Peter Heylyn, *The Historie . . . of St George*, London, 1631.

[2] When Shakespeare's fancy plays around the Garter badge he uses 'fairy' imagery; see *The Merry Wives of Windsor*, V, v, 70–80.

[3] See below, pp. 194–6.

the continuity of its ceremonial and mystique with pre-Reformation times. It thus provided an outlet for modes of thought and feeling for which there was little place in the new order. The hermit imagery of Sir Henry Lee may owe something to this. Monasteries and their pursuit of the contemplative life had been swept away; the hermit of chivalry leading his retired life of contemplation under the greenwood tree was something of an imaginative substitute.

Yet the chivalrous cult was far from being only a nostalgic survival; it belonged to present Italianate fashions as well as to past traditions. The Italian cult of the *impresa* was said to derive from the impression made by the brilliant spectacle of French chivalry, with its badges, during the French invasions of the peninsula. The feudal traditions of courtly love underlie the modern Platonism of the *Cortegiano*; and it is fascinating to study how the Italian, Giordano Bruno, places the Platonic *furores* into the context of Elizabethan chivalry and its fictions.

In the fifth dialogue of Bruno's *Eroici furori*, written during his visit to England and published with a dedication to Sir Philip Sidney in 1585, the heroic enthusiasts come in bearing shields on which are *imprese* with mottoes,[1] for all the world like knights at an Accession Day Tilt. If one wishes to study the abstruse philosophical meanings which could be drawn out of such *impresa* shields one cannot do better than read what Bruno has to say on, for example, a shield bearing a Flying Phoenix with the motto *Fata obstant*;[2] or on one which showed an oak, with the words *Ut robori robur*;[3] or, still more profound, on the one on which there was nothing but a sun and two circles with the one word, *Circuit*.[4] At the beginning of this work, there is an address to the ladies of England and to the one great Diana who is among them as a sun amidst the stars;[5] so that it is hardly an exaggeration to say that the shield-bearing philosophic enthusiasts are to be fancied as displaying the travail of their souls before Queen Elizabeth and the ladies of her court – as it were tilting for the prize of illumination by the highest divine light. And at the end of the *Eroici furori*, nine blind men receive their sight and become nine *illuminati* when they arrive under the temperate sky of the British Isles and come into the presence of the lovely nymphs of Father Thames, one of whom – the greatest among them – opens an urn and divine splendour is revealed.[6] One is reminded of the Hermit of Woodstock who received his sight when he came into the best country in the world and into the presence of the best ruler. The *Queen's Majesty's Entertainment at Woodstock* was published in 1585, the same year as the *Eroici furori*. Bruno, who elsewhere shows himself in sympathy with the Elizabeth cult,[7] may have been intentionally linking his philosophical dialogues with the chivalrous romance woven around the Virgin Queen.

[1] G. Bruno, *Opere italiane*, ed. G. Gentile, Bari, Laterza, 1927, II, pp. 394 ff.   [2] *Ibid.*, p. 404.   [3] *Ibid.*, p. 411.   [4] *Ibid.*, p. 406.   [5] *Ibid.*, p. 330.   [6] *Ibid.*, pp. 510, 514.   [7] See above, pp. 84–6.

The purpose of this essay is to draw attention to the importance of a neglected subject. It is intended to be impressionistic, rather than conclusive, and it has used only some fragments of the documentary evidence even now known and available. More may be unearthed by future research. It is hoped that enough has been said to suggest that the Accession Day Tilts speak in the language of pageantry a story which belongs to the heart of the age. Strung out as they were all through the reign, with the Earl of Essex becoming the most prominent figure in them in the later years, they reflected the pressures of the time. For the chivalrous formula suited the aristocratic structure of Elizabethan society; and it was the vehicle for the expression of its hopes and fears, whether personal, patriotic, or religious.

THE TRIUMPH OF CHASTITY

There is a side of the Elizabeth cult which, although it has been alluded to in the foregoing essays, has not been quite fully brought out in them. Some pages are therefore inserted here to fill this gap, using both the published Hatfield House Booklet (which is reprinted in an appendix to this book)[1] and material in unpublished lectures and seminars.[2]

Petrarch's famous poem, *I Trionfi*, is in the form of a series of Roman triumphs, allegorized as a moral sequence. First comes the Triumph of Love: Cupid rides triumphant on a chariot beside which walk examples of famous lovers. This is followed by the Triumph of Chastity, with famous examples of this virtue shown walking in the triumph. There follow the Triumphs of Fame, of Death, and finally of Eternity. It is a mark of the influence of the imperial idea on Petrarch that he sets out these thoughts in the form of triumphs. In the earlier Middle Ages, the virtues and vices and their 'examples' would be set out in churches or within the vast perspectives of Heaven and Hell, as in Dante's *Divine Comedy*. Though intensely Christian, Petrarch's imagination is profoundly attracted by the imperial panoply of the triumph, and he uses it as the setting of his moral teaching on successive triumphs of love and chastity.

This remarkable poem was extremely well known, and its influence was spread through its popularity as a subject for the visual arts.[3] The triumphs were displayed in countless paintings and tapestries and frequently also they were enacted in court and public pageantry. A fixed scheme was early arrived at for the representation of the poem which does not entirely correspond to the text. Petrarch describes the first triumph as Cupid entering on a chariot drawn by horses; but he varies this in the other episodes. It became, however, a convention for artists to represent all the divisions of the poem according to the same plan as Petrarch had laid down for the first one; that is to say, they presented the triumphs as a series of triumphal chariots, drawn by various animals, with the 'examples' of the various themes walking beside the chariots.

Petrarch dedicates his Triumph of Chastity to Laura, the heroine of his sonnet sequences. In a typical representation of the Triumph of Chastity (Plate 15) we see Laura riding in a chariot drawn by unicorns, creatures symbolic of virginity. The Love over which she has triumphed is represented as a naked winged figure, carried below her in her chariot, who is being

[1] See below, pp. 215–19 ff.   [2] See Preface, above, p. xiii.
[3] See V. M. Essling and E. Muntz, *Pétrarque: ses études d'art, son influence sur les artistes*, Paris, 1902; A. Venturi, 'Les "Triomphes" dans l'art représentatif', *Revue de l'art ancien et moderne*, XX (1906), pp. 81 ff.

bound and rendered powerless. A leader in the triumphal train carries a banner showing an ermine, symbol of chastity.[1] Beside the chariot walk ladies famed as 'examples' of chastity. One such 'example', mentioned by Petrarch, was Tuccia, a Vestal Virgin[2] who was supposed to have proved her chastity by carrying water in a sieve, unspilt. In the visual Triumph of Chastity here reproduced, Tuccia can be seen walking in the triumph carrying her emblem of the sieve.

We have seen that Protestant propagandists, collecting criticisms of the Papacy, enrolled both Dante and Petrarch on their side as having, at some time or another, ventured to call the Pope the Whore of Babylon.[3] I am not here concerned to unravel Petrarch's real opinions on these problems, only to register the fact that his name was brought into the Protestant propaganda. Thus Puritan associations were tinging the Elizabethan image of Petrarch, and his poem, *I Trionfi*, already fashionable in England,[4] became more fashionable still.

Petrarchizing poetry was associated with contemporary religious issues in the publication by Jan van der Noot, a refugee from the Duke of Alva's persecutions in the Netherlands, of a collection of French Petrarchist verses. The volume, entitled *Het Theatre*, was first published in 1568 by John Daye, the Puritan printer of Foxe's *Acts and Monuments*. The English translation of the little book, now called *A Theatre for Worldlings*, was published in 1569 with a dedication to Queen Elizabeth which contains an early formulation of the Astraea theme in relation to the Queen: 'The Kingdom of Saturn and the Golden world is come again, and the Virgin *Astraea* is descended from heaven to build her seat in this your most happy country of England.'[5] There is an anti-papal tone to the collection, yet a theme of charity and reconciliation also runs through it. Van der Noot was later to become a member of the sect called the 'Family of Love'[6] which sought to avoid doctrinal differences in a mystical interpretation of the Bible. Thus the 'Astraea' of the dedication here introduces a reformed and anti-papal Petrarch, who teaches rejection of earthly love and worldliness, is against religious persecution, and is associated with apocalyptic visions. This Petrarch was endorsed by Edmund Spenser, for some of the translations in the book are by Spenser and constitute his earliest published work.[7]

Thus the Elizabethan and Spenserian Petrarch may be coloured with

---

[1] The ermine is not actually mentioned by Petrarch in the *Trionfo della Castità*, but the ermine banner became a fixed feature of illustrations of the poem.

[2] *Trionfo della Castità*, 148–51. The legend is mentioned by Valerius Maximus, VIII, i; by Augustine, *De civitate Dei*, X, xvi, and was often illustrated.   [3] See above, pp. 41, 44.

[4] See Ivy L. Mumford, 'Petrarchism in early Tudor England', *Italian Studies*, XIX (1964), pp. 56–63.

[5] Quoted J. Van Dorsten, *The Radical Arts*, Leiden–Oxford, 1970, p. 79.

[6] *Ibid.*, p. 75.

[7] Spenser himself acknowledged his authorship of these verse translations by republishing them under his own name in 1591.

notions connected with Astraea and the imperial reform, with attitudes and aspirations arising out of the religious situation in England and on the Continent. With these hints in mind, we now turn to look at the portraits of Elizabeth as a Petrarchan heroine.

There is a well-known portrait at Hatfield House known as the 'Ermine' portrait (Plate 16a) because of the prominence of the little ermine shown on the sleeve. I have analysed this portrait in the Hatfield House Booklet to which I refer the reader for detailed discussion of it,[1] though it is necessary to resume here very briefly the use in this portrait of the Petrarchan theme of the Triumph of Chastity.

There is no doubt that the 'ermine' allusion relates this portrait to the Petrarchan triumph. We are intended to see in this picture Elizabeth as Petrarch's Laura, as a most chaste and beautiful lady, fit heroine of a sonnet sequence. Yet, as in Spenser's Gloriana-Belphoebe combination, the lady of the 'Ermine' portrait is not only a Petrarchan heroine in her private aspect; in her public aspect she is also a 'most royall queene or empresse'. Beside her left hand lies the sword of state, and the ermine's collar is in the form of a crown. In addition to the personal allusion, her purity symbolizes the righteousness and justice of her government. The private and public aspects are joined when we think of Astraea, and of the Justice and Purity of the imperial reform. The 'Ermine' portrait fuses Gloriana and Belphoebe in a composite statement expressive both of the triumph of her reformed imperial rule and of her personal triumph as a chaste Petrarchan heroine. If we follow the relentless argument of the Elizabeth symbolism to its logical conclusion, we may begin to see this Chaste Lady as a Pure Church, the opposite of an unreformed Whore of Babylon.

There is another famous Elizabethan portrait which uses the theme of the Petrarchan Triumph of Chastity in a way which is logically similar to its use in the 'Ermine', though more complicated. The two portraits are very different in style, but through their themes they demand to be considered together. The 'Sieve' portrait has been mentioned in the 'Astraea' and 'Chivalry' essays, but it has not yet been thought over with care. Since this portrait is one of the most important of all for the imperial theme and its complexities, let us conclude the second part of this book by looking at it.

The 'Sieve' Portrait

There are different versions of the 'Sieve' portrait in existence, all of which ought to be considered in any final attempt to solve its problems.[2] However,

---

[1] See below, pp. 215–19.

[2] On the various versions of the 'Sieve' portrait, see R. Strong, *Portraits of Queen Elizabeth I*, Oxford, 1963, Paintings, nos 43–9, pp. 66–9. The earlier versions date from 1579. Strong discusses the allegories of the 'Siena Sieve' on p. 68.

my discussion here is based solely on the most famous and finished version of the portrait which is now in the public gallery at Siena (Plate 16b). The artist and date are unknown; nor is it known how this portrait reached Siena.

We can already recognize the object which she holds. It is a sieve. This must be Elizabeth as the Vestal Virgin, Tuccia, who, with her sieve, appears in Petrarch's Triumph of Chastity. And the point is emphasized by an inscription on the picture. At the base of the column, below the Queen's right hand, are written the words: *Stancho riposo e riposato affano*, 'Weary I rest and having rested I am still weary'. This is a quotation from the Triumph of Love in Petrarch's *Trionfi*.[1] It establishes the point in the Petrarchan sequence in which Elizabeth is here appearing as a Triumph of Chastity. The Triumph of Love, with its pains and struggles, is over for her; and she is joining, in the character of the Vestal Virgin Tuccia, in the Triumph of Chastity.

In the Spenserian terminology, this would be Elizabeth as Belphoebe, the chaste lady whose fame surpasses that of Laura. Where, then, in this portrait, is the allusion to Gloriana, the imperial ruler?

On the column in the background, behind her right arm, is a series of medallions (Plate 17a). The lowest one shows an imperial crown. The crown is definitely in the shape of an imperial crown, not a royal crown. The other nine medallions tell the story of Dido and Aeneas in little scenes. The three medallions immediately above the imperial crown show, reading from right to left, Aeneas fleeing from Troy; the Trojans arriving at Carthage; Aeneas meeting Dido in the Temple of Juno. The row of medallions above these shows Dido and Aeneas together; the banquet at which they fell in love, with the blind harper, Iopas, in the foreground; Dido and Aeneas at the hunt. The top row shows Mercury warning Aeneas to depart; Dido on the funeral pyre; the departure of the Trojans.[2]

The column thus tells the story of Pious Aeneas, the Trojan ancestor, through Brut, of the British imperial line of which Pious Elizabeth is the descendant. The little scenes on the medallions tell of his love for Dido, from which he extricated himself and sailed piously away, whilst she succumbed to the Triumph of Love and perished on the funeral pyre. The extraordinarily elaborate and ingenious allusion seems to be that, unlike Dido, the chaste descendant of Aeneas has achieved a Triumph of Chastity and wears the imperial crown of pure empire. She is Gloriana, the empress of the pure imperial reform, combined with Belphoebe, the chaste Petrarchan lady.

There are further allusions to her pure empire in the globe on her left, in which the British Isles appear in light, together with much shipping moving towards the West, whilst the rest of Europe is in darkness (Plate 17b). Here we see the emerging Idea of the British Empire, perhaps as John Dee con-

[1] *Trionfo d'Amore*, III, 145.
[2] These scenes were identified by Helen Roeder. See Preface, above, p. xiii.

ceived it, an Idea involving both a religious reforming influence, a growth of sea power, and the suggestion of western expansion and rights for the Imperial Virgin in the New World.

There is an inscription on the sieve, *A terra il ben mal dimora in sella*, which may mean, 'On earth the good has difficulty in remaining in the saddle (or in command)'. There is also a motto on the globe, *Tutto vede e molto mancha*, 'I see everything and much is lacking'. An interpretation of these mottoes may be that the Imperial Virgin sees that the good has not yet triumphed, that much darkness yet surrounds the light of her imperial reform. This may account for the melancholy of her expression, and for the purposeful attitudes of the knights in the background who might be devoting themselves to the great task of dispelling the rule of evil in the world and establishing the rule of the pure empire of the chaste Imperial Virgin. If Elizabeth ever saw this portrait, she would have seen herself, as advised by Spenser, in mirrors more than one,

> But either Gloriana let her choose
> Or in Belphoebe fashioned to be:
> In th'one her rule, in th'other her rare chastity.

The fantastic logic of the Elizabeth symbolism reaches a climax in this fantastic portrait. It is related to the simplest form of the statement of the cult, the sword of the imperial reform on the Bible, or to slightly more complex but still simple statements of it, as in the civic pageantries hailing Astraea as the reformed Virgin. And it is most intimately related to the most complex forms of the cult, as in the Spenserian type of involved allegory.

In this portrait one can realize how the Elizabeth cult used every ingredient of the Elizabethan Renaissance. It used the Renaissance in its literary sense, the revived classical learning, the techniques of classical allusion, invigorated, as in the Italian Renaissance, by the imperial idea. It used the Dantesque imperial idea, the Petrarchan literary influences, the whole heritage of the Italian Renaissance, including Neoplatonic allegory. And it used all this in the service of the Reformation idea, turning the allusions towards the concept of imperial reform and the spread of a reformed empire. This included the idea of the British Empire, of the descent through Brut from the Trojan imperial line, of the *renovatio* of this empire in the Tudor imperial ruler, an empire of purified religion with a spreading influence in Europe and a destiny of expansion towards the West, beyond the seas into the New World.

As a final allusion in the 'Sieve' portrait there can be detected a modification of the device of Charles V. There is here a column, marked at its base with an imperial crown, recalling the crowned columns of the famous imperial device (Plate 3a. There is also a globe suggesting an empire spreading out beyond the columns of Hercules to the West, as in the allusion in the imperial device to worlds beyond the seas. It is not fanciful to see the allusion to the device in this picture, for we have seen it alluded to in other expressions of the Elizabethan imperial cult.[1] The Imperial Virgin is here the Virgin of expanded empire, using the echo of the device of Charles V for her own ends and purposes.

Most of the allegorical Elizabeth portraits are probably reflections of some great occasion of pageantry. It was suggested in the 'Chivalry' essay that the 'Sieve' portrait might relate to Sir Henry Lee's retirement tilt of 1590, at which a temple formed of white taffeta appeared, representing the temple of the Vestal Virgin. Before this temple was a crowned column on which were Latin verses extolling the Vestal Virgin and her empire which was spreading out beyond the Columns of Hercules into the New World.[1] Sir Henry Lee's pageant at this tilt seems to express so exactly the idea of the 'Sieve' portrait that the thought suggests itself that the most likely person to have designed the portrait is Sir Henry Lee, who would thus be commemorating in portrait form the pageantry of his retirement tilt. And as one gazes at the knights in the background of the 'Sieve', one can surely imagine that one of them is old, and is handing over his leadership of the tilt to a younger man, in a setting of what might be the tilt-yard at Whitehall. This suggestion must remain conjectural, since the scene with the knights does not occur in other versions of the portrait.[2] Nevertheless, whether or not actually true as to fact, this suggestion of a reflection of the retirement tilt of 1590 in the picture is interesting. To put it cautiously, let us say that the right preparation for looking at the 'Sieve' portrait is to study the history of the Accession Day Tilts up to 1590, the date at which their designer resigned, amid a setting of Vestal Virgin worship.

Shakespeare need not have seen the 'Sieve' portrait in order to absorb the kind of imagery which it represents, which was propagated in the pageantry of the times. The Elizabethans were accustomed to the exercise of following the imagery of the cult.

> That very time I saw (but thou could'st not)
> Flying between the cool moon and the earth
> Cupid all arm'd. A certain aim he took
> At a fair Vestal, throned by the West
> And loos'd his love shaft smartly from his bow,
> As it should pierce a hundred thousand hearts.
> But I might see young Cupid's fiery shaft

[1] See above, pp. 57–8.

[2] As the earlier versions date from 1579 (see above, p. 114, note 2), one would have to assume that Lee in his Retirement Tilt was using an already existing 'Sieve' tradition, and that his elaboration and perfection of this in the Retirement Tilt pageant was reflected in a perfected portrait, the 'Siena' Sieve, which would thus have to be dated in 1590 or later. This is not an impossible suggestion, but more precise work needs to be done on all the 'Sieve' portraits before reaching a conclusion.

> Quench'd in the chaste beams of the wat'ry moon,
> And the imperial votaress passed on,
> In maiden meditation, fancy free.

Shakespeare has picked up all the allusions. Here are the Triumphs, the Triumph of Cupid effaced by the Triumph of Chastity. Here is the fair vestal who is an imperial votaress throned by the West. He has compressed the imagery into one inclusive statement, fused it into words now perhaps too familiar, but that is not his fault. They were new at the time when they were uttered, and the audiences at *A Midsummer Night's Dream* would have heard with satisfaction Shakespeare's brilliant new coinage of the ubiquitous imperial theme.

Why is the 'Sieve' portrait at Siena? Apparently it was found 'rolled up in the attic of the Palazzo Reale, Siena, in 1895; the house was formerly occupied by the Medici.'[1] I have no solution to offer to the problem of how this portrait reached Siena, and what I have to say now has no direct bearing on that problem. Yet the fact that we have to go to Italy to see the original of one of the most striking portraits of Queen Elizabeth raises the question of whether the image of that queen had a meaning outside her own country, whether she stood for something in Europe as a whole in ways which we have hardly, as yet, sufficiently investigated, preoccupied as we have been with her purely English reputation.

There is an unimportant work by an insignificant author which was published in Italy in 1588, with a dedication, in Italian, to Elizabeth, Queen of England. The author is Giorgio Rizza Casa; his little book is an Italian treatise on physiognomics.[2] In the dedication he expresses a veneration for this wonderful queen and her heroic virtues, which is as great, he claims, as that felt by any of her fortunate subjects. He had wished to publish a prognostic of a favourable outcome of her undertakings against the King of Spain but was prevented from doing so by the Inquisitor, so he has been obliged to speak of her covertly, by spelling names backwards or in other ways, or by naming her simply as 'Donna'. He hopes much from her. When the King of Spain sought to make himself tyrant of the whole world his great Armada was defeated by her and her subjects, and he hopes to see in the future that the poor afflicted peoples will be delivered, through her most glorious aid, from tyranny, as Judith delivered the people of Israel from the tyranny of Nebuchadnezzar. So there may one day be an end to fear, to fire and sword, prison, chains, and death. He prays God for the success

---

[1] Strong, *op. cit.*, p. 68.

[2] Giorgio Rizza Casa, *La fisionomia*, Carmagnola, 1588. On Rizza Casa, see L. Thorndike, *History of Magic and Experimental Science*, New York, 1941, VI, pp. 160-1.

of this queen's undertakings, praying, at the same time, for the holy Catholic and Apostolic Church. The book was published at Carmagnola with an ecclesiastical permit dated 10 November which states that there is nothing in the work against morals or against the holy Catholic Church.

By what freak of local circumstances this book managed to get published with such a permit it would be interesting to investigate, but my point is only that Queen Elizabeth appears in it as a potential liberator from tyranny, the tyranny of the King of Spain and his effort to impose his will on all the world by tyrannical means of war and persecution. Rizza Casa is speaking a language which Giordano Bruno had been able to use with impunity in Protestant England when he praised Elizabeth, foretold for her a wide rule, and prophesied the eventual expulsion of the Triumphant Beast of tyranny.

As one other example of the use of the Elizabeth cult for politico-religious aspirations by those not natives of England one may cite Paul Schede, known as Melissus,[1] a German from the Rhineland, who had many contacts with English, French, and Dutch liberal thinkers. He was an enthusiastic member of Baïf's Academy of Poetry and Music in Paris, a great admirer of Philip Sidney (he was the first to mention Sidney as a poet)[2] and the predecessor of Janus Gruter as librarian of the Palatine library at Heidelberg.[3] Some of the Latin verses in his *Schediasmata*[4] are addressed to 'Rosina'; the poems are divided into books, each book preceded by a poem to Queen Elizabeth. To quote Jan Van Dorsten: 'In perfect agreement with the subtle fashions of Eliza's court his (Melissus's) mistress of perfection, Rosina, was the mirror of those ideals of courtly love exemplified by the Virgin Queen. Rosina was, so to speak, Melissus' Tudor Rose.'[5] So the Elizabeth cult, and its recondite courtly and chivalrous mode of expression, was current in those European circles touched by Philip Sidney's missions, and had a meaning wider than that of a purely national enthusiasm. 'Imperial reform' was an idea which could touch chords in Europe. Beyond the English Queen's obvious rôle of protectress and patron of the Protestant cause in Europe, one senses that her fame transcended the Protestant-Catholic antithesis, that she might stand for those wider and deeper aspirations for some universal solution of religious problems which were circulating below the surface in sixteenth-century Europe. After the Armada victory, a hope of freedom from the fear of the tyrant shone out, not only for England but for all Europe. As the Queen stands on the map of England (Plate 13) she is dispelling a universal darkness

---

[1] On Paul Schede (Melissus), see P. de Nolhac, *Un poète rhénan ami de la Pléiade*, Paris, 1923; J. Van Dorsten, *Poets, Patrons and Professors*, Leiden, 1962, and *The Radical Arts* (many important references to Melissus in both these books); James E. Phillips, *Neo-Latin Poetry of the Sixteenth and Seventeenth Centuries*, William Andrews Clark Memorial Library, Los Angeles, 1965.

[2] Van Dorsten, *Poets, Patrons and Professors*, pp. 50–1.   [3] *Ibid.*, p. 109.

[4] Paul Schede (Melissus), *Schediasmata poetica. Secundo edita*, Paris, 1586.

[5] Van Dorsten, *Poets, Patrons and Professors*, p. 97.

with her light, and many, besides her own countrymen, were looking towards her in hope.

Looking at the 'Sieve' portrait, the curious thought strikes one that Queen Elizabeth may here prefigure Queen Victoria and her Protestant British Empire, with its combination of moral earnestness and reforming missionary zeal, its *pax Britannica* which (whatever its faults and social limitations) did, at its best, and for a very limited time, provide a rule of peace and justice in which some part of the human race was free to develop its powers.

PART III

THE FRENCH MONARCHY

THE IDEA OF THE FRENCH MONARCHY

The French monarchy had a much better and older claim to imperial descent that had the upstart Tudor monarchy. It had a mythical Trojan ancestor, Francus, corresponding to the British Brut, but it claimed, as a real historical ancestor, Charlemagne,[1] thus directly partaking in the idea of that translation of the Empire to Charlemagne which kept a hold on men's imaginations as the living link with the universal *pax* and *justitia* of Rome. The French kings shared the claim of descent from Charlemagne with the Holy Roman Emperors; the French monarch was the rival of the Emperor for imperial leadership of Europe.

There was also a peculiar Christian sacredness attaching to French kingship. The French king did not have the title of Emperor, but he did have a very significant title, that of *Rex Christianissimus*, the Most Christian King. This was related to the peculiarly sacred character of the anointing of the kings of France with the holy oil at their coronation.[2] According to legend, the coronation oil had been brought down from heaven in a phial – the 'sainte ampoule' – at the baptism of Clovis. Charlemagne was not anointed when he was made emperor, for he had already been anointed as King of the Franks. Though it was not admitted that the royal anointing endowed the French king with priestly functions (he could not celebrate Mass) yet it gave a peculiar sanctity to French royalty. The English kings also had a peculiarly sacred anointing tradition, perhaps related in its origins to the French one, and this is one of the many significant parallels between French and English monarchy.

The imperial potentialities inherent in the French king were theorized, at about the same time that Dante was theorizing those inherent in the Emperor,

[1] The legend of the descent from Charlemagne was maintained throughout the *ancien régime*. For a typical example of the traditional historiography, see Jacques de Cassan, *Recherches des Droits du Roy et de la Couronne de France*, 1632, with dedication to Richelieu.

[2] See Marc Bloch, *The Royal Touch*, London, 1973; Jean de Pange, *Le Roi très chrétien*, Paris, 1949.

by a French lawyer, Pierre Dubois.[1] Dubois was associated with the revival of Roman law going on in France in the reign of Philip IV (Philip the Fair) and his theorization of the French monarch as *Dominus mundi* has the same background of revived Roman law as that discussed in the first essay in this book in connection with the definition of the Empire. Dubois was passionately imbued with the belief that the world must be under one ruler to ensure peace and justice, but for him the bearer, the channel of the Roman universality was not the Emperor, but the Most Christian King, the King of France, true descendant of Charlemagne and marked out by his peculiar holiness for such a mission. Dubois argues in various pamphlets which he wrote as jurist in the service of Philip the Fair that elections of Holy Roman Emperors are a fruitful source of war, and that it would therefore be a much better arrangement to make the Empire hereditary in the French monarchy,[2] to which in any case it belongs through the descent from Charlemagne. The Empire should therefore be 'translated' back to the French monarchy. In his *De recuperatione terrae sanctae*, Dubois set out a theory of world government to be established under the *Rex Christianissimus*, which was to have its centre in the recovered Holy Land. The theme of the Empire, in this French form, as the reformer of the Church is present in this work which rebukes the avarice and immorality of the clergy, and proposes an enforced return of the church to apostolic poverty through the confiscation of all ecclesiastical lands. Dubois was a dreamer, like Dante, and his theory of world government remained, like Dante's, a pure abstraction.

The idea of the French monarchy exercised a great influence in Italy. Italians, always inclined to look towards the north for the chivalrous and imperial hero who would come to save Italy, could choose as their hero either the *Sanctus Imperator Romanus* or the *Rex Christianissimus*. In practice, this choice very often followed the party line between Guelphs, or papalists, and Ghibellines, or imperialists – the Ghibellines believing, like Dante, in the Holy Roman Emperor and the Guelphs in the Most Christian King. Still, in the sixteenth century, Italians can make a choice between the two imperialisms. Ariosto, as we know, chose the Holy Roman Emperor, Charles V. So did Giangiorgio Trissino, who wrote a long poem, *L'Italia liberata dai Goti*, to glorify the eternal empire now living again in Maximilian and Charles V. Luigi Alamanni, on the other hand, chose the *Rex Christianissimus*, and went to live in France where he wrote a long Arthurian chivalrous epic, *Girone il Cortese*, which he dedicated to Henri II after the death of his first patron, François Ier. The only difference between the imperialism of Trissino and that of Alamanni would seem to be that the former chose Charles

---

[1] For a bibliography of works on Dubois, see W.-I. Brandt, 'Pierre Dubois: modern or mediaeval', *American Historical Review*, XXXV (1930), pp. 507 ff.

[2] Dubois, *De recuperatione terrae sanctae*, ed. C.-V. Langlois, Paris, 1891, pp. 8 ff. Langlois in his introduction gives a useful discussion of the imperialist theory of Dubois; see also C. L. Lange, *Histoire de l'internationalisme*, Christiana, 1909, p. 100.

V as Emperor, whilst the latter chose François Ier.[1] (Spenser would later choose an Imperial Virgin as the heroine of his chivalrous epic.)

Around François Ier there was an immense 'golden age' propaganda, hailing his reign as an imperial *renovatio* and celebrating the rebirth of letters, arts, and sciences. This propaganda echoes throughout the century. Though François Ier was less fortunate in establishing an imperial image than Charles V, and was indeed defeated by his rival, the cult of the French monarchy grew in intensity and was expressed in recondite symbolism around his son Henri II. When Henri II was killed in a jousting accident in 1559, his widow, Catherine de' Medici, became the custodian of the destiny of the French monarchy in a dangerous world – a trust which she exercised to the best of her ability in favour of her sons François II, Charles IX, and Henri III.

Though the monarchy might seem weak in the reigns of these unfortunate last Valois kings, the Idea of the French monarchy was elaborately expounded during the period by Guillaume Postel, who put forward in many books and pamphlets, particularly *Les Raisons de la monarchie*, published in 1551, theories of world unity under the French monarchy which recall those of Dubois. Some of Postel's notions are wildly extravagant, and indeed he was thought mad, even in his own times. His main programme belongs, however, into the tradition of world unity through the spiritual and temporal monarchies. He believed that it would be possible to find by abstruse mystical arguments a formula for a world religion which would be congenial to Christians, Turks and Jews. Beside the Pope, as the head of this world religion, he would place, as temporal head, the King of France.[2]

It is significant that Postel's vision includes the Pope. The break with the Papacy which the Tudor monarchy made was never made by the French monarchy, though it came perilously near it, and though Postel and other French monarchy theorists were insistent in demanding reform of the church.

How far was the development of vast mystiques in connection with a national monarch (that of Postel is in some ways comparable to the wilder aspects of the build-up of Elizabeth of England as the Just Virgin of Imperial Reform) evoked by that phantom which the career of the Emperor Charles V had raised of the rule of One? We shall see that the influence of the device of Charles V plays a part in the French monarchy symbolism of the period, as we have seen that it did in the Tudor monarchy symbolism. The device of Charles IX (Plate 20a), an obvious imitation of the two columns of the imperial device, was prominently displayed at his entry into Paris in 1571. And there were overtones of holy imperialism, of a sacred universal

[1] See G. Toffanin, *Il Cinquecento*, Milan, 1929, pp. 457–8.

[2] On Postel and the French Monarchy, see W. J. Bouwsma, *Concordia Mundi: The Career and Thought of Guillaume Postel (1510–1581)*, Harvard University Press, 1957, pp. 216 ff.

destiny, of a Postel-like mysticism, in the imagery of this entry as a whole.

The emphasis on empire mysticism around the *Rex Christianissimus* is continued in succeeding reigns. Giordano Bruno sees a form of peaceful religious imperialism, as opposed to the aggressive ambitions of the Spanish monarchy, in the device of the Three Crowns of Henri III.[1] The conversion of Henri IV aroused hopes that some universal solution of both political and religious problems would be found through this French monarch.[2] There is a growth of religious imperialism around the French monarchy in the latter part of the sixteenth century which reaches a climax in the religious-imperial rôle assigned to Henri IV. Particularly is the monarchy used as a means of conciliating the opposite religious parties by bringing them together in common loyalty to the crown. This had been Catherine de' Medici's aim throughout her long life, and the royalist conciliatory policy, though painfully interrupted at a crucial moment by the Massacre of St Bartholomew, eventually bore fruit in Henri III's religious movements, which led on to the conversion of Henri IV and so to a solution of the religious problems in a Catholic monarchy which allowed a limited toleration to Protestants in the Edict of Nantes. Thus the religious movements associated with monarchy in France did not lead to a Gallican break with the Papacy and a Gallican reformed national church, as did the Anglican reform in England. Yet the monarchy did develop in the direction of liberal solutions of the religious problem. And, as in the case of the build-up of the Tudor monarchy, there was the aim of building up for the French monarchy a strong spiritual position against Hispano-Papalism. Throughout the period, Hispano-Papalism and the ambitions of Philip II of Spain were a threat to the French monarchy, as they were to the English monarchy.

The religious importance of the Idea of the Monarchy in a country distracted by wars of religion helped to preserve its legends and mythology from the criticism of new schools of historical thought. The critical and scholarly approach to history, as opposed to uncritical acceptance of myths of empire and monarchy, made great progress in sixteenth-century France, yet in the royalist propaganda the old myths were allowed to stand. Ronsard knew that Francus was not really the Trojan ancestor of the Kings of France, just as it was known in England that Brut was not really the ancestor of the British-imperial line, yet Ronsard retains Francus in his *Franciade* in honour of Charles IX as a new Augustus, just as Spenser retains Brut in his British-imperial epic.

There is a sense, too, in which the cosmic setting of the monarchical-imperial Idea, the presentation of the One Monarch as the expression, in the world of human society, of the unified governance of the world of physical

---

[1] G. Bruno, *Spaccio della bestia trionfante* (*Dialoghi italiani*, ed. G. Aquilecchia, pp. 826–7). See my *Giordano Bruno and the Hermetic Tradition*, London, 1964, pp. 228 ff., and below, pp. 167–9.

[2] See below, pp. 210–13.

nature, was not merely a reaction into medievalism. It was consonant with contemporary philosophical attitudes, particularly those of an esoteric type, an expression of the macrocosm-microcosm analogy which had such an intensive revival in the Renaissance Hermetic tradition. Elizabethan imperialism was developed, not by some survivor from the Middle Ages, but by John Dee, Hermetic Magus and scientist, a figure thoroughly representative of the most 'modern' trends of the age in which he lived. The mystique of the French monarchy was developed by Guillaume Postel, the Cabalist, a visionary of a somewhat similar type to Dee. It is important for the history of thought not to neglect the monarchical Idea as a factor in the Renaissance magico-scientific outlook. The great, illuminated, revolving model of the heavens which showed forth the destiny of the French monarchy during the festivals of 1581 was a highly 'modern' expression of the latest mathematical-mechanical techniques, though its purpose was talismanic and magical.

In the following essays, the symbolism and imagery used of French monarchy are studied at work on specific occasions. The official entry of a French king into Paris was always the occasion for the presentation of an elaborate programme of decoration in the streets; one such entry is here studied in detail, namely the entry of Charles IX into Paris in 1571. The traditions of French chivalry were deployed in honour of the monarch at the great court festivals; the festivals here studied in detail are those for the wedding of the Duc de Joyeuse in 1581.

It is, I believe, a new departure to present within the covers of the same book studies of both English and French propaganda for monarchy. Resemblances and contrasts will occur to the attentive reader of the two parts of the book. Perhaps the greatest contrast is that between what one may call professional and amateur modes of production. The aldermen of the City of Paris, who were responsible for the design of the entries, could draw on a great, established, European art tradition, the School of Fontainebleau, for their artists; they use poets and humanists in the employ of the court for the invention of the programme to be followed by the artists. Compare this with the Elizabeth propaganda in England, where there was no established court school of art, no poet-humanists officially in the pay of the court. All seems, compared with the French system, haphazard and accidental in England, and we do not really know, although we can guess in a few instances, who were the people who designed the Elizabeth symbolism. The French court festivals, based on the traditional exercises of chivalry, with their teams of artists, poets, musicians employed in the production of magnificent shows, of central importance for the evolution of certain basic European art forms, contrast strangely with the Accession Day Tilts, the organization and design of which seem to have been due to an enthusiastic amateur, Sir Henry Lee, and not to any initiative from the court.

Yet, however different in their modes of expression, in their cult of monarchy both the English and the French traditions belong to the same age, in which the Idea of monarchy was a basic theme, and a theme intimately connected with the religious problems of the age. In England, the leadership of monarchy was towards imperial reform and a predominantly Protestant temper. In France it was to lead eventually towards a version of Counter Reformation; Henri III's leadership of the distinctively French type of Counter Reformation will be studied in the essay on religious processions in Paris in 1583. A short final essay sketches the religious solution under Henri IV, hailed as the return of Astraea, a golden age of prosperity and purified religion, an imperial *renovatio* which provided a tolerant solution for the problems of religious schism.

THE ENTRY OF CHARLES IX AND HIS QUEEN INTO PARIS, 1571

The Treaty of Saint-Germain in 1570 had brought to a temporary conclusion the wars of religion in France. Liberal terms had been allowed to Protestants in this treaty, who were permitted to exercise their cult within certain limits, and this attempt at toleration aroused a hope amongst 'politiques' and moderates that a new age might be dawning in which war in the name of religion might become a thing of the past. The hope of religious peace had been further aroused by the recent marriage of Charles IX to Elizabeth of Austria, daughter of the Emperor Maximilian II and granddaughter of the Emperor Charles V. The Emperor Maximilian II, like his father, took seriously the imperial rôle in religious matters. Influenced by Melanchthon, he was interested in ideas of reform. The French king's marriage to the daughter of this tolerant emperor seemed like another step in the direction taken by the Treaty of Saint-Germain, a step towards an increase of tolerance and the establishment of religious peace.

Moreover, to sixteenth-century minds saturated in the imperial idea, the union of two great royal lines, both claiming descent from Charlemagne, in the marriage of a *Rex Christianissimus* of France with a daughter and granddaughter of emperors, was seen as something in the nature of a portent, an event of tremendous significance which might lead to a world religious empire in which religious peace would be finally established. The traditional French-monarchy symbolism for a royal entry is expanded in the entries of Charles IX and Elizabeth of Austria into vast imperial perspectives, which undoubtedly owe something to the mysticism of Guillaume Postel concerning the destiny of the French monarchy, and its rôle of world religious leadership, which included a world-wide solution of problems of religious disunion.

Charles IX had adopted as his device two columns, linked together, with the motto *Pietate et justitia* (Plate 20a). This was obviously an imitation of the famous device of Charles V. The young French king saw himself in a wide imperial rôle. In the symbolism of his entry, the two columns of his device are constantly alluded to, but the columns are straightened so as to make them an even closer imitation of the imperial device of Charles V, an allusion both to the empire of the young queen's grandfather and to the monarchy of her husband, a descendant of Charlemagne, like herself. The two main themes of the entry are Peace and Empire. Thus the symbolism of this entry becomes a remarkable example of the imperial theme, viewed from a French angle.

And a profoundly melancholy interest is aroused by the symbolism of this entry. The hopes expressed in its themes of peace and empire, the nervous exaltation induced by the ending of religious war and the fantastic perspectives of imperial peace through the French monarchy, were to be shattered in the following year by the dread event from which it would be hardly an exaggeration to say that Europe never recovered – the Massacre of St Bartholomew's Night.

The major source for the entries (the Queen entered later than the King, and separately) is the illustrated account of them by alderman Simon Bouquet, published in 1572 with a very long title which will here be abbreviated as the *Recueil*.[1] This account is illustrated with engravings of the triumphal arches and other decorations for the entry, fully describing the mythology and symbolism of these in words, and also fully explaining the meaning of the symbolism. Bouquet's account can be supplemented with much documentary material from other sources.[2]

It was the responsibility of the mayor and aldermen of the City of Paris to design, and pay for, the decorations erected in the city for a royal entry. At a meeting of the mayor and aldermen in September 1570, it was decided that the preparations for the royal entries in March of the following year, of which they had been notified, must begin immediately, and that no effort must be spared to make these occasions very splendid.[3] It was decided to ask Pierre de Ronsard and Jean Dorat 'poètes français très doctes', to come to the Hôtel de Ville for a consultation.[4] After the matter had been 'amply communicated' to them, these two poets undertook, not only to provide poetry to be inscribed on the erections for the entries (Ronsard, French verses, and Dorat, those in ancient tongues) but also to be responsible for the scheme of the decorations. And in accordance with their advice the city fathers made contracts with those who were to execute the decorations.

Of the seven French poets so influential throughout the sixteenth century and known as the 'Pléiade', Ronsard was the most famous. Jean Dorat was the oldest of the group and considered the most learned. He it was who instructed Ronsard and the others in the Renaissance type of Greek and Latin

---

[1] Simon Bouquet, *Bref et sommaire recueil de ce qui a esté faict & de l'ordre tenu à la joyeuse Entrée de très-puissant . . . Prince Charles IX de ce nom, Roy de France, en sa bonne ville & cité de Paris . . . le Mardy sixiesme jour de Mars. Avec le couronnement de très-haute Princesse Madame Elizabeth d'Autriche, son epouse . . . et Entrée de ladicte Dame en icelle ville, le jeudi xxix dudict mois de Mars, MDLLXXI*, Paris, 1572.

A facsimile reproduction of this work is to be published by Theatrum Orbis Terrarum Ltd, Amsterdam, in the series 'Renaissance Triumphs and Magnificences'. See Preface, above, p. xiv, note 1.

[2] The published archives of the City of Paris include the 'devis et marchés' or contracts with the artists for the decorations, giving detailed specifications for the work; see *Régistres des deliberations du Bureau de la Ville de Paris*, ed. P. Guérin, vol. VI (1891), pp. 236 ff. An unpublished manuscript (Bibl. Nat., MS. Français 11691) is a 'Compte particulier' which gives accounts of payments made to those who worked for the entries.

[3] *Régistres*, VI, p. 232.   [4] *Ibid.*, p. 233.

erudition in which he excelled.[1] It used to be a question widely and vaguely debated in critical works on sixteenth-century French poetry whether the poets were, or were not, interested in art, or whether they preferred poetry to art. This question was put, for the first time, on a refreshingly factual basis by the discovery of the documents which record the employment of two leading poets of the Pléiade as advisers to artists on the decorations for these entries. These documents shows us Ronsard and Dorat as learned humanist experts in complete control of an artistic scheme which the artists bind themselves to execute faithfully as part of the contract which they make with their employers. The old artificial distinction between 'literature' and 'art' prevented any real understanding of the social rôle of the poets of the Pléiade, as humanist experts able to advise artists on the visual presentation of the images which they used as poets in their own poetry, and as experts in the royalist propaganda which, as court poets, it was their loyal duty to devise and propagate.

Triumphal arches and other decorations made for royal entries were temporary erections formed of canvas stretched on to wooden frames. On to this flat surface the artists painted figures, using illusionist techniques to give the effects of sculpture or architectural ornament. Free-standing figures, sculptured in stucco, were used on the tops of the arches or for large groups. The artists to whom the city fathers entrusted the execution of the decorations for the Charles IX entry were Niccolo dell'Abate, who was to provide the paintings on them; Pierre d'Angers, also a painter but employed in a humbler capacity, for he was to do all the painted festoons, perspectives, and such matters; and Germain Pilon, who was to provide the sculpture. All these were pledged to work incessantly at the preparations during the next six months, giving their whole time to this work, and working 'suivant les pourtraicts, compositions, desseings et ordonnances desdits sieurs de Ronsard et de Dorat'.[2] This team included the most eminent French sculptor of the day, Germain Pilon, and the most eminent Italian painter then in France, Niccolo dell'Abate. And these artists were working from the plans and descriptions of Ronsard and Dorat and under their supervision. In the contract between the city and Dell'Abate and Pilon it is expressly stated that Dell'Abate is to execute his paintings 'as advised and ordered by the poet having charge of this'; similarly, Pilon must work under orders, and the contract speaks of 'pourtraicts' which have been given to Dell'Abate and Pilon which they must follow exactly.[3]

These two artists were both late descendants of the School of Fontainebleau; both had worked with Primaticcio. Pilon was an expert on work in stucco; among the surviving bronze busts by him is one of Charles IX

---

[1] See F. Yates, *The French Academies of the Sixteenth Century*, Warburg Institute, 1947 (Kraus Reprint, 1967), pp. 14-15.
[2] *Régistres, loc. cit.*   [3] *Ibid.*, p. 243.

(Plate 44), probably close in date and spirit to his work for the entry. Niccolo dell'Abate was an old man, helped in his work for the entry by his son Camillo. He died later in the same year, 1571, as that of the entry.

There exists in the National Gallery of Stockholm a design for a triumphal arch with figures (Plate 18a) which corresponds almost exactly to one of the arches for the Charles IX entry in Bouquet's *Recueil* (Plate 18b). This design brings us a stage nearer to the actual artistic work done for the entry than do the rather clumsy engravings in Bouquet's account. The Stockholm drawing has been attributed to Camillo dell'Abate.[1] It brings us close to that collaboration between poets of the Pléiade and artists of the late School of Fontainebleau which, as finally executed, presented in the streets of Paris a series of temporary works of art representing the fine flowering, both of the humanist scholarship of the Pléiade School, and of the brilliant professionalism of the School of Fontainebleau.

Ronsard was paid two hundred and seventy 'livres tournois' for 'les Inuentions deuises et Inscriptions qu'il a faictes pour les dites Entrees', and a supplementary payment of fifty-four 'livres tournois'.[2] Dorat was paid one hundred and eighty-nine 'livres tournois' for having made 'tous les carmes grecs et latins' for the entries, and 'partie des inuentions'.[3] That is to say, Ronsard was responsible for the invention of the programme of the entries, though Dorat helped a little with this. Dorat provided all the Greek and Latin inscriptions, Ronsard the French inscriptions, though Bouquet himself did some of these.

Thus, at this French entry, one can watch the imperial themes being evolved by the poets, can see them translated into visual imagery by the artists, and all in the most business-like way, with accounts kept of all the transactions and almost every detail described. This world of organized humanist scholarship, geared to organized artistic production, contrasts strangely with the vague lack of definition, and of documentary evidence, concerning the production of the symbolism of the Imperial Virgin in Tudor England. And yet the actual imperial themes are, many of them, the same in France as in England.

Imperial Themes. The Trojan Descent

It had long been Ronsard's ambition to write a great epic poem on the theme of the glorious imperial origins of the *Rex Christianissimus*. All the monarchies of Europe sought Trojan ancestors through whom to link their destinies and origins with imperial Rome. The French parallel to Brut, the Trojan ancestor of the British-Tudor imperial line, was Francus, supposed

---

[1] Sylvie Béguin, 'Niccolo dell'Abate en France', *Art de France*, II (1972), p. 114; and *Il cinquecento francese*, Milan, 1970, fig. 31.
[2] 'Compte particulier', fol. 88.   [3] *Ibid.*, fol. 88 *verso*.

to have been the son of Hector and to have escaped from Troy to found the legendary race of the mythical early kings of France. It was Ronsard's ambition to crystallize this legend in an immortal epic, decked out with all the learning of a member of the Pléiade. It was to be a French *Aeneid*, with the Trojan Francus in the rôle of the Trojan Aeneas, and leading up to Charles IX as the French Augustus. Ronsard was on terms of intimacy with Charles IX, who admired his poetry, and in recent years, with royal encouragement, he had begun to write this great work. When the city authorities called upon him to provide a programme for the entry, he had one ready to hand in his material for the *Franciade*. Like Spenser, Ronsard never completed his epic poem. The first four books of the *Franciade* were all that he ever wrote; they were published in the year after the entry, in 1572, and they connect very closely indeed with his programme for the entry.

The theme of the Trojan descent was not only a normal element of French monarchy propaganda. It was also peculiarly well suited to the occasion of the entry, since the Queen, Elizabeth of Austria, the young bride whom Charles had recently married, was also, mythically speaking, a descendant of the Trojan imperial line. In their marriage, two Troy-descended personages were united, and a vast, a portentous, imperial future might be expected from such a conjunction. It was a re-uniting of French and German Trojan-imperial lines which both went back to one source. Francus was supposed to have founded a kingdom in 'Sicambria'. One of his descendants, Pharamond, was supposed to have been the first king of France. From Pharamond descended Pepin, and also Charlemagne, the great imperial ancestor of both the French kings and the German emperors.

Upon the first of the triumphal arches (Plate 19a) erected for the entry of Charles IX, the one at the Porte Saint-Denis, stood two great figures of stucco sculpture, one representing Francus, the other Pharamond.[1] The close links between the programme for this arch and Ronsard's *Franciade* are made very evident by the insertion in Bouquet's account of forty-two lines of verse by Ronsard which were to have been inscribed on the arch, but unfortunately there was not room for them.[2] These verses tell the story of Francus and Pharamond in language which is practically identical with what may be read in Ronsard's unfinished epic. According to the legend (particularly as recounted by Jean Lemaire des Belges in his poem *Les Illustrations de Gaule*) there was German blood in Pharamond, Francus having taken a wife in Germany, and so Pharamond becomes the prototype for the uniting of French and German blood in the marriage of Charles and Elizabeth. This was briefly stated in a quatrain by Bouquet, in which he reduced to manageable size the gist of Ronsard's peroration, and which was written on a tablet in the centre of the arch.

[1] Bouquet, *op. cit.*, pp. 8–13.
[2] *Ibid.*, p. 10.

From the contracts made by the city with the artists who executed this arch we learn that they were to do all 'selon l'ordonnance de monsieur de Ronsard, poète'.[1] These instructions describe exactly what we see on the arch in the engraving of it in Bouquet's account. Francus is to have an eagle near him; Pharamond a crow; the two figures are to hold swords and to look towards one another; every detail of the 'Majesty' and 'Victory' to be painted in the illusionist niches on the arch is laid down in the contract, even to the style of the painted architecture.

These exact instructions about the iconography of Francus and Pharamond, though drawn up by Ronsard for the benefit of the artists, were not entirely invented by him, for there was an existing tradition for the representation of Francus and Pharamond in pseudo-antique armour. An important personage behind the design of French monarchy propaganda in the sixteenth century was Nicolas Houel, an apothecary, designer of tapestries, and general virtuoso who worked for Catherine de' Medici. Houel wrote an *Histoire des anciens rois de France* which is lost, but the drawings by Antoine Caron and other artists made as illustrations to it have been preserved.[2] One of these designs shows a group of Pharamond and other ancient kings, with, in the centre, a 'Majesty' and a 'Victory'. This composition compares closely with the Porte Saint-Denis arch at the entry, which represents a visual tradition for the legends about the ancient kings of France which Ronsard knew and used.

Just as, in England, the Brut legend about the Trojan ancestry of British kings had been demolished by Polydore Vergil and modern scholarship, so in France contemporary historiography was abandoning the Francus legend for more realistic approaches to history.[3] There was a campaign going on amongst French historians against basing French history on the mythical Francus and his bogus story. Ronsard was aware of such criticisms and dealt with them in the preface to his *Franciade* where he says that he has used the old annals in his poem 'sans me soucier si cela est vrai ou non, ou si nos rois sont Troyens ou Germains . . . si Francus est venu en France ou non'.[4] Such questions are the business of historiographers, he says, and not of poets. Great poets have always used old legendary annals in their epics. Even Aeneas, says Ronsard, may not have really existed, may never have come to Italy from Troy, as Virgil describes. In the same spirit of poetic rather than literal truth, Ronsard intends to make Francus the hero of the *Franciade*. This attitude to the Francus legend would of course also apply to Ronsard's use of it for the decorations for the Charles IX entry. He was using it, not as literally true, but as poetic panegyric of the French monarchy, and

[1] *Régistres*, VI, pp. 238–9.
[2] They were published by J. Guiffrey, *Les Dessins de l'histoire des rois de France par Nicolas Houel*, Paris, 1920.
[3] See George Huppert, *The Idea of Perfect History*, Illinois, 1970, pp. 72 ff.
[4] *La Franciade*, preface (Ronsard, *Œuvres*, ed. I. Silver, Chicago, 1966, IV, p. 19).

its present representative Charles IX, just as Virgil's panegyric of Augustus used his supposed Trojan ancestor, Aeneas.

Even so in England would Spenser in his epic about the Fairy Queen retain the Brut legend as poetic truth for expressing the imperial sanctions of the Tudor monarchy. But we have no records of Spenser as designer of visual representations of the imagery of his poem for some royal entry.

Imperial Themes. Peace and Catherine de' Medici

The imperial theme of peace is very strongly present in the symbolism of the entry. The peace to which the decorations allude is a religious peace, the establishing of harmony between Catholics and Protestants, and the architect of such a peace, built under the imperial auspices of French monarchy, is assumed to be the Queen Mother, Catherine de' Medici.

One of the decorations at the entry (Plate 20c) showed a woman holding up a map of Gaul and resembling the Queen Mother. She is surrounded by hieroglyphs referring to Catherine de' Medici's vigilance and promptitude, and to her efforts at pacification. Most of these hieroglyphs are taken fairly directly from the usual Renaissance handbook, the *Hieroglyphica* of Pierio Valeriano. The designers had only to look up *Pax*, *Concordia*, in the index to this work to find suggestions for what they wanted.

These crowded symbols of concord and harmony referred to how this queen 'a si bien et heureusement accordé les parties discordantes, qu'il en est sorty une tres desirée paix, union, et concorde'. This was an allusion to the Peace of Saint-Germain of 1570 which had ended religious war, given good terms to Protestants, and which had aroused hopes that a permanent settlement on a basis of religious toleration had been arrived at.

It was just that the image of peacemaker in the religious wars should here be assigned to Catherine de' Medici, whose policy had always been Erasmian and tolerant, who had supported the Colloquy of Poissy which had attempted a solution of the problem of schism, who had surrounded herself with representatives of the 'politique' party, or middle party of conciliation. The festivals organized by her throughout her regency had built up a symbolism of peace and concord around her young son, Charles IX, in an effort to draw together the discordant religious parties in loyalty to the monarchy.[1] The Peace of Saint-Germain looked like the crown of all her efforts in this direction, and the symbols of peace and union which abound throughout the entry take their rise from the 'Gallia' decoration, devoted to the Queen Mother, as from their source.

One may compare Catherine as a royal religious symbol holding the map of Gallia with Elizabeth as a royal religious symbol standing on the map of England (Plate 13). No influence of the former image on the latter is sug-

[1] See F. Yates, *The Valois Tapestries*, Warburg Institute, 1959, pp. 51 ff.

gested, but the comparison is interesting, indicating how the predominant theme of the age, monarchy or empire in its religious rôle, found similar expressions. Catherine could not take the Virgin Astraea rôle, since she was not a virgin but a widow. The character of pious widow, devoted to the memory of her royal spouse, Henri II, was one of Catherine's most emphasized public images, and it is alluded to in the 'Gallia' decoration at the entry. The four seated figures below 'Gallia' represent virtuous classical heroines whom the Queen Mother resembles. Amongst them is Artemisia, the famous classical widow who built the first mausoleum in memory of her husband, Mausolus. The history of Artemisia as an allegory of the widowed Queen Mother was worked out by Catherine's propagandist, Nicolas Houel, the apothecary, in his *Histoire d'Artémise*[1] in which the monumental tomb of Henri II, erected by Catherine, is compared to Artemisia's erection of the mausoleum. The *History of Artemisia* was illustrated by artists whose designs survive and which were to have been executed in a great tapestry sequence in honour of the Queen Mother.[2]

The theme of the pious widow was carried on at the next decoration at the entry[3] (Plate 18b) of which we have already seen a sketch in the Stockholm drawing (Plate 18a). On the top of the arch, at the centre, is a heart and an urn supported by four children. The 'devis', or instructions from the poet as to how the artist (Pilon) was to execute this group, quotes what may be Ronsard's actual words, which correspond exactly to what we see in the Stockholm drawing and in the engraving.[4]

Another of Catherine's public rôles, not virginal but matriarchal, was Juno. The colossal Juno (Plate 20d) at the entry, 'faicte d'estuc si bien et si bien taillé qu'il n'avoit celluy qui ne le print pour vray marbre',[5] was evidently a work which showed forth something of Pilon's genius. She was a 'nocière Junon', presiding over marriages, and referred to the Queen Mother's skill in arranging splendid matches for her children. The imperial splendours of the alliance of Charles with Elizabeth are emphasized by the eagles below the statue, and the rainbow, prominently introduced, was Catherine's device (Plate 23b), used with the meaning of peace. Catherine, the peacemaker, with her rainbow, is here amalgamated with Catherine, the Juno, who arranges splendid imperial peace-bringing marriages.

Another great statue at the entry was a Hymen,[6] corresponding to the Juno, and also with eagles at its base. The verses by Ronsard inscribed on it

[1] The unpublished manuscript of Houel's *Histoire d'Artémise* is in the Bibliothèque Nationale, MS. Français 308.

[2] Most of the designs for the Artémise sequence are reproduced in M. Fenaille, *Histoire générale des tapisseries de la manufacture des Gobelins*, vol. I, Paris, 1903–7.

[3] Bouquet, *op. cit.*, pp. 18–27.

[4] *Régistres*, VI, pp. 240–1. The allusion is to the urn containing the heart of Henri II on the monument to that king by Germain Pilon (see A. Blunt, *Art and Architecture in France, 1500–1700*, Harmondsworth, 1953, Plate 63).

[5] Bouquet, *op. cit.*, p. 26. [6] *Ibid.*, p. 28.

ensured that no one would miss the connection of the monument to Hymen with the basic theme of the entries, the *Franciade* theme of the alliance of two Troy-descended monarchs in the marriage of Charles and Elizabeth.

Gallia-Artemisia-Juno, or the Queen Mother, Catherine de' Medici, presides over the symbolism of the entry in her well-known and established rôles. She is the peace-bringer from religious war, always on the side of concord and harmony. As widow of Henri II, she had represented French monarchy during the minority of her son. Now she establishes peace and concord in the Treaty of Saint-Germain, ushering in her son's reign on this note, and further encouraging an even wider imperial peace in her rôle of Juno, presiding over a marriage union between the two great representatives of Empire.

Castor and Pollux bring Peace to the Ship of France

On one of the arches at the entry[1] a great ship was to be seen (Plate 19b). A ship is the emblem of Paris, and also of France; this ship is both Paris and France. On it can be seen the fleurs-de-lys, crowned, and surrounded by the collar of the Ordre de Saint Michel. Two figures stand beside it, aiding and encouraging its voyage. On their foreheads are stars. The allusion is to the well-known emblem, popularized by Alciati, based on the legend that the appearance of Castor and Pollux to sailors in a storm at sea means that calm weather is at hand.[2] The emblem usually showed the brothers as stars or flames appearing on the rigging. The meaning of the arch is that Charles IX and his brother Henri are two brothers who are bringing the Ship of France into peace, appearing like Castor and Pollux to announce calm weather after storms. The emblematic language would have been understood by the beholders of the arch, for the Castor and Pollux emblem and its application to the Ship of France was part of the usual language of royal propaganda. It had been used at this same point in Paris at the entry of Henri II, the father of Charles IX, where there had been an arch showing a ship protected by Castor and Pollux.

As an example of Ronsard's specifications for the decorations for the Charles IX entry, I quote here, in English translation, the directions laid down by the poet for the artists to follow in creating the Castor and Pollux arch:[3]

For the form (of the arch) and of the statues on it, as ordered
by Monsieur Ronsard, a strange and rustic style must be used, in

[1] *Ibid.*, p. 33.

[2] The ship and stars with the motto *Spes proxima* is the forty-third emblem in Alciati's collection (Plate 23c). The meaning is expanded in Claude Mignault's commentary (see Andres Alciati, *Omnia emblemata*, 1574, pp. 148–50). The lights on the ship were sometimes shown as flames, referring to the legend of St Elmo's fire, which has the same meaning.

[3] *Régistres*, VI, pp. 242–3.

such a way that from the base [of the arch] up to the architrave, there will appear, as it were, rocks. . . . There will be snail-shells and fishes around the water, the appearance of which is imitated on the arch. At the key of the arch, there will be two dolphins, or sea fishes, with a crab hanging between them, and these fishes will seem to sustain a large tablet on which will be the inscription. On each side of this tablet will be two great statues, one of an old man with a beard, the other of a woman with long hair; these figures lean against great vases out of which water is pouring.

Above the said tablet and the simulated cornice, there will be a great vessel resembling an antique ship, with water around, and reeds and islands. On each side of the ship there will be great statues, seven or eight feet high. The ship will be ornamented with fine decorations, in the antique style, with a mast and sails. And as to the said figures, they are to be made in accordance with the description of the said poet, as follows:

There must be . . . beside the said antique vessel or ship, two handsome young men, having each a star on their heads, who will be seen to be touching the ship and aiding it. And below each of the figures there will be placed the bit and bridle of a horse.

Comparing these instructions with the engraving of the arch in Bouquet's account (Plate 19b) it will be seen that the artist who painted the rustic and river effects on the arch (the artist was Pierre d'Angers[1]) has followed Ronsard's instructions most precisely. And Germain Pilon, too, when creating the stucco sculptures on the arch, had Ronsard's directions in front of him and followed them faithfully, even to the detail of the bits and bridles at the feet of Castor and Pollux, also known as the Dioscuri, an allusion to their rôle of horse-tamers.

The poem by Ronsard on the royal brothers who protect the Ship of France from storms, like the Dioscuri, is well known.[2]

Sur le navire de la ville de Paris Protégé par Castor et Pollux, ressemblants de visage au Roy et a Monseigneur le Duc d'Anjou

Quand le Navire enseigne de Paris
(France et Paris n'est qu'une mesme chose)
Estoit de vents et de vagues enclose,
Comme un vaisseau de l'orage surpris,
Le Roy, Monsieur, Dioscures esprits,
Freres et filz du ciel qui tout dispose,
Sont apparus à la mer qui repose
Et le Navire ont sauvé de perilz.

[1] *Ibid.*, p. 245.
[2] Bouquet, *op. cit.*, p. 34; Ronsard, *Œuvres*, ed. P. Blanchemain, IV, Paris, 1860, p. 205.

The poem loses its colour and meaning, its very precise relevance to its times, when it is read as one item in the literary works of a Renaissance poet. It was originally read by the crowds who examined the decorations for the Charles IX entry, anxiously searching for hopeful signs of the times. They read it as inscribed on the tablet on the Castor and Pollux arch.

The Imperial Theme at the Queen's Entry

When the King's entry was over, no one thought that it would be closely followed by the Queen's entry, for it was believed that the Queen was pregnant and that her entry was put off for another year. This rumour was current until 11 March, when the city authorities were informed by the Queen Mother that the new Queen would enter on 29 March. This threw everyone into a turmoil. The demolition of the decorations for the King's entry, which had begun, was stopped and frantic efforts were made to re-arrange or alter them in accordance with the Queen Mother's instructions that nothing must be the same as at the King's entry. So far as was possible this was done, though the city authorities lament that, owing to the hurry their designs could not be executed as they would have wished.[1]

The most important changes were made at the Francus and Pharamond arch, where Francus and Pharamond were replaced by Pepin and Charlemagne. Bouquet explains that Charlemagne, through Clovis, was the descendant of Pharamond, that his empire included both France and Germany, that the present union of Charles and Elizabeth is a prognostic of the restoration of a universal empire which will subdue even Asia and will plant its banners on the whole of the universe. The wide extension of the imperial theme is the note struck by the Queen's entry; all the modifications of the King's entry programme tend in this direction. Castor and Pollux were replaced by Europa and the Bull to signify that, as Jupiter ravished Europe, so the Dauphin who will be born of this marriage, through which Europe is joined, will ravish Asia and the rest of the world and become the monarch of the universe.[2]

The expansion of French monarchy symbolism into an imperial symbolism of such vast pretensions is no doubt accounted for by the fact that the French King had married the Emperor's daughter. Yet the imperialist symbolism of this entry, with its emphasis on expansion of empire to the east, reveals an influence of Guillaume Postel whose fantasies about the destiny of French monarchy emphasized the theme of expansion towards the east. The influence of Postel on the imperial propaganda surrounding Charles IX will be suggested again later on.

[1] Bouquet, *op. cit.*, Queen's Entry, pp. 1–4 (a new pagination begins for the Queen's Entry). The details of all the transformations are given in *Régistres*, VI, pp. 251–3.
[2] Bouquet, *op. cit.*, p. 6.

The Imperial Device

At the King's entry, an illusionist perspective was set up, near the Châtelet, so brilliantly painted that it was difficult to believe that this was not a real view of ancient Rome, with colonnades in grey marble, but only 'platte painture'.[1] Beyond the painted marble columns a street scene appeared, continuing the perspective of the columns. The whole was framed by the two pairs of columns in the foreground; the pair on the left exhibited the motto *Pietate et Justitia*; the identical pair on the right showed the words *Felicitas et Abundantia*. The allusion was to the device of Charles IX turned into the device of the Emperor Charles V. The twisted columns of Charles IX's device (Plate 20a) were straightened to make them conform more closely to the famous device of the bride's grandfather. The words Felicity and Abundance announce the happiness and prosperity to be introduced in this new golden age of empire.

The perspective introduced classical and Roman vistas into the streets of Paris, making a fitting background for the passing of Charles IX as a new Augustus on his entry into his city of Paris or New Troy.

The imperial device was the theme of the present[2] given to the King by the city (Plate 20b) on the day after his entry, in accordance with tradition. Made of silver gilt by Jean Regnard 'maître orfèvre', the present showed Charles riding on the two columns of the device. He rides as emperor, in the typical Marcus Aurelius pose (Plate 1) and a crown is held over his head, rather precariously, by an imperial eagle. Below him, in a chariot, rides the Queen Mother as Cybele, gazing up adoringly at her imperial son, and accompanied by her other children, also in mythological rôles. Beside the chariot walk four monarchs of the name of Charles, two emperors and two kings of France.

The present summed up in an all-inclusive statement the theme of the entries. It was indeed an imperial theme, blended with the peace theme of the ending of the wars of religion. Whatever the various influences at work may have been, it is clear that the purpose of all this propaganda was to build up the Idea of the French Monarchy, now that the King had come of age, now that the weakening wars of religion were over, now that the Idea had received a fresh infusion of the Imperial Idea through the marriage.

The Entry and Baïf's Academy of Poetry and Music

Royal entries were governed by traditions which hardly changed through the centuries. The decorations were always put up at the same points in

---

[1] *Ibid.*, p. 31 (King's Entry).

[2] Bouquet, *op. cit.*, pp. 52–3; *Régistres*, VI, p. 244. A version of the present, with twisted columns, had been ready by 1567; Regnard was ordered to straighten the columns in the version which was actually presented (*Régistres*, VI, pp. 197, 244).

Paris along the same route. On the day of the entry, the monarch took up a position outside the Porte Saint-Denis, and thither there went out, to greet him and to offer him the loyalty of the city, a cortège which was always made up of the same elements in the same order, the mayor and aldermen, representatives of the university, of the city, and so on. There were no deviations from these usual customs at the entry of Charles IX, and, also as usual, the entry was enlivened with music.

Bouquet says that Charles took great pleasure in the triumphal arches and other decorations and also in the 'diverses instruments de musique' which sounded as he passed.[1] The accounts speak of making 'planches' at the arch at the Porte aux Peintres 'servant aux joueurs d'instruments'.[2] The same source records payments to hautbois players for their performance at this arch on the day of the King's entry.[3] And the same manuscript mentions payments to Noel Durand and to Jacques Hemon, 'maîtres joueurs d'instruments à Paris' for their performances at the Queen's entry and at the banquet given to her by the city.[4]

A minor poet who had been present at the entries seems to associate the vision of the street decorations with the sound of voices rising from them:[5]

> Quelles superbes tours, colosses & statues,
> Quels grands pegmes aislez se voyant par les rues
> Entez dedans les cieux:
> Iò, quelz ieux publics! quelles voix eclatantes
> Par les theatres haults!

One may perhaps hazard a surmise that Jean-Antoine de Baïf's Academy of Poetry and Music,[6] founded in the preceding year under the patronage of Charles IX, might have contributed something towards the musical side of the entries, which Baïf's colleagues of the Pléiade, Ronsard and Dorat, had done so much to design. There are verses by Baïf in Bouquet's account of the entries,[7] and there are other poems scattered through Baïf's works referring to these occasions. One is a 'Presage Hieroglife' of the golden age of peace which Charles as Augustus will usher in.[8] Another promises that peace and the healing of all discord will come with the marriage of Charles and Elizabeth, ending with the words:[9]

> Chantâmes cet accord, qui le trouble acoysa:
> Soit le lien durable, & la Paix eternelle.

This word 'acoyser' (to calm, tranquillize) is used, in the Statutes of Baïf's

[1] Bouquet, *op. cit.*, p. 49.   [2] 'Compte particulier', fol. 24.
[3] *Ibid.*, fol. 84.   [4] *Ibid.*, fol. 127.
[5] J. Prevosteau, *Entrée de Charles IX à Paris*, Paris, 1571, reprinted Paris, 1858, p. 19.
[6] *French Academies*, Ch. II, III, and *passim*.   [7] Bouquet, *op. cit.*, pp. 50–1.
[8] J. A. de Baïf, *Evvres en rime*, ed. Marty-Laveaux, Paris, 1881–90, IV, pp. 342–3.
[9] *Ibid.*, p. 393.

Academy, of the 'effects' which he believed that his 'measured poetry and music' was capable of producing.[1] The poem would have been a very suitable one for a choir, placed at one of the decorated points, to sing as the royal patron of the Academy passed on his entry, surrounded by symbols of the coming Augustan age of eternal peace.

Baïf's Academy of Poetry and Music belonged very much to the peace movement encouraged by the Treaty of Saint-Germain. It was founded in 1570, the year of the peace; Charles IX was its protector. Its aim of measuring together poetry and music after what was believed to be the manner of the ancients was not only aesthetic in purpose. Baïf and his poets and musicians hoped to recover the 'effects' of ancient music, as recounted in the stories about Orpheus, Amphion, and other musical heroes of antiquity. And the 'effects' were to be used towards tranquillizing religious passions. Catholic and Protestant musicians worked together in the Academy, providing musical settings, not only for 'profane' songs but also for the songs of David, the Psalms, hoping in this way to help towards that concord and harmony, that peace from religious wars, which the Peace of Saint-Germain, followed by the imperial wedding, had seemed to promise.

Baïf was one of the seven poets who formed the Pléiade; his Academy was the latest expression of the whole 'Pléiadist' movement of 'politique' royalism. Though there is no factual evidence that the new 'measured poetry and music' was actually used at the entries, the influence of Baïf would have been at one with the influence of Ronsard in propagating the meaning of the imperial wedding of their hero, the *Rex Christianissimus* as fraught with deep significance for France and for the world.

Bacchus and the Imperial Theme; Jean Dorat's Programme on the Marriage of Cadmus and Harmonia

The programme designed by Ronsard and Dorat for the entries was a public programme, intended to be exhibited publicly to the people in the streets. The theme, the Trojan-Imperial descent of the Kings of France, was an ancient and well-worn theme, thoroughly familiar in the traditional royal propaganda. The city fathers did not want the programme to be startlingly original; they wanted it to be on the same lines as the entry of Henri II in 1549, which it did, in fact, frequently echo. The presentation of Catherine de' Medici and her children in mythological rôles – Artemisia, Juno, Castor and Pollux, and so on – was a tradition which had been carefully built up by the poets as royalist propagandists. The peace theme of the programme was also expressed in traditional symbolism; similar symbols had been promulgated after every cessation of the religious wars. The Renaissance public was able to read off symbolism of this kind through its long training

[1] *French Academies*, p. 393.

in public shows. The Renaissance scholar, with Alciati's emblems, Valeriano's hieroglyphics, and the other usual handbooks of symbolism on his shelves, would not have found anything very novel or surprising in the programme of the entries, though the traditional symbols were skilfully adapted to the present occasion by the highly trained poets of the Pléiade. There was, however, a strain of wild exaggeration in the imperialist symbolism, particularly at the Queen's entry, which struck a note unusual in a conventional French royal entry, but which was still more distinctly evoked in the programme for a sequence of paintings in honour of the King and Queen, designed by Jean Dorat.

For as well as the public programme in the streets, mainly designed by Ronsard, there was a private programme, devised entirely by Jean Dorat for the élite, painted by Niccolo dell'Abate and his son, Camillo, and first revealed to a very select court gathering on the occasion of the banquet offered to the Queen by the city, which was held in the Palais Episcopal on 30 March, the day after her entry. This programme was of astonishing originality and interest; it expressed the imperial theme in terms of Bacchus, the world-conquering god of the East, and with a mystic enthusiasm quite out of the usual key of normal royalist propaganda.

Bouquet tells us that when the guests arrived for the banquet they began to gaze at the pictures. There were nineteen pictures running as a frieze round the walls and five pictures on the ceiling. They displayed a very fine history or programme such as had never before been seen, says Bouquet, adding that it was taken from the book of the Greek poet, Nonnos.[1]

Unfortunately we cannot see these pictures. They were painted for the occasion, possibly not actually on the walls and ceiling but on canvasses which may quite soon have disappeared in the disastrous confusions of the years ahead. But we know quite a lot about these invisible pictures; we know who designed them, who painted them, and, roughly, what their subjects were.

In a contract with the city of 8 January 1571,[2] Niccolo dell'Abate and Camillo, his son, engaged to paint the pictures for the great hall of the Palais Episcopal in accordance with the directions to be given to them ('telles que le devis leur sera baillé'). On 22 March they were paid for this work.[3] It is thus certain that Niccolo and Camillo dell'Abate painted the pictures.

On 5th April the city paid Jean Dorat for the inventions and poems furnished by him for the Queen's entry 'and also for the translation and allegory which he made of the history of Tifre invented by him in 24 pictures for the frieze of the hall of the Palais Episcopal'.[4] 'Tifre' refers to

---

[1] Bouquet, op. cit., pp. 52-3.   [2] Régistres, VI, pp. 247-8.
[3] 'Compte particulier', fol. 106-7.
[4] 'A. M. Jean Dorat poete du Roy la somme de cinquante-quatre liures tournois . . . pour les Inuentions carmes Latins et fictions poetiques par luy faictes pour lentree de la Royne. Aussi pour la traduction et allegorie quil a faict de lhistoire de Tifre par luy inuentee en xxiiii tableaux pour la frize de la salle de leuesche [l'Evêche?]', 'Compte particulier', fol. 107 verso.

Typhoeus, or Typhon, the giant who plays a large part in Nonnos's poem. It is thus certain that it was Dorat who devised the programme for these pictures, based on Nonnos.

Nonnos was an Alexandrian poet of the fifth century A.D.,[1] author of a very long poem, the *Dionysiaca*, which tells the history of Bacchus. When Nonnos wrote his poem, the library of Alexandria was still in existence and many Greek authors, now lost, were accessible to him. It is understandable that this confused but rich poem, impregnated with the astrology and occultism of its Alexandrian milieu, would have had a strong attraction for Dorat, whose Greek erudition was infused with the spirit of Alexandria.

In the fifteenth century, a manuscript of the *Dionysiaca* reached Italy from Byzantium and was placed in the library of the Medici at Florence, but the text was not printed in Italy. It remained unpublished until a copy, bought in Italy by Johannes Sambucus, was published at Antwerp by Plantin in 1569. Dorat thus drew his programme from a very obscure Greek work, the *editio princeps* of which had only just been published. It was thus with justifiable complaisance that Bouquet announced that the pictures in the Palais Episcopal contained a history 'non auparavant veue ne mise en lumière'. Sambucus was historiographer to the Emperor Maximilian II, in honour of whose daughter, Elizabeth of Austria, the banquet was held. The choice of this author for the cycle might therefore have been an indirect compliment to the scholarly tastes of the bride's father. Dorat's interest in the poem dated, however, from before the first edition of it; he knew of the Latin translation of it which his friend Charles Utenhovius, a savant in the circle of Sambucus, was preparing.[2]

This newly discovered poem might also have seemed suitable as an allegory of the new hopes of religious harmony for another reason. The hero of the earlier part of the poem is Cadmus, the ancestor of Bacchus. Cadmus was one of the great examples of music in all its aspects, practical, philosophical, mystical; he was the 'saviour of the harmony of the world'. In a long passage on the art of Cadmus,[3] Nonnos describes how Cadmus had discovered the secrets of language and taught the Greeks

> the organization of meaning and sound, which he accorded together
> and of which he regulated the connections and the intimate harmony
> by placing vowels and consonants in their order. . . . It was he who
> first intoned the magical and inspired hymn which is sung in a
> mysterious voice.

In short, the Cadmus of Nonnos is a hero who thoroughly understood 'the music of the ancients'; it was through the effects of his music that he

---

[1] See Nonnos, *Dionysiaca*, preface to the edition in the Loeb Classical Library, 1940.
[2] P. de Nolhac, *Ronsard et l'Humanisme*, Paris, 1921, p. 106. [3] *Dionysiaca*, IV, 259–73.

conquered the giant, and his history is directly connected with that of another musical hero, Amphion, who built the walls of Thebes with music.

Cadmus married Harmonia, and in Dorat's programme this marriage stands, of course, for the marriage of Charles IX and Elizabeth of Austria. Thus the whole theme could connect with Charles as the patron of the Academy of Poetry and Music, founded to recover the music of the ancients and its effects, an effort now consecrated and enhanced by the marriage of Cadmus-Charles to Elizabeth-Harmonia.

Though we cannot see the pictures in the Palais Episcopal, their subjects can be roughly reconstructed. Bouquet quotes twenty-four Latin couplets by Dorat which were inscribed on the pictures as titles.[1] It is possible to trace the passages in Nonnos's poem to which these couplets refer. Though one cannot be absolutely precise as to what the pictures showed, the couplets tell us enough to enable the story depicted by the cycle to be reconstructed in outline.

The couplets for the nineteen pictures of the walls in the Palais Episcopal indicate that the story which they told was roughly as follows.

Whilst Jupiter is reposing with a nymph, the giant Typhon seizes his thunderbolts and begins to attack the heavens.[2] Jupiter arranges with Cadmus that the latter shall disguise himself as a shepherd and enchant Typhon with his melody, for Cadmus is very wise in music and magic.[3] The giant succumbs to the enchantment, and whilst he is asleep Jupiter regains the thunderbolts.[4] The giant awakes, furious, assembles his brother giants, and war between gods and giants ensues.[5] Victorious Jupiter buries the giant, and the gods organize a great triumph in heaven.[6] Jupiter promises Cadmus that Harmonia shall be his bride as a reward for his services.[7] Cadmus sails to Thrace and makes his way to the magnificent palace where Harmonia lives.[8] Harmonia is persuaded by divine intervention to accept him as her husband.[9] Their glorious wedding festival is attended by all the gods.[10]

This sequence gave Dell'Abate and his son plenty of scope for exercising their gifts for romantic landscape. And the guests at the banquet noted, after gazing at the pictures, that the story which they told was 'apropos'.

For the five pictures of the ceiling, Dorat was conditioned by the need to concentrate on the emblem of Paris and of France, the Ship; he also tried to make the pictures work as an allusion to the four estates of the realm living in harmony under the monarch. And he had to make the five central pictures depend on the pictures of the frieze and the story from Nonnos

---

[1] Bouquet, op. cit., pp. 22–3. These couplets are examined in detail and related to the passages in the Dionysiaca to which they refer in the appendix to my introduction to the facsimile reprint of Bouquet's Recueil to be published by Theatrum Orbis Terrarum.

[2] Dionysiaca, I, 145–54, 163 ff.   [3] Ibid., 363–407.   [4] Ibid., I, 409 ff.

[5] Ibid., II, 20 ff., 170 ff., 356 ff.   [6] Ibid., II, 626 ff., 699 ff.   [7] Ibid., III, 16 ff.

[8] Ibid., III, 124–79.   [9] Ibid., I, 181.   [10] Ibid., IV, 207–9.

which they told. In the large central picture of the ceiling, Cadmus and Harmonia were shown sailing in a ship. This ship was the Ship of France, now brought into peace and harmony. Four other ships in the four corners of the ceiling contained the four daughters of Cadmus and Harmonia, with their sons. Wild stories of religious frenzy are associated by Nonnos with these four women. By a remarkable *tour de force*, Dorat contrived to make them symbolize Religion, Justice, Nobility, and Merchandise, or the four estates of the realm.[1]

One of the four daughters was Semele, whose son was Bacchus. The main subject of Nonnos's poem is the recounting of the victories of Bacchus through which he subdued the East and became a universal world ruler. Bacchus might symbolize the expected Dauphin, to be born of Charles and Elizabeth, whose universal empire, western and eastern, is prophesied on one of the arches of the Queen's entry.

The Dionysiac enthusiasm, the prophetic hints of extension of empire to the East, which the Peace and Empire themes take on in Dorat's Nonnos programme, were also expressed at the banquet in the perishable medium of sugar.

The confectionery served at the banquet was designed by Dorat and executed by the confectioner under the supervision of Pilon.[2] It was an old tradition to present serious allegories in 'sucreries' at state banquets; in the series of sugar pieces described by Bouquet, the King was in the rôle of Perseus and the Queen was Minerva. The last of these symbols in sugar was a ship coming from the East which submitted itself to Perseus and Minerva to show that Asia would one day submit itself to them, or to their descendants, in accordance with prophecies which foretell that of the union of French and German blood will be born a prince who will dominate the world.

The prophetic note, and the insistence that the future French world ruler will dominate both East and West, strongly suggest an influence of Guillaume Postel on this mystical French imperialism. Postel, in his theories on French monarchy and on the destinies of the *Rex Christianissimus*, envisaged the movement of the centre of world government from West to East, from Rome to Jerusalem, whence the future French world ruler would dominate the world, effect a general reformation, and bring in the earthly Paradise.[3]

---

[1] For detailed analysis of the ships on the ceiling, see appendix to my introduction to the reprint of Bouquet's *Recueil*.

At the entry of Henri II, that king was presented as the Gallic Hercules drawing the four estates of the realm after him on the chains of his eloquence. It would appear that the four ships at the corners of the ceiling were attached by chains to the central Cadmus-Harmoniaship.

[2] The 'Sucreries' are described by Bouquet, *op. cit.*, pp. 24-6. The 'Compte particulier' gives the devis or specifications for them (folio 124-6) and notes (fol. 88 *verso*) that Dorat was paid for the 'ordonnance des six figures de sucre' made for 'la collation de la Royne'.

[3] W. J. Bouwsma, *Concordia Mundi: The Career and Thought of Guillaume Postel*, Harvard, 1957, pp. 216 ff. Postel was concerned with reconciling the claims to world leadership of the French King and the Emperor.

Postel's theories were a continuation of the medieval theory of French imperialism expounded by Pierre Dubois who had also envisaged the transfer of the seat of empire to Jerusalem. With Postel, the Cabalist, these views were expanded with enthusiasm and he had urged them on French monarchs.[1] In latter years, he had been living in semi-confinement, for his sanity was doubted, yet his influence was considerable.[2]

> Learned men came to see him, and he would sit with them, his white beard falling to his waist and his eyes shining, discoursing on strange lands and peoples and telling once again of his hopes for the world. Charles IX would listen to him, and referred to him affectionately as 'his philosopher'.

When seen in the perspective of the traditional rôle of French monarchy, the astonishing imperialist propaganda of the Charles IX entry falls into place as an effort to revive the position of the French monarch, the position which had been outlined by Dubois in the Middle Ages and immensely re-emphasized by Postel in the sixteenth century, the position which gave him a claim, equal or superior to that of the Emperor, to world leadership in both East and West.

There is a painting by Antoine Caron (Plate 21) which it is instructive to look at after this analysis of the themes of the Charles IX entry. It shows a city en fête, decorated with great temporary structures such as were erected for entries and festivals. The dominant structure shows two great columns, surmounted by a crown. Perched on the festoon which links them is an imperial eagle, and the motto Pietas Augusti hangs from the festoon. This must surely be a version of the imperial device of Charles IX. Charles IX himself, as Augustus, is kneeling to the Tyburtine Sybil who points to the skies, where a vision of the Virgin and Child announces a tremendous religious destiny awaiting this king-emperor.

Antoine Caron was a disciple of Niccolo dell'Abate, like him employed on work for entries and festivals. He did some work for the Charles IX entry[3] and would certainly have been very familiar with its themes. The imperial device, ubiquitous at the entry, is placed in the Caron picture on a base to emphasize its dominating importance in this festival scene, and the two columns have been strangely transformed into twisted columns decorated with vine tendrils bearing grapes.

We have seen that Charles IX's device was capable of new formulations and adaptations. Originally in the form of twisted columns (Plate 20a) the columns of the device were straightened at his entry (Plate 20b) to make them

---

[1] Postel urged his views on French monarchy on François Ier, Charles IX, and Henri III; see F. Secret, 'De quelques courants prophétiques et religieux sous le règne de Henri III', Revue de l'histoire des religions, 171-2 (1967), pp. 1 ff.
[2] Bouwsma, op. cit., p. 26.   [3] See below, p. 224, note 2.

conform more closely to the device of the Emperor Charles V. And here the columns are altered again, twisted, and enriched with a pattern of growing vines. There can be no doubt that the allusion is to the Temple at Jerusalem, the columns of which were represented as twisted and vine-encrusted. The French artist could have seen the Temple columns so represented in French artistic tradition, notably in the wonderful representations of the Temple in Jean Fouquet's *Antiquités Judaiques*. Fouquet had seen in Rome the *Columnae Vitineae* (the Vine Columns) which were supposed to have come from the Temple of Solomon and which afterwards disappeared.[1] Once one sees the allusion to the columns of the Temple at Jerusalem in Caron's version of Charles IX's device, one understands that the *Rex Christianissimus* is being promised a universal empire, based on the Holy Land, as in the prophecies of Guillaume Postel.

Simon Bouquet's account of the entries of Charles IX and his Queen contains at the end a long poem by Etienne Pasquier on the Peace of Saint-Germain, full of admiration for the generosity of that treaty and arguing passionately that religious differences cannot and must not be solved by violent methods, which are both unchristian and futile. It has been proved, says Pasquier, both in France and in Germany, that wars and tyrannical repression do not solve these problems; neither side benefits from them and their only result is the discrediting of Christianity. The publication of this poem with Bouquet's account of the Charles IX entries shows that the city took this view of the meaning of the symbolism of the entries with its insistence on peace, union, charity, and concord. It is strangely ironical that Pasquier's poem should have been published, attached to Bouquet's account, in 1572, the very year in which the next series of court festivals were interrupted by the Massacre of St Bartholomew's Night.

When a match was arranged between Henry of Navarre, the leader of the French Protestants, and Marguerite de Valois, daughter of Catherine de' Medici and sister of Charles IX, this move naturally looked like another step towards religious toleration, or towards the solution of religious differences by peaceful means. The marriage of the King to the daughter of a tolerant Emperor was to be succeeded by a yet more significant step, the marriage of a Protestant to a Catholic within the royal circle. So this

[1] See Trenchard Cox, *Jehan Foucquet*, London, 1931, p. 121, and Plates XLVIII, XLIX, showing the *Columnae Vitineae* in the Temple in two of the illustrations in Fouquet's *Antiquités Judaiques*. The Temple in the 'Marriage of the Virgin' in Fouquet's *Livre d'Heures d'Etienne Chevalier* (reproduced in H. Martin, *Les Foucquet de Chantilly*, Paris, 1926, p. 41) also has the twisted vine columns.

On Bernini's use of the vine columns, see Irving Lavin, *Bernini and the Crossing of St Peter's*, New York, 1968, pp. 14 ff. There was an association between the vines on the columns and the Sacrament. The vine columns appear in the cycle by Rubens in honour of James I (the 'British Solomon') in the Banqueting House at Whitehall.

marriage looked to the world, and in August 1572, the French Protestants and their leaders came to Paris to join in the festivities for this wedding. And to Paris, too, came an embassy from England to confer the Order of the Garter on Charles IX. Amongst those in the train of this embassy was Philip Sidney. All the 'politiques' in Europe were either in Paris for that wedding or were watching it from afar.

All the more terrible was the fall from these heights of hope for Europe into despair. The attack on Coligny interrupted the wedding festivals; fear, gloom, and suspicion enveloped Paris; and then the Massacre broke.

The old sensationalist approach to the Massacre of St Bartholomew is gradually giving way to more critical views in which it is seen that the attack on Coligny was the crucial issue, for Coligny and his Huguenots were about to join forces with Louis of Nassau in an attempted invasion of the Netherlands to rescue them from the Spanish tyranny.[1] The side which benefited from the Massacre was the Spanish side, for it destroyed Louis of Nassau's projected move, in which Charles IX was to some extent interested. This is the true background to the Massacre, one of the chief casualties of which was its destruction of the Idea of the French Monarchy as a liberal force to which opponents of Spanish tyranny and intolerance might rally. By a strange injustice of history, Catherine de' Medici, whose patient Erasmianism had built up over the years the climate of opinion which made possible the tolerant Treaty of Saint-Germain, became the ogress on whom responsibility for the Massacre was fastened.

Much still remains mysterious about this immensely important event in European history, and all possible lines of evidence about it should be examined. The symbolism of the Charles IX entry is important for this problem, indicating, as it does, the state of mind of the French court in the year before the Massacre. How should one interpret the Idea of the French Monarchy? Was it a liberal force making for toleration, as Pasquier thought, and encouraging harmony, as Baïf and the poets of the Pléiade seem to have thought? Or could it at times revert to methods of elimination, to the 'liquidation' of religious dissidents in a manner which made it no alternative for liberals to the tyranny of the Spanish monarchy? Though the Massacre was almost certainly the work of enemies of the monarchy, not of its friends, its shadow could not easily be dispelled.

Though there is much in this dark mystery which still remains unsolved, it is now becoming clear that the real issue was the threatening power of Philip of Spain. It was that power which benefited from the Massacre, for the death of Coligny and his followers prevented the movement of Louis

---

[1] See Yates, *The Valois Tapestries*, pp. 51 ff., 64 ff., 75 ff.; N. M. Sutherland, *The Massacre of St Bartholomew and the European Conflict 1559–1572*, London, 1973; this book effectively takes the Massacre out of the short-sighted approach to it, and shows it as one episode of a wider European struggle against the domination of Spain.

of Nassau for the liberation of the Netherlands from the terrible tyranny of Alva, and set back all the plans of William of Orange. And it also crushed, and set back for years, the emergence of French monarchy into its former, and future, position of leadership in Europe. France slipped back into the old misery of the religious wars, into the old uncertainties under a weak monarchy beset by dangerous enemies bent on its destruction.

THE MAGNIFICENCES FOR THE MARRIAGE OF THE DUC DE JOYEUSE, PARIS, 1581

In the few years of peace preceding the outbreak, in 1585, of the last and most disastrous of the wars of religion, a great outburst of poetry and music was to be heard in Paris. At court, in 1581, all the resources of poets, artists, musicians, and mechanics were expended on the splendid entertainments with which the King, Henri III, honoured the marriage of his favourite, Duc Anne de Joyeuse, to the Queen's half-sister, Marie de Lorraine. The 'Magnificences' for the Joyeuse wedding lasted for about a fortnight, and during this time a different entertainment was given nearly every day. One of these entertainments, the *Ballet comique de la reine*, is well known because a printed edition of it was published in 1582.[1] It is less well known that this performance was one of a series, the other items in which can be reconstructed, to some extent, from various sources. Neither the politico-religious intention of these festivals nor their artistic importance can be fully realized through study of the *Ballet comique* alone which is, in some ways, not quite characteristic of the series as a whole, though closely linked with it in imagery and intention. It is the purpose of the present essay to study the Joyeuse Magnificences as a whole, as far as possible in all their aspects, but with particular attention to their reflection of the themes and images of French monarchy. In these dark years of the century which lead up to its darkest years, the final cataclysm of the wars of the League which was for a time to blot out the monarchy in France, the court of the Valois is making a last effort to oppose the oncoming storm with the weapons of art.

Festivals of this type are ultimately based on the exercises of chivalry: tournaments, combats on foot, running at the ring, and so on. French and Burgundian chivalry had been noted throughout the Middle Ages for the exquisite splendour of its trappings, and in the chivalric Magnificences of the Valois court those traditions were continued and expanded with the addition of all the wealth of Renaissance learning in iconography and symbolism, and the refined artistry which made of this court one of the last great expressions of the Renaissance spirit. In this atmosphere, the exercises of chivalry expanded into exercises in poetic declamation, with musical accompaniment, carefully staged and costumed. These little dramas,

---

[1] Baitasar de Beaujoyeulx, *Balet comique de la Royne, faict aux nopces de Monsieur le Duc de Joyeuse*, Paris, 1582; see H. Prunières, *Le ballet de cour en France*, 1914, pp. 82 ff., F. Yates, *The French Academies of the Sixteenth Century*, Warburg Institute, 1947, Kraus reprint, 1967, pp. 236 ff. and *The Valois Tapestries*, Warburg Institute, 1959, pp. 8–10, 82–8, etc.; Margaret McGowan, *Le ballett de cour en France*, Paris, 1963, pp. 42 ff. The *Ballet comique* is to be reprinted in facsimile in the series 'Renaissance Triumphs and Magnificences'. ed. M. McGowan, Theatrum Orbis Terrarum Ltd, Amsterdam (forthcoming).

interspersed among the splendours of highly theatrical jousting and other sports, were the genesis of a new art form, the French *ballet de cour*, one of the ancestors of that art form so characteristic of Europe, opera.

The Joyeuse Magnificences were the culmination, the quintessence, of a series of entertainments of this type as established at the Valois court many years previously and as perfected throughout the sixteenth century.[1] At Bayonne in 1565, a great series of Magnificences had been held to grace the meeting of Catherine de' Medici with her daughter, the wife of Philip II of Spain. The series was based on chivalric exercises in fancy dress, jousts, foot combats, running at the ring and so on, but included one of the earliest examples of a *ballet de cour*. Such a series was repeated, with variations, throughout the regency of Catherine de' Medici, who was herself an excellent producer. She no doubt deeply enjoyed expressing in this way the artistic gifts which were her Medici inheritance, and she also used these festivals with political purpose. She hoped to draw together the opposite religious parties in common loyalty to the monarchy, through encouraging Catholics and Protestants to take part together in the festivals. The central figure in these highly dramatized chivalric events was always the king, and thus the function of chivalry as an appanage of monarchy survived in them.

There is a series of drawings by Antoine Caron illustrating typical episodes of a series of Magnificences at the French court. The series belongs to the reign of Charles IX and not to that of Henri III, but one of them is reproduced here (Plate 22a) to give an idea of what such scenes were like. The sport in progress is a running at the quintain, taking place, probably, in the courtyard of the Louvre, and watched by the ladies of the court. Several of the episodes in the Joyeuse Magnificences took place in the court-yard of the Louvre and no doubt resembled pretty closely the scene depicted in this stylized drawing by Antoine Caron. Moreover, this drawing formed the basis for one of the Valois Tapestries (Plate 22b) in which Henri III stands in the foreground of the running at the quintain, attired in masquerade costume probably typical of costumes at the Joyeuse Magnificences, though these tapestries were not made in France but in the Netherlands and may not always reproduce quite accurately the French styles. Still, the object of the tapestry is obviously to depict a festival in the reign of Henri III, very probably one of the Joyeuse Magnificences, and it gives a striking impression of the splendour, the pomp, the high artistic quality of the royal chivalrous sports at the Valois court.[2]

In 1581, the problem facing Henri III, now king of France, was more complicated than that of conciliating Huguenots, as in the days of his late brother, Charles IX. The chief danger to French monarchy now was the

[1] *Valois Tapestries*, pp. 53 ff.
[2] The whole set of the Caron drawings of French court festivals, and the tapestries based on them, are reproduced in *Valois Tapestries*.

growth of the Catholic League, the party purporting to represent an extreme Counter-Reformation Catholicism, which would be made use of by Hispano-Papalism, and its representative, Philip II of Spain, to foment sedition against Henri III. This extreme development, which would drive Henri from his throne, was as yet in the future. In the present, Henri, who was himself strongly affected by Counter-Reformation influences, seemed to favour the Catholic League, the two most powerful members of which, in France, were the Duc and the Cardinal de Guise, supported by their relatives of the House of Lorraine. Henri had married a member of this house. His Queen, Louise de Lorraine, was the queen who took part in the *Ballet comique de la reine*. And the king would appear to be strengthening still further his sympathetic connections with this house by celebrating with such infinite pomp and circumstance the wedding of his favourite, the Duc de Joyeuse, to the Queen's half-sister, Marie de Lorraine, also a relative of the Guises. Thus the Joyeuse festivals would appear to be an occasion on which French monarchy is conciliating, drawing towards itself, the Guises and the nascent party of the Catholic League. Yet the tensions were already apparent through which the Guises would eventually become the heads of the militant League movement which in a few years' time would almost succeed in obliterating the French monarchy, as part of a general movement towards the Spanish hegemony of Europe.

The artistic team employed by the French court for the Joyeuse Magnificences was the same, or very nearly the same, as the one which we saw working for the Charles IX entry, though with a few changes. Niccolo dell'Abate was dead; the dominant artist at the Joyeuse Magnificences was his disciple, Antoine Caron. We know from a poem by Jean Dorat[1] that Caron worked on the decorations for the Joyeuse festivals, assisted by Germain Pilon. It would appear from this poem that Dorat was working for these festivals in his usual capacity of humanist designer of the works to be executed by the artists. Most of the artistic work for the Joyeuse Magnificences has not survived, nor do we have anything like the detailed programes for it such as exist for the entry.

The poetic team was even closer in its membership to the traditional one. The poets of the Pléiade, though now getting on in years, all loyally co-operated in using their talents to support this brilliant court occasion. Ronsard wrote verses for it; Dorat, as already mentioned, designed for it. One newer and younger member of the group, Philippe Desportes, also contributed verses. And Jean-Antoine de Baïf and his Academy of Poetry and Music were a very strong influence behind the production. Though

[1] Jean Dorat, 'Epithalame, ou Chant Nuptial sur le très-heureux et très-joyeux mariage de Anne Duc de Joyeuse et Marie de Lorraine' in J. Dorat, *Œuvres poétiques*, ed. C. Marty-Laveaux, Paris, 1875, pp. 22–3. There is a Latin version of the poem in Dorat, *Poematia*, Paris, 1586, pp. 251 ff. Cf. *French Academies*, p. 271, and below, pp. 162 ff.

Baïf's Academy and its ideas were briefly touched on in the last essay it will be necessary to give a slightly more extended account of this movement before describing its influence on the Joyeuse Magnificences.

The stories told by classical writers about the effects of music are many and various. The poets speak in their fables of Orpheus who with his music turned men from slaughter and their foul way of life and soothed the animal in them to sleep. Or of Amphion, whose lyre had power to move the rocks and who built the walls of Thebes with music. A more literal story was the one which told how Timotheus excited Alexander so much by his playing that the king bounded to his feet and rushed to get his weapons; whereupon Timotheus, by modulating into another mode, was able to calm by his music the martial frenzy which he had aroused by the same means.

Baïf and his musician friends wished to revive ancient music and its effects, but musical humanism, as such an endeavour is called, was beset with difficulties because hardly any ancient music survives. It is hard to imitate something which is not there. Though much was written in classical sources about the modes of ancient music, so important for the different psychological effects, little was known in practice about them. Undeterred by these difficulties, Baïf and his friends set about creating what they believed to be an ancient music by very exactly measuring the words of a song to the music for it.[1] They believed that the effects depended upon this close measuring of words with music, and on the audibility of the words. Baïf wrote French verses in what he believed to be ancient metres, assigning long and short values to the syllables in the effort to make the verse quantitative rather than accented; these long and short syllables were married very exactly to long and short notes of music. Baïf invented schemes of phonetic spelling in the effort to make his measured verses as exactly matched to the measured music as possible. The philosophical background was the Platonic and Neoplatonic philosophy, with its emphasis on number and harmony as fundamental in the structure of the universe and in the soul of man. The mere name 'Academy' used of Baïf's institution implies Platonism; the union of poetry and music was, in one of its aspects, a symbol of a phase of initiation into higher harmonies. The Academy was encyclopedic in scope, ideally including under music all the arts and sciences. Baïf was a mathematician as well as a poet-musician.

Both Catholic and Protestant musicians wrote music for Baïf's *vers mesurés*; the best musician of the Academy was a Huguenot, Claude Le Jeune. The Academy of Poetry and Music, beyond, or as well as, its purely

---

[1] D. P. Walker, 'Musical humanism in the 16th and early 17th centuries', *Music Review*, II(1), pp. 1 ff.; II (2), pp. 111 ff.; II (3), pp. 220 ff.; II (4), pp. 288 ff.; III(1), pp. 55 ff.; Yates, *French Academies*, pp. 36 ff.

aesthetic aims, had the aim of fostering the *détente* of religious passions by encouraging Huguenots and Catholics to make music together in the Academy. Sacred music was cultivated as well as the measured songs, and the psalms in French *vers mesurés* were set to measured music by Catholic and Protestant musicians. For the sacred counterpart of Orpheus was David, calming through his psalms the passions of men.

The year after the founding of the Academy, in 1570, the entry of Charles IX into Paris took place, as described in the previous essay. The following year saw the Navarre-Valois wedding and the Massacre of St Bartholomew. Wars broke out again, followed by the interval of peace during which the festivals for the Joyeuse wedding took place. And it has been discovered that *vers et musique mesurés*, written by Baïf and Le Jeune in accordance with the purest principles of Baïf's Academy, were used at these festivals, showing that the influence of the Academy was still operative in 1581. Thus, in spite of the terrible interruptions of wars and massacres, and in spite of the fact that Henri III at the time of the Joyeuse festivals appeared to be cultivating the Guise faction and the Catholic extremists, he was yet employing the Huguenot musician of the Academy for his own rôles in the festivals.

Various facts had already seemed to point to participation by Baïf and members of his Academy in work for these festivals. The bridegroom, the Duc de Joyeuse, was a financial supporter of the Academy.[1] That Baïf was paid for his work for the Joyeuse wedding is stated by the diarist, Pierre L'Estoile.[2] Jean Dorat mentions Baïf as having collaborated with other poets in working for it.[3] And in the dedication to Joyeuse of a poem written just after the festivals were over, Baïf speaks as though he had been present at all of them:[4]

> I have only just collected my wits which have been overwhelmed
> amidst the dazzling diversity of so many magnificent theatres,
> spectacles, jousts, masquerades, ballets, pieces of poetry and music,
> paintings, which in this city of Paris have called upon the best masters
> in every art to celebrate your happy marriage.

The words call up the whole series of the Magnificences, the chivalric exercises in fancy costumes with poetic and musical accompaniment, the ballets, the theatres, or temporary erections set up in the courtyard of the Louvre and elsewhere, the paintings with which these were adorned.

And tradition has maintained that Claude Le Jeune composed music for this wedding which actually had 'effects' like those attributed to ancient music. The following is an English translation of the account, published in

---

[1] *French Academies*, pp. 28–30, 141, 237, 260–1.
[2] L'Estoile, *Mémoires-Journaux*, ed. J. Brunet *et al.*, Paris, 1888, II, p. 23.
[3] *Œuvres poétiques.*, p. 22.
[4] J.-A. de Baïf, *Evvres en rime*, ed. C. Marty-Laveaux, Paris, 1881–90, V, p. 5.

1611, through which music by Le Jeune for the Joyeuse wedding became an example of 'effects' of music and a proof that Baïf's Academy had succeeded in its aim of reviving the psychological power of ancient music:[1]

> It was by a Phrygian and a Subphrygian song that Timotheus gave proof of his skill to Alexander. By a Phrygian song, he excited Alexander, who was sitting quietly at table, to rush to take up arms, then, suddenly modulating to a Subphrygian song, he caused him to return to his previous tranquillity. I have sometimes heard it said of Monsieur Claudin Lejeune, who has penetrated much more deeply than any musician of former times into the understanding of the modes of ancient music, that he composed in parts an air for the 'Magnificences' at the wedding of the late Duc de Joyeuse, in the time of Henri III . . . when this air was rehearsed at a private concert, it caused a gentleman who was present to take up arms, swearing loudly that he felt absolutely impelled to rush to fight someone. And when they commenced to sing another air in the Subphrygian mode, he became quite tranquil again. This has been confirmed to me by some of those who were present, so great is the force and the influence on the spirit of the modulation and movement of the music closely conjoined to the voice.

By associating the story about the power of Le Jeune's music with the famous Timotheus and Alexander story, it is implied that Le Jeune, with his deep knowledge of ancient music, had indeed succeeded in producing effects equal to those described in the stories about ancient music.

It is possible to identify the very piece of Baïf–Le Jeune poetry and music which achieved fame for its 'effects'.

There exists a manuscript programme of the various entertainments planned for the Joyeuse wedding festivals which gives brief descriptions of their subjects. This programme is given in full in English translation at the end of this essay.[2] And there exists a volume of pieces of music by Le Jeune with words by Baïf which was published in 1608 as the *Airs* of Claude Le Jeune. In 1951, F. Lesure and D. P. Walker published a new edition of these *Airs*.[3] The availability of the Le Jeune *Airs* in this edition enables one to realize that many of these *Airs* must have been written for the Joyeuse festivals, for the words of some of the songs fit exactly with the themes and settings described in the programme of the festivals. Comparison of the programme with the words in the *Airs* makes it possible to reconstruct the settings in which this music was first performed.

---

[1] Philostrate, *De la vie d'Apollonius Thyanéen*, ed. Blaise de Vigenère, 2nd ed. Artus Thomas, Paris, 1611, I, p. 282; cf. *French Academies*, p. 59.

[2] See below, pp. 169–71.

[3] Claude Le Jeune, *Airs (1608)*, Rome, 1951, vol. I, introduction by F. Lesure and D. P. Walker.

According to the programme, the entertainment planned for the evening of 19 September was a combat on foot between the King and the Dukes of Guise, Mercoeur, and Damville, 'la bande du Roy combattant en la défaveur d'amour'. This was evidently a masquerade combat between the King and three prominent courtiers of a type traditional in these French court festivities. The subject of the mock fight was also a traditional Renaissance theme, the debate 'for and against Love', in which the King's band took the side 'against Love'.[1]

> They will enter on a rock at the base of which Love will be bound,
> beneath the King's feet. The musicians, dressed in some elegant
> antique fashion, as men and women, will sing insults to Love, with
> menacing gestures, as though to shake him, pinch him, bind him, and
> injure him in other ways.

We can easily imagine this entry, on one of those property rocks which must have served again and again in these shows. And it can be shown that the musical accompaniment to the warlike attack on the bound Cupid was actually the piece by Le Jeune which had the 'effects'.

In the Le Jeune *Airs* there is a long piece in four parts beginning 'Arm! arm!', with the sub-title 'La Guerre de Claude Le Jeune'.[2] This significant sub-title already makes one wonder whether this may be the celebrated war-like piece which was rehearsed for an entertainment at the Joyeuse wedding. This supposition becomes a certainty when we find from the words of the song that the 'war' is waged against Love; the terrible combat ends with the conquest of Love, who is made prisoner and insulted by the victors.[3] This corresponds exactly to the directions of the programme, that the musicians must sing insults to love, with menacing gestures. Further the line 'Chevaliers approchez de ce Perron'[4] indicates that the piece was sung at a knightly exercise; and another line specifies that it is 'nostre Roy'[5] who is the leader of the warriors against Love. The programme states that it was 'la bande du Roy' which was to fight 'en défaveur d'amour'.

Thus there can be no doubt that the piece 'La Guerre de Claude Le Jeune' in the *Airs* of 1608 represents (though in a partially altered or revised form so far as Baïf's words are concerned) the *poésie et musique mesurées* composed by Baïf–Le Jeune for the 'bande du Roy' on the occasion described in the programme. And it is possible to point to the exact passage at which the gentleman who heard it at the rehearsal passed from his war-like excitement to a gentler mood. This would be at the moment when the music modulates from the combative mood to the gentle mood of 'Rendez-vous tous mes loyaux pensers doux'.[6] The fame of this piece reached Marin Mersenne, who was told in a letter from a friend who had known Le Jeune that it was with

---

[1] See Programme, below, p. 170.   [2] *Airs (1608)*, no 24, p. 90.   [3] *Ibid.*, p. 114.
[4] *Ibid.*, p. 98.   [5] *Ibid.*, p. 94.   [6] *Ibid.*, pp. 106–8.

'vers français mesurés' such as Baïf had written, 'that he had put a captain in a rage with musical movements joined to the words'.[1]

The other 'bandes' in the combat for and against Love also had verses written for them, no doubt also set to music. The music has not survived but the poetry can in two cases be identified.

A vigorous defence of Love by Ronsard, written, according to its title, for a 'Mascarade pour les nopces de Monseigneur Ann, Duc de Joyeuse', begins thus:[2]

> J'aurois ingrat soldat combatu sous Amour,
> Porté ses estendars, et suivi ses armées,
> Si voyant maintenant ses armes diffamées,
> Et luy fait prisonnier, lie contre un rocher,
> Je ne venois icy ses liens détacher . . .

Obviously this belongs to the scene of the rock, to which Cupid is bound and insulted. Ronsard's defence of the prisoner, bound to a rock, is a reply to the insulting of Love in 'La Guerre de Claude Le Jeune'.

From Desportes's collected works can be culled verses 'Pour la Masquerade des Chevaliers Fidelles aux Nopces de Monsieur Duc de Joyeuse', in which nine knights come to fight in defence of Love:[3]

> Amour est le sujet de leur juste querelle:
> Ils ne sçauroient souffrir que l'audace mortelle
> Le conduise en triomphe à la honte des dieux . . .

This must surely have been written for a 'bande' in the for-and-against-Love controversy.

This whole performance was clearly a musical dramatization of Petrarch's *Trionfi*, with the King's band representing the Triumph of Chastity. The Petrarchan formulae are here being acted out in a chivalrous context which is most closely relevant to the moods and anxieties of the times. It is strange to think that Le Jeune's exercise in rousing and calming the passions by the effects of music took place at an entertainment in which the French King took part together with his enemy, the Duc de Guise, soon to lead the revolt of the League.

There are other pieces in the Le Jeune *Airs* which can certainly be related to the Joyeuse festivals, particularly the very long *Epithalamium*[4] with words

---

[1] Marin Mersenne, *Correspondance*, eds C. de Waard, and R. Pintard, Paris, 1932, I, p. 75.

[2] 'I would be an ungrateful soldier under Love's banners and follower of his armies, if, seeing him now conquered and made prisoner and bound to a rock, I did not come to free him from his chains' (Ronsard, *Œuvres*, ed. I. Silver, Chicago, 1966, V, p. 175).

[3] 'Love is the subject of their just quarrel. They cannot permit that Love should be led in a triumph by mortal audacity, to the shame of the gods' (Desportes, *Œuvres*, ed. A. Michiels, Paris, 1858, p. 461).

[4] See Programme, below, p. 170, note 2.

in *vers mesurés* by Baïf. And it is now possible to reconstruct, from the *Airs* and the programme, what was evidently an event of central importance in the series, the King's entry in a ship to the accompaniment of solemn measured poetry and music promising the blessings of heaven upon French monarchy.

The programme states that the representation decided upon for Sunday, 24 September, was to be a combat between the King and the Dukes of Guise and Mercoeur. The King was to make his entry into the court of the Louvre in the following manner:[1]

> His entry will have the form of a marine triumph, being in a great ship, before which there will be two or three rocks like little floating islands, on which will be Tritons and Sirens playing various instruments and sorts of music, with drums, to excite and accompany the King's triumph.

This scene used properties traditional in French court festivals, the rocks and islands bearing singing tritons and sirens. It belonged into the tradition of Catherine de' Medici's festivals in which she had invoked the deities of nature to shed their blessings on the monarch.[2]

In the *Airs* of Claude Le Jeune we can find the musical accompaniment of this scene in the song 'O Reine d'honneur'[3] sung by marine deities addressing themselves to the Queen and her ladies and written in Baïf's *vers mesurés* most accurately wedded to Le Jeune's music. The words of the song speak of a ship advancing on land, bearing a king, and followed by musical rocks, reflecting precisely the scene of the King's entry described in the programme.

The theme of 'O Reine d'honneur' is that the King in his marine triumph announces peace, happiness, and prosperity for France. One may look upon it as a prophecy, as a prayer, as an incantation. There are four verses, each followed by the same refrain, sung first by five voices and then by seven. The tone of this refrain is most solemn and heavily emphasized. As can be realized from the quotation of the words with their musical accompaniment (shown overleaf), the measured poetry and music here sounds like an incantation; the powerful ancient music is to draw down the influences of fortunate stars on the French monarchy.

The song is in hexameters, and it is unusual amongst those in the Le Jeune volume in having been left unaltered in Baïf's original, unrhymed *vers mesurés*. Those who published the 1608 edition of the *Airs* altered, in most of the songs, Baïf's original text into rhymed verses. (The song 'La Guerre

---

[1] See Programme, below, p. 171.
[2] Compare the sirens and tritons used at Bayone, see *Valois Tapestries*, pp. 56–7 and Plates III X (a).
[3] *Airs, ed. cit.*, pp. 87 ff.

de Claude Le Jeune' was so altered.) Was 'O Reine d'honneur' left unaltered because of some particular importance or significance attached to it? D. P. Walker has pointed out to me that the hexameter is a very unusual metre for *vers mesurés*. The Latin song *'Ut candore micans assurgit Lilium'* in this same volume of 1608 is one of the very few others in hexameters. This

ASTRES HEUREUX TOURNEZ, TOURNEZ CIEUS, TOURNE LE DESTIN.
Turn, O fortunate stars, turn heavens, turn destiny.

Figure 2 Music from Claude Le Jeune, *Airs*, 1608

solemn song on a vision of the Lily of France, the symbol of French monarchy in its holiest aspect, was apparently addressed by Le Jeune to Henri IV early in his reign. Perhaps 'O Reine d'honneur' was also regarded as a grave affirmation in hexameters of the sacred destiny of French monarchy.

The identifications of Le Jeune's music with festivals for the Joyeuse wedding which have here been put forward prove that Baïf's Academy, far from having receded into the background in the reign of Henri III, was still very much to the fore in 1581 and was providing 'ancient music' in large quantities for a significant court occasion. Prunières's impression that Baïf and the Academy were not much patronized by Henri III, and were not much interested in the Joyeuse wedding festivals, was based on the fact that the *Ballet comique de la reine* is not in the pure *musique mesurée*.[1] The printed *Ballet comique* was the only specimen of the Joyeuse festivals that Prunières knew. When it is placed in the sequence of these festivals as a whole it can be seen that it is not characteristic of the festivals as a whole. The King employed the Baïf–Le Jeune combination for his own part in at least two

---

[1] It is above all Augé-Chiquet in his book *Jean-Antoine de Baïf*, 1909, so invaluable to all those interested in Baïf, who gives the impression that Henri III abandoned Baïf's Academy. I disputed this idea in *French Academies* (pp. 27 ff., and *passim*) but I did not then know that Henri employed Baïf–Le Jeune for his own parts in the festivals of 1581. This proves that the Academy was still high in royal favour in the reign of Henri III.

of the entertainments and for the important *Epithalamium*, probably ordered by him, thus giving his own strong royal support to the academic music. The *Ballet comique* was ordered by the Queen, and the musicians and poets she employed – Beaulieu and La Chesnaye – would reflect her taste. Or perhaps it reflected what was available for her to use, after the King had monopolized for his own use the best musician, Le Jeune, and his poetic partner in the *vers et musique mesurés*, Baïf.

That most of the other entertainments in the series had been ordered by the King is stated in the introduction to the printed edition of the *Ballet comique*:[1]

His Majesty ordered . . . many kinds of superb combats . . . both on foot and on horseback, with ballets on foot and on horseback, arranged after the manner of the ancient Greeks and of remote nations; the whole was accompanied by most excellent concerts of music, never before heard.

The exotic character of the festivals was indicated in the costumes; their effort after pseudo-antiquity was expressed in the 'ancient music', in a great outpouring of music 'never before heard', on which the influence of Baïf and his Academy was paramount.

As we think of these attempts at reviving 'ancient music' and its effects through poetic and musical techniques, the question arises as to how far the aims of Baïf and his Academy were affected by that Renaissance climate of thought in which a refined and learned type of magic played an important part. Marsilio Ficino in the fifteenth century had propagated such an outlook in his *De vita coelitus comparanda*, with its precepts on how to 'draw down the life of heaven', or the *spiritus* of the stars, through various techniques, one of which was the kind of musical incantation which he believed to be ancient Greek, or Orphic, in origin.[2] Was there any connection in the minds of the French musical humanists between their methods of recovering the power of ancient music and the theories of Ficino on the incantatory power of what he believed to be 'Orphic singing'?

This problem was examined by D. P. Walker in a paper given at the same colloquium as that to which my contribution on music and poetry at the Joyeuse wedding festivals was addressed.[3] Walker points out that one of the magical techniques expounded by Ficino was that of the 'Orphic singing', the singing to the lyre of songs addressed to favourable astral influences,

[1] *Ballet comique*, p. I.

[2] D. P. Walker, *Spiritual and Demonic Magic from Ficino to Campanella*, Warburg Institute, 1958 (Kraus Reprint, no. 22, 1969), pp. 14 ff.; Yates, *Giordano Bruno and the Hermetic Tradition*, London, 1964, pp. 62 ff.

[3] D. P. Walker, 'Le Chant Orphique de Marsile Ficin', *Musique et Poésie au XVIe Siècle*, ed. Jean Jacquot, Centre National de la Recherche Scientifique, 1954, pp. 17 ff.

which were in effect a species of learned incantations, mentioning the colours, plants, metals and so on of the planet addressed, after the manner of incantatory formulae.

In Ficino's type of Renaissance astral thinking we are in the presence of an attitude which is not the same as astrological determinism. In this way of thinking, man has free-will and power to mitigate the influences of 'unfortunate stars' by cultivating in various ways the influences of 'fortunate' or 'happy' stars. The most harsh and unfortunate of the stars, or rather planets, were believed to be Mars and Saturn, but their influences could be, it was believed, tempered and made productive, rather than destructive, by being combined with the influences of 'fortunate stars' of which the chief were Sol, Jupiter, Venus, and, to a lesser degree, Mercury.

The address to the 'astres heureux' in the song 'O Reine d'honneur' certainly sounds like an incantation, and it is more than probable that the 'happy stars' so addressed are the fortunate planets. That is to say, the techniques of Baïf's 'ancient music' are aiming also at magical and incantatory effects; the object of this powerful poetry and music is to draw down the influences of fortunate stars upon the French king and the French monarchy.

In a Renaissance court, like that of the Valois, a solemn appeal to the 'astres heureux' must surely have been more than a poetic metaphor. One of the strongest influences at the Valois court was precisely that of Ficino, and of the type of revived, late Alexandrian Neoplatonism of which he was the exponent and which had spread all over Europe from the court of the Medici in Florence. Let us remember that the most influential member of the Valois court, the Queen Mother, was herself a Medici. Catherine de' Medici was a devout believer in the occult sciences, employing many Magi, not merely for private interest but in the belief that they could aid her in her political ends. These interests were strongly shared by her son, Henri III. It is difficult to believe that the Queen Mother, and the King himself, when they heard the appeal to the 'astres heureux' in the powerful ancient music at a tourney between the King and Messieurs de Guise would have taken this lightly as nothing but a metaphor and a compliment. They would have understood it for what it was, a most learned incantation, an effort to influence events through the latest magico-scientific techniques, an attempt to avert the influence of dark stars of war and treason, represented by the Guises, soon to be leaders in the revolt of the Catholic League against the monarchy, counteracting those influences by invoking the influences of 'astres heureux' upon the menacing situation.

Another example of how the techniques of Baïf's Academy might be combined with Ficinian magical techniques is the song of which the first line is 'L'un émera le violet'. This is Baïf's phonetic spelling for 'L'un aimera le violet', in English 'One person will love the violet colour'. The song is all about colours, violet, white, black, grey, tan, carnation, and finally, and best of all, the orange colour, the favourite colour of the singer of the song:

> I will praise, I will wear,
> I will love so long as I live, the orange colour.

The orange colour is the most adored amongst all this rainbow choice of colours because it is the colour of the Sun:

> The radiant, all-animating, all vivifying beautiful Sun,
> Approaching the beautiful season,
> Whence comes summer,
> Wears the orange tint.

Other verses name the sun's flower, the heliotrope; the sun's metal, gold; and the golden apples of the Hesperides, or the zodiac.

This song is clearly a solar incantation of the Ficinian type, applying the technique of an incantation, the naming of a colour, a flower, a metal, and so on, associated with the sun through which to attract solar influences. And it is also a song in the strictest measured poetry and music of Baïf's Academy, with words in Baïf's phonetic spelling and music by Le Jeune. It is using 'ancient music' to achieve 'effects' and combining this with magical incantatory methods.

'L'un émera le violet' is not to be found in the Le Jeune *Airs* of 1608 in which we have found so much material connected with the Joyeuse festivals, but in another volume of Baïf–Le Jeune music, *Le Printemps*, published in 1603.[1] I believe, however, that one of the décors described in the programme of the Magnificences is very likely to have been the setting in which this song was first heard.

As the setting for an evening entertainment, the programme describes the following scene, in which twelve or fifteen musicians were to recite the verses which had been given them:[2]

> The twelve torch-bearers will be men and women disguised as trees,
> such as orange-trees, lemon-trees, pomegranate-trees, and others, the
> golden fruits of which will carry lamps and torches.

This evening scene at the Joyeuse wedding festivals, when the musicians recited their verses under the illuminated, golden-fruited trees, would surely have been the perfect setting for the Baïf–Le Jeune song about the sun, with its many-times-repeated protestation of devotion to the orange colour. And the theme of the different colours which the song elaborates reflects an outstanding characteristic of the Joyeuse Magnificences, as described in the

---

[1] Claude Le Jeune, *Le Printemps*, Paris, 1603, reprinted in H. Expert, *Les Maîtres musiciens de la Renaissance Française*, Paris, 1900, part 14, no. XXVII; and in *French Academies* (Kraus Reprint), pp. 342 ff.

[2] See Programme, below, p. 171.

programme, that the participants in these festivals wore different colours, and changed their costumes several times a day to fit the symbolic colours of the entertainments.[1]

One begins to grasp the plan of the Joyeuse Magnificences as a whole. They were one vast moving talisman, formed of figures in different colours moving amongst incantatory scenes designed to draw down favourable influences on the French monarchy, the influences of fortunate stars, the most powerful of which was the sun. It was out of these splendid settings that there poured music which even Pierre L'Estoile, who deplored the mad extravagance of these festivals, could not forbear admiring. 'The greatest excellence of all', says L'Estoile, 'was the music of voices and instruments, the most harmonious and subtle that any man there present had ever heard.'[2]

If we could have the opportunity of wandering through Paris at the time oi the festivals for the Joyeuse wedding, and of seeing the many triumphal arches, arcades, and other temporary erections, decorated with paintings, we might gain visually the impression that the theme of the festivals was the drawing down of fortunate influences on the French monarchy. And to some extent the opportunity of making this tour is given us, though in a rather confused and obscure manner, by Jean Dorat who in his *Epithalame ou Chant Nuptial* describes the festivities which he had had some part in designing.[3] All the poets, he says, are hurrying to play their part, 'Desportes le doux', and 'Baïf le nombreaux', and 'le grave Ronsard'. And he, too, Dorat, must make his contribution. This contribution probably consisted in helping to design the schemes of the visual decorations and of writing the verses to be inscribed under the pictures, on the triumphal arches. We know that this was Dorat's usual rôle in court festivals. It is therefore not surprising that his poem dwells mainly on the wonderful 'arcades', and the 'théâtres pompeux' which are being erected for the occasion.

L'Estoile speaks of the new lists which had been erected in the garden of the Louvre in which, as one of the Magnificences for the wedding, an evening tournament between 'fourteen whites and fourteen yellows' was held by torchlight.[4] This is probably the event alluded to in the programme as the *carrousel* in the courtyard of the Louvre planned for Saturday evening, between a band dressed in carnation and white and another in pale yellow and white.[5] Dorat describes the 'arcades' which had been erected for this

---

[1] L'Estoile notes with astonishment that throughout the whole series of the 'festins', the participants were continually changing their costumes (*Mémoires-Journaux*, II, p. 22). This would have been in accordance with the directions of the programme which always specifies the colours to be worn; see below, pp. 169–71.

[2] *Ibid.*, II, p. 34.

[3] Dorat, *Œuvres poétiques*, pp. 22 ff.; *French Academies*, p. 271.

[4] *Mémoires-Journaux*, II, p. 33.   [5] See Programme, below, p. 170.

tournament.[1] One of these 'arcades' shone like a full moon; it was dedicated to the happy bridal pair. The other was seen from afar to represent a flaming sun, and was dedicated to the King. This moon-and-sun theme explains the white and yellow liveries of those who took part in the night tournament.

The 'arcades' were connected with a 'théâtre pompeux' evidently the most striking of the temporary erections for the festival. In his poem, Dorat sees many workmen hurrying after him to construct these festival buildings:[2]

> . . . Me sembloit il voir apres moi acourir
> Un grand nombre d'ouvriers pour auec moy bastir
> Un théâtre pompeux & deux braves arcades,
> Pour au Tournoy roial seruir de deux entrades . . .

The poet wishes us to know that the workmen were constructing these erections according to his designs.

Dorat devotes a long passage at the end of his poem to the description of the 'théâtre pompeux', which seems to have been a great amphitheatre[3]

> Qui du ciel estoilé representoit l'exemple

that is to say, it was a model of the heavens, perhaps not unlike the one which we know was designed by Leonardo da Vinci for a wedding festival at Milan in 1489. Within it were 'cabinets' representing the planets and constellations. The whole elaborate design seems to have been a working model of the heavens, for lights representing the planets were seen to move, weaving their way amongst the constellations of the zodiac:[4]

> . . . on voioit au milieu des eschaffauts reluire
> Sept grands globes ardens, qui en tours & retours
> Par erreur non errant entresuiuoient leurs cours.

And this whole representation seems to have been organized to show forth, or to bring down, a fortunate destiny for the French royal house. Amongst these artificial heavens were to be seen allusions to the 'Rainbow' device of the Queen Mother (Plate 23b), to the 'Three Crowns' device of Henri III (Plate 23a), and to that emblem so often used in earlier festivals and entries of Henri and his brother Charles, namely that of the lights of the twin stars, Castor and Pollux (Plate 23c), alighting on the Ship of France to announce peace:[5]

> Autres feux vagabons descouroient par la lice,
> Comme l'astre iumeau qui sur le mas se glisse.
> [Other wandering lights were to be seen near the lists,
> Such as the twin star which glides onto the mast.]

---

[1] Œuvres poétiques, p. 26. These 'arcades' can perhaps be seen in the painting of a night tournament attributed to Antoine Caron, reproduced in Valois Tapestries, Plate XII.
[2] Œuvres poétiques, p. 23.   [3] Ibid., p. 29.   [4] Ibid., p. 30.   [5] Ibid.

It seems that this construction formed the background for some dramatic entry of the King as the Sun, on a sun-chariot:[1]

> Mesmement quand le Roi sur son char y entroit,
> Qui comme un grand soleil estival se montroit,
> Et iectant son aspect vers la lampe lunaire,
> Plus il s'en esloignoit, plus il la rendoit claire.
> [And when the King entered on his chariot,
> Showing himself like a great summer sun,
> And throwing his aspect towards the lunar lamp,
> The more he withdrew from it the more clearly it shone.]

The Sun King is playing a part in the artificial heavens like that of the real sun in relation to the moon, which shines more brightly as the sun withdraws in the night.

In very many ways the court and circle of Henri III laid down patterns which, though apparently submerged in the wars and confusions of the years to come, were to reappear in new forms when the French monarchy entered on its period of greatest glory in the seventeenth century. Henri III as the Sun King prefigures Louis Quatorze as Le Roi Soleil, the centre of the great symbolic festivals and ballets of his reign.

The 'théâtre pompeux', or moving model of the heavens, was probably a triumph of the latest mechanics, and we know the name of the engineer who created it. Dorat says that the great model of the world shown at these festivals, which he likens to that created in ancient times by Archimedes, was designed by Louis de Montjosieu.[2] This was a remarkable man. He is said to have been interested in the mechanics of the ancients.[3] Perhaps he was influenced by what may be called mechanical humanism, the revival of the mechanics of the ancients, a movement comparable in its own sphere to the humanist attempts at reviving the music of the ancients. He was a protégé of the Duc de Joyeuse to whom he is said to have taught mathematics. He was also interested in sculpture and painting, and in the dedication to Joyeuse of his essays on these topics he draws an analogy between colours and musical tones.[4] Evidently this was an all-round scholar, who would have seen the various aspects of the Joyeuse Magnificences, their use of colours, music, painting, mechanics – his own contribution – as all part of a whole, as the combined use of culture in the service of court festival.

At this time mechanics were still associated with magic, as in the earlier magico-mechanical tradition. This does not mean that the mechanics used by Montjosieu in the creation of the 'théâtre pompeux' were not actually

[1] *Ibid.*, p. 29. [2] *Ibid.*, p. 23; cf. *French Academies*, pp. 103, 271, 273.
[3] La Croix Dumaine and Du Verdier, *Bibliothèques Françoises*, 1772 ed., II, p. 55; cf. *French Academies*, p. 103.
[4] Ludovicus Demontiosus (Louis de Montjosieu), *Gallus Romae Hospes*, Rome, 1585, part 3, pp. 8 ff.; cf. *French Academies*, p. 103.

mechanics in the scientific sense, perhaps enriched by mechanical humanism, or the recovery of the mechanics of the ancients. But the science would be used with magical intention. The use of mechanics with magical intention has been well defined by Robert Evans in his book on Rudolph II.[1] As an art which could create movement, thereby simulating life, mechanics could (it was believed) make a magical contact with the living universe. Thus Montjosieu's 'théâtre pompeux' for the Joyeuse wedding festivities would be yet another magical procedure for drawing down the life of heaven on the French monarchy; it was a moving talisman, exercising, through mechanics, similar incantatory effects to those hoped for from the ancient music.

With these impressions of the festivals in mind, we can now look with new eyes at the most famous, because the best preserved, of its entertainments. The *Ballet comique de la reine*[2] was published with full text, music, and illustrations in 1582, whereas the entertainments we have here been studying were never fully published and can only be pieced together from the programme and the other sources here used. The *Ballet comique* was contributed by the Queen, Louise de Lorraine, to the series of the Magnificences. She used other poets and musicians than those used in the teams for the other entertainments, and the poetry and music of the *Ballet* is not in the measured poetry and music of Baïf's Academy. Nevertheless, the introduction claims that the performance was an 'ancient music', and it shows sufficient traces of the theory of humanist music to allow us to suppose that it aimed at producing 'effects'. Moreoever, the plot and the themes of the performance relate it to the themes of the Magnificences as a whole, the invocation of cosmic forces in aid of the French monarchy.

The theme of the plot is the transference of power from the hands of Circe, the enchantress, into the hands of the French royal family who watch the performance. This must have been clear from the layout of the hall and the progress of the action. At one end of the hall was the brilliantly lighted garden of Circe and before her passed the forms of animals, men whom by her spells she had transformed into beasts. At the opposite end sat the royal party, the Queen Mother, the King, the bridegroom (the Queen and the bride took part in the performance). The action opens with the escape of a 'gentilhomme fugitif' from the garden of Circe; he crosses the hall and implores the King to deliver the world from the sorceress. In the mythological drama which follows, the power fluctuates. Circe is not at once defeated but in the end she succumbs to superior powers.

The 'voûte dorée' on the left of the hall, brightly illuminated and covered with star-spangled clouds, represented the celestial world. It contained

---

[1] R. J. W. Evans, *Rudolf II and his World*, Oxford, 1973, p. 186.
[2] Illustrated in *French Academies*, ch. XI; *Valois Tapestries*, pt II, ch. III.

singers and players divided into ten 'concerts de musique', and its music represented the true harmony of heaven.

The elemental world of nature, represented by the mythological beings, Sirens and Satyrs, amongst whom the first action takes place, is under the control of Circe. She is only defeated by an alliance of the Virtues and Minerva with the celestial world, expressed through the brilliant ballets, danced by the Queen, the bride, and other ladies, which were based on symbolic geometrical figures. When the Four Cardinal Virtues enter, in star-spangled robes, they appeal to the gods to descend from heaven. The music of the 'voûte dorée' replies to their music, and it is at this point that the celestial world begins to get the upper hand of Circe. The final victory is assured by the descent of Jupiter. The descent of the god, on his eagle, took some time, and was accompanied by a great outburst of the 'most learned and excellent music that had ever been sung or heard'. The words sung to this music were:

> O bien heureux le ciel qui de ses feux nouueaux
> Jaloux effacera tous les autres flambeaux
> O bien heureux encor sous ces princes la terre
> O bien heureux aussy le nauire Francoys
> Esclairé de ses feux, bienheureuses leurs loix
> Qui banniront d'icy les vices & la guerre.
> [O happy heaven, which, with these new lights,
> will jealously efface all other torches
> O happy earth beneath [the rule of] these princes
> O happy Ship of France, lighted with its lights,
> Fortunate are their laws which will banish from hence
>   all vice and war.]

The song would have reminded spectators, as did the musical golden vault, of the vault of heaven shown forth on Montjosieu's great amphitheatre, with its allusion to the Ship of France, lighted by Castor and Pollux, announcing peace for France and a fortunate destiny for the French royal house written in the lights of heaven. Jupiter, as he descends to the music of the golden vault, would appear, not as a decorative figure from a dead mythology, but as an 'astre heureux' brought down by the powerful music to keep far from France the horrors of war and to strengthen and bless the French monarchy.

As an artistic product, the *Ballet comique de la reine* may not have been of such high quality as other events in the Magnificences. Nevertheless, the scheme of the Queen's contribution fitted into the series as a whole as yet another poetic and musical talisman.

These festivals are the last product of Renaissance tradition as developed throughout the sixteenth century at the French court. This world is already under severe pressure and in a few years' time the Renaissance universe of the Valois court will go under and disappear in the chaos of the wars of the League.

The politico-religious slant behind the Joyeuse Magnificences is made very clear by Baïf in his poem *Les Mimes*, dedicated to Joyeuse, and full of reminiscences of his wedding festivals. Baïf in this poem expresses passionate loyalty to the French crown, and earnest Catholic piety, but he is very much against the Catholic League which he warns the Papacy not to support, for it hides treachery. He calls for a non-violent Counter Reformation which should use, not political weapons and tyrannical repression – he fears the introduction of the Inquisition into France – but only the weapons of genuine virtue and piety made attractive by art, with the praises of God sung in all languages and to 'new music'. And he appeals most fervently to that 'noble and valiant blood', the Guises, not to support the seditious faction but to remain loyal to the throne.[1]

The words uncover the drift of the Magnificences, support of the monarchy and appeal to the Guises not to betray it, a plea set forth with all the attractiveness of art and in 'new music'.

The last Valois king represents a complex moment in religious history; at his Palace Academy he listened to debates at which poets and scholars expounded the religious syncretism of the Renaissance, that all things are full of gods, that the fables of the poets and the myths of many religions refer to one religious truth, expressible in many forms.[2] This liberal Renaissance sycretism was combined in Henri with Counter-Reformation influences to form what one may call a movement (as yet little studied) of liberal Counter Reformation led by the French monarchy. The Guises, leaders of the Catholic League, represent the newer reactionary fanaticism, allied to pro-Spanish political motives, ultimately bent on destroying Henri. Baïf, in *Les Mimes*, sees the situation quite clearly, and calls for the kind of 'musical' and non-violent movement which Henri was trying to lead.

The effort to conciliate the Guises was proving hopeless. Henri was looking for support towards Elizabeth of England. Shortly after the Joyeuse Magnificences, which he had certainly seen, Giordano Bruno passed from Paris into England, there to expound his mission of Hermetic reform, with which he associated heliocentricity and Henri III.

As a Hermetic philosopher of the Renaissance, Bruno needed an imperial theme to which to anchor his philosophico-religious outlook, and as an Italian who hated Spanish repression, he chose the French monarch as European leader. The appearance of Henri III with his device of the Three

[1] Baïf, *Evvres*, V, pp. 110–11; cf. *French Academies*, p. 213.
[2] *French Academies*, chs VI, VII.

Crowns in the heavens of Bruno's *Spaccio della bestia trionfante*[1] (published in London in 1585) could be, among other things, a reminiscence of the great model of the heavens at the wedding festivals in which Henri's device had appeared among the artificial stars, presaging an imperial destiny. The heliocentric philosophy would fit in well with the solar mystique of French monarchy.[2] It is strange to notice that, when expounding the new philosophy in the *Cena de le ceneri*, Bruno uses a figure which is really an emblem. He is arguing in favour of the movement of the earth from the analogy of a stone dropped from the mast of a moving ship on to its deck. This is illustrated by a woodcut of a ship at sea (Plate 23d). Two flames are visible on the rigging, turning this ship into an emblem, the familiar Castor and Pollux emblem, with two lights on the rigging announcing peace after storms.[3] Hidden in the scientific argument is a message from the French king, and the message is surely one of peace.

Henri's device of the Three Crowns, with its motto '*Tertia coelo manet*', referred to the crowns of France and Poland which he held, and to a third crown in heaven which he hoped to obtain hereafter. It was not an aggressive device, and when Henri appears among the constellations of Bruno's *Spaccio della bestia trionfante* it is as a peacemaker:[4]

This most Christian king, holy, religious, and pure, may securely say:
Tertia coelo manet, for he well knows that it is written: Blessed are
the peacemakers, blessed are the pure in heart, for theirs is the
kingdom of heaven. He loves peace, he preserves his contented
people as much as possible in tranquillity and devotion; he is not
pleased with the noisy uproar of martial instruments which administer
to the blind acquisition of the unstable tyrannies and principalities of
the earth; but with all manner of justice and sanctity which show
the straight road to the eternal kingdom.

Thus does Giordano Bruno transmit to Elizabethan England the peace message from Henri III. We may imagine such an announcement being

[1] Bruno, *Dialoghi italiani*, ed. G. Aquilecchia, Florence, 1957, pp. 826–7; cf. *Giordano Bruno and the Hermetic Tradition*, pp. 228–9.

[2] I have suggested elsewhere that 'Bruno might have picked up the idea of a magical solar reform connected with the French monarchy from notions circulating at the French court' (*Giordano Bruno and the Hermetic Tradition*, p. 202).

Bruno connected Copernican heliocentricity with Ficinian solar magic (see *ibid.*, pp. 155, 208–9).

[3] Bruno, *La Cena de le ceneri*, third dialogue (*Dialoghi italiani*, p. 117, fig. 6). I pointed out that this figure is really the Castor and Pollux emblem, in my article, 'The emblematic conceit in Giordano Bruno's *De gli eroici furori* and in the Elizabethan sonnet sequences', *Journal of the Warburg and Courtauld Institutes*, VI (1943), pp. 109–10 and Plate 34. This article is reprinted in *England and the Mediterranean Tradition*, ed. Warburg and Courtauld Institutes, Oxford University Press, 1945, pp. 81–101.

Bruno's figure is the first emblem to be published in England. He probably cut the block for it himself for he knew how to do this (see *Giordano Bruno and the Hermetic Tradition*, p. 320).

[4] *Dialoghi italiani*, p. 825; cf. *Giordano Bruno and the Hermetic Tradition*, p. 228.

proclaimed, not only from the heavens of the *Spaccio*, but also four years earlier from those artificial heavens at the Joyeuse Magnificences where the Three Crowns device shone among the constellations. The Paris of the Joyeuse Magnificences was a highly sensitized recorder of the storms and strains brooding over Europe. It was the stage on which the Most Christian King strove to calm with the magic of poetry and music the growing uproar of the unstable tyrannies.

English Translation of the Programme[1]

Magnificences which are to be held at the
wedding of Monsieur le Duc de Joyeuse
in September and October 1581

First Day
Thursday, 14 September[2]
Day of the betrothal; the accoutrements will be violet colour with gold embroidery.

Sunday, 17th of the said month
Day before the wedding. After dinner there will be running at the ring.[3] There will be two kinds of prizes. The first and the most honourable will be for putting [the lance] within [the ring]. The second will be for making the best runs. For the King's Troop: it will consist of six persons; three men and three women. The women will be dressed in black with gold and white tinsel trimming. Their horses, and those of their followers, will be white; the harnesses of the horses will be black with gold and silver trimmings to match the costumes. The men will wear white costumes, also trimmed with gold and silver. Their horses and those of their followers will be black with white harnesses trimmed with gold and silver to match the costumes. The men will each have a page on a jennet carrying a javelin. The women will each have a girl attendant carrying their quivers and arrows in a sling. And each of the six will have, to carry their lances, a king of a

---

[1] The French text of the Programme is in Bibliothèque Nationale, Fonds Français, 15,831, fol. 90. It is printed in Pierre de la Vaissière, *Messieurs de Joyeuse*, Paris, 1926, pp. 63–5, and (more accurately) in my article 'Poésie et musique dans les "Magnificences" au Mariage du Duc de Joyeuse, Paris, 1581,' *Musique et Poésie au XVIe Siècle*, Centre National de la Recherche Scientifique, Paris, 1954, pp. 237–63. There is another version of the Programme in Bibliothèque de l'Institut, Fonds Godefroy, 385, fol. 174; this is a revision made after the change in the dates of the betrothal and wedding which altered the dating of the whole programme; the order of the events is also slightly changed in this programme. It gives no description of the events and is therefore of little value except for the revised dating.

[2] The betrothal actually took place on Monday, 18 September, as laid down in the Fonds Godefroy Programme, and as confirmed by L'Estoile, *Mémoires-Journaux*, II, p. 22; and by the English ambassador, *Calendar of State Papers, Foreign, Jan. 1581–April 1852*, p. 318.

[3] For an illustration of running at the ring, or the quintain, see Plate 22a.

foreign country, chained, and they will be accompanied by a recital in a strange language, not understood, and with extravagant music, recited by six Moors, carried *en panier* on a camel or on a tower on an elephant.

Monday, 18th of the said month

The wedding day.[1] The accoutrements will be of white and silver. It will be good to have an epithalamium recited, with concerts of music, by musicians dressed *à l'antique*, partly as men, partly as women, accompanying Hymen, god of marriage.[2]

Tuesday, the 19th

M. de Mercoeur's fête. The accoutrements will be scarlet and silver. The same day in the evening. Combat on foot in the Salle de Bourbon. The King's band fighting against Love. The King dressed in white; Monsieur de Lorraine in black; Monsieur de Mercoeur in scarlet: Monsieur de Damville in green. They will enter on a rock at the base of which Love will be bound, beneath the King's feet. The musicians, dressed in some elegant antique fashion, as men and women, will sing insults to him [to Love], with menacing gestures as though to shake him, pinch him, bind him, and injure him in other ways.[3]

Thursday, 21st, in the evening

Monsieur de Mercoeur's fête.

Friday, 22nd

Nothing on this day.

Saturday, 23rd, in the evening

Tilt in the courtyard of the Louvre. There will be twenty-four combatants, twelve on each side, one band in scarlet and white, the other in pale yellow and white.[4]

[1] L'Estoile states that the marriage took place on 24 September at Saint-Germain-l'Auxerrois *Mémoires-Journaux*, II, p. 22).

[2] The epithalamium can be identified as the piece 'Cherchans de combler, Epithalame à deux Chœurs', in Claude Le Jeune, *Airs* (1608), no. 12. pp. 40 ff.

Ronsard confirms that the 'two choruses' were divided into men and women, as specified in the Programme, in his poem 'Epithalame de Monseigneur le Duc de Joyeuse' describing the two ranks of 'garçons et filles' chanting before Hymen (Ronsard, *Œuvres*, ed. I. Silver, V, p. 199).

The 'Epithalame à deux Chœurs' is in Baïf's *vers mesurés*, in his phonetic spelling, unrhymed and unaltered, and exactly fitted to Le Jeune's music. This long piece is a good example of the academic poetry and music in its pure form.

[3] The piece sung by the musicians was 'Arm! arm!, La Guerre de Claude Le Jeune', in *Airs*, no. 24, pp. 90 ff.; see above, pp. 153-6. Baïf's *vers mesurés* have been altered into rhymed verses, thus losing some of the academic purity. For a visual presentation of a fierce attack on a bound Love in a Triumph of Chastity see Plate 15.

[4] This spectacle perhaps took place on Monday, 16 October; see above, p. 162.

Sunday, 24th of the said month
Combat with three sorts of weapons, on foot and on horseback, after dinner, in the great court of the Louvre where one runs at the ring.

The King one of the combatants, with pike and sword. His entry will have the form of a marine triumph, being in a great ship, before which there will be two or three rocks like little floating islands, on which will be Tritons and Sirens playing various instruments and sorts of music, with drums, to excite and to accompany the King's triumph.[1]

Monsieur de Mercoeur, also one of the combatants, with truncheon, on foot. His entry will be on a triumphal car *à l'antique*, with various trophies, those which are the finest and the easiest to represent. His costume will be gold and grey.

Monsieur de Guise, also one of the combatants, on horseback, with sword, and it might be good that his horse should be winged, like a Bellerophon. His costume to be green trimmed with gold.

For the retreat, and for the platforms of the three combatants which should be expressive of their rôles:

That of the King will be in the form of an island, or of a rock in the sea, and, if it is thought good, there may be fireworks here and there to suggest views of the Sicilian islands(?). And there must be objects suggesting the sea attached to it, as oars of galleys, boats, and so on.

That of M. de Mercoeur will be a rock on land with several trees, and above all a great oak, crowned with trophies, with a cartel hanging on it.

That of M. de Guise will be at the side entry and will be a rock with two pinnacles, at the summit of which will be a fountain springing from the foot of his horse.

The evening of the same Sunday
Twelve masquerades. There will be twelve or fifteen musicians dressed as fauns and dryads of the woods, who will recite the verses which will be given to them. The twelve torch-bearers will be men and women disguised as trees, orange-trees, lemon-trees, pomegranate-trees, and others, the golden fruits of which will carry lamps and torches.[2]

Monday, the 25th, in the evening
The Queen's ballet at the Louvre.[3]

[1] The Baïf-Le Jeune music for this marine entry can be identified as 'O vous Reine d'honneur', Claude Le Jeune, *Airs*, no. 23, pp. 87 ff. Baïf's *vers mesurés* are in their pure form. See above, pp. 157–8.

[2] The music for this masquerade can probably be identified as the Baïf-Le Jeune song, 'L'un emera le violet' in Claude Le Jeune, *Le Printemps*, 1603, reprinted in H. Expert, *Les Maîtres Musiciens de la Renaissance Française*, Paris, 1900, part 14, no. XXVII and in Yates, *French Academies*, musical appendix. See above, pp. 160–2.

[3] This was the *Ballet comique de la Reine*, see above, pp. 165–6. According to L'Estoile (*Mémoires-Journaux*, II, p. 33) the Queen's ballet, which he calls 'un ballet de Circe', was actually performed on 15 October.

Tuesday, the 26th
The Cardinal de Bourbon's fête.[1]

Thursday, the 27th
Tournament on horseback in the form of a ballet in the court of the Louvre. It would be good to have music of hautbois, trumpets, and other instruments.[2]

Evening of the same day
Monsieur de Guise's fête, in his hôtel.[3]

Friday
Nothing on this day.

Saturday the 29th
Monsieur the Cardinal de Guise's fête.

Sunday, in the evening
The Queen Mother's fête in her house.[4]
End of the Magnificences which are to be held for the wedding of Monsieur d'Arques (Joyeuse) and the sister of the Queen of France.

There is a confused late tradition which states that Queen Louise gave a second ballet, some days later, called a 'ballet de Ceres', with music by 'Claudin'; see J. Bonnet, *Histoire de la musique et de ses effets*, Paris, 1717, p. 318. An anonymous eighteenth-century manuscript (*Traité du ballet*, Bibl. Nat. Français, 25,465, fol. 18) speaks of this 'ballet de Ceres' and says that it was immediately followed by a horse ballet. There is no trace of this 'ballet de Ceres', and the story may have arisen through confusion of 'Circe' with 'Ceres'.

On the curious claim of Agrippa d'Aubigné, the Huguenot follower of Henry of Navarre, that he was the real author of the *Ballet comique*, see *French Academies*, p. 257.

Antoine Caron's picture 'The Triumph of Winter' (see J. Ehrmann, *Antoine Caron*, Geneva, 1955, Plate 2) is tantalizingly suggestive of some ballet of this period.

[1] According to L'Estoile (*Mémoires-Journaux*, II, pp. 32–3) the Cardinal de Bourbon planned to transport the royal party across the river from the Louvre to the Abbey of Saint-Germain-des-Prés in a barge accompanied by singing tritons, sirens, and other marine monsters, but the works in the aquatic creatures went wrong, disappointing fifty thousand Parisians gathered on the banks and expecting to see a wondrous spectacle. The King was very annoyed, and after waiting hours for the marine monsters, the royal party went by coach to Saint-Germain-des-Prés where the Cardinal had prepared a marvellous artificial garden, garnished with flowers and fruits. This was on Tuesday, 10 October.

[2] L'Estoile, *loc. cit.*, says that on Thursday, 19 October, there was a horse ballet, performed by horses which had been trained for five or six months, and which danced to music. On horse ballets at French festivals, see *Valois Tapestries*, p. 84, and Plate IXb.

[3] Nothing is known about the entertainments which the Programme hopefully suggests will be given by the Duke of Guise and his brother, the Cardinal.

[4] Nothing is known about an entertainment planned to be given by the Queen Mother.

RELIGIOUS PROCESSIONS IN PARIS, 1583-4

Henri III took himself seriously as a *Rex Christianissimus* and attempted to lead a Counter Reformation. He hoped to overcome the menace of the Catholic League by, at first, identifying himself with it. Hence the orders, *confréries*, and other religious organizations which he founded, which filled the streets of Paris with their processions, with the spectacle of a renewed religious chivalry and of the public devotions of a penitent king. The year 1583 was called in Paris the year of processions, and no study of this confused and dangerous period can be complete without taking into account the strange processional rhythm of the times. For the processional rhythm in Paris in about the years 1583 and 1584 there happens to be a visual record, which is little known,[1] in the drawings here reproduced (Plates 24-34). These drawings give an opportunity of moving along the *quais* of the Seine, and of seeing what was going on. Or rather, one sees emblems and allegories of what was going on, and the real *quais* of the real Seine have a way of disappearing from time to time into Biblical country, which is, however, not misty, because one can find one's way about in it with iconographical precision.

The leading themes reflected in the drawings can be grouped under headings. The main, the predominant theme is Chivalry, for the chief characters in the King's Procession drawings are the Knights of the Holy Spirit, reflecting Henri's foundation of the new Order of the Holy Spirit. Associated with this is the theme of Penitence, and we see in the procession the penitent *confréries*, White, Blue, and Black, which Henri founded. The third main theme is Charity, and this introduces the charity patronized by the King and his knights and penitents. This was the House of Christian Charity, revealed in the Queen's Procession drawings (Plates 35-9), founded by Nicolas Houel, the artistic apothecary whom we have met in an earlier essay, whose experience in formulating themes of royal propaganda went into his very skilful design of these procession drawings.

It is Houel, with his House of Christian Charity in a herb garden, and its possible connection with the secret sect of the Family of Love, who raises important and interesting questions as to the inner nature of Henri III's Counter Reformation.

At the end of this essay there is an analysis of the drawings,[2] with explana-

---

[1] Six of the Processions Drawings are reproduced in my *The French Academies of the Sixteenth Century*, Warburg Institute, 1947, as illustrations to the chapter on Henri III's religious movements, pp. 152 ff.

[2] See below, pp. 197-207.

tions of their scenes and figures, so far as I have been able to identify these. In what follows here, I give a more general account of the themes reflected in the drawings, which the reader may fill in with more detail from the analysis. I hope that everyone who reads this will feel drawn to follow the procession drawings in detail, for to do so is a revealing historical experience.

Chivalry. Processions of the Order of the Holy Spirit

As a major instrument of his religious effort, Henri III founded a new order of chivalry, the Ordre du Saint Esprit.[1] Though the exercises and traditions of chivalry were very familiar at the French court, as we have seen in the study of the festivals, the order of chivalry specifically associated with the French crown in the Middle Ages, the Ordre de Saint Michel, was not in a very flourishing state. Henri wished to renew religious chivalry in relation to the crown, as a focus of loyalty, through his new order. Its ceremonies and rules were modelled on those of the fourteenth-century Ordre du Saint Esprit, or du Droit Désir, the statutes of which had been presented to Henri when he was in Venice. The annual ceremonies of the new Order took place in the New Year and occupied three days. The headquarters of the Order were in a chapel of the church of the Grands Augustins,[2] which has long since disappeared, though the memory of it lingers in the place-name 'Quai des Augustins' in modern Paris, on the left bank of the river near the Pont-Neuf. On New Year's Day, the knights, robed in the mantle of the Order on which glittered the descending flames of the Holy Spirit, and wearing the collar from which depended the cross with the Dove, went in solemn procession from the Louvre to the Augustins carrying tapers. There were other processions on other days and on the last day a banquet. Representations of these annual ceremonies can be seen in the bas-reliefs which adorn the four sides of the square-headed silver mace of the Order, made in the reign of Henri III from the designs of Toussaint Dubreuil and now in the Louvre.[3] One side shows the procession of the Order outside its chapel at the Augustins.

The Order was founded late in 1578; the first of its processions took place on 1 January 1579. Thereafter, the ceremonies took place annually. L'Estoile writes in his Journal:[4]

[1] On the Ordre du Saint Esprit, see A. Favyn, *Théâtre d'honneur et de chevalerie*, Paris, 1620, pp. 643 ff.; P. Helyot, *Histoire des ordres monastiques, religieux et militaires en France*, Paris, 1714–19, VIII, pp. 314 ff.; Yates, *French Academies*, pp. 156–7. My article in *Annales musicologiques* (see above, p. xiv, note 3) has more material on the Ordre du Saint Esprit than I have used here.

[2] On this chapel, see H. Sauval, *Histoire et recherches des antiquités de Paris*, Paris, 1724, II, p. 723; A. L. Millin, *Antiquités nationales*, Paris, 1791, III, p. 60. A plan of the church showing the chapel is in the Musée Carnavalet, Album 102 E.

[3] Illustrated in my article in *Annales musicologiques*.

[4] Pierre de L'Estoile, *Mémoires-Journaux*, ed. J. Brunet, *et al.*, Paris, 1888, II, p. 97 (useful historical notes are given in the more recent edition by L.-R. Lefèvre, Paris, 1943).

On the first day of the year 1583, the King performed his solemn celebration and ceremony of the Order of the Holy Spirit at the Augustins at Paris, in the accustomed manner. . . .

The ritual thus established by Henri III was to continue throughout the *ancien régime*; his new Order became the recognized badge of the French monarch, always to be seen in the portraits of French kings, like the Order of the Garter on the portraits of monarchs on the other side of the Channel. In England, the Order of the Garter had survived undimmed from the Middle Ages and took on new strength in the Elizabethan age. In France, the order of chivalry particularly associated with the monarch was created anew by Henri III, who laid down its statutes, its costume and regalia, its annual ceremonies, its centre in the chapel of the Augustins (which became a rich depôt of works of art connected with it), its meaning as the Order of Chivalry associated with French monarchy in its religious and Catholic aspect.

In the first of the King's Procession drawings (Plate 24, K.P.1), we see the head of the long procession which will be unrolled throughout its twenty-two scenes. That it is the King's Procession is emphasized in its very first group in which a youth is carrying the device of Henri III, the two crowns of France and Poland surmounted by the third crown in heaven. The device is surrounded by the collar of the Order of the Holy Spirit with its pendant, and it is immediately followed by a group of three knights of the Holy Spirit, wearing the robes and collar of the Order and carrying tapers. The basic theme of the King's Procession drawings, underlying and linking together all the other themes to which they allude, is that of a procession of Knights of the Holy Spirit as leaders in a movement of religious renewal.

The three Knights of the Holy Spirit, who are seen for the first time in King's Procession 1, recur again and again in subsequent drawings. This repetition of the group has the function of unifying the whole procession as the presentation of a many-sided religious movement inspired by a renewal of Christian chivalry through the new order of chivalry created by the Most Christian King. Yet though the knights are used in this way as a kind of theme song, in a manner bordering on allegory, there is also in the first six drawings a definite allusion to the actual route followed by an annual procession of the Order of the Holy Spirit. This can be worked out through careful attention to the topography.

The procession is moving along the *quais* of the Seine, on the right bank; views of buildings on the left bank appear on the other side of the river. In the first drawing (K.P. 1) there is a bridge, the Pont aux Meûniers, which the procession is about the cross to reach its destination, the church of the Grands Augustins on the Quai des Augustins. Having crossed the river by this bridge to the Île de la Cité, near the Palais de Justice, the procession would then leave the island by the Pont Saint Michel (not seen in the drawings) where it would turn along the left bank to reach the Grands Augustins. This church, with its long roof and its pignon, a great centre and landmark in the old Paris, is very clearly visible across the river in K.P. 3 (Plate 25). One can even distinguish the large chapel on the side next to the river, which was the centre of the Order of the Holy Spirit and the objective of its processions. Near the Augustins, the beginnings of an unfinished bridge are visible; the great blocks of stone on which its piers will be continued can be seen in the river. This is the Pont-Neuf, built by Henri III, under construction. The state of the building is evidence that this drawing is not earlier than 1582 and not later than 1583.[1]

It is hinted by one writer that Henri had the Pont-Neuf built to facilitate the processions of his Order of the Holy Spirit from the Louvre to the Augustins. However that may be, the route would certainly be easier after the Pont-Neuf was built, leading straight to the Augustins, instead of going round by the Pont aux Meûniers and across the island. This is the kind of consideration which would have seemed important to Henri III, though the modern historian, naturally assuming that a bridge is built because it is needed for normal traffic, may find it difficult to envisage the priorities of other ages.

And the traffic here is not normal but allegorical. Walking in the procession (K.P. 3) between two groups of Knights of the Holy Spirit, are the three theological virtues, Faith, Hope, and Charity, and the four cardinal virtues, Fortitude, Prudence, Temperance, and Justice. These figures indicate the ethical aims of the Order, to cultivate the Christian virtues and to spread them through the world.

Penitence. The Penitent Processions

The most striking and novel, and, to many, alarming feature of the religious processions in Paris in these years were the processions of the penitent confréries. The penitent confraternity is a group of lay persons (not ecclesiastics), who join together in undertaking penitential disciplines, including public processions. The penitent confréries were a southern form of extravagant pietism; they wore a peculiar garb, with a mask covering the face with slits for the eyes, giving a rather sinister appearance to their processions; sometimes they indulged in flagellation. Henri enthusiastically encouraged penitent confréries, which he pressed the courtiers to join, building houses of retreat for them and himself taking part in the processions.[2] The confréries were of different colours, some wearing white robes, others blue, others black, and they moved to psalms and liturgies in most melodious

[1] F. Boucher, Le Pont Neuf, Paris, 1925, I, p. 108.
[2] H. Fremy, Henri III pénitent, Paris, 1885; Yates, French Academies, pp. 154 ff.

music provided by the court musicians. Such processions were an unfamiliar spectacle in Paris; they aroused much disapproval, and indeed it was an unwise move to arouse religious hysteria in this way, and one which was to turn to the King's undoing in the hysteria of the League. These manifestations suited Henri's temperament, corresponding in the religious sphere to the dramatic extravagances of the court festivals in their many-coloured liveries, and he was encouraged in them by his religious advisers.

L'Estoile's diary for the year 1583, which begins with his mention of the New Year ceremonies of the Order of the Holy Spirit, contains a well-known satirical description of the first procession of the Confrérie des Pénitents de l'Annonciation de Notre Dame. This *Confrérie* was begun by Henri in this year; its first public procession took place on 25 March:[1]

> On Friday, 25 March of the present year, 1583, there took place the solemn procession of the Penitent Confrères, who came at four in the afternoon to Notre Dame from the Augustins, walking in pairs in their attire, like that of the Battus of Rome, Avignon, or Toulouse. . . . In this procession the King walked unguarded and without any difference from the other Confrères, either as to attire or position; the Cardinal of Guise carried the Cross, the Duke of Mayenne, his brother, was master of the ceremonies, and Brother Emond Auger, Jesuit (formerly a juggler of which trade he kept all the marks) . . . conducted the rest. . . . The King's Singers and others marched in their ranks, dressed in the same habit, in three distinct companies singing the litany most melodiously in *faux bourdon*.

The 'bon bourgeois de Paris', always cynical about the doings of Henri III, gives some facts which we know from other sources: that the White Penitents were centred at the Augustins, like the Knights of the Holy Spirit, and that, as always in these years, the King's future enemies of the League, the Guises, joined in his activities, and walked in his processions.

We know from the statutes of the Pénitents de l'Annonciation[2] that the Augustins was their base. The annual processions of the Knights of the Holy Spirit and of the White Penitents, both associated with the church of the Grands Augustins and staging their processions at different times of the year, kept an association between the Order and the Penitent *confrérie* in the public mind, and there is no doubt that the King intended such an association. The knights were also penitents, the penitents were also knights, and both associations drew their membership from the court. The Order and the

---

[1] L'Estoile, ed. Brunet, II, pp. 109-10.

[2] *Les Statuts de la Congrégation des Pénitens de l'Annonciation*, Paris, 1583. There is an incomplete reprint of this in M. L. Cimber and F. Danjou, *Archives curieuses de l'histoire de France*, Paris, 1834-40, 1st series, X, pp. 437 ff. And there is an unpublished manuscript of the statutes (Bibl. Nat. Français, nouvelles acquisitions, 7549) which gives more information and names.

Penitent *confrérie* were both aspects of the monarchical Counter Reformation, though the association between the two was afterwards forgotten. The Order of the Holy Spirit survived to become the ornament and badge of French monarchy; the Penitent *confréries* were banned in the seventeenth century from Paris and the court. Thus, whilst the annual processions and ceremonies of the Order of the Holy Spirit were kept up during the whole of the *ancien régime* very much as established by Henri III, the companion foundation of the Pénitents de l'Annonciation was suppressed and its processions were no more seen in Paris. The League was to make a seditious use of these emotional processions, which the King had himself fostered and invited his enemies to join. The deplorable rôle played by some of the penitent associations in Paris under the League had the result that, after the pacification of the country by Henry IV, they were discouraged in Paris and took refuge again in their place of origin, the south.

The King's Procession drawings show the Order and the Penitents functioning together, as originally intended by Henri III. Though knights and penitents seem never to have walked together, in the same procession,[1] the King's Procession drawings (Plates 30 and 31, K.P. 14 and 15) indicate the spiritual link between the two by showing a procession of White Penitents of the Annunciation framed between two groups of three knights. The leader of the Penitents (K.P. 14) carries a banner with the Annunciation. Two others follow him; then two with torches, and one with the crucifix. They wear the penitent habit, with the slits for the eyes, and show on their left shoulders the mark of the White Penitents of the Annunciation (a mark copied from the Gonfalone,[2] an Italian *confrérie*). The bearer of the crucifix is followed by King David with his harp, accompanied by two Jewish priests, swinging censers. David with his harp indicates a musical accompaniment, probably of penitential psalms, and in the next drawing (K.P. 15) are choir boys and men with music books.

From an unpublished manuscript version of the statutes of the Penitents, dated 1583, we can learn the names of the King's singers and musicians who were officially attached to the *Confrérie*. The list is as follows:[3]

M. Le Roux, choriste premier ordinaire
    Chantres:
M. de Beaulieu
    de St Laurens
    Mainguon

[1] It was indeed impossible that they should do so, for the same people belonged to both institutions.

[2] On the Gonfalone and its connection with the Pénitents de l'Annonciation, see Helyot, *op. cit.*, III, pp. 219 ff.

[3] *Les noms des Penitens de l'Archicongrégation royalle de l'Annonciation de Notre Dame erigee aux Augustins de Paris, 1583*, Bibl. Nat. Fr., nouv. acq. 7549.

Salmon
Laurigni (or Lorigni)
De Mesme
Baliffre
Busserat

The same list of names is repeated later in the statutes, where they are described as 'Huit musciens de la Chambre du Roy', and it is stated that these musicians shall be held to be 'confrères et en mesme degré et seront tenus à toutes les corrections excepté à celles dargent s'ils ne ueulent . . .'.[1] That is to say, the musicians were to be penitent *confrères* following all the rules, except that they need not contribute to the charities, unless they wished to do so.

Who is the 'Monsieur de Beaulieu' who heads the list of the 'chantres'? Surely he can be no other than the musician now identified as Girard (not Lambert) de Beaulieu, whom Fabrice describes as having been closely associated with Thibaut de Courville, co-founder with Jean-Antoine de Baïf of the Académie de Poésie et Musique.[2] The preface to the printed edition of the *Ballet comique de la reine* states that the music of that production was provided by Beaulieu, who was assisted by the King's musicians, notably one of the name of Salmon.[3] In 'Beaulieu' and 'Salmon' mentioned as musicians for the Penitents we thus have the two people mainly responsible for the music of the *Ballet comique*. And amongst the other names in the list is 'Monsieur de Saint Laurent', that is, the famous *castrato* singer, Etienne Le Roy, Abbé de Saint Laurent, who sang the part of one of the satyrs in the *Ballet comique*.[4] It is thus not surprising that when L'Estoile saw and heard the penitent processions go by he was unwillingly forced to admire the 'très-harmonieuse musique', for that music was executed by very much the same team as that which two years earlier had produced the famous *Ballet comique de la reine*.

When one is used to the technique of the King's Procession, one learns that the buildings seen in the background relate to the figures passing in the procession. One may therefore fancy that the building seen across the river in K.P. 15 may be one of those many places of retreat erected by Henri for his pious foundations, perhaps a place of contemplative and penitential retreat for the White Penitents of the Annunciation. Such buildings must

---

[1] 'They shall rank as *confrères* on an equal footing with the others, and shall be subject to all the corrections except fines in money, if they do not wish to pay these.'

[2] See *French Academies*, p. 51, note 4.

[3] Baltasar de Beaujoyeulx, *Balet comique de la Royne*, Paris, 1582, preface.

[4] *Ibid.*, p. 32. M. François Lesure informs me that a comparison of this list of names with that in the Etats de la Maison du Roi for 1584 (Arch. Nat., KK 139) suggests that 'Le Roux, choriste premier' is the same man as 'Etienne le Roy, abbé de St Laurens', who thus appears twice in the list. He identifies the other musicians named as Martin Mingon, François de Lorigny, Mesme Jacquinot, Claude Balifre, and Jacques Busserat.

have been quite a feature of Paris and its environs before the days of the League, during which most of them were violently destroyed.

Among other penitent *confréries* much favoured by the King, which he himself joined, and for which he built retreat houses, were the Pénitents Bleus de Saint Jerome, or 'Hieronymites', for whom he erected retreat houses in the Bois de Vincennes.[1] Keen members of the 'Hieronymites' (and of the other organizations) were the Duc de Joyeuse and his brother the Comte de Bouchage, who afterwards entered the Capucin order. In the King's Procession (Plate 30, K.P. 13) St Jerome and a group of his followers pass, framed between two groups of the Knights of the Holy Spirit. St Jerome carries a stone with which to beat his breast, as do his followers, and they are, perhaps, all wearing hair shirts. The group expresses severe forms of penance and may refer to the austerities of the 'Hieronymites'. Still harsher is the aspect of the group in K.P. 16 (Plate 31) who carry scourges with which to discipline themselves. They are led by St John the Baptist, carrying his head, and accompanied by two prophets. This may refer to the Confrérie des Pénitents Noirs de Saint-Jean-Décollé,[2] particularly as the charitable work characteristic of this *confrérie* was to accompany condemned criminals to their execution, a Work which is being performed in the next drawing (Plate 32, K.P. 17).

Charity. The Works of Mercy

Penitence was intimately connected with Charity, as defined in the statutes of the Pénitents Blancs de l'Annonciation, which state that the two main objects of the White Penitents were the cultivation of both Penitence and Charity. The Penitence was to be both public, in processions through the streets, and private, in places of devotional retreat (this throws light on the places of contemplative retreat shown in the King's Procession drawings as backgrounds to the penitent *confréries* walking in the procession). Charity demanded both time and money of the Penitents. Money was to be collected as fines, subscriptions, donations, and officers were appointed to administer its distribution. The Penitents must also themselves do charitable acts. On Holy Thursday they must wash the feet of thirteen very poor persons, then take them to the Augustins and see that they were reclothed and given a meal and money. Every Good Friday there was to be a collection for ransoming a prisoner from the Turks or from the prisons of Paris. The Penitents must also visit hospitals and the sick; attend the funerals of colleagues; visit prisons and console prisoners; accompany those condemned to death to the place of execution.

These are the Works of Mercy which in the propaganda of Counter

---

[1] Helyot, *op. cit.*, VIII, p. 264; *French Academies*, pp. 159-61.
[2] Helyot, *op. cit.*, III, p. 219.

Reformation had been given a set iconographical programme, and classified under set scenes: giving food and drink to the poor; clothing the poor; receiving pilgrims; healing the sick; relieving prisoners; burying the dead.

In the King's Procession drawings, when the theme of Charity is being illustrated (Plates 28 and 29, K.P. 10, 11 and 12), the Works of Mercy are shown in progress in the backgrounds, where can be seen little scenes of feeding and clothing the poor, receiving pilgrims, visiting prisoners, burying the dead; the Work of healing the sick is alluded to through the story of the Good Samaritan. In front of these Works of Mercy scenes there marches a procession of Charitable Men, wearing long buttoned uniforms and carrying objects which show that they have been doing the Works – food, drink, and clothing for the poor, medicines and herbs for healing the sick, and so on.

As the themes of Chivalry and Penitence in the King's Procession drawings had definite contemporary reference to a real Order of Chivalry and to real associations of Penitents, so the theme of Charity had reference to a real charity in which the King and Queen, the Order of the Holy Spirit, and the Penitent *confrères*, were interested. This was the 'Maison de Charité Chrétienne', founded by Nicolas Houel, the apothecary, as an institution for growing herbs and compounding them into medicines, combined with an orphanage for bringing up and educating poor children and training them to work in the herb garden and the 'apothicairerie'.

The King's Procession drawings are paralleled by another closely related set of drawings, the Queen's Procession. In the Queen's Procession drawings (Plates 35-9) we see Queen Louise de Lorraine starting out to visit the Maison de Charité Chrétienne, the various activities of which are set out in fascinating detail. We see the herb garden, the 'apothicairerie', the orphans, the school, the chapel, and amongst the busy staff of the institution can be clearly seen men wearing the long buttoned uniforms of the Works of Mercy Men in the King's Procession. Moreover, the Work of healing the sick is expressed in the King's Procession through the Charitable Men who carry phials, alembics, and dried herbs (K.P. 11, 12), an obvious reference to the most characteristic activity of the Maison de Charité Chrétienne, the herb garden and the drugs made from it, dispensed to the sick poor in the 'apothicairerie'.

This method of presenting the scenes of the Works of Mercy in conjunction with people who are actually doing the Works in a House of Christian Charity is, so far as I know, original. It is extraordinarily close to the method employed by Spenser in *The Faerie Queene* when he shows the personified Works of Mercy acting as 'beadsmen' in a 'holy Hospitall'.[1]

---

[1] *Faerie Queene*, Bk I, X, xxxvi-xliv. The seven beadsmen in the holy hospital are doing the Works of Mercy: receiving travellers (xxxvii); giving food and drink (xxxviii); giving clothing (xxxix); relieving and ransoming prisoners (xl); tending the sick (xli); burying the dead (xlii);

This Spenserian House of Charity is presided over by Charissa, a Counter-Reformation type of Charity with many children, such as can be seen throughout the Procession drawings. The Red Cross Knight, it will be remembered, had arrayed himself in sackcloth and met with 'bitter Penance with an iron whip'[1] before he is led to the 'Holy Hospital'. Spenser's presentation of the themes of Penitence and Charity in a framework of Chivalry is a remarkable parallel to what we see in the Procession drawings.

Processions as Prayers for the Birth of a Dauphin

The revival of religious chivalry, the devotional movements of penitence and charity, should surely influence heaven in favour of the French monarchy, and the most pressing need of the French monarchy was the birth of an heir to the throne, through which to silence the murmurs of the Catholic League about heretic heirs and to continue the line of the Valois. The attempt at drawing down the influences of heaven to produce an heir to the throne had been one of the themes of the *Ballet comique*,[2] and it is certainly a theme of the King's Procession, though expressed through Biblical allegory instead of the pagan imagery of court festival.[3]

At one point in the King's Procession drawings, Biblical personages take a prominent part, chosen because they were parents of holy children. Abraham walks with Sarah and the little Isaac, followed by Hannah with her son Samuel (Plate 26, K.P. 7); the parents of the Virgin are seen with their daughter; the parents of St John the Baptist with their son (Plate 27, K.P. 8). All this leads up to Queen Louise de Lorraine, surrounded by imaginary children and carrying a model of a church (Plate 28, K.P. 9). A holy child is expected, a Dauphin and future Most Christian King of France, the fulfilment of prophecy, and the reward of pious works of mercy and the support of religious and charitable foundations.

This theme of supplication for a Dauphin was urged with painful intensity in the pilgrimages and processions of these years. The caustic L'Estoile notes that on 9 March 1584, the King left Paris, accompanied by forty-seven penitents, on a pilgrimage to Notre Dame de Cléry: on 22 March

---

caring for orphans (xliii). Spenser makes one Work, instead of two, of giving food and drink, and therefore has a Work to spare, which he calls caring for orphans, not usually named as one of the Seven Works. He seems to think of his seven charitable men, or beadsmen, as an Order, with Charissa as its 'chiefest founderesse' (xliv).

[1] *Ibid.*, Bk I, X, xxvii.   [2] See *French Academies*, pp. 259-60.

[3] The satyrs and sirens through whom supplication had been made for the birth of a Dauphin in the *Ballet comique* could be used in such a way at such an extremely orthodox Catholic shrine as Notre Dame de Lorette. I have found it stated in a work on penitent *confréries* that a present which Henri III sent to Notre Dame de Lorette in the hope of obtaining an heir was a lapis lazuli cup held by an angel, supported by four satyrs, enamelled and jewelled, and three sirens holding a little gold child (Jules Giéra, *Confrérie des Penitents Blancs d'Avignon*, Paris, 1858, p. 68). The gift was taken to the shrine by the Duc de Joyeuse, as mentioned by L'Estoile, *op. cit.*, II, p. 127.

he returned, very tired, from his pilgrimage to Chartres and Cléry.[1] These were famous shrines of the Virgin and the object was to pray for an heir.

We know more of what this pilgrimage was like from other sources. A document in the Vatican published by Godefroy de Paris in his history of the Capucins in France states that the cortège left Paris on 9 March, the King being attired in the penitent garb of Holland cloth, with eyeholes, and girded with a cord from which hung a discipline. He was accompanied by forty-seven penitents 'belonging to the highest nobility of France'.[2] Six members of the Order of the Minimes were in the procession, and it stopped at the convent of the Capucins at Meudon to recruit five Capucins. They arrived at Chartres on 13 March in the evening and went on again the next day, reaching Cléry on 17 March. Having paid their devotions there, they set out for Orléans, the King still accompanied by his forty-seven penitents and the Minimes, and the number of the Capucins had risen to twelve. They arrived at Orléans by torchlight, paid their devotions in the cathedral, stayed at the Capucin centre in the town, and set out for the return journey to Paris the next day. Another account in the archives at Chartres confirms the presence of the Minimes and Capucins in the pilgrimage, and states that there were more than sixty, attired as penitents, in the procession, 'cardinals, princes, and great lords of the realm', most of them walking barefooted and chanting litanies. One of the penitents carried a great crucifix.[3]

The last two drawings of the King's Procession (Plate 34, K.P. 21, 22) reflect this procession. In K.P. 21, between two groups of knights of the Holy Spirit, there is a group, obviously of members of a religious order, not of lay *confrères*. From their habits they can be identified as Minimes. They are followed by another group from a religious order (the first part of this group is in K.P. 21, the rest of it in K.P. 22). These men, with the peaked cowls, are certainly Capucins. Following them is a penitent carrying a huge crucifix, and then, at the very end of the procession, the King and Queen appear as penitents, wearing tiny crowns on their sackcloth. Between them is Jonah, uttering some prophecy.

These two drawings seem to be by a different hand from the others, and were probably added to include reference to the famous pilgrimage of 1584.

Religious Influences on Henri III

Henri III was the first King of France to have a Jesuit confessor, Emond Auger, believed by L'Estoile to have been an important influence on the

[1] L'Estoile, pp. 148-90.
[2] Godefroy de Paris, *Les Frères-Mineurs-Capucins en France*, Rouen-Paris, 1937-9, I, ii, pp. 21 ff.
[3] Edouard d'Alençon, 'Notre-Dame de Chartres, le roi de France, et les Capucins', *Annales franciscaines*, XVI, (1888-90), pp. 885 ff.

penitent processions. He certainly admired them and wrote a defence of the Pénitents Blancs[1] which is useful for the King's Procession drawings, though it does not contain much that we do not already know from the Statutes of the *Confrérie*. More important, I believe, was the influence of the Minimes, and more important still that of the Capucins. These two are the only religious orders portrayed in the procession drawings.

The Minimes, founded in 1461 under Franciscan influence, were very much favoured by Henri III[2] who built a house for them in the Bois de Vincennes. In the early seventeenth century a man famous as the friend of Descartes joined the Minimes. Mersenne was an intense admirer of Baïf's Academy of Poetry and Music and is the main source for information about it. Possibly, therefore, the sixteenth-century Minimes, so much favoured by Henri III, would have been tolerant of academic influences.

The Capucins were reformed Franciscans, representatives of the Counter Reformation in its Franciscan aspect and noted for their abnegation and fierce zeal. They were introduced into France[3] about 1567 and were favoured by Catherine de' Medici and by the family of Lorraine. Their first public appearance in the streets of Paris was at the funeral of Charles IX. Thereafter they grew in influence and had convents at Meudon and in the Rue Saint Honoré. Henri III was utterly devoted to the Capucins; he was constantly going into retirement with them either in their convents or in those various hermitages and retreats which he was so fond of erecting. It is possible that he became a member of the Third Order of St Francis, and if so this was through Capucin influence. An important personage behind the Capucins in France was Bellintani da Solo, who may have entertained Joachimist notions, and mystiques characteristic of the Franciscan spirituals.[4] Another Capucin, Bernard d'Osimo, was, as well as Auger, the King's confessor.

The strong Capucin influence at court has a bearing on the whole penitent movement. The idea of lay penitent *confréries* was Franciscan in origin;[5] St Francis's Third Order may be said to have suggested it. It was followed forty years later by St Bonaventura's confraternity of Our Lady of the Gonfalone on which the Pénitents Blancs de l'Annonciation were explicitly

[1] E. Auger, *Metanoeologie, Sur le suget de l'Archicongrégation des Penitens de l'Annonciation de Notre Dame*, Paris, 1584; see *French Academies*, pp. 165 ff. On Blaise de Vigenère and Auger and the penitent movement, see the valuable references in F. Secret, 'De quelques courants prophétiques et religieux sous le règne de Henri III', *Revue de l'histoire des religions*, 171-2 (1967), pp. 18 ff.

[2] Helyot, *op. cit.*, II, pp. 412 ff.; L. Dony d'Attichy, *Histoire générale des Minimes*, Paris, 1624; Hilarion de Nolay, *La gloire du Tiers Ordre de S. Francois*, Lyons, 1694, II, p. 178.

[3] On the Capucins in France, see the very full history by Godefroy de Paris, cited above, p. 183, note 2.

[4] See Fredegand Callaey, 'L'infiltration des idées franciscaines spirituelles chez les Frères-Mineurs-Capucins au XVIe siècle', *Miscellanea Fr. Ehrle*, Rome, 1924. For Bellintani, the Capucin reform is the final reformation announced by prophecy from Joachim of Flora onwards. Bellintani and Bernard d'Osimo were the chief Capucin influences behind Henri III.

[5] On the Franciscan origin of the penitent confraternities, see Helyot, *op. cit.*, III, pp. 158 ff.

modelled. The Franciscan character of the new devotions at the French court is emphasized in a work published in 1583.[1]

Both Jesuits and Capucins were interested in using scenes and characters from sacred drama in processions and propaganda, and the King's Procession drawings abound in evidence that personages representing saints and Biblical characters walked in the processions. The Capucins went to extravagant lengths in the use of sacred scenes in processions, which reached strange heights of exaggeration in later hysterical years. After the Day of the Barricades in 1588, when the League drove the King out of Paris, he took refuge first at Chartres, and thither, on 17 May, a procession went out from Paris. It was both an embassy from the League to the King and a religious procession of the type which he had himself done so much to encourage. It was composed of Capucins and a large number of penitents, and was led by Frère Ange, a Capucin, formerly Henri de Joyeuse, Comte de Bouchage, a brother of the Duc de Joyeuse, the bridegroom of the Magnificences. From the satirical description of this procession by De Thou[2] it is clear that it was a walking mystery-play. Frère Ange himself took the part of Christ carrying the Cross, and beside him walked 'two young Capucins disguised as two young virgins, one representing the Virgin Mary, the other Mary Magdalene, who lifted their eyes towards heaven, shedding false tears, and prostrating themselves, as though in rhythm, every time that Frère Ange allowed himself to fall'. The dramatic instincts of the Joyeuse family were here taking a religious form. It may well be that the King's Procession drawings reflect Capucin dramatic effects in processions.

Gazing at the appearance of Henri III in the last of the King's Procession drawings (K.P. 22), it is strange to think that this pathetic figure is the grandson of François Ier. It was shocking to Frenchmen like L'Estoile to see the King walking in these processions with nothing to mark his rank. As we remember the tremendous Renaissance build-up of the monarch, the ceremonial all through the century celebrating the grandeur of the *Rex Christianissimus*, the contrast with what appears to be Henri III's concept of that rôle is striking. His device of the Three Crowns, with which the King's

[1] C. de Cheffefontaines, *Apologie de la Confrairie des Penitents*, Paris, 1583. Like Auger, Cheffefontaines warmly defends Henri's penitent movements from their critics.

Such movements spread widely among the people generally in these years. L'Estoile describes (*op. cit.*, II, pp. 134-5) how hundreds of people came to Paris from the country in September 1583, walking as penitents in processions. A learned canon of Rheims describes the popular processions of multitudes of people, dressed in the penitent garb and traversing long distances on foot. He compares the movement to that of the Bianchi in Italy in 1399 (H. Meurier, *Traité de l'institution et vrai usage des processions*, Rheims, 1584, pp. 22 ff.).

[2] J. A. De Thou, *Histoire universelle*, The Hague, 1740, VII, pp. 207-8; see also Agrippa d'Aubigné, *Histoire universelle*, ed. A. de Ruble, Paris, 1893, VII, p. 218; Louis de Gonzague, *Le Père Ange de Joyeuse*, Paris, 1928, p. 151. From documents quoted by Louis de Gonzague, it is clear that Bernard d'Osimo was the organiser of this procession in which Ange de Joyeuse took the part of Christ. This is also explicitly stated in the annals of the Capucins published by Z. Boverius (Lyons, 1632, 1639, II, p. 465).

Procession opens, strikes the note of lack of worldly ambition, seeking only a Third Crown in heaven. And now, at the end, he appears in Franciscan abnegation as though this was his idea of how a Most Christian King should lead. Certainly we see here an image of the monarch which is highly unusual in the Renaissance gallery of kingship.

Yet Baïf and his friends of the Pléiade and of the Academy of Poetry and Music, those loyal co-operators in the royalist 'politique' movement, might have recognized an imperial theme in the spectacle of the Penitent King. On his accession to the throne, Baïf had dedicated to Henri a poem in which he outlined the imperialist view of history as a series of renewals. The splendours of the Roman Empire were succeeded by the darkness of the barbarian invasions; this darkness gave place to the light of the new Christian Rome; the Christian light was again gradually eclipsed by the growth of abuses in the Church which opened the door to heresy, the mother of Division; Division brought war and all the miseries of the terrible present. Out of his present darkness, Baïf calls passionately upon Henri, who has a mission to lead the world into a new light period in which peace, the arts, and virtue may flourish:[1]

> O mon Roy, Dieu te fauorise:
> Dieu te conduise a l'entreprise,
> T'en doint le coeur & le pouuoir.

And in the poem Les Mimes, addressed to Joyeuse after the Magnificences of his wedding, Baïf outlines the kind of religious movement for which he hopes. 'What is now required is not a renewal of the horrors of war in an already exhausted country but a true moral reformation, a great revival of piety and genuine holiness, and of charity towards one's neighbour'.[2] With such a movement, Baïf contrasts the aggression and repression, the cruelty and intolerance of other contemporary professedly religious movements. This is surely what we see in the King's Procession drawings, a liberal, non-aggressive religious movement, a continuation of Catherine de' Medici's 'politique' policy which she had tried to express in her court festivals. The King's Procession shows us the French court passing into an early Counter Reformation stage, yet, in spite of its intensely devotional appearance, it is moving to the musical rhythms of ballets and masques. It is a transposition into Counter Reformation forms of the rhythms of the ballets and the masquerades of court festival. This was indeed noted, with extreme disapproval, by Agrippa d'Aubigné. Satirizing the 'invention of Orders', the processions of 'mad Capucins' absurdly disguised, the courtiers now going

---

[1] Baïf, *Evvres en rime*, ed. C. Marty-Laveaux, Paris, 1881–90, V, p. 256; quoted *French Academies*, p. 230.

[2] *French Academies*, p. 260, quoting Baïf, *Les Mimes*. See also the quotations from *Les Mimes*, above, p. 167.

through the streets in penitent masks, D'Aubigné proclaims that such *processions* are really nothing but *ballets*.[1]

The French royal Counter Reformation has an artistic accent of its own. And in its purely religious aspect it is not in line with the Catholic League, for its apparently fantastically Catholic penitent processions hide an attitude more in line with the Erasmianism of Catherine de' Medici's policy than with the contemporary forms of Catholic revival which the League was trying to enforce. It was to be a leading theme in the violent League propaganda against Henri III in the terrible years to come that he was a 'hypocrite', that all his pretensions of extreme piety in his various religious activities were a mask behind which he hid intentions inimical to the Catholic religion. This propaganda was basically political, paid for with Spanish money as part of the campaign for the Spanish hegemony of Europe. Yet these intimations of secret purposes, of something enigmatic behind Henri's movements, persisted.

Nicolas Houel and the House of Christian Charity

The charity which was supported by the royal movement of penitence and charity was the Maison de Charité Chrétienne, founded by Nicolas Houel, artistic adviser to Catherine de' Medici. It was situated in the Faubourg Saint-Marceau, not far from Baïf's Academy of Poety and Music. Obviously, it becomes important to find out all we can about this House of Charity in case it may contain clues as to the inner meaning of the whole movement. First, let us look again at the Queen's Procession drawings which purport to describe the Charity.

In the first drawing (Plate 35, Queen's Procession 1), the Queen and her ladies are seen leaving the Louvre, stepping out with an eager dancing measure. The following drawings use a technique with which we are familiar from the King's Procession drawings: in the foregrounds marches a procession of dignitaries and representatives of the Charity; in the backgrounds, the Charity itself is unrolled. In Q.P. 2 (Plate 35), the procession includes Nicolas Houel himself, followed by the officials of the town; behind the

---

[1] 'Les ordres inventez, les chants, les hurlements,
Des fols capuchonnés, les nouveaux regiments
Qui, en procession sottement desguisées,
Aux villes et aux champs vont semer de risées
L'austerité des voeux & des fraternités,
Tout cela n'a caché nos rudes veritez.
Tous ces desguisements sont vaines mascarades
Qui aux portes d'Enfer presentent leurs aubades,
Ribauds de la paillarde, ou affectez valets
Qui de *processions* luy donnent des ballets'

(Agrippa d'Aubigné, *Les Tragiques*, in *Œuvres*, ed. Réaume and Caussade, IV, pp. 99-100).

wall in the background we see a countrified district in the Faubourg Saint-Marceau, watered by the little stream of the Bièvre. The procession (continuing in Plate 36, Q.P. 3) now includes, according to the captions on the drawings, 'preceptors and masters for teaching the poor orphan children', who wear long-sleeved gowns of 'escarlatte violette' colour. This colour is always specified in the captions as that of the uniforms of the House of Charity. In the background, the herb garden begins; the pavilion on its wall is labelled 'Hall for conferring about medicine, pharmacy, and surgery'.

The teaching staff of the Charity continues in the procession in the next drawing (Plate 36, Q.P. 4) revealing a remarkable curriculum for the orphans. A teacher of Hebrew and a teacher of Greek – 'in the dress of their countries' specifies the caption – are followed by five other language teachers, all in the dress of their countries. These costumes give the teaching staff the air of a masquerade, and suggest a breadth of interest in languages, including oriental languages, surely very unusual in a Counter Reformation orphanage. In the background, the herb garden continues, and under an arbour 'doctors and apothecaries are disputing about the properties of simple medicines.' The procession in the next drawing (Plate 37, Q.P. 5) presents widows with their female orphan pupils, and in the background the herb garden is being watered.

In the remaining drawings (Plates 37–9, Q.P. 6–10), the main buildings and activities of the Charity are suggested; the 'apothicairerie' (Q.P. 6–7) where the medicines made from the herbs grown in the garden are distributed to the sick poor; the chapel (Q.P. 8); the school (Q.P. 9); the hospital, combined with a school of music and a 'French Academy for various kinds of artisans' (Q.P. 10). The drawings are alive with figures engaged in all these numerous activities and give an extraordinary impression of eager effort.

Looking back to the King's Procession, where the Charitable Men in long buttoned gowns (Plates 28–9, K.P. 10–12) represent the Works of Mercy, it is clear (as suggested earlier) that these men are the staff of the House of Charity. If these drawings were coloured, their uniforms would be scarlet-violet. They represent the Work of healing the sick through carrying phials, alembics, and dried herbs, alluding to the characteristic activity of the House, and to its emphasis on medicine as the Work of Love with which it associated its other works.

Nicolas Houel[1] was an unusual kind of apothecary, a bourgeois virtuoso

---

[1] For a brief account of Nicolas Houel, see my *French Academies*, pp. 157–8. The fullest study so far is still J. J. Guiffrey, 'Nicolas Houel apothicaire parisien fondateur de la maison de Charité Chrétienne', *Mémoires de la Société de l'Histoire de Paris et de l'Ile de France*, XXV (1898), pp. 179–270. The documents about the charity are printed in M. Félibien, *Histoire de la ville de Paris*, Paris, 1725, II, pp. 1133 ff. On Houel as apothecary, see M. G. Planchon, 'Le jardin des apothicaires de Paris', *Journal de pharmacie et de chimie*, XXV (1893), pp. 251 ff. There is a biography by S. E. Lepinios, *Nicolas Houel*, Dijon, 1911. Other studies bearing on Houel will be mentioned below.

who had long been in contact with Catherine de' Medici, for whom he had designed important artistic projects. Houel was the author of the *Histoire d'Artémise*, which as illustrated by Caron and other artists, was the basis of the build-up of Catherine in her rôle of Artemisia, widow of Mausolus, which was so much used in the court mythology and was alluded to at the entry of Charles IX.[1] The illustrations to Houel's lost *Histoire des anciens rois de France*[2] provided conventional iconography for the mythical ancient kings upon which Ronsard drew for his designs for the same entry. Houel was a man drenched in the iconography and mythology of French court festivals and entries, a man who had been professionally employed in drawing up large artistic schemes full of contemporary reference.

It must surely have been Houel who designed the procession drawings. Probably he used artists in his circle to make the actual drawings, but the plan for them must surely have been formulated by Houel himself, a design revealing his intimate knowledge of contemporary royal interests. Houel's long-standing association with court artistic schemes gives authority to the procession drawings as the design of a man intimately acquainted with artistic work for court circles.

The proximity of Houel's House of Charity to Baïf's Academy of Poetry and Music suggests that the apothecary would surely have known much about that centre. There is actually a concert in progress in one of the Queen's Procession drawings (Plate 39, Q.P. 10). There had been a curious institution, centred on an apothecary's garden and near Baïf's Academy in the Faubourg Saint-Marceau, before the time of Nicolas Houel. This was the 'Lyceum' of Jacques Gohorry, or Leo Suavius, alchemist, magician, and Paracelsist physician. Gohorry's establishment is thus described by D. P. Walker:[3]

> It was in an apothecary's garden, where he prepared Paracelsan medicines, did alchemical experiments, made talismans 'suivant l'opinion d'Arnaud de Villeneuve, & de Marsilius Ficinus', and where he received learned visitors who admired the rare plants and trees, played skittles, and performed vocal and instrumental music in the 'galérie historiée'.

Gohorry's centre seems to have come to an end at his death in 1576, and Walker suggests that[4]

> it is possibly more than a coincidence that in that year Nicolas Houel began to work for the foundation of his *Maison de Charité* which included an apothecary's garden, a medical laboratory, and a music school, and which was situated in the Faubourg Saint-Marceau.

[1] See above, pp. 134-5.   [2] See above, p. 132.
[3] D. P. Walker, *Spiritual and Demonic Magic from Ficino to Campanella*, Warburg Institute, 1958, p. 100.
[4] Walker, *loc. cit.*

It certainly sounds as though Houel might have taken over something from Gohorry's establishment, though, as far as one knows, Houel was not a Paracelsist, and the striking side of his institution, that it was a charity as well as an apothecary's garden, would seem to have owed nothing to either Gohorry or Baïf.

The earliest documentary reference to Houel's charity is his request to King and Parliament in 1576 for permission to establish an orphanage in which poor children should be trained in the cultivation of medicinal herbs and the manufacture of medicines from them for the benefit of the sick poor.[1] After various false starts, this charity was established by 1578 in an old house with a long history, the Hôpital de Lourcine in the Faubourg Saint-Marceau. This suburb was then a countrified district through which ran the river Bièvre (seen in Plate 35, Q.P. 2), the pure waters of which were to be utilized by the dyers of the Gobelins tapestries. In 1579 there were serious floods in which the Bièvre overflowed its banks. Twenty-two poor persons asleep in the Maison de Charité Chrétienne narrowly escaped drowning; the orphans were much alarmed; the drugs in the 'apothicairerie' for the poor were spoilt by the water; and the chapel was flooded. These details are quoted from an appeal for help which Houel published in 1579;[2] they show that a charity on the lines indicated in the drawings really existed.

Houel lived in hopes that his charity would expand to magnificent proportions through funds to be obtained from his interest at court. A manuscript account of the charity by Houel,[3] dated 1578, expatiates in sonnets addressed to the King and the two Queens (Queen Louise, and Catherine, the Queen Mother) on this work of mercy. This account, without the introductory part with the sonnets, was printed in 1580 with the title *Advertissement et déclaration de la Maison de Charité Chrétienne*. Houel says that when it pleases God to increase the wealth of this poor house by inspiring the King, princes, and other persons to bestow on it their alms, he hopes to expand the scope of the school by having taught in it the seven liberal arts and other disciplines and sciences, including the Hebrew and Greek and other tongues.[4]

The King's movements of chivalry and penitence, which involved a great extension of funds available for charitable purposes through the alms contributed by all the court,[5] aroused the hope that Houel's charity, encouraged and patronized by royalty, would benefit enormously from the movements. The Queen's Procession drawings have a title-page with three coats of arms; in the centre, the King's device, surrounded by the collar of the Saint Esprit,

---

[1] Félibien, *op. cit.*, III, p. 721; cf. Lepinois, *op. cit.*, p. 95.

[2] N. Houel, *Ample discours de ce qui est nouvellement survenu és Faulxbourgs S. Marcel*, Paris, 1579.

[3] Bibl. Nat., MS. Fr. 5726.

[4] *Advertissement*, p. 23.

[5] Auger (*Metanoeologie*, p. 107) indicates that very considerable sums of money may have been made available by the penitents for charitable purposes.

is flanked by the arms of the two Queens. A sonnet on penitence and charity is signed with Houel's monogram and motto, and the date, 1584.

In the Queen's Procession drawings we therefore see an institution which was already functioning more or less on the lines indicated, but which it was hoped to expand greatly through funds expected from the religious movements. Some of what we see in the drawings was no doubt only at the project stage, particularly the lofty scope of the education in the school. This also applies to the buildings, as projected rather than actually in being. The school and the hospital (Plate 39, Q.P. 9 and 10) are based on a design in one of Philibert Delorme's books for a large building which can be erected at small cost.[1] Houel appears to have been able to begin to carry out new building projects, for in a letter of May 1585, it is said that he has 'already begun several fine buildings necessary for the upkeep of our foundation, including a chapel . . . placed out of the danger of flooding'.[2] Further information about the house, and Houel's plans for it, can be derived from a set of miniatures, formerly at Cracow,[3] but these cannot be considered here. The outbreak of the wars of the League, in 1585, no doubt put a stop to new building. Houel died in 1587.

The Family of Love

When I was working on the meaning and iconography of the Procession drawings, years ago, I knew nothing about a secret sect, the Family of Love, which the work of several scholars has made better known in recent years.[4] Many very important people secretly belonged to this sect, amongst them Ortelius, the geographer, Justius Lipsius, the classical scholar, and, above all, Christopher Plantin, the printer. The Familists taught that inner spiritual life alone mattered and that, in comparison with this, adherence to officially established forms of religion was of little importance and might be changed as circumstances dictated. The Familist, secure in his inner life, would conform as a Protestant if that was the dominant form in his surroundings, or as a Catholic in a Catholic country, or – as might happen in the troubled sixteenth century – if the dominant confessional form changed in his country, he could move from one side to the other with changing governments. This may seem a somewhat ambiguous and deceptive mode of life, but both Catholic and Protestant extremists were illiberal, persecuting, and bigoted,

[1] Philibert Delorme, *Nouvelles inventions pour bien bastir à petits fraiz*, Paris, 1561, p. 31.

[2] Archives de l'Ecole de Pharmacie, Notes par Julliot, fol. 18; printed in Félibien, *op. cit.*, III.

[3] These miniatures were destroyed in the war but had fortunately been well reproduced; see A. de Laborde, *Nicolas Houel, fondateur de la Maison de Charité Chrétienne*, Société des Bibliophiles Français, Paris, 1937.

[4] H. de la Fontaine Verwey, 'Trois hereiarques', *Bibliothèque d'humanisme et Renaissance*, XVI (1954), pp. 312-30; J. A. Van Dorsten, *The Radical Arts*, Leiden, 1970, pp. 27 ff. The fundamental work by B. Rekers, *Benito Arias Montano*, published in Dutch in 1960, is now available in English translation, Warburg Institute, 1972.

equally distasteful to persons of tolerant and mystical temper; secret member-ship of the Family of Love could provide a solution for such persons. Plantin was a most ardent member of the sect, and at his printing presses in Antwerp he printed the works of the Familist prophets, first those of Henry Niclaes, known as 'H.N.', and later those of Henry Barrefelt, known as 'Hiel' or the Light of God.

An extraordinary aspect of the influence of this sect is that it could flourish in the most unexpected places. Arias Montanus, who was librarian at the Escorial, belonged to it under the very eyes of Philip II. Montanus was a Hebrew scholar, and, with the French Hebrew scholar, Guillaume Postel, and others, he was engaged on the famous polyglot edition of the Bible, printed by Plantin and sponsored by Philip II. Such sponsorship would seem to ensure extreme Counter-Reformation orthodoxy, but in this Bible Familist influences have been uncovered, with the discovery that Montanus introduced into its commentaries mystical and allegorical interpretations of Biblical texts emanating from the Familist prophet, Hiel. This whole strange movement was, in some respects, a continuation of the Erasmian tradition of tolerance and Biblical study; the Familist editors of the Polyglot Bible were drawing on Hebrew sources for their new Bible in their effort to return to the Scriptural text. Their Hebrew scholarship was looked at askance by the rigorously orthodox, and they lived dangerously, having to keep their mysticism concealed under a code language.

The usual name for this sect was the House of Love, an affirmation of its belief in charity as the chief of virtues. It had strong French connections: Plantin himself was French, and amongst the scholars who worked for the polyglot Bible were Guillaume Postel, the believer in French monarchy, and Guy Le Fèvre de la Boderie, the author of La Galliade. The sect was certainly well diffused in Paris through Pierre Porret, one of Plantin's oldest and closest friends, the manager of a branch of the Plantin business in the rue Saint-Jacques. Porret is known to have been an agent, not only for the Plantin publications, but also for the diffusion of Familist teachings.[1]

The other salient fact that is known about Porret is that he was an apothe-cary. (He was known to Jacques Gohorry who called him 'homme tres-ingenieux & bon simpliste'.)[2] There is an association of ideas here, 'Parisian apothecary' and 'Familist', which suddenly seems significant in relation to Nicolas Houel, Parisian apothecary and founder of a House of Love.

The resemblance of the name of Houel's foundation to the name of the sect need not necessarily have any Familist significance. Houel's orphanage was a Christian work of mercy whose main emblem was a most orthodox

[1] On the importance of the apothecary, Pierre Porret, in disseminating Familism in Paris, see Wallace Kirsop, The Family of Love in France, Sydney University Press, III (1964-5), pp. 103-18.
[2] Ibid., p. 107.

Counter-Reformation type of the virtue of Charity. Nevertheless, there are some points in the Processions drawings which might indicate Familist influence. There is the point noticed earlier, the insistence on *Hebrew*, Greek and other languages as subjects to be taught in Houel's school. Apparently this linguistic side of the school was a project rather than anything actually in existence. Nevertheless, it is an indication that Houel attached importance to the study of Hebrew, which, in view of the current controversies for and against 'Hebraizing' influence in religious movements, may have some meaning in relation to the House of Charity. To this hint may be added the figure of the Jewish priest who appears in the Procession drawings (K.P. 8, 14). The type of the Jewish priest used here is similar to the Aaron in the Polyglot Bible, and such as can be seen in the *Humanae salutis monumenta* (published by Plantin at Antwerp in 1571) by Arias Montanus. Several of the Biblical scenes in K.P. 7-9 (Plates 26-8) are reminiscent of illustrations in this book by Arias Montanus, the Familist. There is a long allegory about Jonah the prophet who preached penitence to the King of Nineveh, in Montanus's commentary on that prophet, which is illuminating to read when looking at the last scene in the King's Procession[1] where Jonah is preaching penitence to the French King (Plate 34, K.P. 22). Others, with ·uller knowledge of Familist modes of expression, may see other meanings in the Procession drawings. Their delicate and allusive use of allegory seems to add another dimension to the stereotypes of Counter-Reformation propaganda.

These suggestions must be left in the form of an enigma or a question, rather than a statement of fact. Statements of fact are, in any case, hard to come by in relation to secret sects or societies. Looking at the Charitable Men in the King's Procession (Plates 28-9, K.P. 10-12) and considering the emphasis on healing the sick poor for nothing in Houel's charity, one thinks also of a later mystery, of the Rosicrucian manifestoes published in Germany in 1614 and 1615, with their emphasis on the rule of the Rosicrucian Order concerning healing the sick, and that gratis.[2] Is it possible that Houel's House of Christian Charity shows us a kind of Familist anticipation of Rosicrucianism? Such questions may never be answered, but the asking of them may serve to focus the attention of scholars interested in these problems on Nicolas Houel and the Procession drawings.

It is not historically improbable that, at this late stage in the French sixteenth century, the disgust of civilized persons at the continual resumption of the absurd wars of religion, the horror of Christians at the frightful tyranny inflicted on the Netherlands in the name of Catholic Counter Reformation (a horror deeply felt by Plantin, the mystical printer) would have resulted in retreat into secrecy. The evolution of a Pléiadist into a

---

[1] See Analysis, below, p. 204.
[2] See my *The Rosicrucian Enlightenment*, London, 1972, p. 44 and *passim*.

Familist is a phenomenon which one might expect at this date, even if there were no evidence for it. The French monarchy was moving towards association with the Imperial Virgin of England, in the effort to counteract the menacing encirclement with which it was threatened by the Catholic League. Henri III's brother, François d'Anjou, suitor of Elizabeth of England and for a time ruler of a state in the southern Netherlands in which religious toleration was attempted, was the centre of an important 'politique' group of thinkers. A student of Familism in France has said:[1]

> Thin as the evidence is, it does not run counter to the view that the intellectual climate of the French court, and singularly of Monsieur's household, could not be hostile to the Familist retreat from religious war into a spirituality, even a mysticism, largely indifferent to outward forms.

It is therefore not impossible that Houel's House of Christian Charity, interpreted in a secretly Familist sense, might represent the final attitude of the Valois court before its disappearance, a last attempt to avert, and escape from, disaster.

Knights of the Holy Spirit and Knights of the Garter: the Garter Embassy, February 1585

In February 1585, the *rapprochement* between France and England in the face of their common enemy, Spain, found expression in the visit of a special embassy from the English court for the purpose of conferring the Order of the Garter on the French King.[2] The bald facts are noted by L'Estoile. The embassy arrived on 23 February, and on the last day of that month the King, attired in the robes of the English Order of the Garter, was received into that Order after vespers in the church of the Augustins.[3] Elias Ashmole, the historian of the Order of the Garter, gives a more detailed account of the proceedings,[4] from which we can picture the Elizabethan Knights of

---

[1] Kirsop, *op. cit.*, p. 113. As an example of Familist penetration in court circles, Kirsop (p. 108) points to the poet Hesteau de Nuysement who was closely in contact with Porret and with Familism, and who was nominated secretary to Henri III and his brother in 1578, probably recommended by Dorat and Baïf. It may also be significant that, in 1577, Plantin received an offer from Henri III to establish himself in Paris as 'royal printer for ten languages' (L. Voet, *The Golden Compasses*, Amsterdam, 1969, I, p. 91). The offer, which was refused, was made through Pontus de Tyard, *doyen* of the Pléiade, and the exponent of its musical philosophy.

That Henri III was interested in oriental languages is stated by Guy Le Fèvre de la Boderie in his dedication to the King in 1584 of a New Testament in Syriac; this dedication abounds in prophecies about the *Rex Christianissimus* (see F. Secret, *op. cit.*, pp. 11–13).

[2] The festivals for the Garter embassy are discussed in relation to the desperate contemporary situation in *The Valois Tapestries*, Warburg Institute, 1959, pp. 111–19.

[3] L'Estoile, *op. cit.*, II, pp. 181–3.

[4] Elias Ashmole, *The History, Laws, and Ceremonies of the Noble Order of the Garter*, London, 1672, pp. 406–11.

the Garter moving with the Knights of the Holy Spirit in the Paris which we see in the Processions drawings.

Ashmole relates how the Knights of the Saint Esprit turned out in their full robes and regalia and accompanied the Knights of the Garter to the Augustins. They did not walk in procession from the Louvre but from a specially prepared house near the Augustins, and the route was heavily guarded. The streets were dangerous through the rising fanaticism of supporters of the Catholic League, to whom the royal reception of the heretic knights was most obnoxious. The French King received the Order after vespers to avoid any difficulty about the Protestant knights being present at Mass. The church of the Augustins was hung with rich arras and cloth of gold; within it were erected two cloths of state, one for the Queen of England (who was not, of course, present), and the other for the King of France. The two French Queens (Catherine, the Queen Mother, and Queen Louise) were present, and all the ladies of the court. That evening there was a splendid banquet and after it a ball and a masque. 'I omit the description of the Masque', adds Ashmole, 'and other singular Musick both costly and curious, whereby the evening was spent till three of the Clock of the next morning.' Fortunately, Ashmole's omission has been filled in by the discovery of a letter to Queen Elizabeth from the Earl of Derby, the head of the embassy which brought the Garter, and Sir Edward Stafford, the English ambassador in Paris, which gives a remarkable description of the masque and the 'singular Musick'.[1]

The Englishmen were sitting with the royal party at one end of the hall, and towards them advanced the music, divided into companies. They came forward 'singing and playing all the way as they marched with such a consort and harmony as nothing could be devised more pleasant and delightfull, as well for the rarenesse of the musicke, both voyces and Instrumentes, as strangenes of the attyre and apparele'. Afterwards, the King himself entered as leader of a masque of twenty-four persons, attired in white doublets and hats of cloth of silver embroidered with pearls. The musicians having taken their places, the masque came on dancing,[2]

> the king foremost, and therein did express by the variety of casting themselves all the letters both in the King and Queenes name: a matter wondered at of all beholders for the good decorum kept at all handes in so strange a manner of dancing.

It was a delicate way of expressing the alliance to the English, by dancing the letters in HENRI and ELIZABETH[3] in one of those marvellous ballets for

---

[1] Bodleian, Tanner MS. 78. The letter was discovered by R. Strong and published in his article 'Festivals for the Garter Embassy at the Court of Henri III', *Journal of the Warburg and Courtauld Institutes*, XXII (1959), pp. 60–70.

[2] Quoted, *ibid.*, p. 67.

[3] It was clearly the names of the King of France and the Queen of England that were spelled

which the French court was famed. The consummate artistry of this performance, and the utter brilliance of the King's dancing, was fully appreciated by the Englishmen, who try to express to Queen Elizabeth, in words almost broken with their enthusiasm, the astonishing nature of this spectacle. They can neither 'appraise, nor any way conceyve the commendation it deserveth', and 'the king deserveth the greatest honor that conducted and led all the rest.'

There was desperation in the King's dancing. The Guises were not present at the Garter festivals; they were busy raising their armies for the wars of the League which shortly broke out. The King was driven from Paris, and eventually, in 1589, the *Rex Christianissimus* disappeared from the European scene in those desperate assassinations of the Guises and the King which ended the tragedy of the Last of the Valois.

The processional frenzy was kept up by the League in a militant direction. In the well-known 'Procession of the League' (Plate 40) reflecting a procession in Paris in 1593, Capucins can be seen, heavily armed, and some penitents with their hoods down because they are wearing helmets. The League made a seditious use of those emotional processions which the King had himself fostered, and the penitent *confréries* were used as militant associations against him. The propaganda of the League, in its distortions of the King's religious movements, gives information about them which is indirectly valuable. The League preachers associate Henri with magic and sorcery and with devil-worship, the devils being in the form of pagan satyrs and sirens, alluding to the artistic magic of the court festivals.[1] And this sorcerer and devil-worshipper, cry the League preachers, had accepted the Garter from the heretic Queen of England, and encouraged the heretic, Henry of Navarre![2] The frantic frenzy, and the malicious use of religious imagery against their victim by the propagandists of the League, remind one of the tone of the propaganda against Frederick of the Palatinate after his defeat.

The English alliance and the Imperial Virgin's Armada victory of 1588 came too late to save Henri III, but his movements had repercussions on such themes as the Spenserian view of Chivalry and the Shakespearean interpretation of Kingship which have not yet been examined. The Garter Festivals, which drew together Knights of the Garter and Knights of the Holy Spirit in common celebration of HENRI and ELIZABETH, are expressive of those interactions between French monarchy and English monarchy which run all through the century and are not fully understandable on the purely political level, involving as they do the Idea of the Monarch in its religious aspect.

---

out, the two monarchs concerned in the alliance, and not the names of the King and Queen of France, as Strong assumed (*ibid.*, p. 69).

[1] *French Academies*, pp. 170 ff.
[2] *Ibid.*, p. 231.

The Procession Drawings

Procession de Henry III, Roy de France et de Pologne, dite des Penitens et des Flagellans: avec les Chevaliers du St. Esprit, de la première création, marchant trois à trois; et partant du Louvre pour se rendre aux grands Augustins, longeant les quais du Louvre, le Pont aux Meuniers, dit aujourd'hui le Pont au Change, et le Pont St. Michel, en 1579, le Ier janvier (Paris, Cabinet des Estampes, Pd. 29 Réserve).

'Procession de Louise de Lorraine femme de Henry III allant du Louvre au Faubourg St. Marceau pour poser la première pierre de la Nouvelle Maison dite Maison Chrétienne, projetée même commencée en 1584' (Paris, Cabinet des Estampes, Pd. 30 Réserve).

The above titles are not in a contemporary hand and some of their information is suspect. The date 1579 cannot be right for the King's Procession, which must be later than the founding of Pénitents de l'Annonciation in 1583. There is no evidence in the Queen's Procession drawings or elsewhere that the Queen was going to lay a foundation stone for new buildings.

The Queen's Procession is preceded by a page containing poems and other prefatory matter in a contemporary hand, and there was probably a similar preface to the King's Procession which is now missing.

The drawings may originally have formed two uninterrupted friezes, but they are preserved as thirty-two separate drawings, the average size of which is about 35 by 55 centimetres, and which are pasted into two albums. They are pen and wash drawings with some very slight colour in the Queen's Procession.

With them is a rambling account in an eighteenth-century hand which states that they had been preserved in the family of the Vicomte de Beaune who presented them in 1765 to the King's Collection. The ancestor from whom the drawings had descended in the Beaune family was probably Renaud de Beaune, Archibishop of Bourges, who was a member of the Pénitents Blancs de l'Annonciation.

The artists of the processions are unidentified. In the King's Procession there are at least two different hands.

Analysis of the Procession Drawings

King's Procession (Captions on the drawings are given in italics)

K.P. 1 (Plate 24) *Le pont aux meusniers. La porte du chateau*
Background   The Pont aux Meûniers (the Millers' Bridge), connecting the

right bank of the Seine with the Ile de la Cité. The water-wheels which drove the mills can be seen under the bridge.

Procession Three youths, the one in the centre carries the King's device of the Three Crowns, surrounded by the collar of the Order of the Holy Spirit.

Three Knights of the Holy Spirit, wearing the robes and collar of the Order and carrying tapers.

Three boys carrying the Instruments of the Passion.

K.P. 2 (Plate 25) *Jardin du Palais. Les femmes et filles penitentes. Le Palais*

Background The Palais de Justice and its garden.

Procession Three Knights of the Holy Spirit.

Mary Magdalene, with the alabaster pot of ointment.

Mary of Egypt, with her long hair and carrying the three loaves of her legend (see A. Jameson, *Sacred and Legendary Art*, Boston, New York, 1897, I, p. 408).

Penitent women.

K.P. 3 (Plate 24) *Les femmes penitentes qui embrassent les vertus et bonnes œuvres*

Background Church of the Grands Augustins and chapel of the Order of the Holy Spirit.

The Pont-Neuf under construction.

Procession Three Knights of the Holy Spirit.

Hope; Charity; Faith;

Fortitude; Prudence;

Temperance; Justice.

K.P. 4 (Plate 25) *Les bonnes œuvres des femmes penitentes*

Background The Hôtel de Nevers?

Procession Knights of the Holy Spirit.

The Three Maries, with their vases of ointment and the angels who awaited them at the sepulchre.

Wise Virgins with lighted lamps.

K.P. 5 (Plate 26) *Ste Cecile. Les vierges qui* (caption continued on next drawing) *chantent hymnes et cantiques*

Background Tour de Nesle.

Procession Wise Virgins continued.

Three Knights of the Holy Spirit.

St Cecilia, with women playing musical instruments.

K.P. 6 (Plate 27) *Vierges presentant la virginité*

Background Saint-Germain des Prés?

Procession   Women with musical instruments.
Three Knights of the Holy Spirit.
St Ursula, bearing a crown, and followed by Virgin Martyrs.

K.P. 7 (Plate 26: no caption)
Background   The real backgrounds in the real Paris cease and give way to Biblical backgrounds. (The Biblical scenes in this and the following drawing have been identified by comparison with illustrations in Gabriel Simeoni, *Figure de la Bibbia*, Lyons, 1577.)

Angels announcing the birth of Isaac to Abraham and Sarah, dwelling in tents in the desert (Genesis 18).

Hannah, with Eli, praying in the Temple for a son (1 Samuel 1).

Procession   Three Knights of the Holy Spirit.
Charity, with burning heart and many children.
Abraham with crucifix (as a type of Christ).
Isaac, carrying the faggots for his own sacrifice and followed by his mother, Sarah.
Hannah, with her son Samuel.
(These characters have very much the look of actors in sacred drama; the Sacrifice of Abraham was a popular subject for mystery plays.)

K.P. 8 (Plate 27) *Les femmes steriles rendues fertiles*
Background   (Left) Elisha arriving at the Shunamite woman's house, and praying in the 'little chamber on the wall' over her dead son who comes to life (2 Kings 4).
(Centre) Clothing being distributed to the poor.
(Right) The birth of the Virgin.
(The left and right scenes look like street stages.)
Procession   Eli (he belongs with Hannah and Samuel in the preceding drawing).
The Shunamite woman with her husband and child and Elisha.
The parents of the Virgin, with the Virgin as a child.
The parents of John the Baptist, Zacharias and Elizabeth, with John the Baptist as a child.

K.P. 9 (Plate 28) *Les roynes et princesses saintes. Les vefues* [widows] *qui vesto-yent* [clothe] *les pauvres.*
Background   (Left) The annunciation of the birth of John the Baptist in the Temple; devout crowds listen to the news.

(This scene is rather close to the illustrations of the same subject in Arias Montanus, *Humanae salutis monumenta*, Antwerp, 1571, no. xxxiv, 'Zacharias'.)

(Right) A modern building and a street in contemporary Paris. Could this be the convent of the Capucins in the rue St Honoré?

Procession   Queen Louise de Lorraine holding a model of a church and surrounded by children.

Group of other 'queens and holy princesses', including Catherine de' Medici, all holding models of pious foundations.

Group of women with banner of St Stephen, perhaps representing some association of 'widows who clothe the poor'.

K.P. 10 (Plate 29: no caption)

Background   The Works of Mercy: (Left) giving food and drink; (Centre) giving clothing; (Right) receiving pilgrims.

Procession   Three Knights of the Holy Spirit.

The leader of the Charitable Men, in long buttoned robe, carrying a banner with the Last Judgment and accompanied by two angels.

Four Charitable Men, carrying food and drink.

K.P. 11 (Plate 28: no caption)

Background   The Work of healing the sick; the story of the Good Samaritan told in three episodes.

Procession   Two Charitable Men carrying clothing.

Two Charitable Men carrying pilgrims' staffs, ewers and towels.

Four Charitable Men (one in next drawing) carrying phials, alembics, bundles of dried herbs.

K.P. 12 (Plate 29: no caption)

Background   (Left) The Work of relieving prisoners.

(Right) The Work of burying the dead.

Procession   Charitable Man carrying dried herbs (belongs with the last group in the preceding drawing).

Charitable Men as knightly figures, wearing crosses (suggestion of a military Order concerned with rescuing prisoners from the Turks).

Charitable Men with skulls (work of burying the dead).

K.P. 13 (Plate 30: no caption)

The preceding drawings have been about Charity and the work of the Maison de Charité Chrétienne. This and the following drawings are about Penitence, exemplified from the Penitent *confréries*.

Background   Here, and in the following drawings, the river reappears. Buildings seen across the river do not refer to a topographical sequence, but are connected with the figures in the procession. The building seen here may refer to an erection by Henri III at Vincennes for the Blue Penitents of St Jerome, or 'Hieronymites' (*see French Academies*, pp. 159–60).

Procession   Three Knights of the Holy Spirit.

St Jerome as a penitent, beating his breast with a stone (for the type, see E. Mâle, *L'art religieux après le Concile de Trente*, Paris, 1932, fig. 289).

Blue Penitents of St Jerome carrying stones and wearing hair shirts.

Knights of the Holy Spirit.

K.P. 14 (Plate 31: no caption)

Background   A river scene. These quiet river scenes are suggestive of private penitence in contemplative retreats as compared with the public penitence seen in the procession.

Procession   The White Penitents or Congrégation des Pénitents Blancs de l'Annonciation, founded in 1583, and closely connected with the Ordre du Saint-Esprit.

They wear the penitent garb, covering the face and with eyeholes. The mark on the left shoulder was copied from the 'Gonfalone' penitent association.

The leader carries a banner with the Annunciation.

Others carry torches, suggesting a night procession.

One carries a crucifix.

King David with his harp, attended by two Jewish priests, swinging censers.

The group suggests that the penitents may be singing the penitential psalms of David.

K.P. 15 (Plate 30: no caption)

Background   Across the river is seen a walled building, perhaps a house or retreat connected with the White Penitents.

Procession   The White Penitents continue. The choirboys and the group of singers with music books do not wear the 'Gonfalone' mark, indicating the slightly different footing of the musicians.

K.P. 16 (Plate 31) *Les prophetes*

Background   Continuation of the river scene, with distant ecclesiastical buildings.

Procession   Knights of the Holy Spirit.

St John the Baptist, carrying his head, and flanked by two prophets, prophesying from scrolls.

A group of penitents carrying scourges and wearing hair shirts. This is probably an allusion to a confraternity of Black Penitents, or Pénitents Noirs de St Jean Décollé (the beheaded St John), on which see Helyot, III, pp. 219 ff. The special Work of these penitents was to attend condemned criminals to the place of execution, a Work illustrated in the next drawing.

K.P. 17 (Plate 32) *Les enchaisnés criminels*

Background   This is rather indistinct. The curious suggestion of walls may be an allusion to prison walls.

Procession   Three Knights of the Holy Spirit.

Chained criminals being accompanied to the place of execution by Charity, with burning heart, and others.

Knights of the Holy Spirit.

K.P. 18 (Plate 33) *Les Enfans de la Charité. Les Confrères de la Charité*

Background   A large building, or complex of buildings, which continues in the backgrounds of the next two drawings. This, as Guiffrey suggested (article cited above, p. 188, note 1), is almost certainly Nicolas Houel's Maison de Charité Chrétienne, perhaps not as it actually was, but enlarged as he hoped it would be through the funds made available by the penitent movements.

Procession   The 'enfans de la Charité' are like the orphans seen in the Maison de Charité Chrétienne in the Queen's Procession (see Plate 37, Q.P. 6). There was a *confrérie* attached to the House of Charity, members of which can be seen in the same drawing (Q.P. 6), barefooted, as they are here, and carrying a reliquary.

This scene is therefore expressive of Houel's charity, as were also the scenes in which the staff of his charity represented the Works of Mercy (Plates 28 and 29, K.P. 10, 11 and 12).

The long procession here arrives at its object, the House of Love.

K.P. 19 (Plate 32: no caption)

Background   The Maison de Charité Chrétienne continues.

Procession   Three Knights of the Holy Spirit.

Two priests swinging censers.

A canopy, supported by Knights of the Holy Spirit, under which a bishop carries the Host.

K.P. 20 (Plate 33: no caption)

Background   The Maison de Charité Chrétienne continues.

Procession   Continuation of the canopy seen in the last drawing, supported by Knights of the Holy Spirit.

Two priests with censers.

A very important-looking figure wearing a 'bonnet Henri III' and the robes of the Order. Beside him, as tall as himself, is a handsome cardinal. Perhaps this is the Duc de Guise with his brother the cardinal.

Near them is probably the little Cardinal de Bourbon, whom they afterwards tried to make king.

In the group following them, Catherine de' Medici can be distinguished.

K.P. 21 (Plate 34: this drawing, and the following one, was probably added in 1584, to include the processions of that year.)

Background   Buildings in the background perhaps refer to the convent of the Minimes at Nigeon. A procession of Penitents went to the Minimes at Nigeon in February 1584 (L'Estoile, *op. cit.*, II, p. 148).

The main allusion of this and the following drawing is to the King's pilgrimage of March 1584, in which large numbers of Penitents were joined by detachments of Minimes and Capucins.

Procession   Three Knights of the Holy Spirit.

Group of Minimes, the leader carrying a crucifix.

Three Knights of the Holy Spirit.

Group of Capucins, the leader carrying a large wooden cross (the Capucins are continued in the next drawing).

K.P. 22 (Plate 34) *Les Capucins*

Background   The building with the large wooden cross in its grounds alludes to the convent of the Capucins at Meudon. There was a famous 'Croix des Capucins' at Meudon (see E. Houth, 'La première maison des Capucins en France, le couvent de Meudon', *Etudes franciscaines*, XLI (1929), pp. 45 ff.). Since we know that the procession of 1584 was joined by Capucins at Meudon (see above, p. 183) it seems certain that we have here a view of Meudon.

As always in the Processions drawings, topography is mingled with allegory. The grounds of the convent at Meudon merge, most improbably, with cliffs and a seashore upon which Jonah is cast up by the whale.

Procession   Capucins (continued from the preceding drawing).

Three Knights of the Holy Spirit.

Penitent in sackcloth carrying a complicated crucifix.

Jonah, holding up a composite representation of the ship from which he was thrown and the whale which rescued him. Jonah is flanked by Queen Louise de Lorraine and King Henri III, as penitents, wearing tiny crowns on their hoods of sackcloth.

The Jonah story was normally depicted in three episodes; he is thrown from the ship, cast up by the whale, and goes to Nineveh to preach penitence to its king. The casting from the ship and the throwing up by the whale are shown in the background of this drawing. The third episode is in the foreground; Jonah preaches penitence to the King of France as King of Nineveh, who repents in sackcloth with all his people.

Arias Montanus was the author of a very long allegory of the Jonah story, urging on kings the importance of humbling themselves in sackcloth and sordid clothing (Arias Montanus, *Commentaria in duodecim prophetas*, Antwerp, 1571, pp. 493 ff), and leading their people in a penitent movement. It may be that there is a clue here of importance for the association of penitence with a House of Love in Henri III's movement.

The Queen's Procession

(There are many captions and inscriptions in a contemporary hand on drawings 2–14. English translations of these are printed in italics to distinguish from my commentary the information actually written on the drawings.)

Q.P. 1 (Plate 35)   Queen Louise de Lorraine and her ladies leaving the Louvre. The part shown is the wing built by Pierre Lescot in the reign of Henri II, with sculpture by Jean Goujon.

Q.P. 2 (Plate 35)

Background   Scenery near the Bièvre in the Faubourg Saint-Marceau.

Procession   *The two Notaries of the House of Charity. The Intendant and the Receiver of the House, dressed in scarlet-violet colour* (one of these two figures is Nicolas Houel). *The Clerk to the Hospitals, in scarlet-violet. The President and Counsellors of the Court of Parliament deputed by the King to direct the House of Christian Charity and keep accounts of the hospitals and orphanages of the kingdom, in their scarlet robes.*

Q.P. 3 (Plate 36)

Background   Men are catching snakes and putting them into jars, an allusion to the manufacture of the drug *theriacum* from snakes. Houel wrote a treatise on this drug (*Traité de la thériaque et mithridat*, Paris, 1578). Walls and a pavilion mark the entry into the herb garden. The pavilion, which is labelled *Salle pour conférer de ce qui appartient a la medicine, appoticairerie, et chirurgie,* is regarded as the forerunner of the Parisian Ecole de Pharmacie (see article by Planchon, cited above, p. 188, note 1).

Procession   *Preceptors and masters for instructing the poor orphan children in various arts and trades; they will wear sleeved robes of scarlet-violet colour* (compare the uniform seen here with that of the Charitable Men in the King's Procession, 10–12); *the children will wear breeches of this colour. The Clerk of the Medicine in scarlet-violet. Four barber-surgeons wearing vests of scarlet-violet. The two doctors in their capes. The three servitors destined for the 'apothicairerie' for the poor sick people wearing mantles of scarlet-violet.*

Guiffrey, 'Nicolas Houel', p. 233, commenting on the 'escarlatte violette' colour worn at the House of Charity, notes that the Gobelins tapestry works on the banks of the Bièvre was famous for its scarlet dye.

Q.P. 4 (Plate 36)

Background   Under an arbour in the herb-garden, *Doctors and apothecaries are disputing about the properties of simple medicaments.* To the left is a fountain on which is a figure of Charity with her children.

Procession   *Seven teachers for instructing the poor orphan children in humane letters, dressed in long robes of scarlet-violet and wearing doctors' caps. A child aged twenty* [an 'enfant' of the school] *dressed in white who will carry a white taper. Two teachers, one of Hebrew, one of Greek, dressed in the costume of their countries. Teachers of foreign languages, dressed in the costume of their countries, but the colour* [of their dress] *will be scarlet-violet.*
The clerk, wearing a vest of scarlet-violet.

Q.P. 5 (Plate 37)

Background   The 'jardin des simples' continues. Gardiners are carrying buckets for watering it.

Procession   *The children's teacher in his surplice. Thirteen girls dressed in scarlet-violet and wearing straw hats (chappeaulx de feurs) who are maintained in various trades through the alms of the widows. Five widows appointed to teach the said girls.*

Q.P. 6 (Plate 37)

Background   The 'Apothicairerie' where the drugs and medicines compounded from the herbs grown in the herb garden are distributed to the poor.

Procession   *Two priests wearing scarlet-violet copes. A priest who will carry the reliquary of Charity* (the figure of Charity with her children is on the reliquary). *Two men in white who will carry two white tapers. Six Confrères in white and barefooted carrying the reliquary of the Face of Jesus Christ* (compare the Confrères de la Charité in Plate 33, King's Procession 18). *Seven children dressed in white and wearing straw hats, destined for the service of the chapel. The children's teacher in his surplice, and below it will be seen his scarlet-violet robe. Seven children in scarlet-violet, maintained by alms, carrying tapers.*

Q.P. 7 (Plate 38)

Background   The 'Apothicairerie' continues.

Procession   *Three children in white, wearing straw hats and girded with a violet-coloured girdle. Thirteen children in honour of Our Lord Jesus Christ and his twelve apostles, carrying rosaries at the girdle and dressed in scarlet-violet, with the mark of charity on the right shoulder. They will be destined for service in the 'Apothicairerie' and for treating the sick. The four chaplains of the chapel in their surplices, over their scarlet-violet robes, singing hymns and canticles.*

Q.P. 8 (Plate 38) The Chapel   Nicolas Houel's monogram, with the cross of Lorraine, and his motto *Scopus vitae Christus*, is prominently displayed.

Procession   *He who carries the banner of Charity, dressed in scarlet-violet enters* the chapel. On the banner is the figure of Charity with her children.

Q.P. 9 (Plate 39) The School   Classes in progress can be seen through the windows below which is inscribed: *College of all disciplines and languages for the poor scholars and poor orphan children, 1583.* At other points on the building are the inscriptions: *Lodging for the poor widows; School for the poor girls to be married who will be instructed in various métiers and sciences; School of writing and arithmetic.*

On the wall is Houel's monogram and the date, 1583.

Q.P. 10 (Plate 39) This building has many uses as the captions on it explain: *Lodgings for the teachers of the girls; Lodgings for the poor crippled and blind children; School of music; French Academy for various kinds of artisans; Lodgings for the retirement of old people; Various arts and métiers for crippled soldiers.*

In the School of Music, a concert is in progress.

A soldier with a wooden leg is drawing water from the well *(crippled soldier for drawing the water for the house).*

The hospital for wounded soldiers was continued under Henri IV and can be regarded as a distant ancestor of the Invalides (Planchon, article cited above, p. 188, note 1).

ASTRAEA AND THE GALLIC
HERCULES

Our sequence cannot end without some brief mention of the solution, both of the religious problems and of the problem of Monarchy, achieved by Henri IV when he assumed the sacred title and destiny of *Rex Christianissimus*. Very little detailed attention has been paid by historians to that important event in European history, the conversion of Henri IV, which used often to be dismissed by hurried quotation of his supposed remark 'Paris is worth a Mass', interpreted as cynical indifference to the religious question. When the complex material surrounding the conversion is sifted, a task which must sooner or later be undertaken, it may perhaps be discovered that what made possible the conversion of Henri IV was Henri III's Counter Reformation, with its 'politique', and perhaps even secretly Familist, undertones.

One of the more virulent of the League propaganda pamphlets against Henri III complains bitterly of his hypocritical religious movements and his encouragement of heretics. This king, cries the League, could never be persuaded to make war on Henry of Navarre. That mortal enemy of Catholics, the Queen of England, was favoured by him above any other prince. He accepted the Order of the Garter from her. He refused aid to the Armada of the King of Spain as it passed along the French coasts, going to deliver the Catholics of England from the cruel tyranny under which they lived. He surrounded himself with favourites so as to keep at a distance the Catholic princes (the Guises). To show his spurious devotion he invented Penitents, White and Blue. He has been heard to say that he wished both Huguenots and Leaguers could be abolished for he hates them both. Of what religion is he, then, since he is neither a Calvinist nor a Catholic? And the counsel that he gave to the King of Navarre was that he should feign to be a Catholic so that the people would more readily receive him.[1]

---

[1] *Histoire veritable de la plus saine partie de la vie de Henry de Valois*, Paris, 1589. The title alludes to one of Henri's pious foundations; see Yates, *The French Academies of the Sixteenth Century*, Warburg Institute, 1947, p. 231.

Interpreted more kindly as a 'politique' Counter Reformation this description would fit Henri III's movements and efforts, which may have helped to make possible the conversion of Henri IV, and led on into the remarkable spiritual climate of early seventeenth-century France. Thus, in the end, Henri's Counter Reformation succeeded, though it failed to avert the immediate danger, and the last of the wars of religion had to be endured before the great Gallic Hercules could establish peace and justice and ensure the return of Astraea.

The waves of death and destruction began to break over the Valois court and its artistic brilliance after the outbreak of the wars of the League in March 1585 (almost immediately after the visit of the Knights of the Garter). The Duc de Joyeuse was killed at the battle of Coutras in 1587; Guise and his brother were assassinated by order of the King in 1588; in 1589, the King himself was assassinated by emissaries of the League. In this final tragedy of Valois Monarchy, all the leading characters were left dead upon the stage, as in the bloodiest style of Elizabethan tragedy. The long-drawn-out siege of Paris under the League brought indescribable suffering to the Parisians. Hating Henri III and everything connected with him, the Leaguers in Paris made systematic efforts to destroy all vestiges of his movements. The paintings of the Knights of the Holy Spirit in the chapel of the Augustins were torn down; vestments, vessels, prayer books, works of art connected with his religious activities were ruthlessly eliminated.[1] The art of a whole period was broken and can now only be pieced together from scattered fragments.

With the death of Henri III in 1589, the French monarchy itself seemed to have disappeared. The institution of the *Rex Christianissimus*, revered, not only in France, but also in Europe as a prop of order, was no more. Chaos was come again.

Then the tide turned. Henry of Navarre won the decisive battle of Ivry in 1590 (the Imperial Virgin had won her decisive naval victory in 1588) and finally destroyed the League by his long and successful siege of Paris.

There is a woodcut of his entry into Paris (Plate 41) showing the King riding in like an Emperor amid scenes of death and horror. The history of the French royal entry of the sixteenth century, on which poets and artists had expended their best gifts, has come to this. What a contrast to the decorations, the gifts, the banquet, with which the aldermen of the city of Paris had welcomed Charles IX in 1571! Navarre enters the city as conqueror, at the head of his army. Here at last was the outcome of all the years of misery. Navarre the Huguenot is king. He has broken the power which all through the century had prevented a solution of the religious problem, and he will solve the problem by becoming a tolerant Catholic (he was absolved in 1595). Order was not immediately fully restored, but gradually Henri

[1] *French Academies*, pp. 173–4.

established his *pax*, and the country welcomed with deep relief and gratitude the Bourbon holder of the title of Most Christian King.

This summary of events is but the introduction to what must be only a brief indication of the symbolism which surrounded Henri IV as King of France. A full survey, with many illustrations, and an understanding analysis of the meaning of the symbolism, has been made by Corrado Vivanti[1] in an article to which I am deeply indebted for the following remarks.

The favourite image of Henri IV, as Vivanti emphasizes, was that of the Gallic Hercules (see Plate 42a), the slayer of the monsters of war and dis-union, the restorer of an imperial peace in which civilization might flourish again. The Gallic Hercules has chains issuing from his mouth through which he draws the people after him by peaceful eloquence rather than by tyran-nical exercise of power. This image, like most of the symbolism used of Henri IV, is merely the use of an old counter of French monarchy propa-ganda. Like the descent from Charlemagne and the columns of empire, the Gallic Hercules had appeared all through the century in connection with the monarchy.

Yet there is a sense in which the imperial theme, as applied to Henri IV, takes on a true universalism, a message of religious peace and union which could be applied to other peoples and nations. Henri IV had not only op-posed with success the threatened Spanish-Catholic hegemony of Europe. As a Catholic monarch who tolerated Protestants within his dominions, a toleration ratified and legalized in the Edict of Nantes (1598) he also represented the 'politique' solution of the religious problem at last embodied permanently (it was hoped) in the French monarchy. He was the religious imperial *pax* made manifest. Through a generous application of *justitia* he restored order and peace; in the years of his reign, fertility and abundance returned to France, and, in this peace and plenty, civilized life and pro-gressive thought revived. As Vivanti shows, the Return of Astraea was the most constantly used symbol of the reign of Henri IV,[2] and that in no merely conventional way but with real hope that a new golden age was beginning, a new era.

There was a widespread belief that the conversion of Henri IV signalized a new and more liberal era dawning in the religious history of Europe, and it is this universal religious hope which gives a particular poignancy to the French Astraea, whose Return becomes an elaborate and esoteric cult in *L'Astrée* (Plate 42b), the pastoral romance by Honoré d'Urfé[3] in which Henri IV himself appears under a thin disguise.

One of the representations of the French Astraea is strangely reminiscent

[1] Corrado Vivanti, 'Henri IV, the Gallic Hercules', *Journal of the Warburg and Courtauld Institutes*, XXX (1967), pp. 176–97. Cf. also the chapter on Henri IV and the Gallic Hercules in Vivanti, *Lotta politica e pace religiosa in Francia fra Cinque e Seicento*, Turin, 1963, pp. 74–131.

[2] Vivanti, 'Henri IV, the Gallic Hercules', pp. 192 ff.

[3] Referred to in the 'Queen Elizabeth I as Astraea' essay, see above, p. 86.

of the Elizabeth symbolism. The engraved title-page of Pierre Matthieu's *Histoire de la France* (1605), reproduced in Vivanti's article[1] and here (Plate 42c), shows a woman on a throne, bearing in her right hand a wreathed sword, in her left a cornucopia. Behind her are the two columns of Empire supporting the royal crown of France. Piety, Justice, and Peace appear on the steps of her throne; peaceful pursuits of arts and sciences are symbolized around her; scenes of peaceful pleasure take place in the background. And that she is truly Astraea is indicated, not only by the profusion of corn in her cornucopia, but also by the tiara of ears of corn which she wears. The French Astraea sits there with her sword in her hand in a pose and a setting which must surely be modelled on images of the Elizabethan Imperial Virgin. This image brings home to us how closely parallel were the English and French politico-religious situations in the sixteenth century. The French Astraea reflects Gallican independence of the Papacy which, though it did not go so far as a break, as did the Anglican position, moved at times very close to it, and close to Anglicanism.

It has been one of the purposes of this book to suggest comparisons between the images of Tudor monarchy and imperial reform, and the images of French monarchy, reflecting the continued effort in France to achieve religious peace through the Idea of the Monarchy. This image of the French Astraea, so obviously reflecting the Imperial Virgin, comes as a fitting conclusion to our study.

The hopes of a pacification of religious issues through Henry of Navarre's accession to the title of Most Christian King were certainly shared by many besides Frenchmen. The significance of the name 'King of Navarre' used by Shakespeare for a character in a play presented at court before Queen Elizabeth at Christmas, 1598[2] (the year of the Edict of Nantes), becomes very obvious in the sequence of our studies in this book. The play is *Love's Labour's Lost*. The chief male characters include bearers of names representing opposite sides in the French wars of religion. Navarre was the Huguenot leader; Dumain (Mayenne) was the Guise governor of Paris under the League. The choice of such opposing names was not muddle or ignorance on Shakespeare's part but a deliberate allusion to the wars.[3] The activities of the Shakespearean French court sound very familiar. The King founds a court academy ('Our court shall be a little académe'). There is much sonnet-writing and discourses for and against Love in the *Trionfi* tradition. The Shakespearean King and courtiers do not come in on property rocks or ships to the accompaniment of measured poetry and music, but to our eyes and ears, attuned to French festival scenes, the comparison comes at once to

[1] See Vivanti, 'Henry IV, the Gallic Hercules', p. 189.

[2] The date 1598 is that of the first printed text of the play 'As it was presented before her Highness this last Christmas'. The title-page states that the play has been 'newly corrected and augmented', indicating the existence of an earlier version or versions.

[3] Indicated in *French Academies*, pp. 264–5.

mind. A central feature is the dancing of a magical ballet in masquerade costume. In a final phase the courtiers turn to penitence (in some 'forlorn and naked hermitage') and to the Works of Mercy (visiting the 'speechless sick' and conversing with 'groaning wretches'), after which an eventual victory of Love, which is the same as Charity, is promised:

> For charity itself fulfils the law:
> And who can sever love from charity.

Hercules is a hero of love ('For valour is not Love a Hercules, Still climbing trees in the Hesperides'). The Princess whom the King admires is a heroine of chastity (presented by him with the device of 'a lady walled about with diamonds'). The liveliest courtier, Berowne, might perhaps be speaking with the accents of Giordano Bruno whose memorable visit to England had been associated with messages from the French monarchy.

There is no need to suppose that this academy and court were actually at Navarre (though there was an academy and a court festival tradition at Navarre). The mixed French names indicate that Shakespeare has absorbed the conciliatory meaning of French academic and court festival tradition; his French king and courtiers pass through the Henri III phase in which Pléiadist poetry and music merge into Familist charity. Finally, religious toleration and love will triumph in Navarre's restoration of French monarchy. Once this play is taken out of literary tradition and put into the tradition of living imagery, clothing vital contemporary movements, its general drift becomes clear. Though of course there is much other detail, much comedy and elusive comic allusion, which perhaps actually serve to mask its inner meaning.

Shakespeare on the King of Navarre may be followed by Agrippa d'Aubigné on the same theme, reporting somewhat sarcastically on the hopes of a general and imperial solution of disunion through the *Rex Christianissimus*:[1]

> ... at Rome the public disputes had for their usual thesis a comparison between the King of Spain and him (Henri IV). The divines there were finding by the figures of Geomancy, by oracles, by the fatal name of Bourbon, that this prince was destined to convert the hierarchies to the Empire, the pulpit into a throne, the keys into swords, and that he would die Emperor of the Christians. The Venetians were adoring this rising sun with such devotion that when a French gentleman passed through their town they would run to greet him. .... At the court of the Emperor and in Poland one heard public prayers that the Empire might be confided into his fortunate hands, together with disputes concerning the reunion of Religions, or the toleration of them all.

[1] D'Aubigné, *Œuvres*, ed. E. Réaume and F. de Caussade, Paris, 1873–92, II, p. 326; cf. *French Academies*, p. 224.

These vast, Postel-like, perspectives opening up behind the converted Henri IV show how the Idea of the French monarchy had come alive as a hope for Europe.

And Giordano Bruno, the Italian always looking for the true imperial leader, had chosen the French King, linked with the Imperial Virgin, even in the dark days of Henri III. For Bruno, the victories of Henri IV over the tyrant meant the possibility of a universal reform, and it was this hope which encouraged him to return to Italy in 1592.[1] The man who betrayed Bruno to the Venetian Inquisition reported him as having made the following dangerous remarks:[2]

> The procedure which the Church uses to-day is not that which the Apostles used: for they converted people with preaching and the example of a good life, but now whoever does not wish to be a Catholic must endure punishment and pain, for force is used and not love . . . soon the world will see a general reformation of itself, for it is impossible that such corruptions should endure; he hopes great things of the King of Navarre.

When Bruno was burned in Rome in 1600, it was an omen that the new century would not see a triumph of liberal principles nor an end to wars of religion. And when Henri IV was assassinated in 1610 on the eve of that mysterious expedition into Germany, the Venetian liberal, Traiano Boccalini, mourned his death as an eclipse of the sun which made Apollo himself weep bitter tears.[3]

This book ends where my last book, *The Rosicrucian Enlightenment* began, in the years immediately preceding the outbreak of the Thirty Years' War. For the imperial peace of the Henrician age turned out to be but a truce between wars, during which the enemy was massing his forces again. It has now become customary for historians to see the Thirty Years' War as continuous with the wars of religion of the sixteenth century, with a space of uneasy peace between them, like the space between 1918 and 1939 in this century. It will be still more important to trace the liberal and 'politique' movement as continuing from the one war period into the other. The link is to be found in the 'Rosicrucian' movement underlying the attempt of the unfortunate Elector Palatine to achieve some kind of 'imperial reform' in Germany, a movement which drew to itself the religious traditions of Elizabethan chivalry and of French Protestantism, of Hermetic reform such

---

[1] F. Yates, *Giordano Bruno and the Hermetic Tradition*, London, 1964, pp. 340 ff.

[2] *Documenti della vita di Giordano Bruno*, ed. V. Spampanato, Florence, 1933, p. 66: cf. *Giordano Bruno*, p. 340.

[3] See F. Yates, *The Rosicrucian Enlightenment*, London, 1972, p. 134.

as Giordano Bruno had propagated, of secret Familism as disseminated by printers, of Pléiadist poetry and music.

Perhaps Astraea never really quite leaves; rather she has to go underground in the iron ages; and the privileged golden ages are those in which she has no need to hide. The Return of Astraea must always be a *renovatio*, a renewal or rebirth or rediscovery of the past through which a new future is created.

ALLEGORICAL PORTRAITS OF QUEEN ELIZABETH I AT HATFIELD HOUSE

In the dedication of *The Faerie Queene*, Spenser tells Raleigh that the poem is intended to celebrate Queen Elizabeth both as a 'most royall queene or empresse' and as a 'most vertuous and beautifull lady'. The presentation of Elizabeth in the 'Ermine' portrait at Hatfield House illustrates how these two aspects complement one another in the elaborate symbolism used of the Virgin Queen.

The 'Ermine' portrait (Plate 16a), attributed to Nicholas Hilliard[2] and painted in 1585 (the date can be seen on the sword) shows her wearing a magnificent gem-encrusted gown, whilst a little animal rests on her left arm. The ermine symbolizes purity and virginity because of the whiteness of its coat. In Petrarch's poem *I Trionfi*, a banner with an ermine on it is carried before the triumphal car in which sits Laura as the 'Triumph of Chastity'. Petrarch describes this ermine as wearing a collar of gold studded with topazes; with this may be compared the vision in one of his sonnets of a white hind standing under a laurel tree and wearing a collar of diamonds and topazes on which is written '*Nessun mi tocchi*' ('Let no one touch me'), also emblematic of Laura's purity. A white hind with a jewelled collar standing under a laurel tree was the device of Lucrezia Gonzaga, and is illustrated in G. Ruscelli's *Imprese illustri*, a collection of famous devices which was much studied and imitated in Elizabethan England. In his commentary on the device, Ruscelli relates the white hind with the jewelled collar to the white ermine with the jewelled collar of the *Trionfi*, explaining that both are emblatic of Laura's purity and virtue and that diamonds and topazes are stones which symbolize purity.

There can be little doubt that the ermine with the jewelled collar in the portrait of Elizabeth relates her to Petrarch's 'Triumph of Chastity'; the jewels down the front of her dress are bluish white and yellowish in colour, probably diamonds and topazes enclosing this lady in her chastity. (Pearls, the other most-used jewels in the picture, are also symbols of virginity.) From these indications that we are intended in this picture to see Queen Elizabeth as Petrarch's Laura it may be further deduced that the sprig of somewhat indeterminate foliage which she holds in her right hand is laurel. With this picture may be compared the prefatory sonnet by Raleigh before *The Faerie Queene* in which he maintains that the fame of Elizabeth has superseded that of Laura:

[1] Hatfield House Booklet, no. 1, 1952.
[2] Now attributed to William Segar.

> All suddeinly I saw the Faery Queene:
> At whose approach the soule of Petrarke wept,
> And from thenceforth those graces were not seene
> For they this Queene attended, in whose steed
> Obliuion laid him downe on Lauras herse . . .

The beautiful and chaste lady of the picture, fit heroine of a sonnet sequence, is also a 'most royall queene or empresse'. Beside her left hand lies the sword of state, and the ermine's collar is in the form of a crown. In addition to the personal allusion, her purity symbolizes the righteousness and justice of her government. The crowned ermine has a relationship to the Sword of Justice (Sir Artegall in *The Faerie Queene*, who represents Justice, has a crowned ermine on his shield) as well as to the Lady, linking the two together in a composite representation which suggests both the private and the public aspects of the Queen.

The picture of Diana at Hatfield House, attributed to Cornelius Vroom, is stated in an inventory of 1611 to be 'a portrait of her late Majesty'. It is clearly not a likeness, but may reflect some pageantry honouring the queen under the symbol so much used by her poets, that of Diana or Cynthia, the Moon, the Virgin Huntress. The moon as a symbol of Empire was well suited to the woman ruler, and as a symbol of chastity to the Virgin Queen. She is here shown as the huntress, with bow and arrows, and hunting dog.

Elizabeth was the object of an intellectual cult rendered to her by the 'deep wits' among her courtiers, an example of which is the abstruse poetry of Raleigh's *Cynthia*, where the queen, as the moon, represents the Platonic 'idea'. However the atmosphere of the Hatfield picture of the moon-goddess with the strangely compelling, magical glance, may perhaps best be compared with George Chapman's *The Shadow of Night*, an esoteric poem in which, in the deep night of contemplation, arises Cynthia, the Moon,

> Enchantresse-like deckt in disparent lawne,
> Circled with charmes, and incantations . . .

who seems to represent both the 'forces of the mind', and Elizabeth in some mysterious imperial rôle.

The most complicated of the three pictures at Hatfield is the famous 'Rainbow' portrait (Plate 43b) which shows the queen in most elaborate costume holding a rainbow. Every detail in this picture is significant.

One of the most popular handbooks of allegories and symbolism, used by artists all over Europe, was the *Iconologia* of Cesare Ripa. On looking up 'Fame' in this book, we find that it is allegorized as a winged figure, 'having

as many eyes as she has feathers, also many mouths and ears . . .' The source
of this image is Virgil who describes Fame as 'a monster . . . who, for every
feather on her body, has as many wakeful eyes beneath . . . as many loud
tongues and mouths, as many ears that she pricks up to listen' (*Aeneid*, IV,
181–3). The eyes, ears and mouths which are depicted all over the queen's
cloak symbolize her Fame which is flying rapidly through the world, spoken
of by many mouths, seen and heard by many eyes and ears.

Under 'Intelligenza', or Understanding, in Ripa's book, we learn that this
is to be represented by a woman holding in one hand a sphere and in the
other a serpent. The sphere is an 'armillary' or celestial sphere, representing
the heavens, with the band of the zodiac encircling it. On the left sleeve of
the queen's dress, just above the serpent's head, can be seen a celestial sphere,
with the zodiacal band clearly marked. Ripa explains that the combination
of the celestial sphere and the serpent means that in order to understand high
and sublime things we must first go on the earth, as does the serpent, pro-
ceeding in our understanding from earthly things to those of heaven.

From the serpent's mouth, on the queen's sleeve, hangs a red, heart-shaped
jewel. Under 'Elettione', or Choice, in Ripa's book is depicted a woman
wearing a heart-shaped jewel and the reader is referred to Pierio Valeriano's
Hieroglyphica (another important text-book of Renaissance symbolism)
where it is said that the heart is the symbol of Counsel, which comes from
the heart, and which is necessary for making a wise choice.

The combination of the serpent with both the sphere and the heart, which
we have in the picture, is a combination of these two allegories. This serpent
of wisdom, or prudence, is wise both in the things of the intelligence, understanding high and lofty matters, and in the things of the heart, knowing how,
through good counsel, to make wise and virtuous decisions.

We may wonder how the artist, or designer, of this picture, could have
supposed that the beholder of it would understand such complicated allusions.
But in the Renaissance, symbolism and allegory were very widely studied;
text-books such as we have mentioned were in the libraries of most educated
people. Since it looks as though the artist, or his adviser, had used Ripa's
book, the first edition of which was in 1593, this would seem to indicate that
the picture was probably painted after that date.

On the queen's bodice and sleeves is a pattern of flowers, amongst which
can be distinguished roses, pansies, honeysuckle, cowslips, and others. The
motif of showing an assortment of English wild flowers in portraits of the
queen, frequently on her dress, is not uncommon and may relate to one of
her most frequently used symbolic presentations – that of Astraea, the Just
Virgin of the Golden Age, in which as we know from Ovid (*Metamorphoses*,
107–8), 'spring was everlasting, and gentle zephyrs with warm breath played
with the flowers that sprang unplanted.' Verses by the poets on Elizabeth as
Astraea usually introduce the idea that she is restoring to England an eternal

spring like that of the golden age. For example, in Sir John Davies of Hereford's *Hymnes to Astraea* are the lines:

> Reserve (sweet Spring) this Nymph of ours,
> Eternall garlands of thy flowers,
> Green garlands neuer wasting;
> In her shall last our State's faire Spring,
> Now and for euer flourishing,
> As long as Heauen is lasting.

Here the connection of the flowers of spring in the golden age with the spring, or golden age, of 'our state', the state of England, is clearly made; and the poet has chosen the opening words of each line so that the letters with which they begin, when read downwards, read the word REGINA.

The great rope of pearls, the pearl pendant, and the many pearls in the head-dress introduce again the note of virginity, and if the strange head-dress is attentively examined it will be seen that it contains an imperial crown, studded with pearls, and surmounted by a jewel in the shape of a crescent moon, also bedecked with pearls, so that we have in this picture also the allusion to the queen as the chaste Moon.

And what of the most prominent of all the symbols, the rainbow which she holds in her right hand, above which are written the words, *Non sine sole iris*, No rainbow without the sun? The rainbow signifies peace. Another sixteenth-century queen, Catherine de' Medici, used the rainbow as her device (Plate 23b), with the motto, in Greek, 'It brings light and serenity'. Ruscelli in his *Imprese illustri*, referred to above, comments on Catherine's device as meaning that as the rainbow, coming after storms, promises serenity and peace, so Catherine hoped that the reign of her husband, the King of France, would bring serenity to the whole of Christendom. Perhaps it is in some such sense that the rainbow is used in the portrait of Elizabeth. The Virgin Queen, clothed in the allegories of her fame and her wisdom, appears almost like a portent in the sky, announcing new golden ages of peace and coming sunshine after storms.

The so-called 'Ditchley' portrait of Elizabeth (Plate 13), now in the National Portrait Gallery, has close affinities with the 'Rainbow' picture. It shows the queen standing on the map of England; behind her the sky is on one side dark and heavy with storms, whilst on the other side a great sun is appearing. The idea of sunshine after storms which the 'Ditchley' picture shows naturalistically by depicting the storms vanquished by the sun in the sky is the same as that expressed in emblematic form by the rainbow and its motto in the Hatfield portrait, and there are other points of resemblance between the two pictures, though they are clearly not painted by the same hand. The 'Ditchley' portrait is said to commemorate a visit of Elizabeth to Sir Henry Lee at Ditchley in 1592. Sir Henry Lee held the office of Queen's

Champion until 1590, when he resigned it to George Clifford, Earl of Cumberland. In that capacity, he arranged the tilts held on the anniversary of the queen's Accession Day, often in highly elaborate allegorical settings which he was expert in devising. We know, for example, that for the Accession Day tilt of 1590, a representation of a Vestal Virgin was erected in the tilt-yard, involving complex symbolic allusions to the Queen. Since there is a notional relationship between the 'Rainbow' portrait and the 'Ditchley' portrait, and since the latter may reflect symbolism devised by that flower of chivalry, Sir Henry Lee, the suggestion presents itself that perhaps a solution might be found for the hardest problem in the 'Rainbow' picture – namely the jewel in the form of a gauntlet which hangs inside the ruff – by regarding it as a chivalrous motif which may possibly relate this most involved picture to some ceremonial tilt in which Queen Elizabeth's knights showed their prowess in honour of the 'most royall queene or empresse' and the 'most vertuous and beautifull lady'.

BOISSARD'S COSTUME-BOOK AND TWO PORTRAITS[1]

The interesting discovery recorded by E. E. Veevers[2] that books on national costumes served Inigo Jones as sources for some of his designs for masque costumes raises the question as to whether strange costumes in portraits might not be illuminated from the same sources. It is the purpose of this note to compare two portraits, the subjects of which appear to be in fancy-dress, with plates from one of the costume-books in which E. E. Veevers has detected a source for Inigo Jones, namely J. J. Boissard's *Habitus variarum orbis gentium*, 1581.

If the portrait of Queen Elizabeth I at Hatfield House, usually called the 'Rainbow portrait' (Plate 43b), is placed beside Boissard's plate of a 'Sponsa Thessalonicensis' (Plate 43a) it is immediately apparent that the curiously-shaped upturned head-dress of the portrait, with the striped rim and surmounted by an aigrette, has been suggested by the head-dress supposed by Boissard to be that worn by a bride of Thessalonica. The flowing mantle worn in the portrait, and the position of the hand which raises it, might also have been suggested by Boissard's figure.

In the portrait, however, the Thessalonian fancy-dress is worn with a court dress and a ruff, and, moreover, this lady is not in the character of a 'Thessalonian Bride' but of a Queen, for a large jewelled crown has been inserted in the head-dress, surmounted by a jewel in the shape of a crescent moon. The last detail confirms that this is indeed intended to be a portrait of Elizabeth, for it indicates her rôle of Diana, the moon-goddess, the Virgin Queen. The allegories of the picture are also highly applicable to Elizabeth: the rainbow shows her as peace-bringer; the eyes and ears with which the robe is covered allude to her fame;[3] the serpent on the sleeve indicates her wisdom; and above the serpent's head is a celestial sphere, encircled with the band of the zodiac, which is a symbol elsewhere found in connection with Elizabeth (for example in the ear-ornament which she wears in the Ditchley portrait).

The clue to this picture may be that it records Elizabeth's presence at some

---

[1] *Journal of the Warburg and Courtauld Institutes*, XXII (1959), pp. 365–6.

[2] E. E. Veevers, 'Sources of Inigo Jones's masquing designs', *Journal of the Warburg and Courtauld Institutes*, XXII (1959), pp. 373–4.

Boissard's costume figures can be seen taking part in a masque on the subject of Circe in the interesting set of engravings in the Cabinet des Estampes entitled 'Mascarades recueillies & mises en taille douce par Robert Boissart Valentianois, 1597'; the title-page states that Jean Jacques Boissard designed the figures.

[3] *Aeneid*, IV, 181–3. On the Fame, and other allegories, in this picture see Appendix I, above pp. 216–18.

masque in which allegories in her honour were presented by various personages but which are now summed up in a composite portrait of herself. If
this is indeed a masque portrait of Elizabeth, then the resemblance of the
head-dress to that in one of Boissard's collection of costumes would suggest
that the fashion for designing masquing attire from costume-books may
not have been started by Inigo Jones but may go back to Elizabethan times.

Our second comparison is between the well-known picture at Hampton
Court of a lady in a strange exotic costume (Plate 43c) and Boissard's
illustration showing a 'Virgo Persica' (Plate 43d). The lady in the picture
wears a tall head-dress from the apex of which depends a long veil ending
in a fringe, the whole being strikingly similar to the mitre-like cap with
fringed hanging worn by Boissard's 'Persian Virgin'. The possibility therefore arises that the lady in the picture is wearing a masquing costume adapted,
like some of Jones's masque costume designs, from a pattern found in a
costume-book. Her fancy head-dress has been suggested by that supposed
to be worn by Persian virgins, but it does not necessarily follow from this
that she appeared in the character of a Persian at the masque. Perhaps the
allegories in the picture may refer to elements in a masque at which she was
present.

The identity of the lady in the Hampton Court picture remains a mystery
now that the Lady Arabella Stuart theory has been abandoned. George
Vertue believed that it was a portrait of Queen Elizabeth,[1] in which he was
followed by Horace Walpole who described it as a 'picture of Elizabeth in a
fantastic habit, something like a Persian'.[2] The comparison with Boissard
proves that Walpole was right as to the fantastic habit being something like
a Persian. Comparison with the 'Rainbow', in which Elizabeth is seen in a
head-dress something like a Boissard Thessalonian, may suggest that he
could perhaps also have been right as to the identity of the sitter.[3]

[1] Vertue, *Note books*, ed. Walpole Society, London, XX (2), p. 481.
[2] Horace Walpole, *Anecdotes of Painting*, ed. Wornum, 1849, I, p. 162.
[3] The Hampton Court picture appears to me to be very similar in style to another fancy-dress
portrait in which the sitter, Captain Thomas Lee, is in a masquerade version of Irish costume,
(see E. K. Chambers, *Sir Henry Lee*, Oxford, 1936, p. 191) and stands under a tree. This picture,
formerly at Ditchley, is dated 1594. If this comparison is valid, it would allow the Hampton
Court picture to be dated within the Elizabethan period, and to refer, probably, to a masque at
Ditchley.

ANTOINE CARON'S PAINTINGS FOR TRIUMPHAL ARCHES[1]

The fresco in the Castel Sant' Angelo discussed in J. S. Ackerman's article[2] may suggest to those interested in the strange works of the late sixteenth-century French painter, Antoine Caron, some points for comparison. The antique galleys of the foreground scene, whose manœuvres are watched by the elongated figures standing on the wall to the right, remind one of those water fêtes *all'antica* which Caron was fond of painting. In the fresco, the naval scene is used to emphasize the humanist vision of ancient Rome behind the Rome of the present, with a technique not altogether dissimilar to that employed by Caron to suggest visions of ancient Rome behind the Paris of the present.

The elaborate *entrées* which characterized the reigns of the last Valois kings were part of the build-up of those monarchs as 'Roman emperors', descendants of the ancient Trojan line. Artists and architects laboured to transform Paris into an antique city, with triumphal arches, theatres, perspectives, obelisks, erected along the routes of the royal processions. A fairly complete description of the antiquizing of Paris for the *entrées* of Charles IX in 1571, and of his bride, the daughter of the Emperor Maximilian II, has come down to us.[3] Against the background of such pseudo-antique temporary erections as are therein described, were staged jousts, tableaux vivants, water-fêtes on the Seine for which galleys on the ancient model were specially constructed.[4] In verses celebrating the *entrée* of Charles IX, and addressed to that monarch, the Seine has become the Tiber:[5]

> Regarde comme l'eau d'un doux bruit te salue,
> Comme la Seine tend sa teste chevelue

[1] *Journal of the Warburg and Courtauld Institutes*, XIV (1951), pp. 133–4.

[2] J. S. Ackerman, 'The Belvedere as a classical villa', *Journal of the Warburg and Courtauld Institutes*, XIV, (1951), pp. 70–91.

[3] S. Bouquet, *Bref et Sommaire recueil de ce qui a esté faict et de l'ordre tenue à la joyeuse triumphante entrée de très puissant, très magnanime et très chrestien prince Charles IX . . . Avec le couronnement de très haulte . . . princesse Elisabeth d'Autriche . . . et Entrée de la dite dame en icelle ville de Paris*, Paris, 1572. This work contains cuts of the arches and the perspective used at these *entrées*. Bouquet's descriptions can be supplemented from the accounts of the expenses of the City of Paris (*Régistres des délibérations du Bureau de la Ville de Paris*, ed. P. Guérin, Paris, 1891, VI, pp. 231 ff.) which record that Germain Pilon and Niccolo dell'Abate worked on the decorations for these arches from specifications given them by the poets Ronsard and Jean Dorat who designed the iconography and provided the inscriptions.

[4] Details of the fabrication of antique galleys for fêtes are to be found in accounts in the reigns of Henri II and later. See G. Lebel, 'Antoine Caron', *L'Armour de l'Art* XVIII (1937), p. 323.

[5] J. Prevosteau, *Entrée de Charles IX à Paris, 1571*, reprinted Paris, 1858, p. 19.

Te voulant caresser.
Ainsi le Tybre fort aux ondes argentées
Brida jadis posé ses courses alentées
Pour Caesar embrasser.

There is no doubt that many of Caron's pictures reflect contemporary fêtes. In 'Augustus and the Sybil' (Plate 21), for example, we see temporary tribunes, columns, colossi; though the crenellated wall and the two-gabled building behind the tribune on the right have a solidity which contrasts with the flimsy impermanence of the latter. They are probably buildings of the real Paris,[1] upon which the pseudo-antique Paris of the fête is superimposed. In this setting, three performances are taking place, watched by three sets of spectators: the joust in the centre background; the tableau-vivant of Augustus and the Sybil in the centre foreground, with Charles IX as Augustus; and to the right, on the river, a water-fête with antique galleys. The tower on the banks of the Seine-Tiber recalls the Tour de Nesle, but the aqueduct and other buildings beyond it suggest Rome.

The artist of the Castel Sant' Angelo fresco uses the imaginary fête-like water-scene to emphasize the vision of ancient Rome which he draws out of the actual Roman scene before him. The French artist imposes ancient Rome on the actual Paris through the pseudo-antique paraphernalia of some *entrée* and its accompanying fêtes.

Caron sometimes executed paintings for insertion in the architectural setting of temporary triumphal arches. In 1573, Henri, Duc d'Anjou, afterwards Henri III, entered Paris as King of Poland. The accounts of the City of Paris for this year record that four arches were erected for this *entrée*, that Germain Pilon was employed as the sculptor to decorate them, Antoine Caron as the painter, and the poet Jean Dorat was to be responsible for the inscriptions.[2] The accounts give a vague idea of the subjects portrayed on these arches. One arch, for example, was dedicated to the Piety of Paris; it was framed by two great obelisks; surmounted by a figure of Lutetia sacrificing at an antique altar; and inscribed with Latin verses by Dorat, beginning 'Salve urbs magna' and lauding the piety of Paris. On the inner walls of the arch were paintings, presumably by Caron since he is the only painter mentioned in the accounts for this *entrée*; one showing Charles IX and his two brothers ruling the world; the subject of the other was 'Cassiopeia' with

---

[1] Lebel, *op. cit.*, p. 323, and in his article 'Un tableau d'Antoine Caron: L'Empereur Auguste et la Sibylle de Tibur', extracted from *Bulletin de la Société de l'Histoire de l'Art Français*, 1937, p. 14, conjectured that the gabled building was an addition to the Tuileries built by Jean Bullant and that the wall was part of the old city wall.

[2] *Régistres des délibérations du Bureau de la Villa de Paris*, VII, pp. 91 ff. The *équipe* working for the city authorities on this occasion was similar to the one employed for the 1571 *entrées*, except that Ronsard has dropped out, and that Caron has replaced his master, Niccolo dell'Abate, now dead, as the leading painter.

apparently some reference to the 'new star' in that constellation, perhaps as a prophecy or portent.[1]

The description in the accounts of these and the other paintings on the four arches are too brief and generalized to allow them to be identified with any known picture by Caron. One may fancy that 'Augustus and the Sybil' with its imperial allusions, and its celestial vision above the Seine-Tiber, might be not unsuitably placed on a temporary triumphal arch erected by the City of Paris to glorify the French royal house as part of an *entrée* in which 'pious Paris' is *en fête* in antique disguise. The affinities between the presentation of Charles IX in antique dress in the picture and the bust of that monarch as a Roman emperor by Pilon (Plate 44) might also suggest that Caron's picture would go with sculptural decorations by Pilon, such as we know were made for the arches at the Polish *entrée*. No sufficiently definite evidence has as yet been found, however, to enable one to place 'Augustus and the Sybil' within the decorative scheme of any particular *entrée*.[2]

[1] The description of this picture cannot be made to correspond with the 'portent' picture by Caron in the collection of Sir Anthony Blunt.

[2] The most likely ones are the *entrées* of 1571 (for which Caron did some work, see the documents printed by Lebel in his 'Un tableau d'Antoine Caron', pp. 17 ff.) or the Polish *entrée* of 1573. The latter seems to me the more probable, for, in addition to the suitability of its 'Piety of Paris' theme, I agree with Lebel (p. 15) in thinking that the tribune in the left background of the picture, between the colossal statues, contains Henri with a Polish retinue. But, as mentioned above, none of the pictures described in the city accounts in connection with this *entrée* fit 'Augustus and the Sybil' exactly; nor is the meaning of the picture as yet fully explained (see now urther, above pp. 145–6).

1   Marcus Aurelius, Capitol, Rome

2   Charles V by Titian, Prado, Madrid

3a Device of Charles V. From *Magnifica pompa funerale*, Antwerp (Plantin) 1559

3b Charles V and his Enemies. Engraving by Martin van Heemskerck, From *Divi Caroli V Victoriae*, 1556

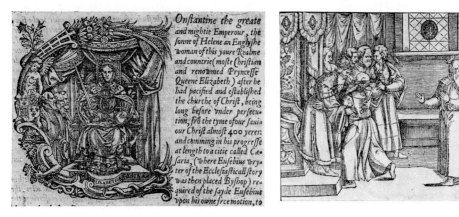

4a (left)   Initial C. From John Foxe, *Acts and Monuments*, 1563

4b (right)   Emperor Constantine embracing Christian Bishops. From Foxe, *Acts and Monuments*, 1570

4c (left)   Pope Alexander III and the Emperor Frederick Barbarossa. From Foxe, *Acts and Monuments*, 1570

4d (right)   Emperor Henry IV at Canossa. From Foxe, *Acts and Monuments*, 1570

5a (above left)   Henry VIII and the Pope. From Foxe, *Acts and Monuments*, 1570

5b (above right)   Henry VIII Enthroned. From Foxe, *Acts and Monuments*, 1570

5c (centre left) The Monk of Swineshead and King John. From Foxe, *Acts and Monuments*, 1570

5d (below left)   Henry III and the Papal Legate From Foxe, *Acts and Monuments*, 1570

6a   Mark of the Printer, John Daye. From Foxe, *Acts and Monuments*, 1570

6b   Queen Elizabeth I. Engraving by Crispin de Passe, senior

7a Initial C. From John Dee, *General and rare memorials*, 1577

Vm in Naui
Gubernator , om=
nia pro ſuo ſolet
arbitrio dirigere ,
quæ ad vectorum
Salutem pertinēt :
T ùm in Exercitu,
Dux, quæ ad Mi=
litum victoriam .
(Alioqui nec ve=
ctoribus , nec Mi=
litibus, vel tantil=
lo tempore res rectè
procederent , niſi
ab Vno vtræq; Vi=
ro regerentur : et
apertiſſimè, maxi=
mis in periculis ,
Monarchiam . ſi=

7b Title-page. From John Dee, *General and rare memorials*, 1577

8a (left)   Queen Elizabeth I. Engraving by Crispin de Passe, senior, after Isaac Olivier
8b (right)   Queen Elizabeth I. Engraving by Vertue after Isaac Olivier

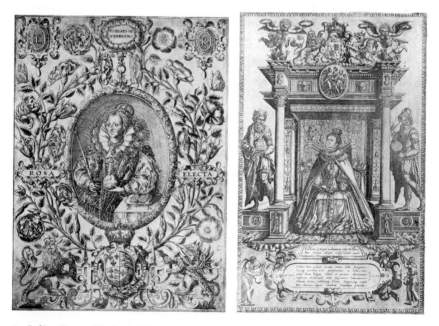

8c (left)   Queen Elizabeth I. Engraving by W. Rogers
8d (right)   Queen Elizabeth I. Engraving attributed to Remigius Hogenberg

9a Queen Elizabeth I and the Judgment of Paris, Hampton Court. Reproduced by gracious permission of Her Majesty the Queen

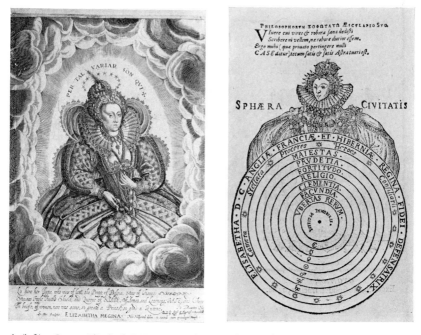

9b (left)   Queen Elizabeth I. Engraving by F. Delaram after N. Hilliard
9c (right)   Queen Elizabeth I. From J. Case, *Sphaera civitatis*, 1588

10a Queen Elizabeth I. Dover Town Hall

10b Queen Elizabeth I. Title-page of the Bishop's Bible, 1569

11a (opposite above) Queen Elizabeth and the Pope as Diana and Callisto. Engraving by Pieter van der Heyden

11b (opposite below) Queen Elizabeth in Procession. Collection S. Wingfield Digby, Sherborne Castle

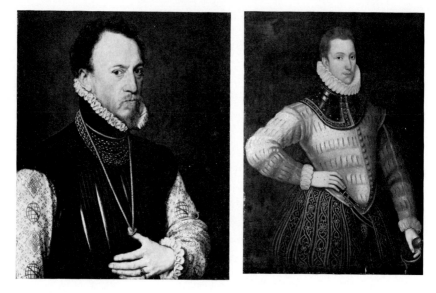

12a (left)   Sir Henry Lee. By Antonio Moro, National Portrait Gallery
12b (right)   Sir Philip Sidney. Unknown Artist, National Portrait Gallery

12c (left)   Armour designed for Sir Henry Lee, *Almain Armourer's Album*, Victoria and Albert Museum
12d (right)   George Clifford, Third Earl of Cumberland. By Nicholas Hilliard, National Maritime Museum, Greenwich

13   Queen Elizabeth I, National Portrait Gallery

15   Jacopo del Sellaio, The Triumph of Chastity, Museo Bandini, Fiesole

Opposite page
14a (above)   Queen Elizabeth I, Windsor Castle. Reproduced by gracious permission
of Her Majesty the Queen
14b (below)   Procession of Knights of the Garter. By Marcus Gheeraerts, senior,
British Museum. Detail

16a   Queen Elizabeth I. The Ermine Portrait. Marquis of Salisbury, Hatfield House

16b   Queen Elizabeth I. The Sieve Portrait, Pinacoteca, Siena

17a, b Details from the Sieve Portrait

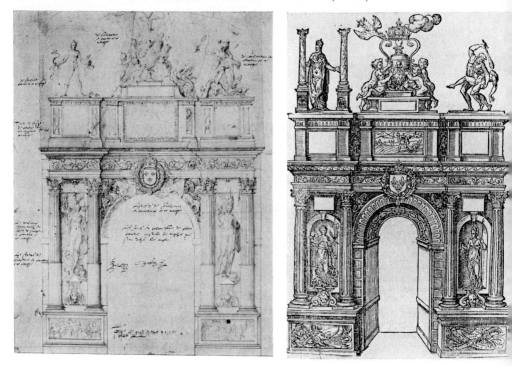

18a (left)   Design for a Triumphal Arch. Nationalmuseum, Stockholm, Cronstedt Collection
18b (right)   Triumphal Arch at Entry of Charles IX. From Simon Bouquet, *Recueil*, 1572

19a (left)   The Francus and Pharamond Arch. From Simon Bouquet, *Recueil*, 1572
19b (right)   The Castor and Pollux Arch. At the entry of Charles IX. From Simon
Bouquet, *Recueil*, 1572

21   Antoine Caron, Augustus and the Sibyl, Louvre

Opposite page
20a (above left)   The Device of Charles IX. From Ruscelli, *Imprese illustri*, 1560
20b (above right)   The Present given to Charles IX. From Bouquet, *Recueil*, 1572
20c (below left)   The Gallia. From Bouquet, *Recueil*, 1572
20d (below right)   The Juno. From Bouquet, *Recueil*, 1572

22a The Quintain. Drawing by Antoine Caron, Witt Collection, Courtauld Institute

22b The Quintain with Henri III in the foreground. Valois Tapestry, Uffizi, Florence

23b   The Device of Catherine de' Medici

23c (below left)   Castor and Pollux Emblem.
From Alciati, *Emblemata*
23d (below right)   Ship with Lights on Rigging
(Castor and Pollux Emblem). From Giordano
Bruno, *La cena de le ceneri*, 1584

23a   The Device of Henri III

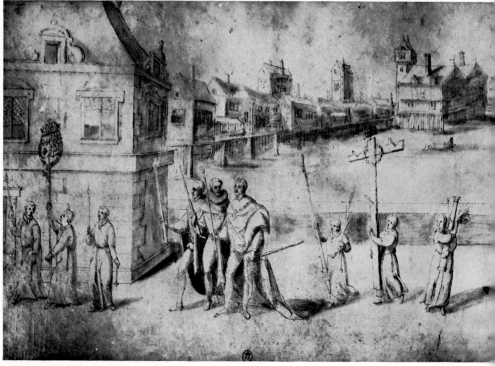

24   K.P. I (King's Procession I)

24   K.P. 3

Plates 24-34   Drawings of Religious Processions in Paris, 1583-4, illustrating H

25   K.P. 2

25   K.P. 4

ous Movements. Bibliothèque Nationale, Cabinet des Estampes, Pd. 29 Réserve

26 K.P. 5

26 K.P. 7

27   K.P. 6

27   K.P. 8

28   K.P. 9

28   K.P. 11

29   K.P.10

29   K.P.12

30 K.P. 13

30 K.P. 15

31   K.P. 14

31   K.P. 16

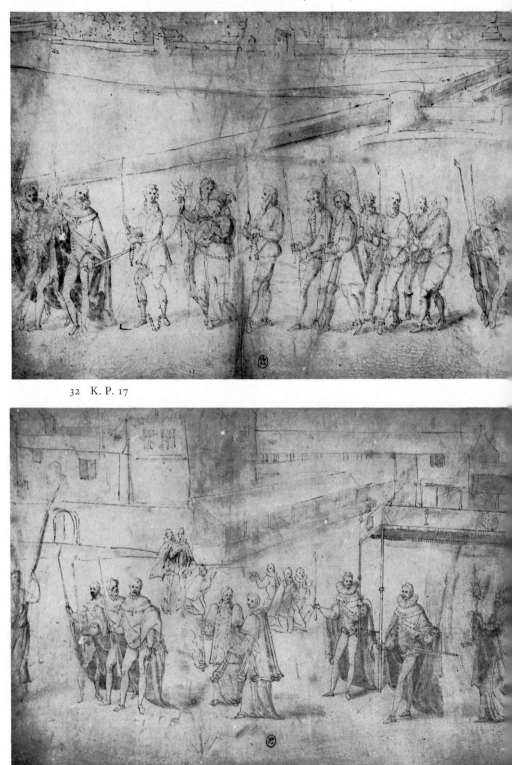

32 K. P. 17

32 K. P. 19

33   K.P. 18

33   K.P. 20

34 K.P. 21

34 K.P. 22

35   Q.P. 1 (Queen's Procession I)

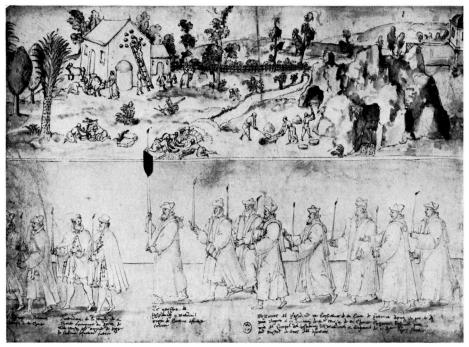

35   Q.P. 2

Plates 35-9   Drawings of Religious Processions in Paris, 1584, illustrating Queen
Louise de Lorraine's visit to the royal charity, Nicolas Houel's House of Love.
Bibliothèque Nationale, Cabinet des Estampes, Pd. 30 Réserve

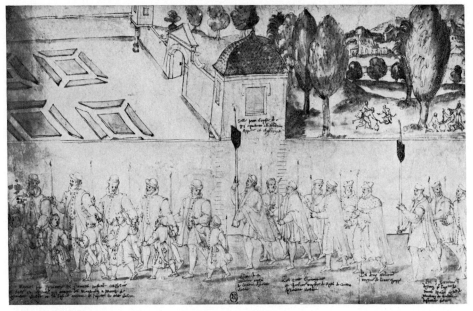

36   Q.P. 3

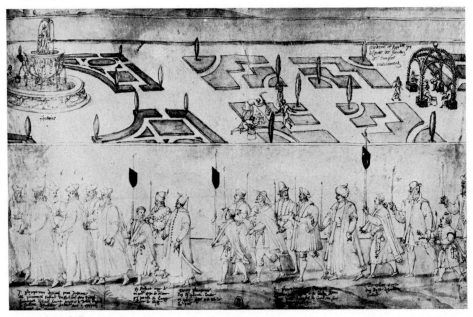

36   Q.P. 4

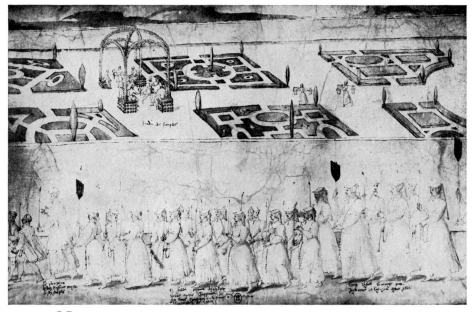

37 Q.P. 5

37 Q.P. 6

38   Q.P. 7

38   Q.P. 8

39   Q.P. 9

39   Q.P. 10

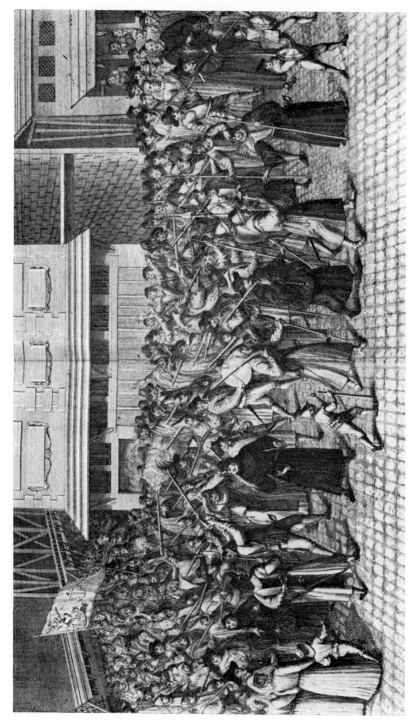

40 The Procession of the League. From B. de Montfaucon, *Monuments de la Monarchie Française*, 1734

Reduction miraculeuse de Paris sous l'obeïssance du Roy Tref-Chreftien Henry IIII. & comme fa Majefté y entra par la Porte Neutue le Mardy 22. de Mars 1594.

41   Entry of Henri IV into Paris, 1594. Engraving by Jean le Clerc after N. Bollery

42a (left) Henri IV as the Gallic
Hercules. Print distributed after the
Consecration at Chartres
42b (above) Honoré d'Urfé,
L'Astrée, 1632, title-page

42c Astraea, title-page to Pierre
Matthieu, *L'Histoire de la France*,
1605

43a (above left) 'Sponsa Thessalonicensis'. From J. J. Boissard, *Habitus variarum orbis gentium*, 1581
43b (above right) Queen Elizabeth I. The Rainbow Portrait. Marquis of Salisbury, Hatfield House
43c (below left) Lady in Fancy Dress, Hampton Court. Reproduced by gracious permission of Her Majesty the Queen
43d (below right) 'Virgo Persica'. From J. J. Boissard, *Habitus variarum orbis gentium*, 1581

44   Charles IX. Bronze bust by Germain Pilon, Wallace Collection, London

Academy of Poetry and Music (*Académie de Poésie et Musique*), xii, 119, 138–40, 143, 151 ff., 179, 184, 187, 189, 211; *see* Baïf; Conciliation, religious; Musical humanism; Shakespeare

Accession Day Tilts, xiii, 61, 81–111, 125, 129; *see* Chivalry; Lee, Henry; Sidney; Spenser

Adam, 8, 12

Aeneas, 33, 50, 115, 131–3

Aeneas Sylvius, 44, 46

Ages, the Four, 30, 33; *see* Golden Age

Alamanni, Luigi, 122

Albigenses, 44

Alciati, Andrea, 46, 135, 141

Alcuin, 3

Alexander, *see* Timotheus

Alexandria, 142, 160

Allegory, 116, 173 ff., 192 ff., etc.

Alva, Duke of, 113, 148

Amphion, 140, 143, 152

Anglicanism, 40–2, 47, 80–2, 124, 211

Antichrist, 40, 45 ff., 80–1

Antwerp, 142, 192, 193

Apothecaries, 173, 181, 188 ff.

Aquinas, Thomas, 11–12

Aratos, 30–2

Arcadia, see Sidney, Philip

Archimedes, 164

Ariadne, 29, 76; Crown of (constellation), 73–4, 107

Arias Montanus, 192–3, 204

Ariosto, Ludovico, 22–3, 26, 51–5, 65, 70, 86, 108, 122

Aristotle, 108

Armada, Spanish, 58–9, 62, 64, 83, 103, 118–19, 196, 208

Arnold of Brescia, 15

Arnold of Villa Nova, 44

Artemisia, Catherine de' Medici as, 134–5, 140, 189

Arthur, King, 5, 48, 50, 107, 109, 122

Ashmole, Elias, 194–5

Astarte, 80

Astraea, Just Virgin of the Golden Age, 4, 9–11, 23, 29–38; Elizabeth I as, xii–xiv, 28–87, 113–14, 217–18; French Monarchy and, 82 n.2, 126, 208–11, 214

Astraeus, 32

Astral influences, xiv, 143, 159–60

Atargatis, 32, 34

Auger, Emond, 177, 183–4, 190 n.5

August, imperial month, 31, 38

Augustine, Saint, 2–3, 12

Augustins (church), *see* Paris

Augustus, Emperor, 4, 11–12, 18, 23, 33–4, 36–7; Charles IX as, 124, 131, 133, 139, 145, 223

Bacchus, 73, 140–2, 144

Baïf, Jean-Antoine de, and the Academy of Poetry and Music, xii, 119, 138–40, 147, 151–65, 179; religious views, 167, 186–90; work for festivals, 138–40, 149 ff.; *see* Academy; Le Jeune; Musical humanism

Ballets, at French court, 172, 186–7, 195–6, 212; *Ballet comique*, 149–51, 158–9, 165–7, 179, 182

Barnfield, Richard, 63

Barrefelt, Henry ('Hiel'), 192
Bayonne, festival at, 150
Beaulieu, Lambert de, 159
Beaune, Renaud de, 197
Bellerophon, 171
Belphoebe, name of Elizabeth I, 69–70, 76, 89, 115
Bernard, Saint, 41
Biblical figures in processions, 182–3, 193, 198, 202, 204
Bièvre (river), see Paris
Boccaccio, 41
Boccalini, Traiano, 213
Boissard, J. J., xiv, 220–1
Bonaventura, Saint, 184
Borromeo, Carlo, 83
Botticelli, 74
Bouquet, Simon, xiv, 128, 130 ff., 141–4, 146
Bourbon, Cardinal, 172, 203
British Empire, 115–16, 120
Bruni, Leonardo, 16
Bruno, Giordano, xi, xii; and the Elizabeth cult, 84–6, 108, 110, 119, 212–14; mission to England from the French court, 83, 124, 167–9, 212–14; see also Henri III
Brut, mythical Trojan ancestor of the Tudors, 50, 62, 116, 121, 124, 130–3, 209
Burgundy, 20, 22, 149
Buridan, 44

Cabala, 125, 145
Cadmus and Harmonia, 140, 142, 144
Callisto, 80
Camden, William, 59, 74, 107
Canon law, 5–7, 10
Canossa, Interview at, 44, 57
Capucin Order, 180, 183–6, 203–4
Carolingian Empire, 16, 23, 82
Caron, Antoine, xiv, 132, 145–6, 150–1, 172 n., 222–4
Case, J., 64–5
Castiglione, Baldassare, 110
Castor and Pollux, symbol of peace, xi, 135–7, 140, 163, 166, 168
Catherine de' Medici: conciliatory policy, 122, 146–53, 165, 172, 186–7, 195; and festivals, 150, 157; mythological rôles, 132–5, 138; in processions, 203; see also, 123, 137, 160, 184, 189, 191, 203; Devices
Caxton, William, 106, 108

Ceres, 32, 34, 78, 172 n.
Chapman, George, 29, 76, 216
Charity, movement of, 146, 175, 180–2, 186–93, 212; see Houel and the Maison de Charité Chrétienne
Charlemagne, 1–5, 11 ff., 20 ff., 121–2, 127, 131, 137, 210
Charles IV, Emperor, 15–16, 37
Charles V, Emperor: and imperial reform, 24–5; influence on symbolism of Tudor and French monarchies, 51 ff., 86, 116–17, 122 ff., 138, 210; revives idea of universal empire, xii, 19, 20–8; see Devices
Charles VIII, King of France, 5
Charles IX, King of France, imperial symbolism and, xiii, 127–48, 150, 189, 209, 222–4; see Augustus; Devices
Chartres, 183–5
Chastity, Triumph of, symbol of imperial reform, 69–70, 112–15, 118, 156, 170, 212, 215; see Petrarch
Chaucer, Geoffrey, 44
Chivalry: chivalrous themes in French festivals, 149 ff.; Cola di Rienzo and, 15, 37–8; Elizabethan chivalry, xii–xiii, 88–111; and the imperial idea, 5, 7, 22, 27, 83; see Accession Day Tilts; Garter, Order of the; Holy Spirit, Order of the
Christianity, and the Empire, 3 ff., 10 ff., 18, 20, 26, 34 ff., 87; Christianizing of imperial symbolism, 3–4
Cicero, 19, 32
Circe, 165–6
Clement VII, Pope, 21, 56–7
Cléry, pilgrimage to, 182–3
Clovis, 121
Cola di Rienzo, 14–15, 18, 37, 45, 83 n.3
Coligny, Gaspard de, 147
Colours, symbolism of, 160–2, 164
Concert of Christian Princes, 55–6
Conciliation, religious, xii, 140; Baïf's Academy and, 152–3; French festivals and, 150, 154; through Monarchy, 86, 124, 133, 140, 167 ff., 192, 194, 210–12; see Toleration, religious
Confréries, 173, 176–80, 184, 196
Conrad II, Emperor, 15
Constantine, Emperor, 2–3, 8, 24, 35, 38, 41–5, 49
Councils: Emperors and, 7, 25, 41, 56, 81; Council of Trent, 40, 82

Counter Reformation, 27, 83, 126, 151, 161, 173, 178, 180 ff., 192–3, 208–9; see Capucin Order; Jesuits; Minimes

Courville, Joachim Thibaut de, 179

Crown, cult of, 107, 115–16, 174; versus papal tiara, 43, 57

Cumberland, George Clifford, Earl of, 94, 102–4, 219

Cupid, 112–13, 155–6

Cusanus, Cardinal, 44

Cybele, 138

Cynthia, the moon, 29, 76

Damville, Comte de, 155, 170

Dancing, see Ballets

D'Angers, Pierre, 129, 136

Dante: Charles V and, 21–6, 51–2; imperialist theory, 8 ff., 36–7, 87; imperial reform, 8–12; Tudor theologians and, 39–47, 64, 76, 112–13; see also 83, 85 n., 116, 121–2

Da Solo, Bellintani, 184

D'Aubigné, Agrippa, 86, 186, 172 n., 187 n., 212

David, King, 140, 153, 178

Davies of Hereford, John, 66–9, 71, 85 n., 218

Daye, John, 49, 57, 113

Dee, John, 48–50, 108, 115, 125

Dekker, Thomas, 29

Dell'Abate, Camillo, 130, 141, 143

Dell'Abate, Niccolo, 129–30, 141 ff., 151, 222 n.2

Della Vigna, Pietro, 8–9

Delorme, Philibert, 191

Descartes, René, 184

Desportes, Philippe, 151, 156, 162

De Thou, J. A., 185

Devices, 61, 212, 215; of Catherine de' Medici, 134, 163, 218; of Emperor Charles V, xii, 23, 54, 57–8, 77, 103, 116–17, 127, 138, 146; of Charles IX, 127, 138, 145–6; of Henri III, 163, 167–9, 175, 184–5, 190, 198

Diana, 29, 76, 80, 110, 216

Dido, 115

Dillon, Lord, 99, 103

Ditchley, Entertainment at, 91, 94 ff.; manuscript, 99, 102–3; portrait, 106, 218

Divine Right, and imperialist theory, 37 ff., 52, 71, 83

Dominus mundi, imperial title, 5, 11, 13, 15, 21, 23, 52, 122

Donation of Constantine, 10, 44–5

Doni, A. F., 37

Dorat, Jean, poet of the Pléiade: at court festival, 151–3, 162–4; programme for decorations at royal entry, 128–30, 139–44, 223; see also 194, n.1

D'Osimo, Bernard, 184–5

Dowland, John, 78

Drake, Francis, 55

Du Bartas, Guillaume, 89

Dubois, Pierre, 122–3, 145

Dubreuil, Toussaint, 174

Durand, Noel, 139

D'Urfé, Honoré, 86, 210

Dyer, Edward, 98, 102

Earthly Paradise, 8, 10, 12, 144

Edgar, Saxon king of England, 48

Edward VI, King of England, 55, 57, 81, 108

Effects, of music, 139–40, 142, 152–6, 159, 165; see Musical humanism

Elizabeth I, Queen of England: chivalrous cult of, 88–111; and the imperial idea, xii–xiv, 29–87; portraits of: Ditchley (National Portrait Gallery), 106, 218, Dover Town Hall, 65, Garter (Windsor), 108–9, Ermine (Hatfield) xiii, 78, 113–14, 215–16, Rainbow (Hatfield), 103 n.1, 216–19, 220–1, Sieve (Siena), xii–xiii, 108 n.1, 114–20, other representations, 43, 58–9, 63–5, 71, 79–80; relations with France and French monarchy, 167–9, 194–6, 208–13; symbolism of and the idea of imperial reform, Astraea, 29–87; Triumph of Chastity, 112–20, 215–19; Virgin of the imperial reform, 123, 125, 130, 133, 139

Elizabeth of Austria, Queen of France, 126, 128, 131 ff., 142–4

Emblems, 97, 135, 168 n.3

Empire, the Idea of, 1 ff.; French monarchy and the idea of Empire, 121 ff.; revival in Emperor Charles V, 20 ff.; Tudor imperial reform, 29 ff.; see Augustus; Charles V; Councils; Dante; Dominus mundi; Renovatio, etc.

Entry, French royal, xiii–xiv, 127–48, 209

Erasmus, 19–20, 24, 26, 55–7, 82, 133, 147, 187, 192

Erigone, 32, 34, 70 n.2, 74
Essex, Robert Devereux, Earl of, 93, 111
Europa and the Bull, 49, 137
Eusebius, 4, 42

Fabrice, Marin Caietan, 179
Faerie Queene, see Spenser
Fame, allegory of, 216–17, 220
Family of Love, xiv, 113, 173, 191–4, 208, 212, 214
Favyn, A., 82–3
Ferdinand I, Emperor, 40, 55, 82
Festivals, French court, xiii, xv, 125, 133, 149–72, 174, 177, 186, 189, 196; see Joyeuse, Anne
Festus Avienus, 32
Ficino, Marsilio, 45 n.1, 48, 159–61, 189
Flacius Illyricus, 41, 46–7
Flagellation, 176, 180
Florence, Italy, 15, 17 ff., 48, 160
Florio, John, 52 n.2, 77 n.3
Fontainebleau, School of, 125, 129–30
Fortuna, 15, 21, 32
Fouquet, Jean, 146
Foxe, John, Acts and Monuments, 42 50, 57, 75, 80, 83
Franciscans, 37, 84–6; see Capucin Order
François Ier, King of France, 21, 55–7, 122–3, 185
François II, King of France, 123
François d'Anjou, 92, 194
Francus, mythical Trojan ancestor of French kings, 121, 124, 130–2, 137
Frederick Barbarossa, Emperor, 44
Frederick II, Emperor, and medieval imperialism, 5 ff., 17, 20–1, 25
Frederick V of the Palatinate, 196, 213

Gallicanism, 82–3, 121 ff., 211
Gallic Hercules, xiv, 144 n.1, 209–10; Gaul, map of, 133–5
Garter, Order of the: and the Elizabeth cult, 90, 108–9, 175; Garter knights in France, 109, 147, 194–6, 208–9
Gascoigne, George, 96, 98
Gattinara, Mercurio, 21, 26
Gawdy, Philip, 103
Geeraerts, Marcus, 71
Gemistus Pletho, 48–9
Geoffrey of Monmouth, 50
Germanicus Caesar, 32

Germany, and the empire, 1, 3–4, 15, 17, 20, 131, 213
Ghibellinism, 7–9, 15, 17, 21–5, 37, 51, 77, 122
Gobelins tapestry works, 190, 205
Gohorry, Jacques (Leo Suavius), 189–92
Golden Age, symbol of imperial renovatio, 4 ff., 30 ff., 47, 50 ff., 61 ff., 84, 113, 123, 126, 138, 210, 214; see Astraea; Renovatio; Saturn; Spenser
Gonzaga, Lucretia, 215
Gower, John, 44
Graces, the, 73–4
Greek Empire, 4, 41, 47–8
Gregory VII, Pope, 44
Greville, Sir Fulke, 102
Grosseteste, Robert, 44
Gruter, Janus, 119
Guelphs, 8, 12, 37, 122
Guevara, Antonio, 22, 51–3
Guicciardini, Francesco, 27
Guise, Henri de Lorraine, Duc de, 151, 155, 172, 203, 209; Guise faction, 153, 156–7, 160, 167, 171, 196, 208–9
Guise, Louis de Lorraine, Cardinal de, 151, 172, 177, 209

Hadrian, Emperor, 34, 38
Hampe, William, 98
Harding, Thomas, 41, 61, 79 n.5
Harington, John, 53, 55
Harmonia, see Cadmus
Hatton, Christopher, 64
Hebrew, teacher of, 188, 192–3
Heidelberg, Palatine Library, 119
Helena, Empress, 42
Heliocentricity, xi, 167–8
Henri II, King of France, 122–3, 134–5, 140, 144 n.1, 218
Henri III, King of France, xi, xii, xiv, 109, 223–4; and court festivals, 135–6, 149 ff.; Giordano Bruno and, 83, 86, 124, 167–9, 212–14; his religious movement, 126, 173 ff., 184 ff., 208–9, 212–13; as Sun King, 163–4; see Devices; Holy Spirit, Order of the
Henri IV, King of France, raises hopes of solution of religious problems through French Monarchy, 86, 124, 126, 158, 172, 208 ff.; symbolism of, 210 ff.; see Gallic Hercules; Navarre, Henry of
Henry IV, Emperor, 44

Henry VII, Emperor, 11, 23, 40

Henry III, King of England, 44

Henry VIII, King of England, 39, 44, 50, 55, 57, 80

Herb garden, 173, 181, 188–90

Hercules, columns of, 23, 103, 116; *see* Gallic Hercules

Hermetic tradition, xii, 125, 167, 213

Hermit of chivalry, 95–6, 99, 105–7, 110

Hesiod, 30, 32 n.4, 71 n.2

'Hiel', *see* Barrefelt

Hilliard, Nicholas, 104

Historiography, 13, 17 ff., 27, 124, 132

Holofernes, 37, 77 n.3

Holy Spirit, Order of the (*Ordre du Saint Esprit*), Henri III and, 83, 109, 173 ff.

Homer, 52

Houel, Nicholas, 132, 173, 181; and the *Maison de Charité Chrétienne*, 187–91, 202–7

House of Love, *see* Family of Love

Huguccio of Pisa, 5

Huguenots, 82, 147, 150 ff., 172, 208–9

Humanism, 12, 16 ff., 27; *see* Musical humanism

Huss, John, 44

Hyginus, 31–2

Hymen, 134

Icarus, 32

Iconography, as a historical discipline, xii, and *passim*

Imperial reform, key idea behind the Elizabeth symbolism, 8, 11, 24, 29–87, 112–20, 211–13; *see* Charles V; Dante; Elizabeth I; Empire

Imperial themes, *see* Justice; 'One'; Peace; *Renovatio*; Virtues, imperial, etc.

Imprese, 107, 110; impresa shields, 91, 93, 104, 110

Incantations, xiv, 157, 159, 160–2

Innocent III, Pope, 6

Inquisition, the, 80, 118, 167

Isis, 32–3, 80

Italy, 5, 6, 14, 16, 23, 27, 122

Ivry, Battle of, 209

Jacquot, Jean, xiii, xiv, xv

Jandun, Jean of, 44

Jerome, Saint, 180

Jerusalem, 144–6

Jesuits, 177, 183, 185

Jewel, John, Bishop, 39–42, 48, 61, 78–84

Joachim of Flora, 37, 41, 44, 83, 184

Joan of Arc, 74, 82

John the Baptist, 180, 182

John, King of England, 40, 44

Jonah, 183, 193

Jones, Inigo, 220–1

Jonson, Ben, 29

Jordanus (Jornandus) of Osnabruck, 45–6

Joyeuse, Anne, Duc de: Magnificences for his wedding, xiv, 125, 149–72; as penitent, 180 ff.; death, 209

Joyeuse, Henri de, Comte de Bouchage (Frère Ange), 180, 185

Judith, 37, 77 n.3, 118

Juno, 32 n.9, 134–5, 140

Jupiter, 30, 32, 52, 143, 160, 166

Justice, imperial virtue, 4–8, 10–13, 20–5, 30–7, 43, 52, 65–70, 114, 121–2, 176, 210, 216; *see* Astraea

Kenilworth, Entertainment at, 95, 98

Kingship: and the imperial idea, 39 ff.; kings of England, 43 ff.; French kingship, 121 ff.; anointing of kings of France and England, 121

Knights, *see* Chivalry

Lactantius, 4, 8, 24, 35–6

Law, Roman, 4–7, 11, 122

League, the Catholic, 82–3, 149, 151, 156, 160, 167, 173, 177–8, 182, 185, 187, 191, 194–6, 208–9, 211

Lee, Henry, and the Accession Day Tilts, 74, 78 n.5, 89–95, 97, 100 ff., 117, 218–19

Lee, Thomas, 221 n.3

Le Fèvre de la Boderie, Guy, 192, 194 n.1

Leicester, Robert Dudley, Earl of, 94

Le Jeune, Claude, musician of Baïf's Academy, 152–5, 157–8, 161, 170–1

Lemaire des Belges, Jean, 131

Leo III, Pope, 3, 12

Leonardo da Vinci, 163

Le Roy, Etienne, singer, 179

L'Estoile, Pierre, 153, 162, 172 n.1, 174 ff., 182–5, 194

Lesure, F., 154

Lipsius, Justus, 191

London, as New Troy, 50

Lorraine, Marie de, 149, 151

Louis XIV, King of France, 164
Louis of Nassau, 147
Louise de Lorraine, Queen of France, in festivals and processions, 149, 151, 157, 159, 165, 181–3, 187, 190–1, 195
Louvre, see Paris
Lucian, 73
Lucius, mythical King of England, 43, 75
Lull, Ramon, 106–8
Luther, Martin, 24–5
Lyra, Nicholas of, 44

Machiavelli, 18–19, 27
Magic, Renaissance, xii, 159–60, 169, 180, 196; and science, 125, 160, 164–5
Maison de Charité Chrétienne, see Houel
Malory, Thomas, 106–7
Manfred, 17
Manilius, 33–4, 73–4
Manuel Palaeologus II, Byzantine Emperor, 48–9
Marcus Aurelius, 22–3, 52, 138
Marguerite de Valois, 146–7
Marsilio of Padua, 39, 41, 44–7
Martianus Capella, 32
Mary Tudor, Queen, 42, 108
Massacre of St Bartholomew, 124, 128, 146–7, 153
Mathematics-magic, 125, 152, 164
Matthieu, Pierre, 211
Mausolus, 134, 189
Maximilian I, Emperor, 122
Maximilian II, Emperor, 127, 142, 146
Mayenne, Duc de, 177, 211
Mechanics-magic, 149, 164–5
Medici, the, 8, 118, 142; see Catherine de' Medici
Melanchthon, 25, 127
Melissus, see Schede, Paul
Mercoeur, Nicolas de Lorraine, Duc de, 155, 157, 170–1
Mercury, 34, 115, 160
Merlin, 37, 53, 70
Mersenne, Marin, 155–6, 184
Michael, Saint, 49
Middle Ages, Popes and Emperors in, 1–3, 13, 16
Minerva, 144, 166
Minimes, Order of, 183–4, 203
Monarchy, the idea of, and the imperial idea, 1–28; Universal Monarchy, see World Rule

Montjosieu, Louis de, 164–6
Moon symbolism, 10, 33, 37, 76–8, 80, 163, 216
Moro, Antonio, 90, 104
Musical humanism, measured poetry and music, 140, 152–9, 161, 165, 170–1; see Academy; Baïf
Music school, 189; musicians in processions, 177–9
Mutability, 99
Mystery plays, 182, 185

Nantes, Edict of, 124, 210–11
Navarre, academy at, 212
Navarre, Henry of, 146–7, 153, 196, 209; see Henri IV
Neoplatonism, 45, 48, 74, 152, 160
Netherlands, 20, 147, 150, 193
New Worlds, and Empire, 23–4
Niclaes, Henry, 192
Nigidius Figulus, 32, 52
Nonnos, 141–4
North, Thomas, 52
Nuysement, Hesteau de, 194 n.1

Ockham, William of, 39, 44, 46
'One', the rule of, 7, 9, 22, 26, 28, 47, 50, 52, 54, 58–9, 64–6, 72–3, 87, 123–5
Opera, 150
Oporinus, 46 n.6
Order of the Garter, see Garter
Order of the Holy Spirit, see Holy Spirit
Oresme, Nicholas, 44
Orleans, pilgrimage to, 183
Orpheus, 140, 152, 155; Orphic singing, 159
Ortelius, 191
Ovid, 29–30, 74, 217

Paracelsus, 189–90
Paris: Augustins (church), 175–7, 179, 194–5, 198, 209; Bièvre (river), 188, 190; festivals in, 149 ff.; Louvre, 150–3, 162, 170–2, 174, 176, 187, 195; as New Troy, 138, 222; Pont-Neuf, 174, 176, 198; processions in, 173 ff.; royal entries into, 127 ff., 209–10, 222–4
Paris, Judgment of, 63
Pasquier, Etienne, 146–7
Paul, Saint, 40, 46
Pavia, Battle of, 21, 27, 36

Peace (*pax*), an imperial theme, 4 ff., 13 ff., 33 ff., 59, 77, 120 ff., 133–7, 140, 146, 163, 168–9, 210

Peele, George, 60–2, 93, 103

Penitents, in processions, 173, 176–85, 190, 197, 201–2, 208, 212

Pepin, 131, 137

Pericles, 48

Perseus, 144

Petrarch, xiii; and the Empire, 13–18, 24, 37; Tudor theologians and, 41, 44, 77 n.3; the *Trionfi* in Elizabethan symbolism, 112–20, 215–16; in French festival, 156; *see* Spenser

Pharamond, mythical French king, 131–2, 137

Philip II, King of Spain, 1, 27, 80–3, 122, 124, 147, 150–1, 192

Philip, Landgrave of Hesse, 57

Phoenix symbol, 38, 58–9, 65–6, 78, 83, 89–90

Phonetic spelling, 152, 160

Pico della Mirandola, 44–5

Pilon, Germain, 129, 134, 136, 144, 151, 222–4

Plantin, Christopher, 142, 191–2, 194 n.1

Plato, 19, 110, 152

Pléiade, the, xii, 13, 128–31, 139–40, 147, 151, 186, 193–4, 212, 214; *see* Baïf; Dorat; Ronsard

Pletho, Gemistus, 49

Plutarch, 19, 22

Poetry and Music, *see* Academy

Poggio Bracciolini, 16

Poissy, Colloquy of, 133

Poland, 163, 175

'Politiques', French party, xiv, 83–6, 127, 133, 140, 147, 186, 194, 208 ff.

Polydore Vergil, 50, 132

Polyglot Bible, 192–3

Pompey, 14, 48

Pontus de Tyard, 194 n.1

Popes: and Catholic League, 167; and Emperors, relative position of, 2 ff., 18, 24 ff., 39 ff.; and French monarchy, 82 ff., 123; 'Pope's Holidays', 100–1, 109

Porret, Pierre, 192

Portraits, of Queen Elizabeth I, *see* Elizabeth I

Postel, Guillaume, 123–5, 127, 137, 144–6, 192, 213

Primaticcio, 129

Procession, religious, 173–207

Protestantism: French and English, 8, 25, 39, 92, 113, 119 ff., 146–7, 191, 213; Protestant chivalry, 88–111; *see* Huguenots

Psalms, 140, 176–7

Puritanism, 113, 115

Quintilian, 16, 169

Rainbow, symbol of peace, 103 n.1, 134, 216 ff.; *see* Devices

Raleigh, Walter, 29, 69, 215–16

Reconciliation, religious, 25–6, 113, 182, 212 ff.

Reformation, the imperial idea and, 3, 8, 25, 39, 42, 60–1, 116, 144, 186, 213

Regnard, Jean, 138

Renaissance, 12, 16, 22, 38, 116, etc.; Renaissance and imperial *renovatio*, 38

Renovatio, imperial theme, 2, 4, 7, 12–14, 16, 22, 27, 37–8, 66, 68, 116, 123, 126, 186, 214

Republic, Roman, 12, 14–15, 18

Reunion, religious, 80, 86; *see* Reconciliation

Rex Christianissimus, title of French king, 121–2, 124, 127, 130, 140, 144, 146, 169, 182, 185–6, 196, 209–12

Rienzo, *see* Cola di Rienzo

Ripa, Cesare, 216–17

Rizza Casa, Giorgio, 118–19

Rogers, William, 58

Roman Empire, source of imperial themes and symbols, 2–3, 10, 14, 17, 23, 33, 37, 109, 121, etc.; Sack of Rome, 21, 24–5, 56; *see* Dominus mundi; Law, Roman

Ronsard, Pierre de, poet of the Pléiade, 82 n.2, 124; and court festival, 151, 162, 170 n.2; designs for royal entry, 128–41, 189; *see* Spenser

Rose, Tudor, 43, 50–1, 59, 78, 209

Rosicrucian movement, xii, 193, 213

Ruscelli, G., 215

Saint Germain, Treaty of, 127, 133, 135, 140, 146–7

Saint John's Gospel, 26

Sambucus, Johannes, 142

Sanders, Nicholas, 81

Sarpi, Paolo, 82 n.3

Saturn: planet, 160; ruler of the Golden Age, 9–11, 30, 33, 35, 61, 70, 113
Savonarola, 41, 44
Saxton, Christopher, 63
Schede, Paul (Melissus), 119
Scipio, Lucius, 14
Segar, William, 94, 102, 215 n.2
Selden, John, 34 n.5
Seneca, 19, 22, 31, 84, 99
Shakespeare, William: and Astraea, 74–80, 82; and the imperial theme, xi, 78–80, 87, 117–18, 196; on a French court academy, 211–12; on the Garter, 109 n.2; on the Imperial Votaress, 117–18, 209
Sicily, medieval kingdom of, 6–9, 20–1
Sidney, Mary, Countess of Pembroke, 67, 98
Sidney, Philip, xiii, 67, 119, 147; the Arcadia and the Accession Day Tilts, 88–97, 101–3, 110
Sieve portrait, see Elizabeth I
Sigismund, Emperor, 3
Soliman II, Sultan of Turkey, 57
Spanish Monarchy, 1, 20, 24, 26, 27, 61, 82–3, 118, 124, 147, 150–1, 167, 187, 194, 208–10; see Armada, Spanish; League, the Catholic; Philip II
Spenser, Edmund: on Astraea, 31–2, 69–74; Spenserian allegory and allegorical portraits of Queen Elizabeth I, 112–20, 215–19; Spenserian epic and Tudor imperial themes, 53–4, 63, 69–74; Spenser's Protestant Petrarchism, 113; The Faerie Queene and Accession Day Tilts, 89, 92, 97–101, 104–8; The Faerie Queene and Ronsard's Franciade, 123, 131–3; the Works of Mercy in Spenser and in French religious chivalry, 181–2, 196
Spring, of the Golden Age, 67–8, 74, 217–18
Stafford, Edward, 195
Statius, 36
Stoicism, 22
Suavius, Leo, see Gohorry
Sun, 10, 31, 90–1, 93, 108, 160; symbol of French monarchy, 160–4, 168, 213; see Heliocentricity; Henri III
Sybils, 26, 33, 35, 96, 145
Sylvester, Joshua, 89, 91, 109

Talismans, 125, 162

Temple at Jerusalem, 146
Themis, 32
Theodulf, Bishop, 36
Theriacum, drug, 203, 205
Thesus, 73
Thirty Years' War, xii, 213
Tiara, papal, 73, 77, 80; see Crown
Timotheus and Alexander, 152, 154
Titian, 22
Toleration, religious, xii, 86, 124, 127, 133, 140, 146, 150–3, 192, 194, 210, 212; see Conciliation, religious
Trajan, 23
Translation of Empire, theory of, 1–2, 4, 13–14, 17–22
Trissino, Giangiorgio, 122
Triumphal arches, 128 ff., 162
Troy: French Monarch's claim to descent from, 121, 124, 130–3, 138, 140; Tudor claim to descent from, 50–1, 60–3, 70, 116; London, Paris, as New Troy, see London, Paris; see also Brut; Francus
Truth, daughter of Time, 80
Tuccia, Vestal Virgin, xiii, 77, 113, 115; see Vestal Virgin
Tudor Monarchy, 24, 41, 48, 54, 121, 123, 133, 211; Tudor imperial reform, 29–120

Udall, Nicholas, 57
Unicorn, 112
Union, unity, imperial theme, 23, 39, 50–1, 146, 210
Universal, universality, imperial theme, 1–2, 51–2, 55, 137, 152, 210, 213
Urania, 33
Utenhovius, Charles, 142

Valdes, Antonio de, 24
Valeriano, Pierio, 133, 141, 217
Valla, Lorenzo, 16, 41, 44
Valois dynasty, 149–50, 160, 166–7, 182, 194, 196, 209; Valois Tapestries, 88
Van der Noot, Jan, 113
Venice, 174, 212, 213
Venus, 32, 73–4, 160
Vernani, Guido, 12, 18
Vestal Virgin, Elizabeth I as, 62, 77, 102–3, 109, 113–17, 219; see Tuccia
Victoria, Queen, 120

Vigenère, Blaise de, 184 n.1, 189
Vine Columns, see Temple
Virgil, xiii, 4, 9–11, 33–8, 69, 87, 115, 131–3, 217
Virgin Mary, 34–6, 78–9, 185
Virgo, sign, 30–5, 44, 52, 59, 63–4, 75
Virgo Caelestis, 34
Virtues, imperial, 14–15, 19, 22, 25, 27, 34, 51–2, 65–6, 68–9, 71–2; see Justice
Virtues, theological and cardinal, 196, 198
Vivanti, Corrado, xiv, 210–11
Von Wedel, Liupold, 91, 101

Walker, D. P., xvi, 154, 158–9, 189
Walpole, Horace, 221

War, opposite of imperial peace, 9, 24, 30, 40, 56, 122; wars of religion, 124, 127–8, 133, 149, 153, 193
Whore of Babylon, 41, 43, 45, 47, 61, 80, 113–14
Wickliff, John, 44
William of Orange, 148
Woodstock Entertainment, 94 ff.
Works of Mercy, 180–1, 188, 200–1, 212
World Rule, idea of, 1–26, 33, 38–9, 64–5, 72, 86, 121–7, 137, 144–5, 192, 196, 208, 211; see Dominus mundi

York and Lancaster, union of, 59

Zodiac, 30–2, 59, 63–4, 75, 85 n.1, 108, 161, 217, 220